CLASSICAL PRESENCES

General Editors

LORNA HARDWICK   JAMES I. PORTER

CLASSICAL PRESENCES

Attempts to receive the texts, images, and material culture of ancient Greece and Rome inevitably run the risk of appropriating the past in order to authenticate the present. Exploring the ways in which the classical past has been mapped over the centuries allows us to trace the avowal and disavowal of values and identities, old and new. Classical Presences brings the latest scholarship to bear on the contexts, theory, and practice of such use, and abuse, of the classical past.

Robert Graves and the Classical Tradition

Edited by

A. G. G. GIBSON

OXFORD
UNIVERSITY PRESS

OXFORD
UNIVERSITY PRESS

Great Clarendon Street, Oxford, OX2 6DP,
United Kingdom

Oxford University Press is a department of the University of Oxford.
It furthers the University's objective of excellence in research, scholarship,
and education by publishing worldwide. Oxford is a registered trade mark of
Oxford University Press in the UK and in certain other countries

First Edition published in 2015
Impression: 1

Published in the United States of America by Oxford University Press
198 Madison Avenue, New York, NY 10016, United States of America

British Library Cataloguing in Publication Data
Data available

Library of Congress Control Number: 2014955875

ISBN 978–0–19–873805–3

Printed and bound by
CPI Group (UK) Ltd, Croydon, CR0 4YY

Acknowledgements

The origin for this collection of essays was three research seminars held under a single title, 'Classics and Robert Graves: a relationship in literature, translation and adaptation'. The seminars were all held in the School of Classics, University of St Andrews, and this event only got off the ground because of a financial grant from the School of Classics, and for that I am very thankful.

The citations in this collection from Robert Graves's literary work are by kind permission of Carcanet Press; although the references have been cited from numerous older editions, they can be found in the following volumes, *Collected Writings on Poetry*; *Complete Poems vols. 1–3*; *Count Belisarius and Lawrence and the Arabs*; *Translating Rome*; *The Golden Fleece and Seven Days in New Crete*; *Goodbye to All That and Other Great War Writings*; *Greek Myths*; *Homer's Daughter and The Anger of Achilles*; *I, Claudius and Claudius the God*; *Some Speculations on Literature, History and Religion*; and *The White Goddess*. The electronic and online copyright consent is by kind permission of A.P. Watt Literary Agency.

The cover image is a previously unpublished photograph of Robert Graves in Majorca, taken about the time of writing *The Greek Myths* for Penguin, and it is reproduced from the private collection by kind permission of William Graves.

William Graves has been extremely supportive of the concept and the subsequent reality of this collection of essays and I am very grateful for all the help he has given me as the project has progressed. I would also like to thank the Librarian and Library staff at St. John's College, Oxford for their generous assistance in researching papers from Graves's working library in Deyá, Majorca held by the St John's College Robert Graves Trust.

I would like to thank all the contributors for their patience, diligence and commitment in this extended process of producing the book, and for buying into the idea that Robert Graves and Classics was worthy of consideration and for producing such considered essays. It is to the immense credit of the contributors that the essays, either from a seminar paper, or a later commission all contribute to make the project much more than the sum of its parts. The Series Editors at

OUP have been supportive throughout and I really appreciate their confidence and guidance. The Subject Editor at OUP, Hilary O'Neill, has been supremely patient with my queries and calm with her guidance which has been a real help in putting the book together. The book's production has been smoothed by Annie Rose at OUP who removed the technical thorns along the way, and Shwetha Panduranganath, Jeff New, and Catherine Macduff tackled the typesetting process coolly and methodically which made it all so much easier than it might have been.

Contents

List of Contributors ix

Introduction 1
A. G. G. Gibson

1. 'It's readable all right, but it's not history': Robert Graves's *Claudius* Novels and the Impossibility of Historical Fiction 21
Andrew Bennett

2. Claudius in the Library 43
Duncan Kennedy and Ellen O'Gorman

3. Homer's Daughter: Graves's *Vera Historia* 57
Sheila Murnaghan

4. Robert Graves as Historical Novelist: *Count Belisarius*—Genesis, Gender, and Truth 77
Shaun Tougher

5. Graves on War and the Late Antique: Count Belisarius and his World 99
Jon Coulston

6. *The Golden Ass* and the Golden Warrior 123
Sonia Sabnis

7. 'Essentially a Moral Problem': Robert Graves and the Politics of the Plain Prose Translation 143
Philip Burton

8. Robert Graves's *The Greek Myths* and Matriarchy 165
Sibylle Ihm

9. Scholarly Mythopoesis: Robert Graves's *The Greek Myths* 181
Vanda Zajko

10. Freedom to Invent: Graves's Iconoclastic Approach to Antiquity 201
Isobel Hurst

11. Restoring Narcissus: The Love Poems of Robert Graves 221
John Burnside

12. Robert Graves at Troy, Marathon, and the End of Sandy Road: War Poems at a Classical Distance? 233
Tom Palaima

13. '*Con beffarda irriverenza*': Graves's Augustus in Mussolini's Italy 255
Jonathan Perry

14. Josef von Sternberg and the Cinematizing of *I, Claudius* 275
A. G. G. Gibson

15. Broadcasting the Common Asphodel: Robert Graves and the Mass Media 297
Mick Morris

16. *The Anger of Achilles*: A Prize-Winning 'Epic for Radio' by Robert Graves 315
Amanda Wrigley

Bibliography 333
Index 361

List of Contributors

Andrew Bennett: Professor of English, Department of English, University of Bristol

John Burnside: Professor of English, School of English, University of St Andrews

Philip Burton: Reader in Latin and Early Christian Studies, Department of Classics, Ancient History and Archaeology, University of Birmingham

Jon Coulston: Lecturer in Ancient History, School of Classics, University of St Andrews

A. G. G. Gibson: Honorary Research Fellow, School of Classics, University of St Andrews

Isobel Hurst: Lecturer in English, Department of English and Comparative Literature, Goldsmiths, University of London

Sibylle Ihm: formerly außerplanmäßiger Professor, Seminar für Klassische Philologie, Georg-August-Universität Göttingen

Duncan Kennedy: Emeritus Professor of Latin Literature and the Theory of Criticism, Department of Classics and Ancient History, University of Bristol

Mick Morris: Tutor, Faculty of Arts, Open University

Sheila Murnaghan: Professor of Classical Studies; Alfred Reginald Allen Memorial Professor of Greek, Department of Classical Studies, University of Pennsylvania

Ellen O'Gorman: Senior Lecturer in Classics and Ancient History, Department of Classics and Ancient History, University of Bristol

Tom Palaima: Robert M. Armstrong Centennial Professor, Department of Classics, University of Texas at Austin

Jonathan Perry: Associate Professor of History, College of Arts and Sciences, University of South Florida Sarasota-Manatee

Sonia Sabnis: Associate Professor of Classics and Humanities, Department of Classics, Reed College, Oregon

Shaun Tougher: Reader in Ancient History, Cardiff School of History, Archaeology and Religion, Cardiff University

Amanda Wrigley: Research Fellow, Faculty of Media, Arts and Design, University of Westminster

Vanda Zajko: Senior Lecturer in Greek Literature and Language and Senior Academic Fellow, Department of Classics and Ancient History, University of Bristol

Introduction

A. G. G. Gibson

In 1965 Malcolm Muggeridge gave a personal and contemporary view of Robert Graves in a preview for a forthcoming interview to be broadcast on the *Intimations* television programme:

> Several times our paths have vaguely crossed.
>
> In my opinion, he is, without any question, the most distinguished practitioner of English letters now living. His output has been prodigious, but none of it is insignificant. Besides being a poet, he is a highly original if unorthodox scholar; a critic, blessedly free of pedantry, a novelist, an essayist, and, in his Claudius books, a popular writer with a following all over the world.
>
> Graves has had the courage and the resolution to live his own way on his own terms, without reference to, or involvement in, the political and moral controversies which have submerged so many writers and poets in our time. In his Majorca retreat he has managed to be an observer rather than a participant; as though the tragic experience of participating as a very young man in the savage buffooneries of war sufficed for a whole lifetime.[1]

In 2010 I was reminded of Robert Graves's continued visibility on a visit to the National Gallery of Scotland, where I happened across a number of Faber & Faber copies of *The White Goddess* in the Gallery shop. This edition was placed alongside art books on subjects as diverse as Robert Mapplethorpe, Goya, Hendrick Golzius, Vermeer, and Christen Købke. It is striking that the poet and author Robert Graves seems to remain in the popular intellectual consciousness of

[1] Muggeridge (1965).

the twenty-first century, even if this tends to be mainly through *The White Goddess* or his novels, *I, Claudius* and *Claudius the God* (the novels having been given additional prominence through the critically acclaimed BBC television adaptation). One would hesitate to argue that, outside of his poetry, the bulk of Graves's work is 'mainstream', and that through these books in particular he entered the popular culture of the twentieth century.

An extended period spent researching the life of Claudius eventually provoked the initiative to examine further Graves's work in Classics, and this was brought to fruition in a series of workshops, 'Classics and Robert Graves: A Relationship in Literature, Translation and Adaptation', at the University of St Andrews.[2] The workshops were to consider the reception and adaptation of Graves's novels for film; his impact via Classics on twentieth-century poetry; his translations from Latin into English; his perception of Greek myth; and the historical novel; however, Graves's books for children are not included in this collection. Other conferences and edited papers have addressed wider issues around Graves's poetry and literature, but this was an opportunity for the relationship between Classics itself and the body of his work to be revisited and reviewed within an interdisciplinary framework. The research material available on Graves is improving. St John's College, Oxford, has an extensive and fascinating collection of papers from Majorca, and the annotated online diaries (1935–9) on the University of Victoria website are a highly useful resource. In addition there are biographies and a complete collection of poetry and novels, as well as collections of Graves's letters and essays.[3] As more material becomes accessible it will allow for more cross-disciplinary studies to be attempted. This collection marks an initial step along that path.

There are a number of impressive biographies of Robert Graves in existence (see the Bibliography), so the following paragraphs will provide only a light biographical sketch. Robert von Ranke Graves was born in London in 1895, son to Alfred Perceval Graves and Amalia

[2] There were three research workshops, held at the University of St Andrews on 19 September, 31 October, and 21 November 2009 respectively; these were hosted through the generous support of the School of Classics, University of St Andrews.

[3] The Robert Graves Trust has excellent research resources at <http://www.robertgraves.org/trust/index.php> and the Poetry Foundation has a short biography and extensive bibliography at <http://www.poetryfoundation.org/bio/robert-graves> (accessed 21/05/2011).

von Ranke. His mother was a great-niece of Leopold von Ranke, an eminent nineteenth-century German historian whose methodology allowed general theories to be constructed from empirical research on the primary sources. Von Ranke's aim was simply 'to see things how they really are',[4] an aspiration, it could be argued, that would be echoed later by Graves in his literary re-creations of 'historical' events.

After attending Charterhouse School, Graves enlisted in the Welch Fusiliers at the outset of World War I and served in France from 1915 to 1917. He was wounded at the Somme in 1916; during his war service he met the poet Siegfried Sassoon, and on his eventual return to England in 1917 he went up to St John's College, Oxford, where he would become a friend of T. E. Lawrence. Lawrence would become a major influence on Graves's life until the former's untimely death. Graves wrote about his friend in *Lawrence and the Arabs*, as well as collaborating with Basil Liddell Hart on publishing their respective correspondence with, in their minds, this inspirational hero figure.[5] In 1918 Graves married the painter Nancy Nicholson, sister of sculptor Ben Nicholson, and settled into a life of bohemian domesticity, first in Oxford, in a house rented from John Masefield, then in London. Graves invited the American poet and writer Laura Riding to work with him on a book on modern poetry, and after a brief sojourn in Egypt in 1926, where Graves taught at the University of Cairo, their theatrical affair developed. It was itself interwoven with other nonconformist relationships, and after a gothic denouement Graves finally abandoned Nancy and their four children for Laura in 1929.[6] Around this time Graves had finished his controversial war autobiography, *Good-bye to All That*, and so he felt free to leave England with Laura that October for a new home in Deyà, Majorca. It was here that he produced many of his works connected to Classics. The initial results were *I, Claudius* and *Claudius the God*, historical novels that Graves considered to be purely literary potboilers. It gives some indication of Graves's work ethic, or perhaps points to the severity of his financial situation, that both novels were published in 1934. Graves and Riding had to leave Majorca with the onset of the Spanish Civil War, and returned to England. He continued to write, and followed the tales of Claudius with a further historical novel, *Count Belisarius*, before venturing into the realms of myth with *The Golden*

[4] Seymour (1995), 4; see Seymour-Smith (1995), 1–11 of 1982 edn. for the family backgrounds in literature, history, and the clergy.

[5] R. P. Graves (1990), 51–6, 229–31.

[6] Seymour-Smith (1995), 122 ff.

Fleece, published in the United States as *Hercules My Shipmate*. A contemporary review in *Time* provides a representative opinion of the relative merits of Graves's creative methodology:

> With Hercules and his shipmates, Graves becomes an ancient Greek, moving among demigods and goddesses, myths and monsters with an easy familiarity and a wealth of erudite detail; both sometimes seem too much of a good thing. Atomic-age readers, ill-attuned to the leisurely, formal talk of Myth-Age Greeks, may find themselves skipping some of the longer speeches.[7]

Graves then took up a number of academic appointments in Britain and the United States; he was Clark Lecturer at Trinity College, Cambridge (1954), and notably following Cecil Day Lewis and W. H. Auden as Professor of Poetry at the University of Oxford (1961–5). For most of his life he continued to write and work in Deyà, Majorca, and after escaping from the turbulent relationship with Laura Riding in 1939 he eventually married Beryl Pritchard in 1950. Throughout his career Graves had a series of influences on his thinking and his work; these would include T. E. Lawrence and W. H. R. Rivers, as well as a number of muses, including Nancy, Laura, and Beryl, among others.[8] Robert von Ranke Graves died in 1985 at the age of 90.

Reading the biographies of Robert Graves, it becomes readily apparent that he was a man with a singular outlook. Stephen Spender wrote: 'All of his life Graves has been indifferent to fashion, and the great and deserved reputation he has is based on his individuality as a poet who is both intensely idiosyncratic and unlike any other contemporary poet and at the same time classical.'[9]

Many questions caught Graves's eye, and once a topic became the focus of intense interest he would try to get beneath its skin. He is someone who willingly and actively chose to plough his own furrow, but his idiosyncratic approach (even though Graves would probably

[7] 'Books: The Golden Fleece', *Time* 15 Oct. 1945; see <http://www.time.com/time/magazine/article/0,9171,792476,00.html#ixzz1NCGqdn2p> (accessed 01/04/2011).

[8] See Seymour (1995), 387–461. For RG's concept of the poet's relationship with and entitlement to a muse, especially later in his life, see Seymour (1995) 387–8. Seymour-Smith (1995), 93-4 and passim, Graves, R. P. (1995), 335–6, 368–9, 416–17.

[9] Spender (1973); Stephen Spender also wrote: 'Of all poets of this time, Robert Graves is the one who, without solemnity but with total dedication, has kept the idea of poetry sacred and the idea of the poet true.'

not see it as such, and would not care if anyone thought that it was) has not always been welcome. Whatever the widespread popularity of his novels and poetry, academia has held a more diffident view of the scholastic value of Graves's output, and classicists especially seem to have baulked at his interpretation of myth and novelization of history. There has been cogent criticism of *The Greek Myths*, *I, Claudius*, and *Claudius the God*,[10] and it is not the aim of the present collection of essays to promote Graves's work or suggest that his writing related (however loosely) to the discipline of Classics should be rehabilitated. Rather, the essays gathered here present individual readings of Graves's unique perspective on the various fields of study he involved himself with, and are intended to energize the debate about the value of his contribution. The essays should enhance and extend our understanding of his works within their original context, and point the way forward to assessing their relevance in how we (so to speak) figure out the ancient world. How did Graves see the classical world? Can Graves's interpretation of antiquity and his translations be seen in a new light that shows their enduring value, or should they be seen as limited by the assumptions and attitudes of his own time? Has his literary success, or even his notoriety, been detrimental to the discipline of Classics? His main publications related to Classics are detailed below, but Graves also produced poetry that used tropes and themes associated with the ancient world, and these are discussed further in Hurst's essay (Chapter 10).

Robert Graves wrote poetry for most of his adult life, producing seven distinct volumes of *Collected Poems*, and other poetry collections, over the working period from 1914 to 1975.[11] Unfortunately the present collection does not contain a comprehensive survey or analysis of the poetry, though aspects of it are examined in the essays by Hurst (Chapter 10), Burnside (Chapter 11), and Palaima (Chapter 12), and discussed incidentally elsewhere in the book. Graves's love poetry falls into five distinct chronological periods—his first marriage; meeting with Laura Riding, 1926–9; the years with Laura, 1930–9; the years before his marriage to Beryl, 1938–45; and the period at the

[10] Beard (2006) compares Graves's laboured novels to Jack Pulman's celebrated TV adaptation; cf. Lowe (2005). One can also find criticism of Graves's poetry; for example, in the *Listener* Donald David (1959), 11–13, wrote that Graves made no allowance for the reader, or hardly even acknowledged their presence and this accounted for the toneless voice of his poetry.

[11] Ward (2003), 96.

end of *Collected Poems 1959*.[12] Numerous poems from different periods of his work feature gods and goddesses or mythic heroes. Examples include 'Prometheus', where the persona Graves adopts opines on 'the intractability of love'; 'Lyceia', his version of the story of Lycoan, the divine wolf and goddess of the Moon; 'Leda', where, like W. B. Yeats, Graves wrote of Zeus seducing Leda, the wife of King Tyndareus of Sparta; 'The Return of the Goddess Artemis'; and his love poem 'Ulysses', first published in 1933, where the amazing adventures, cunning, and tenacity of Homer's hero 'are rearranged and reinterpreted so that his story becomes a classic statement, a paradigm indeed, of man at the mercy of sexual appetite'.[13] D. N. G. Carter's exposition of 'Ulysses' is illuminating and shows how much is yet to be mined from Graves's poetry in relation to the reception of Classics.

> To the much-tossed Ulysses, never done
> With woman whether gowned as wife or whore,
> Penelope and Circe seemed as one:
> She like a whore made his lewd fancies run,
> And wifely she a hero to him bore.

In this first verse of 'Ulysses' Carter maintains that the rhythm of the sea that carried Ulysses on his journey is reflected in the rising and falling of the last two lines (and is evocative of Andrew Lang's 'surge and thunder of the Odyssey'), while the opening phrase suggests Ulysses is flotsam on the sea of love, 'a hero who is essentially passive, the victim rather than the vanquisher in his amatory exploits'.[14] The poem is contextualized in Chapter 3 by Sheila Murnaghan.

While Graves's war experiences became widely read with the publication of *Good-bye to All That*, he had already published poetry written during the war and stands with Siegfried Sassoon, Wilfrid Owen, and Edmund Blunden as a First World War poet of some distinction. His war poetry is also pertinent to the focus of the recent collection, as demonstrated by 'A Dedication of Three Hats', with its reference to Mars, Minerva, and the muse Euphrosyne:[15]

[12] Carter (1989), 62.
[13] Carter (1989), 82. The poem is reproduced in full in Murnaghan's essay.
[14] Carter (1989), 83. [15] Graves (1988).

'A Dedication of Three Hats'
This round hat I devote to Mars,
Tough steel with leather lined.
My skin's my own, redeemed by scars
From further still more futile wars
The God may have in mind.

Minerva takes my square of black
Well-tasselled with the same;
Her dullest nurselings never lack
With hoods of scarlet at their back
And letters to their name.

But this third hat, this foolscap sheet,
(For there's a strength in three)
Unblemished, conical and neat
I hang up here without deceit
To kind Euphrosyne.

Goddess, accept with smiles or tears
This gift of a gross fool
Who having sweated in death fears
With wounds and cramps for three long years
Limped back, and sat for school.

Writing in the *Guardian*, Sean O'Brien concluded that Graves's love poetry should be 'read alongside playful anthology pieces such as 'The Persian Version' and 'Welsh Incident'. No one else offers his precise combination of eroticism, nightmare and epigram'.[16]

'The Persian Version', a poem about the Battle of Marathon first published in 1945 and discussed in the essay of Tom Palaima, warrants a brief excursion here because the reaction to Graves's poem, true to form, touched a collective nerve with classicists. Despite a scarcity of written records other than the account of Herodotus, for over a century scholars have been divided into two camps engaged, as Hoyland notes, in a metaphoric push-and-shove in trying to reconstruct the battle.[17] Tuplin argued from the Persian side and reckoned that Graves has here minimized its importance as part of an imperial invasion to subjugate Greece. The opposing view (see Hölkeskamp) promotes the notion that both Persia and the Greeks saw Marathon

[16] O'Brien (2001). [17] Hoyland (2011), 265.

as purely a minor skirmish. In a short critique on Marathon, in his general history *Early Greece*, Oswyn Murray cites the first two lines of 'The Persian Version' and comments: 'From the Persian side there is something to be said for Robert Graves' analysis.'[18] Graham Trengrove's close reading of the poem shows that the voice in the poem is neither that of the poet nor a historian giving their interpretation of events or even a commentary on the unreliability of the sources, but is that of an official spokesman putting a gloss on affairs. In a new century, seemingly built upon the shifting sands of public-relations spin and counterspin, this poem is as prescient as ever.[19]

Graves was a man well versed in the propaganda of war. He had seen Sassoon rail against the official government line promulgated to justify the allied strategy in France and Belgium; he had been shaped by the enormous loss of life at the Front; and his experience would lead him to question the official version, any version, and the whitewash splashed on by the victors. Considering the passage in *I, Claudius* where Claudius meets Pollio (see the discussion in Chapter 2, by Kennedy and O'Gorman), John Leonard writes, 'I have often thought in connection with this passage whether we have not been misreading Graves's famous satire "The Persian Version". Granted it is a devastating parody of official war-communiqués, but does it not also cast doubt on the "Greek theatrical tradition", and by implication on its historical tradition—a tradition that is the origin of all western historical-writing—as well?'[20]

Another tradition, that of the historical novel, was well established when Graves wrote the *Claudius* novels—one only has to think of Tolstoy and Sir Walter Scott to determine the pedigree. Graves was not the first to adopt figures from the ancient world to the historical novel either; following in the wake of Lew Wallace's nineteenth-century novel *Ben-Hur*, Jakob Wassermann had written *Alexander in Babylon* (Fischer, Berlin 1905) and the basic model has been followed by a number of similar novels into the twenty-first century. Graves's historical novels were designed to make money, and so he had to ensure they were both populist and popular.[21] The *Claudius* novels were so successful that Graves paid the mortgage off outright

[18] Murray (1993), 281. [19] Trengrove (1986), 60–9.

[20] Leonard (2001), 259–72.

[21] R. P. Graves (1990), 187–204; Seymour-Smith (1995), 241–50; Seymour (1997), 199–225.

on his home in Majorca; the film rights to the books were snapped up within a year by Alexander Korda; and these two books have never been out of print since they were first published. Graves had a serious interest in making money, and an as yet unanswered question is how was he so sure that a warts-and-all story of a Roman family, albeit a violent and flashy imperial soap opera, would turn into the gravy train it did? Graves outlined his approach:

> Historical novels are not legitimate if they are an excuse for a thrilling story of modern passion in fancy dress. But they are legitimate if the writer starts with a sudden intimate feeling about a particular character, and believes that the story has been mistold by history. By then soaking himself in the period and reading contemporary accounts so as not to be biased, he is able to build up a story as a zoologist builds up a whole fossil animal from a couple of bones.[22]

This concept can be mapped over Graves's historical novels, and the *Claudius* books in particular. The approach has its problems, however, such as the question of how the figures in a historical novel should speak: should they be made to speak in a modern, conversational tone, or should the author try for authenticity in the manner of their speech, or should there be a third way, a hybrid between the two approaches? The 'voice' of the historical novel is discussed in this volume in essays by Bennett, Kennedy and O'Gorman, and Murnaghan.

Mary Renault and Valerio Massimo Manfredi have each written trilogies about Alexander the Great that are rooted in the sources—just two examples in a burgeoning catalogue of historical fiction that draws on the ancient world of Greece and Rome. Many novelists in this genre do not appear to share Graves's notion of what constitutes historical fiction, but there are better parallels if one looks elsewhere. Hilary Mantel won the Man Booker Prize and the Walter Scott Prize for *Wolf Hall*, a historical novel that took a revisionist stance about the life of Thomas Cromwell, a character, like Claudius, whom history has not treated kindly, and placed him centre-stage in the political milieu around the throne of Henry VIII.[23] In a review for its sequel, *Bring Up the Bodies*, James Woods identifies the qualities Mantel uses to tell her story (in *Wolf Hall*), including how the language of the novels is not that of the sixteenth century but an

[22] RG quoted by Nicholson (1942), 283–6. [23] Acocella (2009).

amalgam of styles that is a model of clarity for the twenty-first-century reader. Woods homes in on the reason for Mantel's success, something that could equally be applied to Graves's historical fiction:

> In short, this novelist has the maddeningly unteachable gift of being interesting. Quite a few readers would be prepared to yawn at a novelistic scene set in 1530, featuring Thomas Cromwell, then one of Henry VIII's privy councillors, and Thomas Cranmer, the Anglican theologian who gained renown as the author of the Book of Common Prayer. Hasn't this material been worked over—in descending order of quality—by Ford Madox Ford, by Robert Bolt, and by the TV series 'The Tudors'? Yet such a scene in 'Wolf Hall' exhibits Mantel's stealthy dynamics. There is nothing dutifully 'historical' about this encounter. Instead, all is alive, silvery, alert, rapid with insight.[24]

Controversy surrounding Graves's work has not been restricted to classicists—*Good-bye to All That* stirred up a hornets' nest of criticism because Graves's war experience was discussed with frankness and openness. Readers and critics were disapproving of his relaying of events, and his unvarnished descriptions of soldiers' behaviour under the stress of war seemed to provoke a backlash from all quarters. The manuscript had been seen by Edmund Blunden and was subsequently closely annotated by Siegfried Sassoon, and both men were deeply angry at Graves's self-centred version of the war; his use of 'poetic licence' and the presentation of certain fictionalized events as fact were additional grounds for criticism.[25] Sassoon in particular was incensed by the unsolicited inclusion of a poem he had sent to Graves in a letter (of 1918), and a section in the book recounting a visit to his mother in 1916 that he felt was an invasion of privacy and not for public consumption.[26] The criticism of Graves for producing such a 'stylized' and even 'manufactured' autobiography still resonates today.

It is worth noting that Graves was also unpopular with the critics for his own performance as a reader and broadcaster in public, discussed by Morris in this volume (Chapter 15). An exercise broadcast on BBC radio, had the actor Anthony Jacobs and Graves reading 'Counting the Beats' then 'The Terraced Valley', with mixed

[24] Wood (2012).

[25] Seymour-Smith (1995), 190–200; R. P. Graves (1990), 131–7; Seymour (1995), 175–86. See Duckworth (2004), 63–7, for a discussion of how two incidents in *Good-bye to All That* have been recycled by the novelist Pat Barker.

[26] R. P. Graves (1990), 132–7.

results. One review concluded that poets are not great at this, pointing to the 'weird creaking chant of W. B. Yeats', and considered Graves's 'flat and jerky' delivery to be harder to listen to than Jacobs's more polished performance—but ponders if this really showed how Graves 'imagined the lines sounded as they formed in his mind'.[27] A reviewer in *Gramophone* writes of Graves reading a collection of his poems:

> It is always interesting to hear a poet read his own works, even if someone else might in the event read them better. But the identity of the voice and the thing said is sometimes blurred when the reader is not the poet, especially in a work so personal as this. Mr. Graves uses a rather dead-pan delivery and he is not really very clear, though one gets used to him as time wears on . . .[28]

Elizabeth Jennings compared Auden's 'splendid rendering of thirteen of his poems for Argo (RG194) which is a triumphant refutation of those who declare that poets are not the best speakers of their own verse' to Graves's jaded delivery:

> His clipped dry donnish voice not only succeeds in ironing out most of the music it also manages to obscure much of the meaning. Only the most attentive Graves addict will be able to isolate these poems from the poet's nearly disastrous handling of them, while the personality-hunter will find Mr Graves quite as elusive as he himself has here made the witty melancholy of his fine lyrics.[29]

The *Observer* critic writes on the third recording Graves produced: 'The reading is what we have come to expect from Graves—determinedly non-rhetorical, meticulous, a trifle hesitant, bringing out what is in the poem but almost overscrupulous in not adding anything extra.'[30]

[27] RGA: uncredited review in the *Mitcham & Tooting Advertiser*; *Wallington & Carshalton Advertiser*, 14 June 1956. The programme, 'A Poet's Reading Compared with an Actor's', was introduced by James Reeves.

[28] RGA: uncredited review in *Gramophone* (Mar. 1960) refers to Listen LPV2.

[29] RGA: Elizabeth Jennings in the *Guardian* 9 June 1960 refers to Listen LPV2.

[30] RGA: John Wain in the *Observer*, 11 Sept. 1960 refers to Argo RG191. Derek Parker in the *Weekly Post*, 3 Dec. 1960 writes of RG191 that Graves 'reads many short poems in a voice that is peculiarly and completely the voice of his poetry: a casual yet apposite voice, hammering away at our ridiculous pomposities, inching mistrust of our human claims to immutability. Never, somehow, on duty, Graves is nevertheless always a sentry at the gates—informally heading off deserters.' Also cf. Jennings (1960).

In a quite different field, Graves again caused controversy when, in advance of writing the *Claudius* novels, he produced a heavily revised and condensed version of Charles Dickens's *David Copperfield*, and its publication as *The Real David Copperfield* (1933) caused indignation among Dickens scholars in Britain.[31] Because Dickens had originally written *David Copperfield* for serialization, Graves surmised that a revision was necessary and proceeded to take out 'all the monthly-part padding and general hysteria . . . putting what's left into some sort of intelligible order'.[32] A contemporary review in *Time* magazine expounded on how, due to the critical white noise, the publishers (Harcourt, Brace & Co.) prevaricated about an American edition. They decided to withdraw it from publication a week before the due date, and opted for producing an abridged version for schools instead.[33] The biographer Richard Perceval Graves provides another perspective, arguing that it was a misconceived project because Dickens was still enormously popular with the public, which may explain the poor sales in Britain. He goes on to add that after sixty years it can be viewed as a valuable exercise, because 'Graves's version is far more accessible to a modern audience than the original'.[34]

The legitimacy of an adaptation, a translation, or a rearrangement of historical facts or motifs by an author is a compelling issue for discussion, and the essays collected here address this among other factors; the chapters by Andrew Bennett, Duncan Kennedy and Ellen O'Gorman, Sheila Murnaghan, Shaun Tougher, and Jon Coulston consider the historical novels; Philip Burton and Sonia Sabnis examine the translations; Sibyille Ihm has analysed myth and matriarchy, and Vanda Zajko discusses *The Greek Myths*; Tom Palaima, Mick Morris, Amanda Wrigley, A. G. G. Gibson, and Jonathan Perry discuss reception in the twentieth century; Isobel Hurst considers Graves's poetry in relation to the classical world; while John Burnside's essay gives a different perspective by providing the essential insight of one working poet into the work of another.

To attempt a synthesis of the similarities and outcomes of this project would have limited value, because readers from different

[31] O'Prey (1982), 219. Seymour-Smith (1995), 223–4.

[32] RG in R. P. Graves (1990), 161.

[33] See Book Review 'Dickens Brushed Up', *Time*, 26 Mar. 1934; the editor of the 1934 US edition was Merrill P. Paine, described by Seymour Smith (1995), 224, as 'a Dickensian pedagogue'. Notwithstanding, the edition was a sales success.

[34] R. P. Graves (1990), 161. Also see Seymour-Smith (1995), 223–5.

disciplines will (rightly) produce a diversity of conclusions. This is not to avoid nailing one's colours to any particular mast, but rather implies a desire for readers to fashion their own opinions about Graves's output and reflect on the current state of their discipline. Twenty years hence Classics will have been transformed again by contemporary culture and/or further academic research—whichever outcome transpires, the body of work represented here can be repositioned accordingly within that world.

However there is an unbridgeable gulf here between Graves's experience in the First World War and those of the reader a hundred years later. The war seems to have shaken the foundations of his very being, and the pointless nature of the killing seems to have led to Graves's questioning everything around him, while also affecting his relationships, sexual and otherwise. His contempt for authority is probably rooted here—why should he take any notice of what anyone thought who had not been through the same experiences as he had? Robert Graves was not an academic but a poet; one who wrote fiction to make money and followed his own star to produce stories, essays, and poems. These may be still popular, or may be unfashionable, or thought to be inaccurate, as though accuracy was the final arbiter of creativity. With a poet's input there will be no uniformity in the results. Reading John Dryden's or Cecil Day Lewis's translation of the *Aeneid*, one becomes aware that these poets draw upon the chaos and darkness of war—for Dryden, the English Civil War and the ensuing revolution that replaced James II; while Day Lewis was writing in the shadow of the Second World War (see Tom Palaima's essay for a discussion of war in poetry). For the translation of the classicist Stanley Lombardo the aftermath of the conflicts in Iraq would not be distant. Their respective translations, and there is no value judgment here, subtly expose the dissimilarities between the translators and illuminate Virgil from another aspect. The opening lines of the Cecil Day Lewis's *Aeneid* are a case in point:

> I tell about the war who first from Troy's frontier,
> Displaced by destiny, came to the Lavinian shores,
> To Italy—a man much travailed by sea and land
> By the powers above, because of the brooding anger of Juno,
> Suffering much in war until he could found a city
> And march his gods into Latium, whence rose the Latin race
> The royal line of Alba, and the high walls of Rome.

Compare it with Lombardo's twenty-first century translation:

> Arms I sing, and a man,
> The first to come from the shores
> Of Troy, exiled by Fate, to Italy
> And the Lavinian coast, a man battered
> On land and sea by the powers above
> In the face of Juno's relentless wrath;
> A man who also suffered greatly in war
> Until he could found his city and bring his gods
> Into Latium, from which arose
> The Latin people, our Alban forefathers,
> And the high walls of everlasting Rome.

In the light of considering other translators the essay of Philip Burton considers three questions regarding Graves's translations from Latin and Greek; firstly, Graves's championing of the plain prose style of translation; secondly, how Graves used his translation to position himself with regards to the original author and other translators; and finally, how far Graves's methodology reflected contemporary culture or just his idiosyncratic approach to the problem of translating the text in front of him. Emily Greenwood's investigation tackles the soundscape inherent in the 'translation' or, more accurately, the 'free adaptation' of the epic poem by the poet Christopher Logue.[35] Warren Anderson, reviewing Logue's 1962 translation of the *Patrokleia* from *Iliad* 16 writes in 1969:

> What we have here is not translation, a carrying-over, but a tradition hardly less honorable which has fallen into desregard [*sic*] since the Renaissance: the practice of *aemulatio*, rivalry in the best sense. Logue is an emulator rather than a translator. Comparison with Lattimore would be entirely beside the point; we look instead (though warily) to Pound's Cantos and the Homage to Sextus Propertius. For Logue's purposes, the text of Homer must be both revered and challenged, given allegiance and also treated as a point of departure. His infidelity follows naturally from his fidelity and is justified by it. The poem he has given us, far from being a "rendering" of Patroclus' last hours, is a reexperiencing [*sic*] of their fevered, death-bound brilliance.[36]

[35] For a discussion of the methodology used by translators of the *Iliad*, namely Fitzgerald, Fagles, and Lombardo, see Greenwood (2009), 503.

[36] Cf. Burton, Sabnis, Murnaghan, and Wrigley in this volume, and Anderson (1969), Folkart (1998), and Greenwood (2009) for an introduction to the intricacies and methodologies of translation.

Amanda Wrigley, in Chapter 16, points the reader to D. S. Carne-Ross the essayist and a translator of Pindar, who said of Graves's *The Anger of Achilles* (in its version for radio broadcast), 'the translations are, so far as possible, poets' translations rather than dons' translations'. Therein lies the dichotomy, between what the reader expects from the translator, and what the translator is trying (or is prepared) to give the audience. The characteristics of a reader, their analytical ability (or the desire to be, or not to be, analytical), and their need for education or entertainment (or both) is not a fixed generic point for an author/translator to aim at. One would expect that though the translator is a fixed point (poet or classicist), they face the impossible task of having to fit into a different set of clothes depending on who is going to pick up the book, or face the wrath of a subset of their potential readership. What should a translation be? Is the translator to be rigorous or entertaining (for which read 'populist'), or if they fall between two stools, risk ending up as neither?[37] Should a translator of the *Iliad* or *The Golden Ass*, for example, expect to achieve the aims of the eighteenth-century essayists Addison and Steele, who were determined to edify *and* entertain their readership? Do we, as readers, expect (or even want) to be 'enlightened'? Barbara Folkart writes that a translator (in Folkart's case, of the medieval poetry of Charles D'Orléans) immediately has to confront their own 'diachronic incompetence' and the fact of being cut off from the poem's 'cultural and pragmatic matrix';[38] however, there is not only an interaction between the text and reader 'but also the linguistic and cultural matrices in which both reader and text are embedded'.[39] The living, breathing language and life and smells of the street in medieval France or archaic Greece or the trenches of the Somme are not available to a reader in the twenty-first century. 'The cultural matrix' only remains in stones and monuments, while flesh and bone perish and ancient value-systems wither away. The result is that the translator immediately faces a deficit because they cannot experience the same milieu as that of the original audience of the poem. Folkart shows that for the modern reader the translator has to become a mediator between the past and present and to do so they should be a 'writer' and not merely a 'replicator'; and to be that 'writer' there is a need to invest as much material as necessary to make the poem the

[37] Folkart (1998), 11. [38] Folkart (1998), 11. [39] Folkart (1998), 20.

translator's own.[40] As a writer Graves could re-imagine the scenarios of ancient Greece and put his experience of the trenches into scenes of war and degradation but they could still be a plausible fabrication (see Sean Tougher and Jon Coulston's essays). Graves faced criticism for his handling of the *Iliad* and the *Odyssey*; he gets into all sorts of trouble because he puts his stamp on a poem or narrative, and imbues it with what Zajko calls 'a literary quality'. Graves's (or another translator's) use of language may take the reader away from the source's literal or metaphorical meanings, and even distort or flatten the song of the Latin or Greek language, so much so that the original subtleties can be lost. However, a translator (or adaptor) creates an alternative version to that which has gone before, and one that brings to life the text in a way a contemporary audience can relate to. Folkart explains how Christopher Logue used a variety of methods to manipulate and create his acclaimed version of the *Iliad*:

> A more recent and no less brilliant example [than Ezra Pound] is Christopher Logue's rewrite of the *Patrocleia* (Book 16 of the *Iliad*). Rather than going for the kind of Wedgwood-china imagery and diction run-of-the-mill translators fall into line with, Logue has worked in a resolutely contemporary idiom, with the sort of technique, diction and structures that would not be out of place in his own, direct poetry: there's absolutely no translating down, here... Logue has been even more audacious with the manipulation of cultural props, using all sorts of anachronisms and 'anatopisms' to get us inside the poem... And since it's impossible for the latter half of the twentieth century to subscribe to Homer's glorification of warfare, Logue has unhesitatingly reversed Homer's stance: his *Patrocleia* reads like a condemnation of war.[41]

Graves shows he is wedded to the idea of using the exact words, even creating them, to describe emotion and action. In an interview in 1969 he talked of love:

> The act of love belongs to two people, in the way that secrets are shared. Hugs and kisses are permissible, but as soon as you start with what's called the mandalot—I invented the word, from the Greek; it comes from *mándalos* (which is the bolt you put in the socket) and means the tongue-kiss or by dictionary definition 'a lecherous and erotic kiss'—these familiarities you should reserve for those whom you really love.[42]

[40] Folkart (1998), 21. [41] RG in *The Paris Review* (1969).
[42] Carne Ross (1962/2010), 152.

The last word, for the moment at least, should go to Carne-Ross, as he argues that readers should not put Logue's translation next to Richmond Lattimore's. His comment in the postscript to Logue's *Patrocleia* may, to some extent, illuminate the translations of Robert Graves:

> The point about good translation is not that it 'gives you the original'. It doesn't and can't and shouldn't try to. There is one place to get Homer's *Iliad* and only one place: in the fifteen thousand lines or so of the Greek text. What a translation does is to turn the original into something else (*vertit anglice*) . . .'[43]

Graves's *The Anger of Achilles*, a narrative translation of the *Iliad*, largely in prose, is an example of the above, but the opening lines in verse demonstrate both the flaws and power of his rendition. Compare this to the 1997 translation of Lombardo;[44] what should the reader take from either version of the epic tale? First Graves:

> Sing, Mountain Goddess, sing through me
> That anger which most ruinously
> Inflamed Achilles, Peleus' son,
> And which, before the tale was done,
> Had glutted Hell with champions—bold,
> Stern spirits by the thousandfold;
> Ravens and dogs their corpses ate.
> For thus did Zeus, who watched their fate,
> See his resolve, first taken when
> Proud Agamemnon, King of men,
> An insult on Achilles cast,
> Achieve accomplishment at last.[45]

[43] See the introduction by Sheila Murnaghan to the Lombardo translation (1997), xvii–lviii.

[44] Graves continues: ' . . . I can tell you: it was Phoebus Apollo, the son of Almighty Zeus and Leto the Fair-Haired, who sent a fearful pestilence among the Greeks, by way of punishing Agamemnon their High King.' This has a poetic resonance with: 'Yet know, my master, God omnipotent | Is mustering in his clouds on our behalf | Armies of pestilence; and they shall strike | Your children yet unborn and unbegot, | That lift your vassal hands against my head | And threat the glory of my precious crown' (*Richard II*, III. iii).

[45] Just two recent examples are Tomas Alfredson's *Låt den rätte komma in* (2008) which became *Let Me In* (2010); and Hideo Nakata's *Ringu* (1998), which was remade as *The Ring* (2002); these Hollywood versions were very successful at the box office. A European success was Sergio Leone taking Akira Kurosawa's *Yojimbo* (1960) and turning it into *A Fistful of Dollars* (1964).

Then Lombardo:

Rage:
Sing, Goddess, Achilles' rage,
Black and murderous, that cost the Greeks
Incalculable pain, pitched countless souls
of heroes into Hades' dark,
and left their bodies to rot as feasts
for dogs and birds, as Zeus' will was done.
Begin with the clash between Agamemnon—
The Greek warlord—and godlike Achilles.
(*Iliad* 1.1–8)

The answer to the question must be subjective. Refashioning the original *Iliad* text, for example, 'into something else' through translation or adaptation is maybe what some scholars object to, because that 'something else' is not Homeric, or not Homeric enough—it is 'Homer-lite'. But if the latter reflects the contemporary milieu and speaks to a current readership, then is that necessarily a negative thing? Maybe a particular translation can suffer from the same critical dismay that proliferates when Hollywood takes a European or Asian low-fi hit and remodels it for the great mass of the cinema-going audience which resists films with subtitles.[46] In the music world, the same can happen when a 'cover version' of a track that has become something of a sacred cow is released; Eater's 1977 cover of *I'm Waiting for the Man*, rather than the original version by the Velvet Underground from 1967, will probably displease most Lou Reed aficionados.

CONCLUSION

In all of his endeavours it seems as though Graves tried to unwrap and expose the world he encountered, and then refashion it; this moulding was influenced by his beliefs about the Goddess or his experience of love, or war. He is insightful and infuriating in equal measure, and while we may not warm to his undoubtedly contrary

[46] Two recent examples are Tomas Alfredson's *Låt den rätte komma* in (2008) which became *Let Me In* (2010); and Hideo Nakata's *Ringu* (1998), which was remade as *The Ring* (2002); a European success was Sergio Leone taking Akira Kurosawa's *Yojimbo* (1960) and turning it into *A Fistful of Dollars* (1964).

nature, as this collection of essays shows, his multifaceted work can still provoke a powerful contemporary response.

As an addendum to the ongoing discussion of Graves's literary output there is one cultural icon of the twentieth century who may (inadvertently) illuminate part of the debate. In the late 1950s Bob Dylan had access to a friend's library in New York, in which, while preferring poetry, he also read works by a range of authors from Thucydides to Balzac to Robert Graves. Dylan writes: 'I read *The White Goddess* by Robert Graves, too. Invoking the poetic muse was something I didn't know about yet. Didn't know enough to start trouble with it, anyway.'[47] He would later meet Graves in London, and as Dylan says, 'I wanted to ask him some things about the book, but I couldn't remember much about it'.[48] So much for fame and influence—but it is noteworthy that Dylan read Graves when he was trying to find his own voice, listening to folk-songs, attracted by the ideas and the stories contained within them, and penetrating humanity in the milieu of fifties New York counterculture. Part of this searching led Dylan to an awakening:

> [Roy] Orbison, though, transcended all the genres—folk, country, rock and roll or just about anything. His stuff mixed all the styles and some that hadn't even been invented yet. He could sound mean and nasty on one line and then sing in a falsetto voice like Frankie Valli in the next. With Roy, you didn't know if you were listening to a *mariachi* or opera. He kept you on your toes. With him, it was all about fat and blood. He sounded like he was singing from an Olympian mountaintop and he meant business.[49]

Dylan's analysis of Roy Orbison gives an insight into the creative process of a great musician and artist, and one that provides a functional allegory for the methodology Graves used in fashioning his work, especially that related to Classics. Orbison had a unique voice and writing style and he attracted many fans from the 1960s onwards—and importantly for Orbison, his peers recognized his talents. Although Graves and Orbison were men of different generations there are similarities in their characters and their writing—both men would mould the rules of their craft to suit themselves. Graves used an 'analeptic' creative technique, an imaginative leap, where he tried to re-create a past and put himself in the mind of his

[47] Dylan (2004), 45. [48] Dylan (2004), 45. [49] Dylan (2004), 33.

protagonist.[50] He would mix fact and fiction, or interchange words, and play with sounds and meaning to get the best literary combination to match his intention.[51] This is not to judge the artistic success or failure of such a process, nor advocate that one should similarly equate artistic prowess across disciplines or genres. The talents of a musician and a writer can be disparate, but correspondence in the innovations and adaptations in technique mixed with ability (in whatever subjective form that may take) may go some way to explain the popularity and durability of their creative labours. Being controversial (whatever that expression may mean and however it manifests itself) can invoke a negativity amongst commentators which can in turn adversely affect the reception of a work in the wider world, although one could argue that *I, Claudius* would be an exception. But should one always equate 'controversial' with the negative? *Good-bye to All That* has provoked much argument and debate. Yet after eight decades the book still exists, it is still in print, and will probably ignite further discussion for years to come. Can this be a bad thing? If so, then on what terms is it a bad thing? Similarly, Graves's interpretation of classical myth has had a bumpy ride, but should his approach be accepted as some part of the critical and scholarly landscape or should it be consigned to the scrapheap? There will be many who will lean towards the latter view, but I would prefer that Robert Graves's works should remain to be rediscovered and debated by future generations of readers and scholars. The closing sentence of Peter Green's critical essay on the diversity and longevity of Graves's poetry stands well with this collection of essays and could equally apply to much of Graves's other literary work:

> Above all, he has inspired generations, win or lose, with the idea of what a poetic vocation should be. Those 'green fields of unrest' that lie at the heart of his last poem form an apt coda to his career. He would, I think, be proud to echo the claim of that other, equally tough, equally woman-oriented poet, the seventh-century B.C. Greek colonist Archilochus, who declared: 'I am both the War-God's servant, and have understanding of the Muses' lovely gifts.' In his rugged, smoldering, island bound old age he stands as a symbol for something above and beyond plain tangible achievement.[52]

[50] Goldman (2003) cites Robert Graves in *King Jesus*: 'To write a historical novel by the analeptic method—the intuitive recovery of forgotten events by a deliberate suspension of time—one must train oneself to think wholly in contemporary terms' (p. 45). Also cf. Presley (1997), 301.

[51] Green (1961/2), 46–50. [52] Green (1983), 118–19.

1

'It's readable all right, but it's not history'

Robert Graves's Claudius *Novels and the Impossibility of Historical Fiction*

Andrew Bennett

Two contemporary academic reviews of Robert Graves's *Claudius* novels—a review of *I, Claudius* in the *Classical Journal* by the American classicist Dorothea Clinton Woodworth, and a review of *Claudius the God* in *Scrutiny* by the British literary critic D. W. Harding—may be said to encapsulate the impossibility of historical fiction. The two reviews, both published in 1935, provide what might seem to be disciplinarily stereotypical and almost diametrically opposed views of the Claudius project, coming at it as they do from a historical and from a literary perspective respectively. It is on this opposition of literature to history, an opposition already at work within the generic mongrel-form of the historical novel, that I want to focus in this essay in order to think about the reception of Graves's Roman novels.

In her review of the novel, Woodworth characterizes *I, Claudius* as 'an interpretation in today's language of a period nineteen centuries remote', and comments that: 'Any student of ancient or contemporary society may profitably read the author's keen juxtaposition of the one against the other.'[1] But the review is focused above all on the question of historical accuracy. For Woodworth, the novel is 'More real than ponderous, documented Roman history' but still historical, and historically veracious, since, she declares, Graves 'uses ancient

[1] Woodworth (1935), 366.

sources as a scholar should'.[2] Woodworth therefore devotes much of her review to detailing points where Graves has silently chosen between 'divergent accounts' of events, or where he has invented events or circumstances of which there is no way of 'filling in gaps' in the historical record.[3] Such 'reconstructions', she considers, are 'skilfully and sympathetically contrived'. 'If this is fiction,' she continues—in a slightly odd equivocation that leaves open the possibility that for Woodworth it isn't, or shouldn't be—'not only is it consonant with historical accounts, but it also reconciles apparent discrepancies in the tradition and builds up the story by supplying motivation.'[4] In other words, Woodworth reads the novel, in the first place, as a piece of historical writing. Indeed, she declares that commenting on the 'literary quality of the book' is 'scarcely within the scope' of her review, and her attempt briefly to do so suggests the limits of her sense of the 'literary'. For Woodworth, the novel's literariness is limited to 'felicitous translations from Homer' and others, and the 'unification' of the narrative, or the various narrative strands (by the device of the Sibylline prophecy in chapter 1 and by what she calls the 'self-consistency' of the characterization of Claudius through which Graves is able to 'reconcile' the 'discordant phases' of the emperor's life).[5] In other words, when Woodworth talks about the 'literary' qualities of the novel, the features she refers to are more-or-less indistinguishable from the qualities that one might expect in a well written and historically reliable work. The important point for Woodworth is the novel's admirable, because accurate, historicality.

By direct and illuminating contrast, on the other hand, D. W. Harding, the author of, amongst other things, a volume of essays on Jane Austen entitled *Regulated Hatred*, doesn't much like *Claudius the God*, and marshals his considerable powers of *Scrutiny*-honed disdain to express his regulated hatred of the novel. 'Mr Graves has well succeeded in what seems to have been his object', Harding begins mildly enough, 'to give by careful reconstruction a convincing idea of the memoirs of an imperial Roman statesman written according to the perspective of the period'.[6] But the next sentence craftily damns with faint praise: 'He has been very thorough', Harding assures the reader. And then comes the sucker-punch: 'Details of

[2] Woodworth (1935), 366–7.
[3] Woodworth (1935), 367.
[4] Woodworth (1935), 368.
[5] Woodworth (1935), 368.
[6] H[arding] (1935), 421.

public works and policies, of ceremonies and campaigns, are all made palatable, and it is easy to go on reading right to the end unless you can think of something you want to do'.[7] As if that final phrase needs emphasis (not 'something better to do', but just 'something'—*anything*—'you want to do'), the next sentence rubs it in: 'For those who prefer reading to gardening at the week-end this book will be thoroughly welcome.'[8] This is the epitome of the kind of laconic, often barely stated but always imperious disdain, the regulated hatred, indeed, for which *Scrutiny* and its chief editor F. R. Leavis were famous—the insinuation being that, for many, gardening might in fact be preferable to reading Graves's novel. Harding also assesses the book's literary qualities, in a brief comment that explains what Graves does well but fails to do enough of:

> The most interesting part of the book, the only part with any pressure behind it, is the end, in its presentation of Claudius's tired cynicism towards the kind of affairs his active years had been devoted to, and his realization that his efforts could have contributed nothing to the ideal he had held for Rome. It is only here for a few pages that the story has any of the interest that one might have hoped for on the strength of some of Mr. Graves' poetry.[9]

Harding concludes, more generally, that the book is 'academic' and that it displays all the 'virtues and lifelessness' of academic writing. I think that we might interpret the 'pressure' that Harding responds to at the end of *Claudius the God* as having something to do with the 'literary' as opposed to the scholarly or historical, and as being related no doubt to what Samuel Johnson calls 'the force of poetry'.[10] Harding associates this 'pressure' with 'some of' Graves's poetry, and it seems to involve the kind of tension—within Claudius's consciousness and between his sense of idealism and his sense of the futility of his efforts to restore the Republic—that we might see as 'dramatic' or 'novelistic' or 'literary': it is this kind of tension or conundrum or aporia or paradox that, for a certain kind of critic at least, *constitutes* the literary itself. But Harding's conclusion is that for the critic who

[7] H[arding] (1935), 421. [8] H[arding] (1935), 421–2.

[9] H[arding] (1935), 422.

[10] Johnson (2000) 247: the essay is from *The Rambler*, vol. 168 (Saturday, 26 Oct. 1751). For Johnson, this is a force 'which calls new powers into being, which embodies sentiment, and animates matter'.

prefers gardening, even, to the reading of dry, academic history, there is just too little of this kind of 'pressure'.

Much of what I want to discuss is encapsulated in these opposing responses to the two novels, this opposition of the response of the classicist to that of the literary critic, indeed of history to literature—an opposition that is in fact already at work in the generic identity of the *Claudius* novels and even in some ways coded within the distinction between the 'readable' and the historical in my title's quotation from *I, Claudius*. I think we can take it that, insofar as Robert Graves may be said to have made a significant contribution to twentieth-century fiction—to fiction as opposed to autobiography, war writing, poetry, translation, the popularizing through rewriting of classical mythology, or elaborations on his own idiosyncratic (if not just plain inaccurate) brand of mythopoetics—it is through the Roman novels, and particularly the two *Claudius* novels. It is these two novels that have reached a wide audience, and not only through film and television adaptations: the novels were immediately popular and have been in print more-or-less continuously since their publication in 1934. One straightforward way to gauge the specifically *literary* impact of Graves's *Claudius* novels, however, is to note their place within—or indeed their absence from—literary-critical discourse. Since their publication there have been only a handful of academic articles on the novels, the most significant of which are a 1995 essay by Philip Burton on their cultural and political topicality or contemporaneity; a rather shorter piece by Chris Hopkins from 1999 on Graves's work in the context of other historical novels of the period; an essay published the following year by Clayton Koelb on the engagement with the past in the *Claudius* novels as well as three further essays in a collection edited by Ian Firla; and, most recently, a technical piece from the field of translation studies from 2005 on the novels in relation to the question of 'pseudotranslation', by Olaf du Pont.[11] There is also a 2004 essay by the critic P. N. Furbank on the weakness of the historical novel in general that treats the *Claudius* novels as exemplary.[12] This seems to me to represent relatively thin pickings, and part of my interest in discussing the novels is to try to tease out some sense of why, despite their continuing popularity over three-quarters of a century, Graves's *Claudius* novels have not been much

[11] Burton (1995); Hopkins (1999); Koelb (2000); Firla (2000); du Pont (2005).
[12] Furbank (2004).

recognized or studied or appreciated or indeed read within the literary-critical institution—why, despite Martin Seymour-Smith's assessment that the *Claudius* novels are 'anything but academic or "historical" in the accepted sense' and his assertion that *I, Claudius* was 'hailed as a masterpiece by reviewers', D. W. Harding's judgement of the literary failings of *Claudius the God* in fact seems accurately to have foreshadowed the subsequent reception of both novels by mainstream literary critics.[13] My suggestion is that this situation has something to do with certain intrinsic difficulties in the historical novel as such, difficulties that Graves fails to resolve and perhaps indeed exacerbates: the *Claudius* novels may be said to bring to our attention the problem of the historical novel itself, its 'impossibility' even.

There is confusion, from the first, regarding this strange tautology, or oxymoron, 'historical fiction'—regarding the relationship between history and the novel or history and fiction. The phrase 'historical novel' is a tautology in the sense that all novels, by their very nature, even those set in the future, are 'historical' because they relate events that have been (or will have been). While it is true that science fiction is often based on an imagined future (Graves's own 1949 novel *Seven Days in New Crete* itself being an example), few if any novels have been narrated in the future tense. And even if they are or could be, even such a futuring in fact acts *as if* it tells of a certain past. But 'historical novel' is also an oxymoron with respect to the fact that that which is historical is precisely not, precisely opposed to, that which is 'novel'—in the sense of 'new', to be sure, but also in the sense that insofar as the novel is identified with 'fiction', it is concerned with what is imagined as opposed simply to recording what happened.[14]

[13] Seymour-Smith (1982), 229, 232; see also Seymour (1995), 222, on the 'eulogistic' reviews of *I, Claudius*, which, with *Claudius the God*, led to the award of the James Tait Black Memorial Prize and the Hawthornden Prize. It is perhaps significant that Jerome de Groot's recent book on *The Historical Novel* makes only a single passing reference to Robert Graves (de Groot (2010), 4).

[14] See Wallace (2005), x. On the rather specialized question of a future-tense narrative, see Abbott (2005), 534–5. Abbott cites Michael Frayn's 1967 novel *A Very Private Life* as, unusually, a novel set in the future, but points out that it is in fact told mainly in the present tense. As Abbott comments, 'even future tense narrative conveys a sense of something already there to be recounted, if only in a place called the future'. For a rather different take on the 'impossibility' of the historical novel, see Furbank (2004), 95: Furbank argues that there are two types of historical novel, the 'modernizing' and the 'archaizing', and that 'both suffer from attempting

It may be that the confusion about historical fiction is generated, paradoxically, by the attempt properly to demarcate the two discourses, to assert their fundamental difference. At the end of his 2006 introduction to the Penguin edition of *I, Claudius*, Barry Unsworth catches himself up on this point. The questions of historical accuracy and of the relationship between historicality and interpretation 'persist', he comments. 'We don't know,' he concludes: we don't know about the past, and we don't know about Claudius's true character and his motivations, 'nobody does':

> But of course it doesn't matter. Yet again we have to remind ourselves of what we are always in danger of forgetting as we read this compelling narrative, with its impeccable research, the tremendous intellectual feat of organization that it represents. It is fiction, after all.[15]

What Unsworth engages with here is the difficulty of reading Graves's novels, and the particular uncertainty, anxiety even, that they present with regard to their own historicity. For Unsworth, this involves an inevitable, unavoidable problem of forgetting that these are not historical accounts, and the need to remember, again and again, that *I, Claudius* 'is fiction, after all'. The problem for Graves, the problem that he faces but fails fully to confront or resolve, is that the historical novel both is and is not historical. It is this ultimately deconstructive logic that, I suggest, cannot be accepted within the terms set by Graves's novels. However much the distinction might be blurred or complicated, Graves cannot rest content within the terms of the unstable, undecidable both–and logic—the logic that may in fact be said to be at work in the literary more generally. This forgetting to which Unsworth alludes is, in the end, the problem: these novels both are and are not historiography, but it often seems that Graves himself would like us to forget that inconvenient truth, to forget that he is *not* writing history.

Graves's own conflicted sense of the significance of history to his novels might be discerned in two remarks in letters to T. E. Lawrence from 1933: he comments that *I, Claudius* is 'largely guess-work &

something impossible'—both, briefly, involve insoluble logical and chronological improbabilities. In fact, Furbank concludes that 'the historical novel cannot be historical', since it 'simply does not work as an art form unless some place is found in it, by fictional means, for the modern consciousness' (Furbank (2004), 112).

[15] Unsworth (2006), x. References to *I, Claudius* are to this edition, Graves (2006b), and cited as *IC* in the text.

imagination'; but he also tells Lawrence that he chose Claudius for his subject and as his narrator because 'he was a historian before he was anything else'.[16] Graves also complains of *I, Claudius* to Julie Matthews in a letter of July 1933, that 'I have to read so many classical authorities to get it anything like historical that it's been a beastly job'.[17] In a letter of May 1934 to Tom Matthews, Graves includes a list of 'historical notes' in case Matthews reviews the novel.[18] The notes include explanations of Graves's additions ('suggestions') to the historical record where there are gaps and an explanation of his method. He has, he says, nowhere '*gone against* history' but has 'felt free to invent' where there are uncertainties or gaps: 'If I had written my version of the story in the second century it would now be taken as authentic', he remarks rather boldly.[19] But again there is a certain ambivalence: while Graves asserts that he is 'not a Classical scholar or anything of that sort', and that if he had been 'my historical conscience would not have let me invent anything', he also warns that reviewers will have to be careful not to claim invention where there are in fact historical sources. The screenplay that he is preparing for Alexander Korda's proposed film of the Claudius novels, he remarks in a later letter, 'will be kept as historical as possible' (O'Prey (1982), 242).

Graves repeatedly seeks to assert the full, proper historicity of his writing, then, not in order to question or to shake up the opposition of novel and history, but simply in order to assert the authenticity of his narrative, and ultimately to confirm the soundness of his own scholarship.[20] The problem is exacerbated in often strangely insouciant ways in relation to the various kinds of text with which the novels are surrounded (the subcategory of paratext that Gérard Genette calls 'peritexts')[21]—most of which seem intended to assert that this is indeed history, and not fiction or literature. So, before they begin, the novels present various peritexts that challenge the reader's sense of the novelistic. In the first place, the title-pages of the two novels

16 Quoted in Seymour-Smith (1982), 255–6.

17 O'Prey (1982), 224.

18 See O'Prey (1982), 236–7 and appendix B (pp. 348–9).

19 O'Prey (1982), 349.

20 As a number of critics have pointed out, Graves may have been influenced in this respect by his great-great uncle, the nineteenth-century historian Leopold von Ranke, often seen as the 'founder' of modern, empirically based historical study (see Hopkins (1999), 131–2; Burton (1995), 209).

21 Genette (1997), 5.

present elaborations on the short titles, *I, Claudius* and *Claudius the God*, which seem to be intended to announce, above all, the historicity of the ensuing texts:

> I, Claudius
> from the autobiography of
> Tiberius Claudius
> Emperor of the Romans
> born 10 BC
> murdered and deified
> AD 54

'From' is both ambiguous here and boldly assertive of autobiographical and therefore historical authenticity. And then there is the longer and even seemingly almost self-parodic title-page for *Claudius the God*:

> Claudius the God
> and his wife Messalina
> The troublesome reign of Tiberius Claudius
> Caesar, Emperor of the Romans
> (born 10 BC, died AD 54),
> as described by himself;
> also his murder at the hands of the
> notorious Agrippina
> (mother of the Emperor Nero)
> and his subsequent deification
> as described by
> others[22]

Everything that is presented in these full titles beyond the short title (the dates, the details of events, the specification of family relations, and that odd and historically anxious phrase 'as described by others') goes to counterbalance or even to eliminate or eradicate the novelistic—including the novelism of the phrases 'I, Claudius' and 'Claudius the God'. In early editions of *I, Claudius* the title-page even included what purports to be a facsimile of the Greek signature of the emperor Claudius, as if as an autobiographical guarantee of authenticity. Next, since the 1941 Penguin edition of the novel, the reader of *I, Claudius* is confronted by a poem, 'the Latin version

[22] Graves (2006c), title-page. References to *Claudius the God* are to this edition and are cited as *CG* in the text.

of the Sibylline verses mentioned in the first chapter', in a translation by 'Mr A. K. Smith, I.C.S.'. In a curious deformation of what we might call the authenticity-effect, the ascription fails to make it clear that the verses are translated from Graves's English rather than from an 'original' Greek inscription.[23] This may be an oversight or it may be obvious to some that the verses are invented by Graves, but it may also be seen as a powerful ambiguity that equivocates over the historicality of the ensuing narrative, allowing again for a certain illusion of historical authenticity. The verses are followed by an epigram taken from the *Annals* of the historian Tacitus, concerning the revenge taken for the death of Claudius's brother Germanicus: Tacitus briefly breaks off from his narrative to make a general comment on the way that 'transactions of pre-eminent importance' are always 'wrapt in doubt and obscurity' because of hearsay, falsehood, and the exaggerations of 'posterity'. At first glance, the framing epigraph might seem to blur the distinction between history and fiction. In fact, though, it may also be understood to have the effect of *reasserting* both the essential truth-value of historical discourse and the historicity of Graves's novel. Graves is as much a historian as Tacitus, the epigraph seems to indicate: if one of Graves's major historical sources is the great classical historian Tacitus (who himself acknowledges the difficulty of distinguishing history from certain forms of fictionality) then Graves's novel may itself be said to constitute a version of history. And while the comment by Tacitus might appear to complicate or undermine the opposition between history and fiction, it only does so in as much as it in fact *reinforces* the truth-value of historical discourse. In the end, it is only because the historian believes in the falsifiability of historical discourse that doubt and obscurity, hearsay, falsehood, and exaggeration ('fictionality', one might say) are conceived as problematic.

But Graves is not done with the framing epitexts to *I, Claudius*. Before we come to the novel proper there is an 'Author's Note' that raises the philological question of the accuracy of the translations in some of the novel's choice of terminology, and that acknowledges the work of Eirlys Roberts in ensuring its 'classical correctness' (*IC* 8).[24]

[23] In chapter 1 Claudius claims that the verses were recorded 'in the original Greek' as well as in 'rough Latin verse translation' (*IC* 16).

[24] Compare de Groot (2010), 6–9 on authors' notes and the question of authenticity in the historical novel.

The effect of the note is again to reinforce our sense that the novel is determinedly historical, that historiographical accuracy is essential to it. And in fact the 'Author's Note' to *Claudius the God* is even more telling in this context: here Graves comments on details of ancient Roman currency, measures of distance, dates, and place-names, and affirms the breadth of his research: since some reviewers had complained that the first novel simply draws on Tacitus and Suetonius, Graves lists as his sources twenty-two historians, the Bible, and the Apocrypha as well as the surviving letters and speeches of Claudius: 'Few incidents here given are wholly unsupported by historical authority of some sort or other and I hope none are historically incredible,' he remarks; 'No character', he affirms, 'is invented' (*CG* 7–9). There is no question of the lengths to which Graves went to guarantee historical accuracy, but what is at stake here is the question of the lengths to which he also went to *frame* the novels, to present them, as historically reliable.

In addition to these preliminary authenticating texts, a number of other peritexts are affixed to the novels as they proceed, serving to reinforce the sense that *I, Claudius* and *Claudius the God* are novels in which history comes before invention or imagination or the literary. In particular, dates are added in the margin at various points, and a number of footnotes, signed 'R.G.', are provided, offering factual information or occasional editorial glosses.[25] Indeed, part of the problem is just the use of the initials 'R.G.'. In as much as 'R.G.' stands for Robert Graves, rather than, say, 'Robert Graves' or 'the author' in a self-consciously metafictional sense, the initials stand for historical authenticity, guaranteeing, so to speak, the truth-value of what is stated. R.G., like Robert Graves, stands outside of the fictionalizing world of the novels, playing no part in the text's language games. And in as much as they guarantee historical authenticity, I suggest, the initials work against the question of literature. In none of this is there any attempt to dwell on or play with the conventions of fiction and the novel form, and no sense that these intrusions by the authorial 'R.G.' might complicate or compromise in interesting ways the illusion of autobiographical immediacy on which the text is based. Graves seems oddly insouciant towards, uninterested in, the fictionality of his fiction, and there is little to indicate an

[25] e.g. *CG* 362 and 404.

awareness of the modernist or proto-postmodernist concern with the literary conventions of authorship, authenticity, and fictionality: instead, Graves seems simply and naively determined to guarantee the historical veracity of his narrative. And this is the effect indeed of the final historical and pseudo-historical documentation with which both novels end: a family tree for the Roman emperors is affixed to the end of *I, Claudius*, and the family tree of the Herods, three historical accounts of Claudius's death, and Seneca's satirical account of Claudius are appended to *Claudius the God*.

In all of these ways, Graves attempts to assert historiographical accuracy and to eliminate fictionality. In fact, little is done to develop what could be highly productive areas of what I am trying to pinpoint as the novels' potential or latent 'literariness'. In particular, there is little sense that Graves is interested in or even aware of the ways in which the question of the relationship between authorial presence and/or absence has informed the novelistic at least from the eighteenth-century in both a problematic and productive way. Despite admitting to T. E. Lawrence in a letter that he particularly 'identifies' with Claudius, the novels give little indication, for example, of the extent to which Claudius is necessarily bound up with the author, Robert Graves. There is little indication that Claudius's narrative *is* Graves's; that Claudius's stammer, his way of speaking and therefore of writing, is also necessarily that of the stuttering Graves;[26] and little or no sense that Claudius's obsession with powerful women, his abasement, even, towards such women might reflect, in complicated ways, Graves's relationship with Laura Riding in the 1930s, and indeed the contemporary development of his zany 'White Goddess' theory of artistic creativity.[27] Instead, both

[26] On Graves's stutter, see his poem 'The Second-Fated', ll. 1–3: 'My stutter, my cough, my unfinished sentences | Denote an inveterate physical reluctance | To use the metaphysical idiom' (Graves (1975), 195); and see Virginia Woolf's comment on Graves in 1925 as 'halfbaked, stammering stuttering' (quoted in Kersnowski (2002), 8).

[27] See Graves's comment in a letter to T. E. Lawrence, that 'I identify myself with [Claudius] as much as with any other historical character I know about . . . I identify myself with him historically, but merely historically' (quoted in Seymour-Smith (1982), 256). And compare: Seymour-Smith's comments on the *I, Claudius* narrative as 'an objective correlative for [Graves's] situation' (p. 231; see pp. 230–2); Seymour (1995), 215, on the 'strength of the *Claudius* books' as involving 'the personality of their imaginary author, the reticent, erudite Emperor in whom Graves recreated himself' (see also pp. 216–17 on Livia and Messalina as versions of Laura Riding); and R. P. Graves (1990), 190.

R.G. and Robert Graves do no more than separately stand, in unexamined and seemingly uncomplicated ways, for extra-textual authorities on historical matters.

Everything in the peritextual apparatus of these novels, in other words, points to their historical authenticity; there is little or nothing that points to or points up their literariness, that emphasizes the novelistic status of the texts, their fictionality: literariness is fended off at almost every opportunity in favour of historical and biographical authenticity. What is missing, in the end, is just the novelistic *play* on or with this question of authenticity—a degree of self-consciousness about the fictionality even (or especially) of the historical that is intrinsic to the English novel from Defoe, Fielding, and Sterne, through George Eliot and Dickens, to—more contemporaneously—Woolf, Joyce, and others. All of these novelists, and the major traditions in English fiction generally, are constitutively alert to the logical, generic, and formal possibilities, paradoxes, and ironies, and to the general conceptual and linguistic *slipperiness* that is necessarily at work in relation to questions of historicity, and of authorship and authenticity in narrative fiction. Graves tends specifically and unrelentingly to fend off such play, to abjure it, to deny himself the force of his texts' own potential 'literariness', their textuality, indeed. Instead, the novels assert, more-or-less univocally, the empirical accuracy, the unproblematic, unproblematized authenticity of a historical account.

There are many references to the fundamental *difference* between history and literature within the novels themselves. The question of the distinction between history and literature appears early on in *I, Claudius*, when Claudius talks about his education and about his decision to start writing history. His tutor, Athenodorus, he says, 'tried to interest me in speculative philosophy, but when he saw that I had no bent that way he did not force me to exceed the usual bounds of polite education in the subject'. Instead, Claudius records, Athenodorus steers him towards history by giving him Livy's *History of Rome* to read, 'as an example of lucid and agreeable writing': 'Livy's stories enchanted me', Claudius remembers (*IC* 64). Throughout this passage, and in the paragraphs that follow, there is a constant, troubled concern with the *literariness* of historical writing. So here Athenodorus suggests that Claudius reads Livy 'as an example of lucid and agreeable writing', and it is the fact that Livy tells 'stories' and that those stories 'enchanted' Claudius that is emphasized in his conversion to historiography. But at the same time a countervailing resistance to or rejection of the literary is at work. In describing Athenodorus in the next paragraph, Claudius uses a simile but denies its poeticality. He tells us that Athenodorus had a 'most wonderful beard' that 'spread in waves down to his waist', a beard that was 'as white as a swan's wing', but then goes on to qualify this figure of speech, indeed to eliminate it *as* a figure of speech: 'I do not make this as an idle poetical comparison, for I am not the sort of historian who writes in pseudo-epic style', he says. Instead, he affirms that he means to indicate simply that the beard was indeed literally 'as white as a swan's wing' (*IC* 65). It is important for Graves, here and elsewhere, to present Claudius as a writer who eschews writerliness, who writes plain history, who eliminates, as far as possible, the play of language: the simile is no figure of speech, is not a metaphor, but rather the statement of a literal truth.[28] For Graves, the distinction between poetry or literature and history needs to be rigorously policed, consistently maintained—precisely because of history's tendency to slip into a form of dangerous 'enchantment' through 'lucid and agreeable writing'.[29]

The most explicit expression of the history–literature distinction is made when the young Claudius banteringly discusses historical writing with Livy and Asinius Pollio, in a passage that is discussed by more-or-less everyone who has written on *I, Claudius*.[30] Pollio and Livy are engaged in a friendly–aggressive sparring match over their respective versions of history-writing. Pollio asks Claudius if he has read Livy's work. 'Isn't that at least trashier writing than mine?', he asks:

> I smiled. 'Well, at least it's easier to read.'
> 'Easier, eh? How's that?'

[28] On this point, see also Claudius's self-critical comments in chapter 24: 'Once you give way to a metaphor, Claudius, which is rare, you pursue it too far. Surely you remember Athenodorus's injunctions against this sort of thing? Well, call Sejanus the maggot and get it done with; then return to your usual homely style!' (*IC* 281).

[29] This distinction is emphasized elsewhere. Talking to Camilla as an adolescent, Claudius asks her if she likes history: 'I think I like poetry the best', she replies, confirming poetry's opposition to the historical. And her elaboration on this reply perhaps confirms one's sense of what history means for Graves (as much as for Camilla): 'there are so many names and dates to remember in history', she complains (*IC* 91). While this is a source of *complaint* for Camilla one would be forgiven for thinking that for Graves it is simply an accurate description of how history works.

[30] See Burton (1995), 208–10; Koelb (2000), 35–6; Hopkins (1999), 131–2; Furbank (2004), 102–3.

> 'He makes the people of Ancient Rome behave and talk as if they were alive now.'
>
> Pollio was delighted. 'He has you there, Livy, on your weakest spot. You credit the Romans of seven centuries ago with impossibly modern motives and habits and speeches. Yes, it's readable all right, but it's not history.' (*IC* 103)

This is an overtly and somewhat heavy-handedly self-conscious moment, and it articulates two related problems in historical fiction with which Graves is grappling: the problem of anachronism and the problem of readability. Anachronism—in the sense of the attempt to modernize historical material—might make fiction 'readable' but it also makes it unhistorical; to be 'readable' in this sense is to not be history. This touches on a point that P. N. Furbank has identified as one of the fundamental problems in historical fiction,[31] and it is one that Graves attempts to overcome by the rather clunky device of presenting Claudius as writing for an audience that will live far in the future (precisely and conveniently 1,900 years in the future). But at this point Graves seems to be questioning the efficacy of such a device: Claudius goes on to describe Pollio's life and work, commenting that although he is a 'distinguished orator and writer of tragedies' he is 'a better historian than he was either tragedian or orator, because he had a love of literal truth, amounting to pedantry, which he could not square with the conventions of these other literary forms' (*IC* 104). Claudius then returns to the three-way conversation in an extended meditation on the opposition between literature and history:

> Livy said: 'The trouble with Pollio is that when he writes history he feels obliged to suppress all his finer, more poetical feelings, and make his characters behave with conscientious dullness, and when he puts a speech into their mouths he denies them the least oratorical ability.'
>
> Pollio said: 'Yes, Poetry is Poetry, and Oratory is Oratory, and History is History, and you can't mix them.' (*IC* 104)

In the end, it is Pollio, the historian who firmly upholds the distinction between history and poetry, that comes out of the discussion best, and when Claudius is made to choose one model for history-writing he chooses Pollio: 'I am sure that I can never hope to attain Livy's inspired literary elegance,' he says, so 'I shall do my best to

[31] See Furbank (2004), 95.

imitate Pollio's accuracy and diligence' (*IC* 106–7). Before the conversation ends (in a rather bitter impasse and with Livy storming out), Claudius attempts to mediate between the two forms of history, suggesting that 'perhaps they are not irreconcilable' (*IC* 109). But Pollio's rather cutting response—'Why, boy, you're an orator'—makes it clear that such a reconciliation would be at the expense of veracity. The enraged Livy then departs and Pollio emerges as Claudius's model historian. Paradoxically, therefore, Graves's historical novels seem to uphold a certain form of non-literary history writing as the ideal, and the idea of the fundamental, finally irreconcilable opposition between two discourses pervades his novels. 'I am a professional historian,' Claudius perhaps rather anachronistically remarks at one point, 'and the one thing that really interests me is to find out how things happen and why' (*IC* 289).[32]

There is at least one other mechanism that Graves's novels employ to assert their historiographical veracity. An important dimension of the persona that Graves creates for his narrator is as an incompetent (rather than necessarily unreliable) narrator. The explicit notification of flashbacks and prolepses, for example, is, along with other forms of narrative signposting, prevalent in the books but often somewhat awkwardly presented, and one might ask what purpose is served by the inclusion of such blatantly contrived narrative links. There are many examples: 'I must now go back a few years to write about my uncle Tiberius', Claudius characteristically begins chapter 6 of *I, Claudius* (*IC* 66); 'I shall explain later how I came to learn all this', he says a few pages later (*IC* 71); 'I went back in time a few years to tell of my Uncle Tiberius, but by following that history through until his adoption by Augustus, I have come out ahead of my own story', chapter 7 begins, in another characteristically incompetent, or at least unsophisticated, temporal adjustment in narrative (*IC* 83); 'But

[32] See also the following comment at the end of *I Claudius*: 'The pillared portrait-busts of Herodotus, Polybius, Thucydides, and Asinius Pollio stood facing me. Their impassive features seemed to say: "A true historian will always rise superior to the political disturbances of his day." I determined to comport myself as a true historian' (*IC* 392). I am not, of course, suggesting that in any simple sense Graves just is historically accurate—knowledgeable and widely read he may be, but as Furbank argues, he distorted his sources to make Claudius appear wiser, wittier, more controlling of his circumstances and more sympathetic than others had allowed: 'Graves, in answer to the question of what the emperor Claudius was "like", represents him as a sensitive modern or near-modern Englishman, somewhat Oxford or Cambridge in style' (Furbank (2004), 101).

before I continue with the story of Postumus I must tell of my meeting with the "Last of the Romans"', he says at the end of chapter 8 (*IC* 102); 'This prosecution was followed two years later—but I put it down here because the Agamemnon story reminds me of it—by that of Cremutius Cordus . . . ', he comments at another point (*IC* 264); 'And so I come to the account of my dinner with Livia', he begins chapter 25 (*IC* 284). 'This ends the first part of the story of Herod Agrippa', Claudius comments at the end of his four-chapter digression at the beginning of *Claudius the God*, 'but you shall hear the rest as I continue to tell my own' (*CG* 62). And then, as the next chapter begins, there is an equally awkward segue: 'So here we are back again at the point where I was being carried round the great court of the Palace on the shoulders of two corporals of the Guard . . . ' (*CG* 62). There is a self-conscious casualness about some of the links: 'Before I forget it, there is another story that I want to tell about a stolen golden cup, and it may as well go in here as anywhere', Claudius remarks at one point in *Claudius the God* (*CG* 139). Such comments are sometimes linked to explicit references to the empirical basis of Claudius's historiography: 'But I shall not record her behaviour in detail here', he says of Messalina's descent into debauchery, 'because I was, so far, wholly ignorant of it' (*CG* 280). At times, as this suggests, Claudius himself acknowledges the awkwardness of his narrative transitions, as in a potentially (but in fact underplayed) Shandyesque moment at the end of chapter 15 of *I, Claudius* (one of the relatively few moments where Graves plays on the meta-narrative conventions of fiction-writing): 'But this has been a very ill-judged digression, leaving Germanicus, as it were, waiting anxiously for his money while I write a book about dice' (*IC* 182). Such awkward narrative links are prominent in the novels and cannot but be seen as important indices of Graves's literary-historical position. Perhaps part of what is at work here involves Graves's attempt to articulate in writing Claudius's verbal 'lameness'—his stammer and his apparent incompetence in making speeches. This is something that Graves explicitly confronts at one point in *I, Claudius*: 'call me Claudius', the historian says to Camilla at one point, 'That's my appropriate name. It means a cripple', he tells her (*IC* 90). And then, when she compliments him on the way that he 'tell[s] things', he demurs: 'But I stammer. My tongue's a Claudian too', he says (*IC* 91). This concern with verbal incapacity may in this context be seen as part of Graves's strategy of historical accuracy, his concern with the documented facts of Claudius's disability. Perhaps it is not too much to say that Claudius's narrative is awkwardly stitched together as a scriptural sign of the emperor's historically verifiable speech-impediment. But I think that the technique also allows for a further level of authenticity, the narrative awkwardness being an effect simply of 'authentic' first-century AD narration: Graves resists the more complex and subtle modes of narration that were developed particularly in the nineteenth- and early twentieth-century novel on the back of new narratological or novelistic technologies such as free indirect discourse, just as he resists to a large extent the representation of interiorized consciousness which may be understood as one of the triumphs of the genre, and we might speculate that this is because the exploitation of such techniques would amount to a form of narratological anachronism. Moreover, and again more specifically, more biographically, in the 'Author's Note' to *I, Claudius* Graves reminds us that Suetonius refers to Claudius's histories as written '"ineptly" rather than "inelegantly"', and that if his novel is 'inelegant' or 'awkward' in places, as well as inept, then this too 'is not out of keeping with Claudius's literary style' (*IC* 8). In these ways, then, Graves insists on the *realism* of his version of Claudius's narrative and its historical veracity and credibility.[33]

So I want to propose that Graves's attempt to ground the novels in historical factuality, in empirical and even stylistic accuracy, may be seen to work against their force as *novels*, as *literary* works, and that rather than questioning or breaking down the opposition between literature and history, Graves's approach seems to reinforce it. It is an opposition that goes back at least to Aristotle's *Poetics*, in fact, in a tradition of which Graves himself is certainly aware, and it is worth briefly looking at the way in which Aristotle's distinction between literature and history is developed in these novels: it is here, I think, that we can most clearly discern the problems that arise in Graves's conceptualization of the historical novel. In his 1982 biography, Martin Seymour-Smith points to the significance in Graves's work of Aristotle's distinction between literature and history. Seymour-Smith argues that the popularity of the *Claudius* novels (and of the TV version in particular) is due to their sense of 'immediacy, of

[33] For a related consideration of the 'translationese' of the novels, see du Pont (2005).

actuality', and he summarizes Aristotle to the effect that fiction 'may be more satisfying than the real' because it can 'present the *general* truth about something more effectively . . . than could some *particular* (or even unique) historical record'.[34] Seymour-Smith is recalling a paragraph from chapter 9 of the *Poetics*, where Aristotle presents his famous distinction between poetry and history, and is also, I think, influenced by Graves's own engagement with this moment in the *Poetics*. In chapter 9 Aristotle seems reasonably clear: 'the poet's task is to speak not of events which have occurred,' he argues, 'but of the kinds of events that *could* occur, and are possible by the standards of probability or necessity.' Aristotle contrasts this function with that of the historian, who 'speaks of events which have occurred'. From this, Aristotle goes on to argue that poetry is therefore 'both more philosophical and more serious than history', since 'poetry speaks more of universals (τὰ καθόλου), history of particulars (τὰ καθ' 'έκαστον)'.[35] It is important to note that Aristotle then qualifies this claim by explaining that there is nothing to stop a poet representing something that has happened, since something that has happened is, by definition, 'in conformity with probability'.[36] But Aristotle's important distinction makes it clear that poetry has an unstable, uncertain status—that, as critics and theorists after him have realized, the 'force' of poetry may be said to rely to a significant degree on a certain undecidability with regard to poetry's relationship with *both* the singular *and* the general (or what Aristotle calls the 'universal'). What is particular, what is singular, about poetry is that it is not history, not *just* an account of what happened, and that it is at the same time not—not quite, not only—philosophy, not *just* the representation of 'universal' truths. Rather, poetry, or literature, inhabits an uncanny, strictly undecidable site that encompasses both and neither within a both–and logic of exemplarity (whereby a poem or literary text can be both unique and an example of the kind of thing of which it is talking, both this unique, singular, one-off poem and an example of a poem, of all poems, of poetry). As Derrida comments: 'Something of literature will have begun when it is not possible to decide whether, when I speak of something, I am speaking of something (of the thing itself, this one, for itself) or if I am giving an example, an example of something or an example of the fact that I can speak of something.'[37]

[34] Seymour-Smith (1982), 229–30. [35] Aristotle (1987), 40–1.
[36] Aristotle (1987), 41. [37] Derrida (1995), 142–3.

Joseph Kronick glosses this as indicating that literature 'witnesses the undecidability between the singular and the general', and comments that, from a Derridean perspective, 'Not to understand this is to have trouble with literature'.[38]

It seems likely, as I say, that Seymour-Smith is recalling Graves's own engagement with Aristotle, specifically a passage from Graves's 1922 book *On English Poetry*, in which he cites precisely this passage from the *Poetics*. In chapter 23 of *On English Poetry* Graves attempts to distinguish the 'Classical' from the 'Romantic' idea of poetry by contrasting the 'probability' of Classicism with the imaginative flights that drive Romanticism. But this distinction is derived in the first place from the paragraph on poetry and history in the *Poetics* that Seymour-Smith uses to explain the popularity of the *Claudius* novels:

> When Aristotle lays down that poets describe the thing that might be, but that the historian . . . merely describes that which has been, and that poetry is something of 'more philosophic, graver import than history because its statements are of a universal nature' so far his idea of poetry tallies with our own. But when he explains his 'might be' as meaning the 'probable and necessary' according to our every-day experience of life, then we feel the difference between the Classical and Romantic conceptions of art—Aristotle was trying to weed poetry of all the symbolic extravagances and impossibilities of the dream state in which it seems to have originated, and to confine it within rational and educative limits.[39]

This seems rather questionable as a reading of the *Poetics*. But I think that Graves's missing of or veering from what I take to be the point of Aristotle is crucial and goes to the heart of the historiographico-literary question in the *Claudius* novels. And it is related to a distinction that Graves makes in the first chapter—indeed, on the first page—of *On English Poetry*, where he distinguishes poetry from prose, and to his often-cited opinion that the *Claudius* novels were 'potboilers', written for money and inferior to some of his other work, his poetry in particular.[40] Graves begins *On English Poetry* by stating

[38] Kronick (1999), 11. De Groot briefly raises the question of exemplarity in the context of the historical novel when he cites William Godwin's 1797 Aristotelian distinction between history and romance (see de Groot (2010), 18–19).

[39] Graves (2000d), 9.

[40] Compare Graves (1955c), 186: 'Of course, I also write historical novels, which is how I make a living. My motive or excuse is usually to clear up some historical problem which has puzzled me, but I never forget that these novels have to support

that poetry involves 'thoughtlessness', the 'unforeseen', 'spontaneity', 'passion'. Even where the poet has some measure of 'control' over his or her output, poetry should be distinguished from prose: while prose is 'the art of accurate statement by suppressing as far as possible the latent associations of words', in poetry 'the implication is more important than the manifest statement' and the 'underlying associations of every word are marshalled carefully'.[41] This conception of poetry—poetry as opposed to other forms, including 'literary' prose, novels—constitutes a fundamental and lifelong belief for Graves and was repeatedly asserted in different ways in essays, books, lectures, letters, and in poems themselves. Unlike prose, poetry is associated with the magical, with inspiration, with the a-rational and with quasi-religious thinking. The poem, for Graves, as he comments in a letter, is a 'miraculous, unpredictable and unassessable event in non-history'.[42]

It is my suggestion, then, that Graves's inaugural statement on the distinction between poetry and prose in *On English Poetry* can be related to the Aristotelian distinction between history and poetry in ways that may help us to understand the relative critical—as opposed to popular—neglect of the *Claudius* novels. Graves seems to equate poetry with the non-empirical, the non-historical, and with language that is unfixed from representational limitations. Prose, on the other hand, is an empirical, linguistically confined, and (therefore) historically specific medium. The *Claudius* novels are 'potboilers' because they are prose and because they are 'historical'. What is problematic in Graves's conception of poetry is also what is problematic about his

me and my large family. So I think of the average, intelligent, educated general reader and try to hold his attention by writing as clearly and simply and unboringly as the subject allows. Money's tight these days, and I should think very ill of myself unless I made the novels as lively as possible . . . Towards my poetry-reading public, however I feel no such tenderness . . . Novels are in the public domain, poems are not . . .'. See also Graves's comments in a 1933 letter to T. E. Lawrence: 'it is a pity that *Claudius* books have to be written because people won't pay a living wage for the essential works'; the novels, he goes on, are 'only the most stupid side-activity, like eating and dressing & going up & down stairs for firewood for the stove' (quoted in Seymour-Smith (1982), 256). For similarly dismissive comments in private letters, see O'Prey (1982), 224, 242, 254–5.

[41] Graves (2000d), 3. The opposition of poetry and prose also appears in *Claudius the God* when Claudius is discussing the ways in which Greek philosophy had led to a 'notable breakdown' in religious belief, and the realization amongst Romans that they had been 'mistaking poetical fiction for prose reality' (*CG* 292).

[42] Unpublished letter to Martin Seymour-Smith from July 1965, quoted in Seymour-Smith (1982), 537.

conception of the novel. Graves resists a thinking of the literary as an undecidable combination of the singular and the general as it (along with the work of art more generally) has been envisaged by critics from Aristotle to Jacques Derrida (via Sir Philip Sidney, Immanuel Kant, William Godwin, Samuel Taylor Coleridge, G. W. F. Hegel, W. K. Wimsatt, and others)—which is to say that what is denied or restricted or limited in Graves's novels is just their literariness, their novelistic or 'poetic' force. While the contemporary reviewers Harding and Woodworth disagree about almost everything else, they agree, in the end, on the fundamental *opposition* of history to literature on which Graves's novels paradoxically, impossibly, insist. And they agree, implicitly if not explicitly, with each other and with Graves himself, in fact, in thinking that what the novels have achieved involves in the end a kind of ersatz historiography rather than anything that has very much to do with the 'force' of poetry, with literature itself.

2

Claudius in the Library

Duncan Kennedy and Ellen O'Gorman

In his Authorial Note prefacing *Claudius the God*, Robert Graves presents his scholarly credentials in one extensive and one very brief citation. His tone, as appropriate for scholarship, is defensive:[1]

> Some reviewers of *I, Claudius* ... suggested that in writing it I had merely consulted Tacitus' *Annals* and Suetonius' *Twelve Caesars*, run them together, and expanded the result with my own 'vigorous fancy'. This was not so; nor is it the case here. Among the Classical writers who have been borrowed from in the composition of *Claudius the God* are Tacitus, Dio Cassius, Suetonius, Pliny Varro, Valerius Maximus, Orosius, Frontinus, Strabo, Caesar, Columella, Plutarch, Josephus, Diodorus Siculus, Photius, Xiphilinus, Zonaras, Seneca, Petronius, Juvenal, Philo, Celsus, the authors of the Acts of the Apostles and of the pseudo-Gospels of Nicodemus and St James, and Claudius himself in his surviving letters and speeches. Few incidents here given are wholly unsupported by historical authority of some sort or other and I hope none are historically incredible.[2]

In the face of an explicit criticism, then—one curiously similar to the accusation usually made against the historian Livy[3]—Graves presents an explicit defence: extensive knowledge of the ancient sources. More

[1] As charted in detail by Grafton (1997).

[2] Graves (1998), 341. All references to *I, Claudius* and *Claudius the God* are taken from the 1998 one-volume Carcanet reprint.

[3] Cf. Walsh (1961), 110: 'The most serious objection to any consideration of Livy as a scientific historian is ... the failure to search out and evaluate the original documentary evidence.' This—thoroughly modern—judgement of Livy (and of Roman historiography in general) is projected onto Graves's Pollio: 'Livy has no conscience ... I asked him once if he always had the same trouble as I had in finding the brass tablets he

interesting, though, is his closing, brief citation: 'I must acknowledge my indebtedness to Signor Arnaldo Momigliano's monograph on Claudius recently published in translation by the Oxford University Press.'[4] Implicit here is Graves's claim that his historical novel is bang up to date with contemporary advances in scholarship.[5] For the English-speaking reader, the publication of Momigliano's translated work in the same year as the *Claudius* novels strengthens Graves's case. The historical monograph and the historical novel emerge together, and together contribute to the revision of Claudius' place in history.

Of course, this parading of historical credentials is part of the rhetoric of every historical novelist speaking in their own voice. But we find the voice of Claudius the narrator imbued with a similar self-consciousness about his status as a historian. On the opening page of *I, Claudius* he claims that 'literature, and especially the writing of history—which as a young man I studied here at Rome under the best contemporary masters—was, until the change came, my sole profession and interest for more than thirty-five years. My readers must not therefore be surprised at my practised style.'[6] He presents himself as scrupulous to the point of fussiness. At the opening of chapter 3 he apologizes for continuing to write about Livia, but, he says:

> It is unavoidable: like all honest Roman histories this is written from 'egg to apple': I prefer the thorough Roman method, which misses nothing, to that of Homer and the Greeks generally, who love to jump into the middle of things and then work backwards and forwards as they feel inclined. Yes, I have often had the notion of re-writing the story of Troy in Latin prose for the benefit of our poorer citizens who cannot read Greek; beginning with the egg from which Helen was hatched and continuing, chapter by chapter, to the apples eaten for dessert at the great feast in celebration of Ulysses's home-coming and

wanted among the litter of the Public Record Office . . . it turned out that he has never once been there to confirm a single fact!' (Graves (1998), 92).

[4] Graves (1998), 342.

[5] Although Graves did not regard *I, Claudius* as 'essential' in the sense he believed mainstream scholarship to be, he defended it in a letter of December 1933 to T. E. Lawrence, who had seen the novel in proof (and hated it): 'I don't want any too great howlers. The book is largely guess-work & imagination but I want it to hold water & have done a great deal of reading to get it passable.' Seymour-Smith (1982), 255–7 quotes this interesting letter at length.

[6] Graves (1998), 5.

> victory over his wife's suitors. Where Homer is obscure or silent on any point I would naturally draw from later poets, or from the earlier Dares whose account, though full of poetical vagaries, seems to me more reliable than Homer's, because he actually took part in the war, first with the Trojans, then with the Greeks.[7]

Claudius's historiographical approach to narrative is highlighted almost to the point of parody when brought to bear on the subject of Homeric epic: an obsession with chronological order, completeness of data, and autopsy as the ultimate grounding of reliable fact. This initiates the stark contrast between history and poetry which Andrew Bennett, in this volume, has observed throughout Graves's writing in these novels, yet the peculiar status of historical writing itself as a form of literature[8] remains a fertile site for Graves to negotiate the boundaries of fact and fiction, and for Claudius to ground himself as a historian.

These issues come to the fore in chapter 9 of *I, Claudius*, where his encounter with the historians Livy and Pollio has important consequences for Claudius's life. This chapter has received more attention than almost any other,[9] for the self-conscious way in which the characters' debate on readability and accuracy in historical writing is sharply relevant for the historical novel. It also represents a turning-point in the young Claudius's career as a historian, as Livy presses him: 'which of us two old worthies will you choose as a model?', to which Claudius essays a diplomatic reply:

> I looked from one face to the other. At last I said, 'I think I would choose Pollio. As I am sure that I can never hope to attain Livy's inspired literary elegance, I shall do my best to imitate Pollio's accuracy and diligence.'[10]

[7] Graves (1998), 25. Echoes here of Graves's own celebrated rewriting of Homer—and Dickens. Cf. O'Prey (1982), 219: 'Before writing *I,Claudius* Graves had "rewritten" Dickens's *David Copperfield*, removing all the superfluous "padding" which its original, serialized form had made necessary (according to Graves). *The Real David Copperfield* was published in March, 1933, and received the most hostile reviews of any of Graves's books.' Graves defended what he did in a heated letter to Siegfried Sassoon, cited in O'Prey (1982), 231.

[8] Marincola (1997), 19: 'the ancient historian was more a man of letters than specifically an historian . . . The modern world is different because it both maintains some of the nineteenth century approach to history, and employs a restricted (and largely poetic) concept of literature.'

[9] Most recently Malamud (2009).

[10] Graves (1998), 88.

Pollio is as delighted with Livy's disgruntlement as he is with Claudius's decision and continues the barbed banter. Livy responds: 'A joke is a joke, Pollio, and I can take it in good part. But there's also a serious matter in question, and that is, the proper writing of history.' As the discussion develops, it becomes clear that Claudius has made a decision which is more than one of stylistics, for Livy defends his 'readable' history on political grounds: his theme is the ancient greatness of Rome, and when he comes across two versions of the same episode he chooses the one nearest to his theme. No 'grubbing around Etruscan cemeteries in search of any third account which may flatly contradict both—what good would that do?' asks Livy. Pollio replies: 'It would serve the cause of truth', and presses Claudius for his response. Claudius replies: 'I see now that there are two different ways of writing history: one is to persuade men to virtue and the other is to compel men to truth. The first is Livy's way and the other is yours: and perhaps they are not irreconcilable.'[11] Yet Pollio in his own way provides an insight into the politics of historiography, when he advises Claudius on the course of action which will ensure his survival and provides him with a clue to his father's murderer:

> You're writing a life of your father . . . you'll see that you won't be allowed to get beyond a certain point in it. And the person who stops you—

Thus Pollio significantly links the suppression of historical research and of Republican politics. What Claudius inherits from this encounter, then, is not merely a proto-Rankean interest in diligently researching and faithfully recording how things happened,[12] but also a sense that through this process he can come to understand the politically charged world of his Julio-Claudian family. Indeed, without the encounter with Pollio Claudius would not be able to consult the ultimate original source, as he does in dining with Livia in chapter 25.

In this debate, moreover, Graves takes on and elaborates the positions held by Livy and Pollio in the tradition of ancient history-writing. In the rich Augustan period of Latin literature Livy and Pollio might be seen to represent in translation the twin fathers of history:

[11] Graves (1998), 91.

[12] Graves was, as he notes in *Good-bye to All That*, the great-nephew of Leopold von Ranke, and in Germany the author of the Claudius novels is habitually referred to as Robert von Ranke Graves. Seymour-Smith (1982), 5 draws attention to a variation between the first and second editions of *Good-bye to All That*: 'In 1929, Graves said that he owed "his historical method" to this famous historian, whose works he had not then looked at; in 1957 he modified this to "I owe him something."'

Herodotus and Thucydides.[13] From its institution by these two Greeks, the discourse of history has arisen from a fruitful dialectic between truth-value and entertainment-value.[14] It is not simply a case of assigning one side of the opposition to one historian, for each historian aims to be read, and therefore to be readable. Rather, the oppositional terms 'truth' and 'entertainment' serve as the frames of a discourse within which each historian positions himself, in part by accusing other historians of being 'unhistorical', often by tendentious readings. So in chapter 9 Pollio gleefully sets Claudius up to expose Livy's disregard of sources, attacking his excessive interest in entertainment ('Our intelligent young friend was criticizing your method, under the respectful disguise of praising your readibility... The truth, boy! Have you ever caught him out in any historical inaccuracies?'); Livy, by way of riposte, elegantly undermines the readability of Pollio's work by ascribing his readers' pleasure to the quality of Pollio's dinners:

> '[Pollio] begins to read. Nobody listens very carefully. Everyone's belly is stuffed. "The cook's a genius," they are all thinking.... Now and then he will pause and ask: "Now which is the right word to use here? Shall I say that the returning envoys *persuaded* or *excited* this tribe to revolt? Or shall I say that the account they gave of the situation *influenced* the tribe in its decision to revolt? Actually, I think, they gave an impartial account of what they had seen." Then a murmur goes up from the couches, "*Influenced*, Pollio. Use *influenced*!"'[15]

In ancient criticism, moreover, Livy and Pollio are positioned within a debate on style which mirrors their wrangling in Graves's work. Livy's monumental history, about a quarter of which survives, is known for its *lactea ubertas*, its 'milky richness' (Quintilian 10.1.32), while Pollio is praised more often for his *diligentia*, his 'scrupulousness' (Quintilian 10.1.113, 10.2.25 and 12.10.11). Similarly, Graves's Claudius praises and Livy parodies precisely this 'accuracy and diligence'.[16] In modern criticism, moreover, the

[13] On Pollio's Thucydideanism: Morgan (2000), 60–5; Woodman (1988), 127–8.

[14] Fornara (1983), 120–30.

[15] Graves (1998), 89. Graves here picks up on the mention by Seneca the Elder that Pollio was the first Roman to recite his works to an invited audience (Sen. *Contr.* 4. *Praef.* 5). Cf. Morgan (2000), 67.

[16] We also have Seneca the Younger's opinion of Pollio's style: *Pollionis Asinii [compositio] salebrosa et exiliens et ubi minime expectes relictura.* 'The style of Asinius Pollio is jagged and jumpy and inclined to leave the reader where he least expects' (Seneca, *Ep.* 100.7).

distinction between Pollio and Livy is opened up in terms of their levels of political engagement, and often leads to a caricature of each: Pollio is the senator and independent critic of Augustus, while Livy confines himself to historical writing, which he explicitly sets up as an escape from the present of Augustan Rome.[17] As we have already seen, these differences in the relation of historical research to political action are important for Claudius, who on Pollio's advice will follow the example of Livy's Brutus (and of Livy himself) and avoid engagement in public life. The methodological opposition of these two historians, then, is an integral part of the tradition of historiographical analysis. Graves thus can be seen in chapter 9 to be dramatizing a moment of literary criticism, projecting it into the mouths of the writers themselves.[18]

If this chapter is touching on debates about how to write history, it is also involving itself in discourses about the historical novel. For example, Claudius defends Livy's history on the grounds that it is 'easier to read':

> 'He makes the people of Ancient Rome behave and talk as if they were alive now.'
>
> Pollio was delighted. 'He has you there, Livy, on your weakest spot. You credit the Romans of seven centuries ago with impossibly modern motives and habits and speeches. Yes, it's readable all right, but it's not history.'

From its emergence in the works of Sir Walter Scott in the early nineteenth century, the historical novel has been enmeshed in an argument that opposes entertainment and accessibility on the one hand against historical accuracy on the other. Thus, in the preface to *Ivanhoe*, which is framed as a 'Dedicatory Epistle to the Rev. Dr. Dryasdust, F.A.S.' (probably meant to stand for Fellow of the Antiquarian Society), Scott himself distinguished his work from 'the

[17] The contrast is drawn explicitly by Syme (1956), I. 136: 'To a general, a diplomat, and a proconsul [Pollio], no greater contrast than T. Livius.' And think of the opening of chapter 9, where Claudius encounters 'Livy and a little brisk old man in the robe of a senator'. Henderson (1998), 128–34 and Morgan (2000), 65–8 present a more subtle analysis of Pollio's political stance.

[18] Graves (1998), 90 also picks up on details of the historians' engagement in antiquity, as, for example, when he borrows Pollio's celebrated (and rather obscure) witticism about Livy's *Patavinitas*—'A decent fellow, Livy is, but there's one thing wrong with him. It's a disease called Paduanity.' For interpretations of what Pollio may have meant by *Patavinitas* cf. Hendrickson (1915) and Latte (1940).

idle novels and romances of the day' on the grounds of its antiquarian accuracy, but at the same time defended its non-antiquarian methods: 'It is necessary, for exciting interest of any kind, that the subject assumed should be, as it were, translated into the manners, as well as the language, of the age we live in.' Macaulay, writing in 1828, proclaimed: 'To make the past present, to bring the distant near . . . to invest with the reality of human flesh and blood beings whom we are too much inclined to consider as personified qualities in an allegory, to call up our ancestors before us with all their peculiarities of language, manners, garb . . . these parts of the duty which properly belongs to the historian, have been appropriated by the historical novelist.' Macaulay's comments reflect the move amongst historians of the time towards empirical research in newly available archives and the professionalization of the discipline which had opened out a gap for dramatic narrative that was being filled by the novelists; thus Carlyle, in an essay of 1838 on Scott, said that 'these Historical Novels have taught all men this truth . . . that the bygone ages of the world were actually filled by living men, not by protocols, state-papers, controversies and abstractions of men'.[19] These debates are staged within the novels themselves. Thus in Bulwer Lytton's *Last Days of Pompeii* (1834), the hero Glaucus, recalling a recent visit to the house of the Elder and the Younger Plinys, castigates them for mixing pleasure and study together, or, as the Elder Pliny puts it more positively, 'mixing the *dulce* with the *utile*'.

When Graves in this chapter presents a debate which reflects two traditions of criticism—relating to history and to the historical novel—he is drawing attention to the continuities which bind these traditions into one: the criticism of narratives which seek to make meaning from events in the past. Emphasis on other aspects of history and the historical novel may serve to divide this critical tradition back into two. But crucially the emphasis on truth and entertainment, and in particular on the 'modernization' of ancient voices, serves to align history and the historical novel. More than this, it adds a self-reflexive dimension to chapter 9; Livy, Pollio, and Claudius are discussing not only a narrative form which they all practise (history), but also the narrative form in which they, and this discussion, appear (the historical novel). Pollio criticizes Livy for crediting archaic Romans with

[19] Macaulay and Carlyle are both cited from Sanders (1978), 4–5.

'impossibly modern . . . speeches', while Graves has Pollio himself speak in 1930s English: 'Young fellows nowadays read only trash', by which he means the poetry of Ovid or Virgil ('some wretched Art of Love, or Arcadian pastoral nonsense').[20] Scott's defence of this translation into modernity as 'necessary for exciting interest of any kind', moreover, holds as good for Livy as it does for Graves. Livy expresses anxiety that his Augustan readers will find nothing entertaining or pleasurable in the history of archaic Rome (Livy, *Praef.* 4). In short, 'translation' might serve as an enabling trope for the various assimilations of this chapter: ancient speech translated into modern; history translated into novel; the historian Claudius translated into the historical novelist Graves.

I, Claudius presents itself as an historical text written in antiquity by the emperor Claudius and now, 1,900 years later, revealed to the world. But *I, Claudius* is also a novel written by Robert Graves. The narrative voice is thus an amalgam of these two identities,[21] and though the 'Author's Note' at the beginning of the book creates the fiction that this is where Graves's voice gives way to Claudius's, one of the greatest pleasures the book offers is the way in which the two identities are played off against each other within its narrative voice: are we reading Claudius or are we reading Graves? Claudius's notional text is written in Greek, but what we are reading is in English, so, encouraged by the 'Author's Note', we might be tempted to regard the voice of Graves as simply that of a translator and editor. But we are also aware that the text we are reading is an imposture. The formal device of a composite narrative voice, and its function within *I, Claudius*, is thematized in the second paragraph of chapter 1, where Claudius refers to his earlier, dull, history of his life in eight volumes written for the City archives:

> To be frank, I was extremely busy with other matters during its composition, which was two years ago. I dictated most of the first four volumes to a Greek secretary of mine and told him to alter nothing as he wrote (except, where necessary, for the balance of the sentences, or to remove contradictions or repetitions). But I admit that nearly all the second half of the work, and some chapters at least of the first, were

[20] Graves (1998), 85.

[21] In the letter to T. E. Lawrence cited in n. 5 Graves remarked: 'I identify myself with him [Claudius] as much as with any other historical character I know about.' Cf. Seymour-Smith (1982), 256.

> composed by this fellow Polybius (whom I had named myself, when a slave-boy, after the famous historian), from material that I gave him. And he modelled his style so accurately on mine that, really, when he had done, nobody could have guessed what was mine and what was his . . . When I consulted this book to-day in the Apollo Library on the Palatine Hill, to refresh my memory for certain particulars of date, I was interested to come across passages in the public chapters which I could have sworn I had written or dictated, the style was so peculiarly my own, and yet which I had no recollection of writing or dictating. If they were by Polybius they were a wonderfully clever piece of mimicry (he had my other histories to study, I admit), but if they were really by myself then my memory is even worse than my enemies declare it to be. Reading over what I have just put down I see that I must be rather exciting than disarming suspicion, first as to my sole authorship of what follows, next as to my integrity as an historian.[22]

We might see Polybius here as a counterpart for Graves as Claudius's ghost-writer. As we read *I, Claudius*, the doubled authorship turns the text into a play of ironies: so, when we read of Claudius's references to his faulty memory and to the Claudian family's predilection for forgery, as we shall see in a minute, do we hear Claudius's rather studied attempts to establish himself as both a good Claudian and a good historian, or the brush of Graves's wit? To analyse a particular point, we may attribute a particular role to each voice (as we might be tempted to attribute the debate on history to Claudius and that on the historical novel to Graves), but the impact lies, as we have seen, in their interplay.

There are dangers, then, in collapsing the novel into the *utile* of truth and accuracy (as Graves comes close to doing in the preface to *Claudius the God*, when he steps out of the composite voice to defend the scholarly credentials of his novel), and ignoring the *dulce* of entertainment and pleasure which it explores: specifically, the way in which the historical novel permits us to entertain the fantasy of a comprehensive recovery of the past.

The historical novel permits us to entertain this fantasy precisely by the way it exploits the relation of history to the past. So closely are these two interwoven that 'the past' is frequently referred to as 'history'. Yet the practice of historical representation simultaneously distances history from the past in all its immanent plenitude. For

[22] Graves (1998), 5–6.

history, the past, is—or rather *was—there*, complete in its presence. History as a form of representation conjures up the past as a completeness which this representation strives towards but never quite reaches. In configuring the past as whole, history at the same time configures itself as partial, fragmentary, incomplete. Far from this being a negative thing, it is this incompleteness that gives history-writing its drive; were the historian ever to attain his goal, a complete representation of the past in all its plenitude, 'from egg to apple', representation would disappear: 'the past' really would be 'history'. Pollio appears fully aware of the incompleteness of historical discourse, as he is seen in the process of completing a supplement to his own *Histories*. Nor is that the final word; at the end of the chapter he authorizes Claudius to write further supplements when they become necessary:

> 'If, when I'm dead, you ever come across any important point in my histories that you find unhistorical I give you permission—I'll stipulate that you have the authority—to put the corrections in a supplement. Keep them up to date. Books when they grow out of date only serve as wrappings for fish'... I kept my promise to Pollio some twenty years later. I found that he had written very severely on the character of Cicero—a vain, vacillating, timorous fellow—and while not disagreeing with this verdict I felt it necessary to point out that he was not a traitor too, as Pollio had made him out. Pollio was relying on some correspondence of Cicero's which I was able to prove was a forgery by Clodius Pulcher... This Clodius was another of the bad Claudians.[23]

History is thus seen as a representation which continually demands supplementing. The historical novel, by way of response, claims to offer a fuller account of the past, one that seems to suggest that no such supplement is required.

One feature of this chapter which might seem to fit this logic is the presence of Livy and Pollio themselves. These historians, known to us partially or in fragments, are *actually* standing there arguing about their histories—a fantasy of the full presence of the past. But if we concentrate on *where* they are standing, we see still further how Graves conveys the plenitude of a past that history cannot quite attain, for the scene begins thus: 'I was reading in the Apollo Library.'

[23] Graves (1998), 93–4. Graves here gestures towards the pseudo-Sallustian invective against Cicero, on which see now Novokhatko (2009). On the Claudians' manipulation of history cf. Wiseman (1979), 57–139.

We moderns are resigned to never meeting Livy in the flesh; our access to the past is predominantly textual. Graves plays on this with his depiction of the Roman public library where nearly *every* text of antiquity is complete and available—*if* you know where to look. And access to the archive is the key to the entire scene; Claudius's meeting with Pollio comes about when Livy calls on the expertise of Claudius's tutor Sulpicius to locate an obscure text:

> I was reading in the Apollo Library when along came Livy and a little brisk old man in the robe of a senator. Livy was saying: 'It seems then, that we may as well abandon all hope of finding it, unless perhaps... Why, there's Sulpicius! *He*'ll know if anyone does. Good morning, Sulpicius, I want you to do a favour for Asinius Pollio and myself. There's a book we want to look at, a commentary by a Greek called Polemocles on Polybius' *Military Tactics*. I seem to remember coming across it here once, but the catalogue does not mention it, and the librarians here are perfectly useless.' Sulpicius gnawed his beard for a while and then said: 'You've got the name wrong. Polemocrates was the name and he wasn't a Greek, in spite of his name, but a Jew. Fifteen years ago I remember seeing it on that top shelf, the fourth from the window, right at the back, and the little tag had just "A Dissertation on Tactics" on it. Let me get it for you. I don't expect it's been moved since then.'[24]

Graves restores for us the archive, in all its contingency,[25] and this exchange gives us the historical Livy (notoriously lax in checking sources) translated—perhaps—into a modern academic who insists on blaming the library for his own scholarly shortcomings.

The archive or the library seems to embody the historical fantasy of filling the gap which will restore the lost plenitude of the past. While the efforts of the three older men in this opening scene mirror the striving of the historian towards a full truth, Graves has Claudius offer us the most tantalizing glimpse of history's object of desire: Pollio's *Histories*. Covering the period 60–42 BC and written from an independently critical viewpoint, these lost *Histories* must be on the wish-list of every scholar of the late Roman Republic.[26] Significantly,

[24] Graves (1998), 85.

[25] As we know from the opening chapter, Claudius can access his own history in the Apollo Library, but cannot determine whether he actually wrote the passages he is reading: Graves (1998), 6.

[26] As they were for Sir Ronald Syme, who in *The Roman Revolution* sought in his own style to repair the loss: 'The great work of Pollio has perished, save for

Graves does not show us his characters hunting out *this* source; it is not sought—it is already possessed. Claudius is in the process of reading Pollio when he is interrupted by the arrival of the author. In omitting the search for Pollio, text and author, Graves underscores the full presence in his discourse of what remains unattainable to the historian.

This glimpse of Pollio's *Histories* is just one example of a favourite way in which historical novels play upon the desire for lost plenitude: by purporting to fill a perceived gap in the documentary record. Suetonius tells us that Claudius wrote an autobiography. What questions couldn't we answer if we had it? *I, Claudius* allows us to indulge that fantasy—whilst, of course, further tantalizing us by its own oblique reference to further texts outside our grasp. Once our attention is drawn to it in chapter 7, wouldn't we just love to have a bit more from Livia's little book, *A Pillow Debate on Force and Gentleness*, 'full', as we are told by Claudius, of its 'intimate touches'? And in chapter 9, what about that little snatch from 'poor Catullus' epigram on the noble Pollio' which is so sadly absent from modern texts of the poet?[27] Claudius attests to this desire for plenitude in the final paragraph of *I, Claudius* when recounting the strange circumstances of his elevation to the emperorship: 'And what thoughts and memories, would you guess, were passing through my mind on this extraordinary occasion?', he asks. Not of the empire or of liberty, he admits, but of being able to make people read his books:

inconsiderable fragments or supposed borrowings in subsequent historians. None the less, the example of Pollio and the abundance of historical material (contemporary or going back to contemporary sources, often biased, it is true, but admitting criticism, interpretation, or disbelief) may encourage the attempt to record the story of the Roman Revolution and its sequel, the Principate of Caesar Augustus, in a fashion that has now become unconventional, from the Republican and Antonian side' (Syme (1939), 6–7). Syme, for whom '[i]t is much to be regretted that he did not carry his *History of the Civil Wars* through the period of the Triumvirate to the War of Actium and the Principate of Augustus', seeks thus to offer his own supplement to Pollio's work, which 'appears to have ended when the Republic went down at Philippi', which Syme interprets as a link between the suppression of historical research and Republican politics ('That Pollio chose to write no further will be readily understood'). He immediately associates Pollio with a familiar figure: 'Another eminent historian was also constrained to omit the period of the Triumvirate when he observed that he could not treat his subject with freedom and with veracity. It was no other than Claudius, a pupil of Livy. His master has less exacting standards' (Syme (1939), 6).

[27] Graves (1998), 91. This epigram is, of course, not to be confused with Poem 12 of the text of Catullus we do have, which mentions Pollio in quite a different context.

That was what I was thinking. I was thinking too, what opportunities I should have, as Emperor, for consulting the secret archives and finding out just what happened on this occasion or on that. How many twisted stories still remained to be straightened out! What a miraculous fate for a historian![28]

[28] Graves (1998), 338.

3

Homer's Daughter

Graves's Vera Historia

Sheila Murnaghan

Within Robert Graves's enormous output, the novel *Homer's Daughter* is easy to miss. Written mostly in hopes of achieving large popular sales and inspired by another book that few people take seriously, Samuel Butler's *The Authoress of the Odyssey*, *Homer's Daughter* has never commanded the same respect as Graves's better-known historical fiction, especially the *Claudius* novels. This is in part because *Homer's Daughter* does not concern what are generally considered real historical events, although, as I hope to show, that difference has positive as well as negative consequences: it allows Graves to raise some of the same questions about writing history that he does in the *Claudius* novels, but with even more freedom. With its light tone and romantic plot, *Homer's Daughter* may seem especially deserving of the label 'potboiler' that Graves applied to all of his prose works. Yet, like the work of Lucian to which my title alludes, it is a playful but challenging exploration of the interplay between history and fiction. The jokey, satirical character of *Homer's Daughter* is less a sign of inconsequence than a reflection of how difficult the main elements of its story—romantic awakening and poetic inspiration—were for Graves, and the book stands as an overlooked illustration of the serious uses of wit.

Homer's Daughter was written in the winter of 1953–4 and published in 1955. Graves hoped to repeat with it the financial success he had achieved with the *Claudius* novels and to make even more money from a film version. This was to star Ingrid Bergman, providing her too with a needed career boost in the aftermath of her scandalous affair with Roberto Rossellini. Plans for the film proceeded on and off until Bergman dropped the idea, offering the excuse that she was getting too long in the tooth to play the heroine Nausicaa. 'The only thing is I'll be a pretty *old* daughter . . . '[1]

According to Graves, the book practically wrote itself. In a letter to Selwyn Jepson, a detective-story writer who was acting as his agent and who became the dedicatee of the book, he reported that: 'Homer's Daughter . . . causes me no trouble. I shall have finished the first draft in about a fortnight and can then concentrate on embellishments. Never have I found a book so easy to write, and the suspense is kept up, and there is a strong love-interest and lots of murders.'[2] Despite these exciting features, the book never achieved the wide sales that Graves was hoping for, and it is not hard to see why. The plot is lively and the central character is engaging, but the real pleasures of the novel are quite esoteric, brought about through reading it in tandem with the *Odyssey* and savouring Graves's complex intertextual moves. *Homer's Daughter* is, in effect, a modern revision of the *Odyssey*, a secondary work derived from the *Odyssey*, but it presents itself as prior to the *Odyssey*: it claims to be the true story of which the *Odyssey* is a revision, and an account of the *Odyssey*'s origins.

Homer's Daughter opens with an account of its own origins, in a 'Historical Note' in Graves's own voice:

> Samuel Butler, the author of *Erewhon*, . . . suggested that the poem, as we now have it, was composed at Drepanum, the modern Trapani, in Western Sicily and that the authoress was the girl self-portrayed as Nausicaa. None of his classical contemporaries, for whom Homer was necessarily both blind and bearded, deigned to pay Butler's theory the least attention . . . Nevertheless, while working on an explanatory dictionary of Greek myths, I found Butler's arguments for a Western Sicilian setting and for female authorship irrefutable. I could not rest until I had written this novel. It recreates, from internal and external evidence, the circumstances which induced Nausicaa to write the *Odyssey*, and suggests how, as an honorary Daughter of Homer, she managed to get it included in the official canon. Here is the story of a high-spirited

[1] Seymour-Smith (1982), 471–8; R. P. Graves (1995), 246–58. Another proposed adaptation that went nowhere was the composer Peggy Glanville-Hicks's idea of using the book as the basis of an opera libretto. See the Gibson essay (Chapter 14) for the context of the film version.

[2] O'Prey (1984), 120.

and religious-minded Sicilian girl who saves her father's throne from usurpation, herself from a distasteful marriage, and her two younger brothers from butchery by boldly making things happen, instead of sitting still and hoping for the best.[3]

This passage displays many of Graves's signature characteristics, including, especially in the magnificent last sentence, his crisp, energetic prose style. The story of the book's origin is typical of his self-presentation as an author. He often portrayed inspiration for one book seizing him while he was working on another. For example, the idea for *The White Goddess* supposedly gripped him while he was writing another of his more obscure classical novels, *The Golden Fleece*, based on the Argonaut legend.[4] The sentence about not being able to rest until he had written this book suggests his characteristic manic productivity and may, as well, be a form of magical thinking, given his aspirations for the book and his earlier claim, in an essay entitled 'PS to *Good-bye to All That*', that 'For a book to be popular . . . it should be written in a state of suppressed excitement and preferably against time and with a shortage of money'. In a further comment that bears strikingly on *Homer's Daughter*, he also adds that 'the most painful chapters have to be the jokiest'.[5]

While this introductory note may give the impression that *Homer's Daughter* was the immediate and spontaneous consequence of discovering Butler's theory, Butler had actually been an important figure for Graves from very early on, first encountered during his time at Charterhouse.[6] *The Way of All Flesh* was a formative influence, which opened up the possibility of exposing the traditional Victorian family as oppressive and hypocritical. The second volume of Siegfried Sassoon's thinly fictionalized autobiography, *Memoirs of an Infantry Officer*, published in 1930, includes a portrait of Graves, under the name of David Cromlech, as unpopular with the other men for his opinionated ranting. He quotes one of those men to the effect that: 'The blighter's never satisfied unless he's turning something upside down. I actually heard him say that that Homer was a woman. Can

[3] Graves (1955b), 8–9. Oddly, this introductory note is omitted from the recent Carcanet edition (2001) edited by Neil Powell, from which subsequent quotations from *Homer's Daughter* are taken.

[4] Seymour (1995), 308–9.

[5] Graves (1930), 21.

[6] Seymour (1995), 30–8.

you beat that?'[7] So Graves had already been championing Butler's theory for many decades before he decided to write *Homer's Daughter*. It makes sense that he would have been immediately attracted to the iconoclastic possibilities of claiming that Homer was a woman, though he also developed further views about women and poetry in the intervening years that would have made Butler's ideas even more congenial.

In *The Authoress of the Odyssey*, which appeared in 1897, Butler argued, as Graves indicates, that the *Odyssey* was written by a Sicilian girl, 'young, headstrong and unmarried' (p. 142), who represented herself in the text as Nausicaa and represented her Sicilian surroundings as the various settings of the *Odyssey*'s events. His argument was based on the poem's domestic focus and close attention to the trappings and rituals of peacetime society, which seemed to Butler evidence of a female sensibility. It was also bolstered by on-the-ground investigations of Sicilian geographical features, which were matched to the settings of the poem in the manner of late nineteenth-century archaeology. Butler's thesis was not taken seriously by the scholarly community of his day, or of subsequent times, and there is even some question whether it was taken seriously by Butler himself; some argue that the book was intended as a parody of scholarship rather than a serious contribution.[8] And yet Butler's hypothesis is one of those theories that gets at something important and serves as a catalyst for the ideas of others, even if it is impossible to credit in the terms in which it is stated. Among students of the *Odyssey* there has been a renewal of attention to Butler in recent decades, although not an embrace of his actual views, as feminist critics have tried to account for the poem's remarkably pronounced and sympathetic attention to women.[9]

At the same time, no current Homeric scholar could accept Butler's thesis at face value, because we now approach Homer though an entirely different model of authorship. Butler treated the *Odyssey* as if it were a modern novel, not unlike *The Way of All Flesh*, in which the individual author's own experience is recast in fictional form;

[7] Sassoon (1937), 357. Cf. Sassoon's comment that 'At that period, Samuel Butler was the source of much of David's ingenuity at knocking highly-respected names and notions off their perches' (p. 384).

[8] On the reception of Butler's theory in his lifetime, see Whitmarsh (2002); Beard (2007).

[9] See Winkler (1990) and, for a survey of other examples, Beard (2007), 331–2.

the Homeric epics are now understood as reworkings of long-standing traditional material transmitted by bards speaking for and to a community. It is therefore not surprising that Butler's impact has been strongest on two twentieth-century novelists who found inspiration for new works of fiction in his vision of the *Odyssey* as itself a kind of novel. One is James Joyce, who, like Graves, was deeply influenced by *The Way of All Flesh* as well as by *The Authoress of the Odyssey*. Butler's conception of the *Odyssey* is fundamental to Joyce's *Ulysses*, a work of covert autobiography in which all of the events of the *Odyssey* have been transposed to a single, circumscribed location corresponding to the author's own home. More particularly, Butler's authoress lies behind Joyce's Nausicaa figure, Gertie McDowell, who constructs an account of her own life along lines inspired by women's novels, and is also behind Joyce's decision to make the final voice in his novel that of a woman, Molly Bloom.[10] The other novelist, of course, is Graves.

Graves's relationship to Butler's theory is much more straightforward and literal than Joyce's; like Butler, he keeps the text of the *Odyssey* itself closely in view. Butler's reconstruction of the *Odyssey*'s genesis follows a scenario that Graves found endlessly attractive and stimulating: the revelation that a valued cultural document, most often a text, is in fact a falsification, or cover-up, that does not disclose but rather obscures the truth that lies behind it. It becomes the role of the scholar or the critic or, in an interesting twist, the novelist to expose this fact and to reveal the authentic truth that has been so long overlooked. This was a role that Graves claimed for himself over and over again, and that he welcomed in his admired model Butler, whose exposure of the hidden truth of the *Odyssey*'s authorship paralleled his exposure of the hidden truths of Victorian family life, truths obscured in that case not by misattribution of authorship but by a set of manners and conventions.

This occult cast of mind shows up throughout Graves's work.[11] In the realm of religion, Graves exposes the works of Paul and others as misrepresentations of the true thought of Jesus; *The Greek Myths* treats all of our myriad sources for Greek mythology as belated distortions, designed to misrepresent an earlier myth of matriarchal

[10] For Butler's influence on *Ulysses*, see Kenner (1956); Müller (2009).
[11] On Graves's relationship to occult religious traditions, see Psilopoulos (1999).

power and male sacrifice.[12] (This approach complicates Graves's obsessive citing of sources, as in his defences of the *Claudius* novels, since it gives him licence to treat those sources as purposely false.) In the realm of literary criticism, Graves's and Laura Riding's influential reading of Shakespeare's Sonnet 129 in *A Survey of Modernist Poetry* argues that the sonnet as generally read is distorted by later editorial interventions that occlude Shakespeare's intentions: 'By apostrophes and accents and changes of spelling the rhythm and consistency in spelling of the original is sacrificed; and without making it an easier poem, only a less accurate one.'[13]

Such thinking also underlies *I, Claudius*, where it applies to a set of texts that no longer exist, the historical works that the real Claudius in known to have written. *I, Claudius* opens with Claudius explaining that his official autobiography, now in the City archives, is 'a dull book', partly ghost-written by the freedman Polybius, in which 'I told no lies, but neither did I tell the truth in the sense I mean to tell it here' (p. 10).[14] The current book, which tells a more urgent and authentic story, is labelled a 'confidential history' (p. 11) and intended for remote posterity. Like Graves, Claudius is not only the author of the truest histories but also the exposer of false ones and a connoisseur of hidden truths. At the end of chapter 9 we learn that he has identified some supposed correspondence of Cicero as a forgery by Clodius Pulcher. At the very end of the novel he confesses that one of the best things about being emperor will be access to secret archives in which he can find out 'just what happened on this occasion or on that' (p. 396).

Nausicaa, as rescued by Butler from her own self-concealment, provides Graves with another, and a very different, protagonist and narrator who, like Claudius, is also the author of an officially recognized and widely credited work that is actually less true than Graves's novel. By adopting her as his heroine, Graves gains a number of significant advantages, to be explored in the rest of this essay, among them yet another opportunity to exploit the pressure that historical fiction places on the boundary between its two components, history and fiction. In this case, however, the supposed author's official work, the *Odyssey*, is not lost, as the historical works of

[12] Murnaghan (2009). [13] Graves and Riding (1927).
[14] Graves (2006b).

Claudius are, but known to us; as a result, it can play a constituent role in the novel's construction.

In the introductory note quoted above, Graves identifies *Homer's Daughter* both as fiction and as non-fiction: he labels it a novel ('I wrote this novel') but also characterizes it as a work of historical reconstruction ('it recreates from internal and external evidence the circumstances . . . '). This doubleness extends to the novel's relationship to the *Odyssey*, than which it is at once more factual, in the sense that it lacks fantasy and corresponds in certain ways to what Graves really believed about Greek history, and more fictional, in that it is clearly a novel of a sort that could never have been written in antiquity. For one thing, *Homer's Daughter* does not, like *I, Claudius*, pretend to be an autobiography, or a story told under particular circumstances, or any other kind of text that would have been produced in antiquity, but simply records the narrator's inner thoughts in the manner of modern fiction. The project of writing a historical novel about a figure who is attested only in a mythological narrative, and one whom nobody but Graves himself and Samuel Butler view as historical, leaves Graves much freer to acknowledge the literariness of his work, and to play with its dual claims as fiction and history—unencumbered by the inhibitions that Andrew Bennett, in his essay in this volume, sees as weighing down the *Claudius* novels and limiting their interest as objects of critical discussion.

The plot of *Homer's Daughter* represents a geographically restricted, down-to-earth version of the *Odyssey*, with many of the events of the Ithacan narrative transposed to Phaeacia, and with Nausicaa in a central rather than a peripheral role. Nausicaa is, as she introduces herself, 'a princess of the Elymans, a mixed race living on and about Eryx, the great bee-haunted mountain', who pride themselves on being 'the remotest nation of the civilized world' (p. 4). She lives with her mother and father and three of her four brothers. The plot gets under way when one of her brothers, Laodamas, disappears after having been nagged by his difficult, superficial wife Ctimene, who wants him to get her an amber necklace. It is widely assumed that Laodamas has gone off on a Rhodian merchant ship, although Nausicaa and her mother both figure out that he has actually been murdered by local rivals. In a nice inversion of the *Odyssey*'s Telemachus plot, Nausicaa's father goes off on a journey in search of his lost son, leaving his kingdom in charge of his brother-in-law Mentor.

In the king's absence the local youths become rebellious. They show disrespect towards Mentor and towards Nausicaa's younger brother Clytoneus, who tries to address the problem in an assembly, and they start regularly feasting in the royal palace on the pretext of being Nausicaa's suitors. Seeking an excuse to meet her loyal friend Procne, Nausicaa goes to the shore to do the laundry, where a Cretan stranger Aethon washes ashore. She grants him her protection on condition of obedience, and lodges him with the swineherd Eumaeus. After the suitors kill Mentor, Nausicaa, Aethon, and Clytoneus work together to defeat them through a plot involving an archery contest, ostensibly for Nausicaa's hand. Nausicaa and Aethon, who turns out to be a long-lost relative of her mother, kidnapped as a baby by pirates, marry for strategic reasons as part of the plot, but also fall in love. Nausicaa's father returns when it is all over to regain his throne and approve his daughter's choice of husband.

In addition to the generally Homeric trajectory of the plot, there are many satisfying reworkings of Odyssean details and motifs. Aethon's name derives from the pseudonym adopted by Homer's Odysseus in one of his false tales; the bitchy Ctimene is named for Odysseus's sister, who is mentioned once in the *Odyssey*. There is a scene of foot-washing involving Euryclea, but she washes the feet of the suitor Eurymachus, and what is revealed as a result is that Eurymachus is wearing one of Laodamas' undershirts—and thus that Laodomas was murdered and Eurymachus was involved. Graves takes the opportunity to correct some of what might be considered the *Odyssey*'s flaws. For example, Nausicaa and her allies make the distinctions among her more and less culpable suitors that Odysseus refuses to make among Penelope's; once the two ringleaders have been killed they offer to let the rest survive if they will only leave the house, a deal that the suitors stupidly reject.

The tone of the narrative is light, high-spirited, and satirical. For example, when Aethon addresses Nausicaa with the same comparison to a palm tree with which Homer's Odysseus ingratiates himself to Homer's Nausicaa, she gives a sceptical reply:

> 'You have visited Delos then?' I asked, much amused, 'Or is this a second-hand compliment borrowed from one of the Sons of Homer? No one ever compared me to a young palm tree; probably because I am neither tall nor slim, and my hair, though long, is by no means my best feature'. (p. 56)

Portraying Nausicaa as practical, unsentimental, and sharp-tongued, Graves makes her an excellent medium for the broader rhetorical project of cutting the *Odyssey* down to size. He makes extensive use of the common satiric procedure of juxtaposing the classically elevated with the grubby details of real life. In Graves's version, Nausicaa's laundry really is dirty; she tells her Uncle Mentor, 'You have gone around in the same tunic this last month—I recognize the wine stain on the hem' (p. 47). And getting it clean really is hard work: 'I was soon jumping on the sheets in the trough, or banging at them with a cudgel' (p. 51).

The deflating jokiness of Graves's approach does not prevent him from raising a basic issue about historical fiction that also pertains to all historical writing and historical inquiry. In this respect, the *Vera Historia* of the second-century AD Greek satirist Lucian provides a useful parallel. The *Vera Historia* or *True History* is also a high-spirited, satirical work cast in the form of a fictional autobiography, and it is also notably dependent on the *Odyssey*. The narrator relays an elaborate and fantastic tale of adventure, including one of the earliest voyages to the moon, that on his own cheerful admission is entirely fabricated. Yet Lucian repeatedly brandishes the same truth-claims that straightforward historians do, making use of such authenticating gestures as the provision of exact numbers of troops or the reporting of first-hand eyewitness information.[15] Lucian's aggressive use of these stylistic features raises questions about what a historian's credibility for his audience is actually based on.

If Lucian's text raises questions about how writers construct a plausible account of the real, Graves's text, in a similarly satiric vein, raises questions about how writers construct a plausible account of the past. When characters in historical fiction speak in ways that seem idiomatic to modern readers and dwell on the mundane details of life as modern readers recognize them, are they being more or less authentic? Is a Nausicaa who speaks in the accents of a twentieth-century girl rather than Homeric hexameters anachronistic or timelessly human? This is an issue that haunts all historical writing, and especially historical fiction, in which invention and historical reconstruction are supposed to converge, as Graves claims in his prefatory note that they do in *Homer's Daughter*.

[15] Greenwood (2006), 109–29.

Graves acknowledges the perennial nature of this issue in *I, Claudius* by retrojecting it into an ancient Roman setting. In the much-discussed ninth chapter of the novel, Claudius is sitting in a library quietly reading Asinius Pollio's *History of the Civil Wars* when in come Livy and Pollio himself, who draw him into a debate about how to write history that, as Duncan Kennedy and Ellen O'Gorman show in their essay for this volume, is also a proleptic debate about how to write historical fiction. Pollio asks Claudius to affirm that Livy's work is trashier than his:

> I smiled. 'Well, at least it is easier to read.'
>
> 'Easier, eh? How's that?'
>
> 'He makes the people of Ancient Rome behave and talk as if they were alive now.'
>
> Pollio was delighted. 'He has you there, Livy, on your weakest spot. You credit the Romans of seven centuries ago with impossibly modern motives and habits and speeches. Yes, it is readable, all right, but it is not history.' (p. 103)

Here a strong distinction is made between real history and what Livy writes, which is readable, accessible, anachronistic, and, as a subsequent discussion of the Lars Porsena episode reveals, fictional. Livy's works would then seem to represent a version of historical fiction not very different from Graves's own.

But the picture becomes more complicated, as Pollio goes on to charge Livy with drawing too much on the non-historical genres of poetry and oratory. Livy asks if Pollio means that he should not write history with an epic theme because that is the prerogative of poetry, and he should not 'put worthy eve-of-battle speeches' in the mouths of his generals because that is the prerogative of oratory. Pollio replies that 'an epic theme' distorts history, which is 'the true record of what people did, how they lived and died, what they did and said', and that Livy's generals' speeches are 'admirable as oratory' but not based on any evidence and also 'inappropriate':

> 'I have heard more eve-of-battle speeches than most men and though the generals that made them, Caesar and Antony especially, were remarkably fine platform orators, they were all too good soldiers to try any platform business on the troops. They *spoke* to them in a conversational way, they did not orate.' (p. 104)

There then follows a description of Caesar's speech before the Battle of Pharsalus, which involved chomping on a piece of bread and waving around a radish, while making earthy jokes about how much chaster Pompey was than himself and telling off-colour anecdotes, illustrated with help of the radish:

> 'Not a word about the coming battles except at the close: "Poor old Pompey! Up against Julius Caesar and his men! What a chance he has"!'
>
> 'You didn't put any of this in your history,' said Livy.
>
> 'Not in the public editions,' said Pollio, 'I'm not a fool. Still, if you like to borrow the private *Supplement* which I have just finished writing, you'll find it there.' (p. 105)

If history like Pollio's, characterized by Claudius as pedantic and unadorned, is truer than Livy's, both Livy's rhetorically elaborated work and Pollio's unadorned work are less true than yet another kind of account, which reproduces the idiom of actual conversation, as observed through first-hand experiences much like the ones that Graves himself had in the trenches of the First World War. It turns out there is a more authentic *Supplement* that stands to Pollio's—now lost—official *History of the Civil Wars* in the same relation that *I, Claudius* does to Claudius's—now lost—official *Autobiography* and in the same relation that *Homer's Daughter* does to the—now still extant—*Odyssey*. All of these Graves-generated fictions are truer than their historically documented substitutes because they capture the 'conversational' tone of real speech, which can only be done by making the people portrayed 'behave and talk as if they were alive now' (p. 103). But one of them, Pollio's *Supplement*, is presented as a lost ancient text rather than a modern novel; in this way Graves slyly raises the question of whether a modern novel might not be more authentic than our surviving ancient sources.

With his tendency to mythic thinking and his scepticism towards almost any document, Graves clearly inclines to the view that a modern reconstruction really could represent past experience better than an ancient source. At the same time, by exploiting the incongruity between ancient original and modern retelling for comic effect, he also acknowledges implicitly the gap between ancient and modern experience. When Claudius praises Livy for making people 'behave and talk as if they were alive now', the episode is provocative in part because the ways that people behave and talk in first-century Rome and twentieth-century England or America are so different. It remains open to question whether, as Pollio suggests with his evocation of real soldiers' talk, that difference is simply a matter of rhetoric, and whether the fact that something rings true to a contemporary reader is really proof of authenticity. In these novels, Graves addresses casually and humorously issues about the claims of historical fiction and the relationship of the epic and the novel that have been taken up much more earnestly and directly by literary theorists, including such twentieth-century heavyweights as Lukács and Bakhtin.

In his comments about *Homer's Daughter* at the time it was being written, Graves stresses the contemporary character of his story and goes out of his way to portray its most modern-seeming elements as the most authentic. In his correspondence with Selwyn Jepson, Graves gives several markedly modern analogues for his emancipated heroine Nausicaa:

> But Nausicaa was a tight little body. She would have made a very good shore-officer in the WRNS.[16]

> I imagine Professor Tush of Columbia and Professor Bush of Harvard are bellyaching about Homeric scholarship. But I have taken expert advice and there is nothing in the world *against* my reconstruction; and every nice Vassar girl will feel flattered that she could have written the *Odyssey* herself.[17]

In one such passage, Graves not only identifies Nausicaa with Eve Gill, the girl detective in Jepson's own novels, but also identifies those features in the *Odyssey* that resemble a modern novel as the most essential:

> The *Odyssey* originally consisted of a straightforward early Homeric saga about the return of Odysseus from Troy, only to find that his wife has been unfaithful—to which (after the first eighty lines) has been added a fairy-tale, unconnected with it, about a hero called Ulysses who escaped various kinds of ritual death. But when these two separate elements have been removed, there remains, as Samuel Butler first pointed out, a substantial mass of realistic modern novel-writing which reflects a domestic and political crisis in a Sicilian court about the year 730 BC. I have worked this background story out and it makes a very exciting drama full of suspense: centered around the Princess Nausicaa (a sort of Ionian Eve Gill) of whom such a charming portrait is given in Book VI of the *Odyssey*.[18]

Graves here makes it explicit that for him, as for Butler, there is no difference between the *Odyssey* properly understood and a modern novel. In *Homer's Daughter*, as he puts the novelistic 'background

[16] O'Prey (1984), 125. [17] O'Prey (1984), 127. [18] O'Prey (1984), 119.

story' into the foreground, he neatly distinguishes and incorporates the 'separate elements' in other genres that have been grafted onto that story to form the *Odyssey*, turning them into discrete embedded narratives, known to Nausicaa but not her actual experiences. As Nausicaa walks through the countryside to Eumaeus's hut with her Uncle Mentor, she gets him to tell her the fairy-tale of Ulysses once again. The 'Return of Odysseus' is sung to the suitors by the bard Phemius; in that saga, Penelope is indeed unfaithful, a consequence of the fact that it is Aphrodite, not Poseidon, who figures as Odysseus's divine opponent.

Graves's willingness to take Butler's thesis seriously gives him an opportunity denied to other historical novelists of antiquity; he can tell the story of a significant historical figure who is also a girl. It is not easy to write a novel about an ancient girl that can claim historical accuracy in which the heroine does anything of public importance. In her reflections on the composition of *Memoirs of Hadrian*, Marguerite Yourcenar comments that she could not have chosen a female subject for that book. 'Another thing virtually impossible, to take a feminine character as a central figure, to make Plotina, for example, rather than Hadrian, the axis of my narrative. Women's lives are much too limited, or else too secret.'[19] During the time that Graves was writing, authors of historical fiction for girl audiences had to perform a balancing act in order to produce narratives set in antiquity that feature both a historically accurate setting and an active, appealing girl protagonist. The strategies they devised include the use of settings on the margins of the classical world, where strict patriarchal practices can be envisioned as somewhat relaxed; the construction of plots in which girls are required to act because of the failures of their brothers; the self-consciously anachronistic introduction of romantic love leading to marriage; and scenes of recognition by the protagonist's father, in which he acknowledges the necessity and value of her unusually enterprising actions.[20]

In *Homer's Daughter* Graves adopts all of these strategies, in effect confirming the constraints that limit writers in any genre who wish to locate active, self-determining girls within the classical world. At the same time, fortified by his belief in the historicity of Nausicaa and by

19 Yourcenar (1990), 327.

20 These are studied in relation to the works of an American novelist of the 1920s and 1930s, Caroline Dale Snedeker, in Murnaghan and Roberts (unpublished paper).

his view of patriarchal society as secondary and impermanent, he gives these strategies much less weight. Nausicaa's Sicilian home is far from the power-centres of the Greek world and the Elymans pride themselves on their remoteness, and this allows for a freer vision of female agency than would a setting like Mycenae or Sparta. In the end, however, by inserting her own poem about her experiences into the Homeric canon, Nausicaa places herself at the very centre of Greek culture. Like other historical novelists, Graves tells the story of a girl who takes over the action in part because of the absence or dereliction of her brothers, of which she has three, and he does invent a violent plot twist to remove one of those brothers, along with Nausicaa's father, from the scene. But Nausicaa's other two brothers do not require such drastic banishment. One is simply too young to be involved, and the other, Clytoneus, is Nausicaa's active, if clearly subordinate, collaborator throughout as she defeats the rebels who are pretending to be her suitors.

In his treatment of Nausicaa's other collaborator, Aethon, Graves allows the romantic plot that is notably curtailed in the *Odyssey* to develop: Aethon and Nausicaa fall in love and marry. But he also mutes this plot-line, playing down the idea that his heroine is motivated by love. The marriage originates as a stratagem for keeping her supposed suitors at bay, and Nausicaa is at pains to conceal her feelings for Aethon, even though he confesses to love at first sight, and even on their wedding night: '... never had I realized how overpoweringly fierce is the Goddess Aphrodite... I must not let Aethon know that I loved him more than the whole world, more than myself, more than anything in existence but the Goddess Athene, whom I invoked silently for strength' (p. 136).

Finally, the novel does include Nausicaa's recognition and acceptance by her father, who returns after his kingdom has been saved to find that his previously reluctant daughter has acquired a husband. 'My father's greeting to me was brief and generous: "Daughter, you did well to delay your choice, having found a husband so acceptable to me"' (p. 154). But this paternal blessing is relatively insignificant and even somewhat absurd, given her father's absence from all the crucial action. A far more important achievement is Nausicaa's self-creation as 'Homer's daughter', author of a poem that enters the Homeric canon and is sung throughout the Greek world.

Nausicaa's gender and her exceptional level of initiative and scope for action set her apart from many of Graves's other depictions both of historical agents and of poets, figures whom he typically portrays as struggling with inhibition, abjection, and compulsion. The off-hand, jokey tone of the novel should not obscure the way in which it addresses by inversion some of Graves's most persistent and fraught concerns. Here it is well to recall Graves's injunction, quoted above, that in a popular work the most painful chapters have to be the jokiest. The energetic heroine who makes things happen instead of sitting still and hoping for the best, and who effortlessly acquires protective colouring through her gender, is an antitype of the passive and genuinely handicapped Claudius. As the author of one of the greatest and most foundational works in the poetic tradition, Nausicaa is also an antitype of the tortured male poet as represented by Graves himself and as described by him in a number of works, notably *The White Goddess*. She experiences her poetic vocation as an untaxing, pragmatic, and down-to-earth matter, very different from the male poet's compulsive servitude to an imperious Muse.

Nausicaa becomes a poet through a calculation. Finding herself preoccupied with death as a moody teenager, she figures out that only poetry is really immortal and takes the decision 'of securing for myself a posthumous life under the mantle of Homer' (p. 4). The moment when she is first visited by the Muses, which she labels 'an important crisis in my life, perhaps the most important' (p. 42), is easy and straightforward. Visiting the family linen factory, she finds the women who work there being told a story, the story of the Cyclops, by an old woman Gorgo. The manageress of the factory, Eurymedusa, laments that 'Homer has no daughters as well as sons', and Nausicaa prays to the Muses: 'enter into the heart of your servant Nausicaa, and teach her to compose skillful hexameter verses!' And then:

> Believe it, or believe it not, my unusual prayer was at once answered! For I heard myself saying:
>
> '*Eurymedusa, the day must dawn when the songs of a woman,*
> *Sound to the well-strung lyre, and are praised by the Delian judges.*' (p. 42)

The one other episode in which Nausicaa is visited by the Muse occurs when she is staying in Eumaeus' hut, where she suffers from the presence of fleas:

> I could not sleep a wink but sat on a stool by the fire, scratching and picking the black torments off my white body. Strangely enough, my head was flooded with beautiful, smooth-flowing hexameter verses . . .

> 'To be a poet is easy,' I thought, 'I could compose a whole fytte in a single night, I believe.' However, I stopped after sixty lines, and memorized them; had I attempted more, I should probably have forgotten all.... Eumaeus, when I told him later about my experience, gave the credit to the goddess Cerdo, who inspires poetry and oracular utterances, as well as protecting swineherds; but I had the fleas to thank for keeping me awake. (p. 104)

In these passages Graves represents effortless poetic composition by making something look easy that is actually very hard: the production of graceful, unforced English hexameters. Not only does this occur in the lines of poetry that Nausicaa quotes, but as she recalls her experience of spontaneous composition her words fall naturally into hexameters: 'I could |not sleep a | wink but | sat on a | stool by the | fire.'[21] This cheerful inspiration by flea-bite is a far cry from the male poet's subjection to the Muse of *The White Goddess*, which calls forth very different insect imagery, 'the Mother of all living, the ancient power of fright and lust—the female spider or queen-bee whose embrace is death', and leads to the formation of true poetry 'in the poet's mind, during a trance-like state of suspension of his normal habits of thought by the supra-logical reconciliation of conflicting emotional ideas'.

Nausicaa's ready production of sixty finished verses is markedly different from Graves's own mode of composing poetry, which involved extensive revisions through multiple drafts, linked in *Good-bye to All That* to his headmaster's parting advice: 'remember that your best friend is the waste-paper basket.'[22] In fact, Nausicaa's poetry-making sounds a lot more like Graves's experience writing *Homer's Daughter*. Both Nausicaa's poetry, which is simultaneously spontaneous and matter-of-fact, and Graves's novel, which is a spontaneously composed prose text based on that poetry, blur the distinctions between prose and poetry that Graves set out in his *On English Poetry*, discussed in this volume by Andrew Bennett.

As a poet, Nausicaa escapes the demands that Graves's Muse imposes on her male worshippers. As a strong female figure, she herself displays very little of the White Goddess' lustfulness or sexual power, although there is perhaps a hint of that allure in the phrase—which has the ring of an authorial intrusion—'white body' in her

[21] My thanks to James Ker for pointing this out to me.
[22] Graves (1957a), 58.

report of herself 'picking the black torments off my white body'. Nausicaa is generally resistant to Eros. Her equally unsentimental mother warns her that a woman is better off if she is not passionately attached to her husband, because she is then able to manage him better. When Nausicaa does fall in love she calmly recognizes the fact through careful reasoning: 'Cautiously examining myself, I decided that I must have well and truly fallen in love, else why should I place such confidence in Aethon's strength and courage?' (p. 89). As noted already, on her wedding night she conceals the depth of her feeling from Aethon, a sign of her self-control as well as a hint of the White Goddess' cruel withholding.

There is one moment in *Homer's Daughter* when Nausicaa becomes a goddess to Aethon, but that is not an occasion of wilful imperiousness, but rather one on which she displays nobler female virtues of good sense, justice, and respect for religion. During the final battle she intervenes to prevent the slaughter of Phemius, which would be unmerited and would bring a curse on the family.

> Picking myself up, I sprang in front of Phemius, and spread my arms wide. Aethon came bounding towards us, drunk with blood lust. 'Aethon, beware!' This time my scream dispelled his trance. He flung away sword and shield, fell at my feet, and worshipped me as though I was a goddess; while the other three methodically continued their horrid task of hunting down fugitives and cutting the throats of the wounded. (p. 148)

Despite its billing as a love story, *Homer's Daughter* purges the *Odyssey* of its erotic character. Graves writes out of the poem not only the seductive goddesses Calypso and Circe, but the central characters, Odysseus and Penelope, whose stories are motivated by their sexual love for one another. He places at the centre of his version a figure who in Homer's narrative pointedly avoids or escapes sexual experience. Homer situates Nausicaa in a scenario that could be expected to lead to seduction or rape, a meeting with a stranger at the wild seashore, but does not allow it to develop in that direction, and he portrays Nausicca as carefully vigilant of her reputation.

Graves thematizes Nausicaa's Homeric function of deflecting sexual content when he portrays Nausicaa herself as cleaning up the *Odyssey*. Nausicaa's *Odyssey*, which we know as Homer's, is supposedly a revision of that version sung by Phemius in which Penelope has sex with all the suitors and Odysseus' main antagonist is not Poseidon but Aphrodite:

> While altering the saga of *Odysseus' Return* to make my Elyman suitors serve as Penelope's lovers, I had to protect myself against scandal. What if someone recognized the story and supposed that I, Nausicaa the irreproachable, had played the promiscuous harlot in my father's absence? So, according to my poem, Penelope must have remained faithful to Odysseus throughout those twenty years. And because this change meant that Aphrodite had failed to take her traditional revenge, I must make Poseidon, not her, the enemy who delayed him on his homeward voyage after the Fall of Troy. (p. 157)

In other words, Graves invents two new versions of the *Odyssey*, one ('the saga of *Odysseus' Return*') that is darker and has more sex in it than the canonical one, and one (*Homer's Daughter* itself) that is sunnier and has less sex. Both are presented as prior to, and thus more authentic than, the *Odyssey* that we actually have, but in *Homer's Daughter* the chaster alternative occupies the foreground, while the more erotic version is cast into shadow.

By contrast, an eroticized version of the *Odyssey* is powerfully foregrounded in another work of Graves's, significantly a poem rather than a work of prose, 'Ulysses', written in 1933:

> To the much-tossed Ulysses, never done
> With woman whether gowned as wife or whore,
> Penelope and Circe seemed as one:
> She like a whore made his lewd fancies run,
> And wifely she a hero to him bore.
>
> Their counter-changings terrified his way:
> They were the clashing rocks, Symplegades,
> Scylla and Charybdis too were they;
> Now angry storms frosting the sea with spray
> And now the lotus island's drunken ease.
>
> They multiplied into the Sirens' throng,
> Forewarned by fear of whom he stood bound fast
> Hand and foot helpless to the vessel's mast,
> Yet would not stop his ears: daring their song
> He groaned and sweated till that shore was past.
>
> One, two and many: flesh had made him blind,
> Flesh had one pleasure only in the act,
> Flesh set one purpose only in the mind—
> Triumph of flesh and afterwards to find
> Still those same terrors wherewith flesh was racked.

> His wiles were witty and his fame far known,
> Every king's daughter sought him for her own,
> Yet he was nothing to be won or lost.
> All lands to him were Ithaca: love-tossed
> He loathed the fraud, yet would not bed alone.[23]

In 'Ulysses', Odysseus, evoked as the 'much-tossed Ulysses', is at the centre of an entirely sexualized version of the *Odyssey*. Every adventure becomes the conquest of a woman. Odysseus' famous mind and will are bent only on the satisfaction of lust, which is portrayed as demeaning and unfulfilling. Unlike Homer's *Odyssey*, which involves the hero's progress from purely physical relations with Circe and Calypso to the deeper pleasures of married love with Penelope, Graves's 'Ulysses' presents Odysseus' erotic encounters as repetitive and indistinguishable ('Penelope and Circe seemed as one'), compulsive re-enactments of a single mythic moment. As a high-spirited, cheerful, and expansive prose narrative, *Homer's Daughter*, with its forward-moving plot and its fresh, active, self-possessed heroine, is the inverse—and the antidote—to the earlier poem, in which the beleaguered hero appears as the passive victim of multiple powerful women, trapped in the endless sexual pursuit that they inspire.

In a passage from *Good-bye to All That* Graves locates the dichotomy, which is also a symbiosis, between the mythic and the satiric at the very beginning of his career as a poet. Writing about Wales, a place that he and his siblings embraced as their own without studying its history, he relates that 'we came to know Wales . . . as a place with a history too old for local legends; while walking there we made up our own . . . above Harlech I found a personal peace independent of history or geography. The first poem I wrote as myself concerned those hills. (The first poem I wrote as a Graves was a neat translation of one of Catullus' satires).'[24] Note here Graves's nice use of punctuation, as he consigns his official satiric parergon to parentheses.

But as many of Graves's poems and other works, such as *The White Goddess*, testify, his personal relationship to myth, as he came to know it as instantiated by the goddess, was not peaceful. The parenthetic alternative is not so easily bracketed or disowned, for it points ahead to the kind of corrective to, and relief from, that stormier realm that he was moved, even compelled, to construct with

[23] Graves (1975), 56. [24] Graves (1957a), 34.

Homer's Daughter. The 'neat' translation suggests the future authoress as a 'tight little body' whose WRNS uniform covers but does not entirely efface the underlying 'white body' of the goddess. Some of Catullus's poems certainly qualify as satires, but satire is not the genre that he is usually associated with, being more readily thought of as a love poet giving voice to the male lover's subjection to a maddening, capricious woman and the torment of mingled love and hate. Graves's 'neat translation' of Catullus seems to carry with it with a distinctive generic choice, a choice like that which underlies *Homer's Daughter*, the neat satire into which Graves translated Homer's *Odyssey*.

4

Robert Graves as Historical Novelist

Count Belisarius—*Genesis, Gender, and Truth*

Shaun Tougher

INTRODUCTION

Robert Graves's popular fame rests largely upon his achievement in the field of historical fiction—his two novels about the Roman emperor Claudius (AD 41–54). (This fame was of course enhanced by the celebrated BBC TV series produced in the 1970s, featuring unforgettable performances by Derek Jacobi as Claudius and Sian Phillips as his ruthless grandmother Livia.) However, Graves also turned to Rome again for a further historical novel, *Count Belisarius*, an account of the life and career of this general who lived in the sixth century AD. As a schoolboy studying Classical Studies and Ancient History, and then as an undergraduate taking Ancient History and Byzantine Studies, I naturally read Graves's *Claudius* novels as well as *Count Belisarius*. I enjoyed the former but found the latter a dull and disappointing book. It may be that prior familiarity with the story of Belisarius blunted the impact of the novel, but general critical reaction suggests that the key problem was the characterization of the hero himself.[1] Martin Seymour-Smith comments that 'Belisarius

[1] Though the noted Byzantinist Cyril Mango thought that the problem with *Count Belisarius* in comparison with the *Claudius* novels was the lack of evidence for Byzantine daily life: Mango (1981), 337 (I would like to thank Ruth Macrides and Roger Scott for alerting me to this comment). I think other problems with the book are that the narrator is not engaging enough and that Procopius should have been developed as a character.

himself is a little stiffly noble'; Miranda Seymour considers that Belisarius 'is made too one-dimensional by his unfailing decency'; and most devastatingly, Graves's own nephew, Richard Perceval Graves, declares that the novel 'suffers from a serious central flaw. Namely, Belisarius himself.'[2] Graves himself, in a letter to the *Sunday Times* published on 17 April 1938, shortly after the publication of the novel, responded to the fact that 'A number of reviewers . . . have taken the same point of view: that . . . I have presented Belisarius as altogether too noble and victorious.' However, whatever one thinks of the quality of *Count Belisarius* as a novel, there can be no doubt that it is a fascinating book: it turns the spotlight on a less well-known but vital period of Roman history; it deals primarily with war in the aftermath and expectation of global conflict;[3] it has as its narrator a eunuch, thirty-six years before the appearance of the most celebrated eunuch narrator in historical fiction, Mary Renault's Bagoas, the eponymous *Persian Boy*.[4] In this essay I aim to demonstrate just how intriguing *Count Belisarius* is, and how rewarding it is to explore for a deeper appreciation of Graves's life and work. I will examine in particular the genesis of the novel, keys themes in it (especially gender), and Graves's attitude to historical accuracy.

THE GENESIS OF *COUNT BELISARIUS*

Count Belisarius was published in 1938, two years after Robert Graves and Laura Riding had returned to England from Mallorca (due to the outbreak of the Spanish Civil War), where they had lived since 1930. *Count Belisarius* was thus published in the wake of Graves's success with his two *Claudius* novels (*I, Claudius*; *Claudius the God and his Wife Messalina*), which had both been published in 1934. Like the *Claudius* novels, *Count Belisarius* is concerned with the Roman empire, but the Roman empire of the sixth century AD, when the west had 'fallen' and Constantinople was now the imperial centre. *Count Belisarius* tells the story of the life and career of Belisarius, the

[2] Seymour-Smith (1995), 297; Seymour (2003), 259; R. P. Graves (1990), 279.

[3] For the theme and treatment of war and generalship in the novel see Chapter 5 in this volume by Jon Coulston.

[4] Renault (1972). For Renault's Bagoas see e.g. Tougher (2008b).

famous general of the emperor Justinian I (527–65), as well as of the times he lived in. It is narrated by Eugenius, the eunuch slave of Belisarius's wife Antonina, a vibrant character in the novel who first meets Belisarius as a tall and handsome 14-year-old youth in chapter 2, when she performs as a dancing-girl at a banquet of Belisarius's uncle Modestus. Eugenius idolizes Belisarius, and tracks his life from his boyhood in Thrace to his death in March 565, but also recounts the subsequent deaths of Justinian, Antonina, and another general, the eunuch Narses (Eugenius declares at the start of chapter 23 that he is writing in the year 571). The novel is primarily preoccupied with narrating in detail the campaigns waged by Belisarius in the service of Justinian (as emphasized by most of the titles of the twenty-four chapters of the book, e.g. 'War with Persia', 'The Expedition against Carthage', 'The Defence of Rome', 'Victory at Carchemish'), which took him from the eastern frontier and conflict with Sassanid Persia to the west, as a key figure in the emperor's attempted reconquest of the lost western parts of the Roman empire. The reconquest started with a campaign against the Vandals in North Africa in 533, and moved on quickly to Italy and engagement with the Ostrogothic rulers there, though the Italian campaign dragged on into the 550s and was concluded by Narses rather than Belisarius (though Graves asserts that it was advice given to the eunuch by Belisarius which was instrumental in the success of Narses: chapter 23). The novel is greatly concerned also with the character of Belisarius as a noble and morally upright man (as well as an excellent general) in an age of corruption, contrasting him especially with the emperor himself, who is depicted as suspicious and treacherous, very much in the mould created by the major historian of the period, Procopius (Belisarius's legal secretary), in his *Secret History* (which also spotlights the wives of both Belisarius and Justinian—Antonina and Theodora respectively, both coming from families involved in the entertainment profession—as Graves does too).[5] The focus on the relationship between Belisarius and Justinian builds in the novel to the emperor's 'Last Ingratitude' (chapter 24) to his general, for in 564 Belisarius is implicated in a plot against Justinian (a situation in which Procopius himself is portrayed as playing a vital part), despite having saved

[5] The nature of Belisarius's and Justinian's Christian faith is also counterpoised in the novel, Belisarius's purity and religious simplicity being contrasted with Justinian's hypocrisy and complexity of religious thought.

Constantinople from an attack by Huns in 558 at the Battle of Chettos (chapter 23). In January 565 Belisarius is put on trial for high treason, and after being convicted is stripped of his honours, estates, and goods. He is also blinded, and takes to the streets of Constantinople with a begging-bowl, proclaiming: 'Alms, alms! Spare a copper for Belisarius! Spare a copper for Belisarius who once scattered gold in these streets! Spare a copper for Belisarius, good people of Constantinople! Alms, alms!' Such is Justinian's alarm at the positive public response to Belisarius, and the consequent hostility to the emperor himself, that he quickly pardons and restores Belisarius to his previous rank, though the great man dies soon after.

Our knowledge of the researching, writing, and finalization of *Count Belisarius* is greatly assisted by the existence of the diary Robert Graves kept between 1935 and 1939.[6] In this diary Graves relates when he began research for the novel; what he read; when he began writing; how the writing progressed; the rewriting process; his dealings with his publishers; the production of maps and the image for the dust-jacket of the novel; and the final submission and publication of the novel. We are told, for instance, that he began reading for the novel on 30 June 1937; he began writing it on 22 July; by 11 September he had written about half of it; on 19 December he finished the last chapter; on 15 January 1938 Laura Riding began checking through the revised draft; on 14 February he revised and sent off the last chapter to his British publisher, Cassell; on 26 February he finished working through the proofs; and on 31 March he was sent copies of the novel.[7]

Although *Count Belisarius* was published four years after the *Claudius* novels, the idea of writing a novel about Belisarius had been on Graves's agenda prior to 1934.[8] Graves himself was to report that the original suggestion came from T. E. Lawrence (1888–1935), whom Graves had known since meeting him at Oxford in 1920, and whose biography he had written and published in 1927. Graves recalled:

6 The diary is available online, as part of the Robert Graves Diary Project based at the University of Victoria, Canada.

7 The writing of the novel coincided with the move of Graves and Riding from London (they initially stayed in a friend's house when they returned from Mallorca) to Highcroft House in Ewhurst village in Surrey on 7 July 1937, and their move back to London, to 31 Alma Square in Maida Vale, on 15 November of the same year.

8 Seymour (2003), 255 dates the idea to 1931.

> some time in the early Thirties . . . Lawrence in a depressed mood wrote to me from India, where he was living disguised as Aircraftman Shaw of the R.A.F.[9] He begged me: 'Spare an obol for Belisarius!'[10] Not understanding the reference, I wrote back inquiring exactly who Belisarius was.[11] He answered that Belisarius was one of the only three really first-class Roman generals in history: Scipio Africanus, Julius Caesar and . . . this Thracian genius Belisarius. And that Belisarius was the only general in Classical history who had ever successfully invaded Italy from North Africa; but that he was eventually blinded by his ungrateful and jealous master, the Emperor Justinian, and forced to beg for small coins at a street corner in Constantinople . . . Lawrence then suggested my writing a book about Belisarius, none of any value having been published since Lord Mahon's in 1828.[12]

The appeal of a reputedly great general like Belisarius for the likes of Lawrence and Graves, men with direct experience of war and command, is unsurprising. Graves described the novel as 'a military manual', and commented that 'tactics interest me'.[13] War is certainly the prime subject-matter of the novel.[14] I for one have to agree with Winston Churchill, who observed to Graves, 'I daresay some of your readers will have felt there was too much war' (though Churchill continued, 'but the vivid accounts you give of those long-forgotten campaigns, in my mind, only enhance the value of the work').[15] Basil Liddell Hart (1895–1970), the military historian and friend of Graves,

[9] Graves's chronology is inexact, since Lawrence left India in January 1929: Wilson (1990), 844.

[10] In a letter to Basil Liddell Hart of December 1935 Graves remarks: 'Have just come across a forgotten passage in a letter [Lawrence] wrote me from the NW Frontier: identifying himself with Belisarius. Most interesting': O'Prey (1982), 259.

[11] It seems, then, that Graves had not had occasion to discuss Belisarius with the noted Byzantinist Henri Grégoire when they worked together at the University of Cairo in 1926: Graves (2000), 267. It is worth mentioning that Graves also met another well-known Byzantinist, Joan Hussey, in Manchester on 14 January 1938, as recorded in his diary.

[12] Graves (1972), 167–8.

[13] Seymour-Smith (1995), 369, citing a letter written in 1952.

[14] See also Jon Coulston's essay, Chapter 5 in this volume. Graves continued with the subjects of war and history in his two subsequent novels, *Sergeant Lamb of the Ninth* (1940) and *Proceed, Sergeant Lamb* (1941). Snipes (1979), 163–72 treats the Sergeant Lamb novels together with *Count Belisarius*, entitling the chapter 'Historical Novels: on Two Soldiers'.

[15] Seymour-Smith (1995), 356. Churchill had been sent a copy of *Count Belisarius* by the publishers at Graves's request. Graves had known Churchill since 1915: Graves (1972), 168.

who had himself published a book on Scipio Africanus in 1926 (*Scipio Africanus: Greater Than Napoleon*), 'thought it a superb book'.[16] In his estimation of Belisarius as a great general Graves clearly took Lawrence's lead, who was himself informed by the biography by Lord Mahon, first published in 1829 (not 1828) and followed by a second edition in 1848.[17] The diary reveals that Lord Mahon's biography was a key secondary source for Graves (he began reading it on 30 June and finished it on 8 July), and it is not without interest that Graves had borrowed the biography from Liddell Hart himself.[18] At the beginning of his life of Belisarius the 24-year-old Lord Mahon sets the scene for the salvation of the Roman empire by his hero:

> At the beginning of the sixth century of the Christian era, the empire of Constantinople was beset with enemies and sinking to decay . . . Frequent insurrections wasted the resources of the state, and deprived the government of all energy and enterprise; while the armies, turbulent and feeble, had thrown off the restraints of military discipline. It is the purpose of this narrative, to show how the genius of one man averted these dangers, and corrected these defects; how the tottering empire was upheld; how the successors of Augustus were enabled, for a time, to resume their former ascendancy, and to wrest from the hands of the barbarians their most important possessions.[19]

In his summing up of Belisarius at the end of the biography, Lord Mahon compares him to the First Duke of Marlborough (John Churchill, 1650–1722, whose biography Winston Churchill had written in the 1930s), 'whom he equaled in talents'.[20]

In his diary Graves also alludes to other secondary sources which informed his knowledge of Belisarius and his times. He refers to Sir Charles William Chadwick Oman's *History of the Art of War in the Middle Ages* (1924); Henri St Lawrence Beaufort Moss's *Birth of the Middle Ages, 395–814* (1935); Sir William Smith's *Dictionary of the Bible* (1860), *Dictionary of Christian Biography, Literature, Sects*

[16] Seymour (2003), 259. Graves and Liddell Hart first met in September 1936, though they had corresponded before this.

[17] Lord Mahon was the parliamentary name of Philip Henry Stanhope (1805–75), Fifth Earl Stanhope. Canary (1980), 116 opines that: 'One suspects that some of Belisarius's heroic qualities come from Graves's good friend T. E. Lawrence, but then Lawrence, too, has always been mysterious.'

[18] O'Prey (1982), 278.

[19] Mahon (2006), 1.

[20] Mahon (2006), 209. The quote continues, 'and closely resembled in his faults of uxoriousness and love of money'.

and Doctrines (1877–87),[21] and *Dictionary of Christian Antiquity* (1880);[22] and Henry Hart Milman's *History of Latin Christianity* (1854). It is clear that Graves did not list all his reading, for he had consulted Gibbon's *The History of the Decline and Fall of the Roman Empire* too, but it is not named in the diary.[23] He does indicate, however, that he also benefited from conversations with those who had knowledge of the period, such as his niece Sally Graves.[24] Primary sources perused by Graves appear in the diary too: he mentions Vegetius; Sidonius Apollinaris; Cassiodorus; Malalas and Theophanes (in Latin); Fronto; Jerome ('Reading that awful Jerome's letters', he records on 29 September 1937); Claudian; and Eusebius. Of course, the key source for Graves, as he acknowledged himself in the foreword to *Count Belisarius*, was Procopius, the most prolific ancient source for Belisarius and the age of Justinian. Procopius worked for Belisarius as his legal secretary from the 520s, accompanied him (like Antonina) on the campaigns in the west (until 540), and, to an extent, idolized him. He wrote a major narrative of the military campaigns of the reign of Justinian (the *Wars*), an infamous exposé of the regime best known as the *Secret History*, as well as an account of the extensive building-work undertaken during the reign (the *Buildings*). In his diary Graves records that he received copies of Procopius' work on 15 July, started reading at once, and was still reading on 29 July. Part of the problem with *Count Belisarius* as a novel is that if one knows Procopius' works the story is no longer a surprise, but Graves is not alone in producing a Belisarius (and an age of Justinian) that is in effect Procopius': Averil Cameron has remarked: 'As Thucydides does for the Peloponnesian War, or Tacitus for the early Empire, so Procopius provides the filter through which we must view the reign of Justinian.'[25] It was Procopius who put Belisarius on the map in the first place, and it was Procopius who set the military agenda.

So Graves's decision to write a novel about Belisarius and his military career appears to have been prompted by a direct suggestion by T. E. Lawrence and encouraged by his general interest in warfare (an interest shared by his friends and contemporaries). Graves's self-confessed ignorance about who Belisarius was suggests that he was

[21] With Henry Wace. [22] With Samuel Cheetham.

[23] For Graves and Gibbon see the discussion later in this chapter.

[24] The diary records that Alan Hodge also assisted with research for the novel.

[25] Cameron (1985), 3.

not influenced (initially, at any rate) by the string of works produced by artists and writers who had taken Belisarius as their subject from Procopius onwards, such as Marmontel's novel *Bélisaire* (1767), David's painting (1781), Donizetti's opera (1836), Longfellow's poem (1845, in *Birds of Passage*), as well as Lord Mahon's biography (1829). However, as will be argued below, it is clear that other factors also motivated Graves to write a book about Belisarius, and other themes that appealed to him were served by the subject-matter.

Before turning to these factors, however, one further aspect of the genesis of *Count Belisarius* deserves consideration: the title itself. Graves's own working title for the novel was simply *Belisarius*. What to call the book was obviously an issue though, as the diary reports that on 6 October Riding suggested an alternative title, *The Faith of Belisarius*, which does reflect well key concerns of the novel. However, the diary also records on 9 November that it was the publishers who had the final say: Graves notes that they preferred *Count Belisarius* as a title. Whether this was an alternative Graves gave them or whether they proposed it themselves is unclear. Why the use of the title 'Count' was deemed so desirable seems rather puzzling, given that it strikes me as hardly fundamental to defining Belisarius's life and career. Perhaps its selection was intended to provide a playful echo of the title of Sir Walter Scott's last historical novel, *Count Robert of Paris* (published in 1832).[26] Intriguingly, this novel also dealt with the Byzantine empire, featured an independent forthright woman, the empress Anna Komnene (and also the Amazonian wife of Robert), and featured a 'British' character as a point of reference, the Saxon member of the Varangian Guard, Hereward.

MONEY, VIRTUE, AND RELIGION

Turning to other factors which motivated Graves to write *Count Belisarius*, one is financial considerations. It is well known that Graves dismissed his novels as potboilers, a means of making money; for him, poetry was the thing. Certainly Graves was in desperate need of money in the 1920s and 1930s. The *Claudius* novels

[26] Scott (2006).

had sold well, and also attracted the attention of the movie business (in the shape of Alexander Korda), thus raising the spectre of further financial rewards. It is probable that Graves thought (or at least hoped) that another novel about the Roman empire would be a money-spinner. However, the sincerity of his assertion that his novels were just potboilers has rightly been questioned. The amount of research he did, and the extent of his investment in his subjects, suggest that his novels were not merely cash-raising vehicles, effective though they could be as such. Graves may have considered his novels less significant than his poetry, but this does not make them intellectually or artistically worthless. It is possible that he felt a certain stigma about writing 'historical fiction'; Laura Riding could be dismissive of the genre,[27] so his own dismissive attitude may have been a form of defence. It is evident that *Count Belisarius* was not just written to be a popular blockbuster. Graves, as has been said, was interested in the subject of war itself, the details of the campaigns, the tactics, the nature of Belisarius's leadership of his men. He was also interested in the character of Belisarius: his nobility in the face of widespread corruption and treachery, and especially his loyalty to the emperor despite his poor treatment at the hands of the jealous and deluded Justinian. King has described the novel as 'another cynical story about the ways of the world', while in an article on historical novels of the 1930s Hoskins notes Graves's interest in 'the possibilities of an individual retaining some kind of integrity' when involved in politics.[28] Graves's swiftness to defend his characterization of Belisarius, which was criticized in reviews of the book, as has been seen, indicates that he considered (or at least posed as considering) the novel to have a deeper message. He wrote in the letter to the *Sunday Times*:

> To me it is a rather shocking comment on twentieth-century literary taste that when, as a rare case, a really good man is shown actively, patiently, loyally at work in his struggle against the forces of confusion, nobody must admire him whole-heartedly: it must be said that he is wooden, humourless, over-correct, that 'he does not come to life'.
>
> That this popular prejudice against a belief in wisdom and virtue is a very strong one seems to be proved by the fact that (so far as I know) no other life of Belisarius has been published in England since Lord Mahon's in 1828.

[27] See e.g. R. P. Graves (1990), 218.
[28] King (2008), 131; Hoskins (1999), 133.

Thus, in addition to the military skills of Belisarius, Graves was interested in the personal virtues of his hero too.

Graves's preoccupation with religion was also well served by writing a novel set in the later Roman empire. In his work he would return time and again to the subjects of biblical history and Christianity (as well as antiquity in general). In 1925 he published his first novel, *My Head! My Head!* (which tells the story of the Old Testament prophet Elisha and the Shunamite woman); the *Claudius* novels touch on Judaism and early Christianity, especially in relation to the figure of Herod Agrippa; and in 1946 he published *King Jesus* (his telling of the life of Christ). Graves's attitude to Christianity is certainly intriguing. In *Good-bye to All That* (his autobiography published in 1929, which took his military experience as its central focus) Graves expressed his disillusion and cynicism about the Church (but not necessarily Christianity), though this may have been a view imposed upon his past, for he had been a committed Christian.[29] In *Count Belisarius* he relished the opportunity to look askance at Christians and the Church, through the eyes of the cynical Eugenius and Antonina, both of whom are not characterized as Christians but as devotees of traditional religion. Especially mocked are the involved theological debates of the time and the hypocrisy of certain Christians, notably Justinian himself, whose religious attitudes are contrasted with the simple devotion of Belisarius. That religion is a key theme of the book is underlined by its conclusion, in which Belisarius is compared to Christ. Eugenius writes:

> 'Under the Old Gods', my former master Damocles used to say, somewhat exaggerating the case, 'virtue was always honoured, ignominy frowned upon; the felon's cross was not gilded and jewelled; man did not revel in self-abasement.' But let anyone believe what he pleases. And if he happens to be a simple devotee of virtue, not a logic-chopping, hypocritical theologian or perverted ascetic, this story will not offend him, but contrariwise confirm him in his principles. For Count Belisarius had such a simple devotion to virtue, from which he never declined. Those of you for whom the Gospel story carries historical weight may perhaps say that Belisarius behaved at his trial before Justinian very much as his Master had done before Pontius Pilate, the Governor of

[29] On Graves and Christianity see e.g. R. P. Graves (1990), 104; Seymour-Smith (1995), 380–1; Seymour (2003), 28–9; King (2008), 18.

Judaea—when unjustly accused of the very same crime, namely treason against the Empire; and that he suffered no less patiently.

So much, then, for these things.

GENDER: WOMEN AND EUNUCHS

Graves was patently also drawn to the age of Justinian by the pair of powerful women who characterize it: Antonina, the wife of Belisarius, and Theodora, the wife of Justinian. Following Procopius's lead (especially in the *Secret History*), but developing it for his own purposes, Graves made these women the potent, intelligent actors, far more clued up than their husbands, who are both ineffectual in their way. In Graves's vision, unlike Procopius's, Antonina and Theodora make an attractive and engaging pair. It is well known that Graves was interested in powerful, independent women. For instance, he had created memorable portraits of Livia and Messalina in the *Claudius* novels; he had relationships with such women (the feminist Nancy Nicholson and the 'prophet' Laura Riding); he was interested in matriarchal societies (influenced by the psychiatrist W. H. R. Rivers in the early 1920s); and was attracted by the concept of the original domination of a Mother Goddess (famously developed in his *The White Goddess*, published in 1948, but which had much deeper roots in his intellectual ideas, prior to his contact with Laura Riding).[30] It is no coincidence that when Graves was writing *Count Belisarius* Laura Riding was engaged in the writing of *Lives of Wives*, a history of antiquity from Cyrus the Great to Herod the Great (and focusing especially on Persia, Macedonia, and Jerusalem), in which, she declared, 'the principal male characters are . . . written of as husbands rather than as heroes';[31] *Lives of Wives* was in fact contracted at the same time as *Count Belisarius*, and published a year after it.[32] Antonina, in particular, gave Graves great scope to develop his ideas about powerful women: she was sexually enlightened, she was sassy and

[30] See e.g. Seymour (2003), 108 and 146–7.

[31] Riding (1939), foreword.

[32] Diary, 28 June 1937. Seymour (2003), 253 asserts that Riding was taking Theodora 'as one of her subjects', but if this was the case she did not make it to the published version, which stops at the threshold of the Christian era.

savvy, she was politically active, and she participated in Belisarius's campaigns. One of the most intriguing things Graves's diary reveals about the writing of *Count Belisarius* is that the narrator was not originally intended to be Eugenius but his mistress, Antonina herself. The diary records that Graves had written up to the start of chapter 12 (of an eventual twenty-four) with Antonina as the narrator; it was only on 28 September (he had begun writing on 22 July) that the decision was taken to write the novel from the point of view of a eunuch, which of course entailed revising what had already been written. Graves's decision to change the narrator is usually thought to have adversely affected the novel. Seymour notes that 'The book suffered a consequent drop in the tension of the narrative', while Richard Perceval Graves observes that 'the most striking aspect of *Count Belisarius* is Graves's complex portrayal of Antonina' and considers that the change of narrator 'probably weakened its emotional force'.[33] Keeping Antonina as the voice of the novel would surely have made it more distinctive and engaging.

The question must therefore be asked, why did Graves alter the narrator from Antonina to Eugenius? In his diary Graves records that the suggestion to make the narrator a eunuch was Laura Riding's, but no explanation for it is given.[34] One might assume that Graves and/or Riding were intrigued by the opportunity of voicing such a figure, but Graves in fact makes very little obvious play of Eugenius as a eunuch.[35] He seems far more interested in Eugenius's origins than in his castration. In his diary he tells us that on 3 November he wrote the story of Eugenius. This is found at the end of chapter 2, and begins: 'The story of how I had come to be in attendance on the dancing-girl Antonina, my mistress.' Eugenius was bought as a slave by Barak, a Syrian who traded in (fake) Christian relics. He purchased the 6-year-old Eugenius from Saxon pirates on the Channel Islands. Eugenius relates: 'My name was Goronwy, the son of Geraint, who was a British nobleman. The Saxons had carried me off, together with my young

[33] Seymour (2003), 259; R. P. Graves (1990), 279. However, some disagree: Seymour-Smith (1995), 297; King (2008), 123.

[34] The diary states baldly: 'Laura advised me to change the outlook of Belisarius from Antonina to a eunuch.' One assumes that Eugenius is meant, but it is ambiguous.

[35] Graves seems to have been intrigued by the queer. It is interesting, for instance, that in *Sergeant Lamb of the Ninth* Graves featured the Indian transvestite Sweet Yellow Head (chapter 14) as well as the story about the fighting cock that had female feathering (chapter 1).

nurse, in a sudden landing in the Severn estuary.' Eugenius recalls his father and his father's castle, where harpers sang ballads. He continues: 'My master Barak starved me and treated me very cruelly, and brought me with him to Palestine, where he changed my name to "Eugenius" and castrated me.' His becoming a eunuch is thus very matter-of-fact, and not explored any further. The story is more concerned with Barak's fake relics, which leads to the explanation of how Eugenius came to be transferred to the ownership of the family of Antonina.

One of the few times that Graves shows sustained interest in the subject of eunuchs per se is in chapter 6, when narrating the preaching of a bishop from Ravenna in Hagia Sophia in Constantinople. The bishop develops the idea that 'the Christian angels . . . are all eunuchs', and asserts that earthly eunuchs are still a prey to lust, as are angels.[36] He argues that eunuchs have a hair fetish, since angels looking down from heaven can only see people's heads and shoulders (Graves seemingly developing this notion from Paul, 1 Corinthians 11: 10, which tells women to cover their heads 'on account of the angels'). This leads on to an attack on women's preoccupation with beautification, including wigs.[37] Thus Graves's concern becomes women rather than eunuchs, and more fundamentally, the mocking of Christian attitudes and hypocrisy.

Having raised the issue of Roman assumptions about the lustful nature of eunuchs, it seems rather odd that Graves never pursues it at length in relation to Eugenius. Indeed, Eugenius's personal life appears to hold no interest for Graves; the eunuch is defined purely by his devoted service to Antonina and Belisarius. It is the figure of the chamberlain Narses who serves to provide more sustained, albeit brief, comment on eunuchs. He comes to the fore in chapter 8, as an envoy from Justinian to Antonina as they are both journeying to Belisarius at Daras on the eastern frontier. It is noted that Narses began his career in the palace working 'at a loom in the company of the Palace women', 'until his education was complete',[38] but he is

[36] The bishop notes that 'the Arch-Fiend himself was an angel who fell from Grace'.

[37] At this point the bishop provocatively gestures at Antonina and Theodora's sister Chrysomallo. The bishop relates in particular Jerome's story of the punishment of Praetextata (who acquired a wig for her niece Eustochia at the command of her pagan husband Hymetius): *Letter* 107.5, To Laeta. Graves gives the lady's name as Praetexta.

[38] Graves (1983), 127. This is taken from later legendary stories about Narses's clash with Sophia and Justin II at the end of his career, but is not found in Procopius.

characterized as having military aspirations. Eugenius observes that 'Narses talked very practically on the problem of frontier defence, and recruiting, and the commissariat problem; and when he addressed the escort of Guards he gave clear, abrupt orders in a very good imitation of a military voice'. Eugenius accounts for Narses's yearning for a military career by the fact that he 'had been captured in battle when he was eleven years old, and had already at that tender age killed a man with his little sword—for he came of a well-known military family in Armenia' (this is all invented by Graves, bar the fact that Narses was of Armenian extraction). Antonina teases Narses as 'a traitor to his sex', since: 'He shows none of the usual traits of a eunuch—luxury, sentimentality, timorousness, and argumentative religiosity. He betrays not the least inclination to comb my fine auburn hair or fondle my pretty feet, and even seems to have no envy of my good looks; which is the most outstanding trait of all in a eunuch.'

The emergence of Narses into the narrative also allows Eugenius/Graves to give a digression on court eunuchs. He asserts that most of them were 'imported . . . from the Black Sea shores, about Colchis'; they are valuable to the emperors for their loyalty, trustworthiness, and support against plots of the nobility; 'rich middle-class families' exploit the demand for eunuchs by castrating their own children; and illegitimate imperial children were also castrated to prevent them from claiming power (though the latter two points apply to subsequent Byzantine practice rather than to that of late antiquity[39]). In addition, he remarks that eunuchs can also be priests ('The City Patriarch himself is now frequently one of our number'), and that eunuch slaves are more expensive than other slaves. This digression then turns to issues of sex. Eugenius describes how men mock eunuchs for being 'debarred from the sweet and wholesome act of love', but asserts that the eunuch is able to retaliate that 'sex is a madness and never brought anyone much luck'. However, he then adds that the eunuch 'secretly, as I confess . . . is apt to envy the man who can take a woman to bed with him and do more than embrace her as a sister and chastely kiss her eyes'. Antonina herself declares that she would rather be a eunuch than a man, 'because men find it most difficult to find a mean, in sex, between debauchery and

[39] See e.g. Tougher (2008a).

asceticism . . . men envy the evenness of women. And this evenness the eunuch enjoys to a certain degree.'

These reflections on sex and gender in relation to eunuchs suggest that Graves was alert to the fact that castrated men could serve these subjects in the novel. Nevertheless, it must be acknowledged that these digressions are few and far between in the focused concentration on military affairs, and arise primarily in relation to Narses rather than Eugenius. Since the idea to make Eugenius the narrator of the novel came late in the day, perhaps Graves plainly did not have enough scope to revise the perspective sufficiently. On the other hand, perhaps he simply did not want to; the appeal of Eugenius may not have been his eunuchood (which as a subject was served by Narses anyway), but his servitude: his utter devotion to his master and mistress. One has to wonder what personal relevance the figure of Eugenius had for Graves and Riding. It is often observed that Graves was in effect the devoted slave of Riding, which raises the possibility that he was Eugenius to her Antonina. Alternatively, and more sinisterly, one might wonder if he perceived himself as the faithful Belisarius to her unworthy Justinian. Biographers of Graves have noted that, despite the public proclamations of his devotion to Riding and of her superiority, Graves's treatment of Livia and Messalina in the *Claudius* novels suggests a more critical view of her.[40] To take Riding's perspective, it has been suggested that she, by advising Graves to make his narrator a eunuch slave, was in fact mocking him. The possibility that the eunuchood of Eugenius is relevant after all is strengthened because it is known that Graves had embraced a life of celibacy for Riding. Seymour asserts that it: 'must have amused [Riding] to create a parallel to her own situation, with Graves appearing as the servile and sexually frustrated Eugenius. Graves, too, could get a morose pleasure out of such an analogy; there was always an element of masochism in the humiliations he chose to undergo.'[41] Here I think one should recall Eugenius's rather odd observation that all eunuchs can do is 'embrace [a woman] as a sister and chastely kiss her eyes'. Eunuchs could surely do rather more than this! Graves may have been thinking more of the limitations placed upon him by Riding. It is possible that eunuchood was on Graves's mind for other reasons too. In *Good-bye to All That*, recalling the injuries

[40] R. P. Graves (1990), 190–1; Seymour (2003), 216–17.
[41] Seymour (2003), 259.

which caused him to be sent home from the Front in 1916, he writes: 'One piece of shell went through my left thigh, high up, near the groin; I must have been at the full stretch of my stride to escape emasculation.'[42] What indicates most strongly that the eunuchood of Eugenius was fundamentally important for Graves and/or Riding is the fact that although Procopius testifies to the existence of Eugenius he does not identify him as a eunuch, only as a slave of Antonina.[43] Thus it looks as if Graves deliberately turned Eugenius into a eunuch for his own ends. This observation brings us appositely to the last aspect of *Count Belisarius* I wish to explore, the relationship between historical fiction and historical accuracy.

TRUTH

In his foreword to *Count Belisarius* Graves is keen to assert his sound knowledge and historical reliability. He identifies his major source, Procopius, as well as alluding to others (Agathias by name, and Cassiodorus). He declares that: 'Wherever surviving records are meagre I have been obliged to fill in the gaps of the story with fiction, but have usually had an historical equivalent in mind; so that if exactly this or that did not happen, something similar probably did.' He notes that there is evidence for the 'Belisarius–Antonina–Theodosius love-triangle, however fictional it may seem', and adds: 'Nor is the account here given of sixth-century ecclesiastical and Hippodrome politics exaggerated.' He records that the 'only invented character' in the novel 'is Belisarius's uncle Modestus, a familiar type of the tinsel-age Roman man of letters'. This apparent anxiety about accuracy (or desire to be thought accurate) is also reflected in Graves's diary. As has been seen, he records key primary and secondary sources he consulted for the production of the novel. Most interesting and illuminating is the entry for 28 February 1938; he records that he 'Wrote a bit about the deposition of [the pope] Silverius and blinding of [Belisarius] in case my facts should be challenged'. It is noteworthy that Gore Vidal, in his original Note to his novel about the last pagan

42 Graves (2000b), 181.

43 *Secret History* 1.27. Seymour (2003), 259 mistakenly thinks that Eugenius was an invention of Graves.

Roman emperor, *Julian*, is likewise keen to assert the wealth of source material he drew upon for his depiction of Julian and his age—not just, he says, 'the history of Ammianus Marcellinus (or even of Edward Gibbon)'—and appeals to the example of Graves himself.[44] Vidal relates that Graves had countered the impression that for *I, Claudius* 'he had simply spun himself a novel from Suetonius' gossip', by including in *Claudius the God* an extensive bibliography.[45]

It is ironic, then, that Graves did find himself challenged concerning historical accuracy in *Count Belisarius*, though he anticipated this. It was the question of the blinding of Belisarius that caused controversy. Soon after publication of the novel the *Sunday Times* published a letter from a J. H. Williams of Fraserburgh, which runs:

> Contemporary evidence supports the estimate of the character of Belisarius given by Mr. Robert Graves . . . It is surprising, however, that the author has chosen to perpetuate the absurd myth that the hero was blinded by Justinian and received alms in the streets of Constantinople. [This] may serve to adorn a 'moral or romantic tale,' but it is pure fiction. Gibbon calls the story 'an idle fable'; [George Frederick] Young, in 'East and West Through Fifteen Centuries,' says it is 'a pure invention of later times, made popular by Marmontel in his romance "Belisaire."' The evidence adduced by both Gibbon and Young is so well documented that there is no need to quote it here. Belisarius did not lose his sight and did not die in poverty and disgrace. He was accused of complicity in the conspiracy of Sergius, and thereafter was kept a prisoner in his own palace for seven months. In July, 564, he was restored to freedom, wealth, and fame.

Graves retaliated as follows, in a letter to the *Sunday Times* published on 15 May:

> In a historical novel the narrative of events is given confidently without the interruptive perhapses and no doubts which historians use. This confidence may mean wilful ignorance of the period, and usually does; it may also mean that the novelist has taken the trouble to read the original sources at least as conscientiously as many professed historians.

[44] It is interesting to note that one of Vidal's first essays, a form he is celebrated for, is on Graves's translation of Suetonius's *Caesars*: Vidal (1963), 204–14.

[45] Vidal (1964), 'A Note'. It is notable that for her historical novels (the first of which, *Last of the Wine*, was published in 1956, though her first novel, *Purposes of Love*, was published in 1939) Mary Renault developed the habit of appending an Author's Note, discussing the ancient sources and interpretation of them.

> Mr. J. H. Williams puts me in the former category, accusing me of 'perpetuating an absurd myth.' He follows popular encyclopaedias which, summarising Gibbon and others, throw doubt on the historicity of Belisarius's blinding by Justinian—on the grounds that no authority for it is found until the 'Chiliads' of the poet Tzetzes, who wrote in the twelfth century. Tzetzes, though a bad poet, was an erudite scholar, and his 'Chiliads' are highly rated by historians: it is clear that he drew on several historical works no longer in existence. Besides—this was unknown to Gibbon—an anonymous eleventh-century historian, who as a signal honour was allowed to dedicate his book to the Emperor Alexis, had anticipated Tzetzes in recording this blinding. A slight discrepancy in the two accounts (in one case a wooden begging bowl is mentioned, in another an earthenware one) suggest that Tzetzes drew his information from another source than this anonymous writer. Moreover, the fifteenth-century historians, Crinitus, Volaterranus, Pontanus, Egnatius, who had access to a number of Byzantine authorities now lost, all firmly believed in the blinding. Nor can any political motive be suggested for the invention of the story, if it was indeed an invention of the anonymous historian, and it surely would have been very difficult for him to foist it on the literary men of Constantinople, who had high critical standards.

Graves thus conveys that he is better informed about the evidence than his critic, and better informed than Gibbon himself. He takes the stance of a scholar, and wears his knowledge on his sleeve.[46] It is salutary (and perhaps startling) to realize, however, that in his letter Graves is merely dependent on the researches of Lord Mahon, who made it one of the unique selling-points of his *Life of Belisarius* that he had discovered new evidence relating to the fate of the general. He declares this in the preface to the biography and then devotes an extensive coda to the evidence, in which he explains his 'grounds for adhering to the original narrative of the blindness and beggary of Belisarius'.[47] It is Lord Mahon who pits himself against Gibbon.

[46] For fascinating comment on the development of the Belisarius legend in Byzantine chronicles see Scott (2006). It is the twelfth-century chronicler Kedrenos who seems to be the key catalyst: Scott (2006), 42 observes, 'we have here the elements that can develop into the romantic tragedy of Belisarios. It is only now, I suggest, that the Belisarios legend begins.'

[47] Mahon (1829), 441–73. He returned to the question again in the preface to the second edition of 1848. It is to be regretted that the modern reprint of the biography does not reproduce the prefaces or the coda. In the coda Lord Mahon asserts, 'I am now about to bring forward a new and authentic testimony, to which public attention has never yet been called, and by which this story may be traced nearly one century

Nevertheless, even if Graves is merely parroting Lord Mahon, he does pose as being committed to historical truth. It is ironic, then, that today Gibbon is still preferred to Lord Mahon. One should ask, however, whether Graves really did believe the arguments of the nineteenth-century biographer. As has been seen, Graves indicates that he did not know about Belisarius at all until T. E. Lawrence mentioned him, and this was in specific relation to the story of his begging. Thus the blinding and begging of Belisarius was a core aspect of the story from the beginning for Graves, so he may have accepted these unquestioningly (or felt saddled with them by Lawrence). The fact that he pre-prepared a defence suggests that he may have had doubts. It is possible that Graves was wedded to the story of the fate of Belisarius regardless of the question of truth.

Graves certainly shows himself quite capable of bending history to his own purposes, inventing freely when it suited him. Most striking of all is the question of the religious affiliations of Eugenius and Antonina herself, who are depicted as devotees of traditional religion, reference even being made to Antonina sacrificing.[48] This clearly assisted Graves's agenda of looking askance at Christianity. Tellingly, his diary remark, 'Reading that awful Jerome's letters', is echoed by Antonina herself in chapter 6 of the novel. It has already been seen that Graves gave Narses a background that is both elite and military, though there is no evidence to support this. Perhaps Graves simply could not conceive of a domestic eunuch becoming a military figure, or was even uncomfortable with the notion. The background ascribed to Eugenius is also interesting. Although he is attested as existing, nothing is known about Eugenius's origins. Graves thus chose to make him British (as well as a eunuch), though the historical evidence indicates that it would be far more likely that, as a castrated slave, he would have come from Armenia or Abasgia, as Graves knew. Perhaps Graves was encouraged to give the eunuch a noble origin because of the name Eugenius (meaning 'well-born'), but the decision to make

earlier'. He reports that this anonymous source, a description of the city of Constantinople in four books and dedicated to Alexios I Komnenos, was first printed in 1711, and can be found in Banduri's *Imperium Orientale*. One wonders why there was discrepancy about the material from which the bowl was made if indeed there was an extant tradition. I am indebted to Roger Scott for assisting me with the question of the evidence for the blinding and begging of Belisarius.

[48] e.g. Graves (1983), 382. Here Antonina alleges that Theodora was a secret pagan too.

him British (and specifically Welsh) says far more about Graves's own life than that of a late antique eunuch. The reference to the bards in Eugenius's father's house strikes one as a reference to the interests of Graves's own father, a noted composer of ballads. These details add to the sensation that Eugenius can represent Graves himself.[49] A further instance of Graves following his own inclination is in relation to the famous whale which dogged Byzantine waterways during the reign of Justinian, and which was eventually run to shore and killed.[50] Procopius records the name of the whale as Porphyrion, but Graves adds the detail that the beast was discovered to be female, thus making a connection between the whale and Theodora, who died at the same time.[51] It should also be noted that while Graves differs from Procopius in his take on Theodora and Antonina, he maintains the historian's deeply hostile attitude to Justinian. In a letter to Basil Liddell Hart, Graves observes: 'Mahon is very good, but he misunderstood Antonina—the Christian prejudice.'[52] Thus Graves was able to deconstruct what he wanted to suit his own purposes. His greater sympathy for Antonina and Theodora may not just be a sign of his historical sensibilities but also a sign of his own uxoriousness.

Ultimately Graves was unwilling or unable to resist the legend of Belisarius. Truth was no obstacle to storytelling, though he posed as a devotee of truth. It was important that readers should believe his version of history, whether it was true or not.

CONCLUSION

Despite its flaws as a novel, there is no doubt that *Count Belisarius* is rewarding to read for the light it sheds on Robert Graves's life and work. It reflects major preoccupations of his writing—history, war, morality, religion, and gender—as well as his pressing need to make money in order to survive. Although for Graves poetry was his priority as a writer, it is evident that it is his achievement in the

[49] One can note also the fact that Graves received a bow-and-arrow set for his birthday in 1937 (recorded in the diary) and that Eugenius utilizes a bow: R. P. Graves (1990), 279; Seymour (2003), 257; Graves (1983), 375.

[50] Procopius, *Wars* 7.29.9–16.

[51] Graves (1983), 381.

[52] O'Prey (1982), 278.

field of historical fiction that has secured his claim to fame. Graves may have considered (or claimed to consider) his historical novels as mere potboilers, but his success with the genre has created a potent legacy, reflected by the likes of Mary Renault and Gore Vidal (both of whom found literary salvation with the historical novel). The claims of research and truth, avowed by Graves, are seen as vital for writers and readers alike. Equally significant, however, is the example Graves sets of the financial rewards of writing historical fiction (though Sir Walter Scott is the ultimate symbol of this, first dramatically increasing his wealth then writing himself out of debt). The *Claudius* novels were clearly money-spinners, but *Count Belisarius* was also commercially successful, having a first edition of 20,000 copies.[53] It is often observed that Graves's example even had an effect on Laura Riding herself, who published her novel on the Trojan War, *A Trojan Ending*, in 1937.[54] This irony was topped by the fact that her novel did not meet with the same critical or financial success as those of Graves. Despite the dim view that can be taken of the genre by critics, it is clear that writing a successful historical novel is an art.

[53] Seymour-Smith (1995), 301.

[54] See e.g. Seymour (2003), 225.

5

Graves on War and the Late Antique

Count Belisarius and his World

Jon Coulston

Robert Graves's *Count Belisarius* is a historical novel based on the life, achievements, and sufferings of the emperor Justinian's most prominent and successful general.[1] Intertwined with this story is the interplay between Belisarius and his master, Justinian; Belisarius and the empress Theodora; and between Belisarius and his wife, Antonina. Graves drew heavily on the *Secret History* and *History of the Wars* by the contemporary writer Procopius of Caesarea,[2] both directly and through the medium of Stanhope's *Life of Belisarius*, itself substantially a retelling of Procopius's narrative.[3] That he relied heavily on Stanhope's work is corroborated in personal diary entries made over the period of writing.[4]

[1] Graves (1938). Page references in this paper are to the Penguin Classics 2006 text of the novel.

[2] Cameron (1985); Kaldellis (2004). For academic studies of the period see Barker (1966); Bridge (1978); Browning (1987); Evans (1996), (2002); Cameron *et al.* (2000), 65–85; Maas (2005); Coulston (2006). For a recent new edition and translation of *The Secret History* see Prokopios (2010).

[3] Mahon (2006). First edition 1829, revised edition 1848, modern edition 2006. Edward Gibbon's great work, first issued in 1776, also dealt in detail with Justinian and Belisarius (Gibbon 1987, chs. 41–3), casting a long shadow over successive perceptions.

[4] Diaries archived and now available online as a searchable database in the Library of the University of Victoria (Australia): <http://spcoll.library.uvic.ca/Digit/GravesDiaryProject/home.htm>. The author is very grateful to Sean Tougher for first bringing this resource to his attention. Reading of Stanhope (Mahon), *Belisarius*, was recorded in entries for 30 June and 1 July 1937, Graves finishing the book on 8 July.

Many readers of *Count Belisarius* come to it after *I, Claudius* and *Claudius the God*.[5] This is an appropriate progression because of the later chronological setting of *Belisarius*, but also because it was the third of Graves's historical fictions to be written. With the intervention of the Spanish Civil War, Graves and his personal White Goddess, Laura Riding, returned to England in 1936.[6] The writing of *Count Belisarius* commenced in 1937 in a house named *Highcroft*, at Ewhurst in Surrey, and was completed in 1938 at 31 Alma Square, London SW8.[7]

Laura Riding's contributions to Graves's work on many levels—textual, philosophical, psychological, and environmental—are explored by Sean Tougher in Chapter 4 of the present volume, and here it will suffice to re-emphasize the relationships between the characters in *Count Belisarius* and the author's domestic situation. Justinian dominated by the empress Theodora, and Belisarius bewitched by the 'entertainer' Antonina find many parallels in the interactions between Graves and the women in his life. In his foreword Graves wrote that, 'I have to thank Laura Riding for the great help she has given me in problems of language and narrative'.[8] It was Riding's idea that the narrator of the novel be shifted from Antonina to the eunuch, Eugenius. The latter introduces himself with the words: 'I, the author of this Greek work, am a person of little importance, a mere domestic; but I spent nearly my whole life in the service of Antonina.'[9] According to Miranda Seymour: 'It must have amused her [Laura Riding] to create a parallel to her own situation, with Graves appearing as the servile and sexually frustrated Eugenius. Graves too could get a morose pleasure out of the analogy; there was always an element of masochism in the humiliations he chose to undergo. The change [Antonina to Eugenius as narrator] was made. The book

[5] Graves (1934a and b).

[6] R. P. Graves (1990), 235–47; Seymour (1995), 239–41; Seymour-Smith (1995), 260–2; King (2008), 119–20. Events of the Civil War, such as Belchite changing hands, were noted in the diaries during work on *Count Belisarius*.

[7] Gross (1938), 12J 48. Writing commenced on 22 July 1937, and work on the proofs ended seven months later, on 26 February 1938. See R. P. Graves (1990), 277–81, 283, 285; Seymour (1995), 253–6, 259; Seymour-Smith (1995), 291–3, 295–7, 299, 301–2; King (2008), 120–3.

[8] Graves (1938), 8.

[9] Graves (1938), 9.

suffered a consequent drop in the tension of the narrative.'[10] The *ménage à quatre* formed by the main protagonists of the book coincidentally reflects the personal situation of Graves, his wife Nancy, Riding, and the fourth member of their gilded circle, Geoffrey Taylor. Someone who did not much like Riding was Graves's friend T. E. Lawrence, who simply said that she 'Bewitched and Bitched' Graves.[11]

Count Belisarius explored the themes of male–female domination, moral corruption and decline, and leadership, all set within a fallen world of imperial tyranny and disintegration, wrapped in Christian bigotry and superstition.[12] Of these elements, generalship was central, both in terms of specific military qualities and of the general's loyalty to higher command in the face of provocation and unjust oppression. The present chapter will explore Graves's treatment of historic warfare and his presentation of Belisarius as commander, placed within the context of the author's own military experiences, and of attitudes towards war in the 1930s. The chapter's title contains a deliberate ambiguity: the 'his' in 'Graves on War and the Late Antique: Count Belisarius and *his* World' refers both to the world of the general and to that of the novelist. The body of the paper is divided between these two aspects.

GRAVES IN BELISARIUS'S WORLD

What strikes the reader from the outset about *Count Belisarius* was the author's commitment to constructing a vivid world around the main characters. They do not merely move through cardboard sets but inhabit a rich environment for which Graves went to some lengths to provide detail. In the manner of the ancient biographical genre, the protagonists' attributes and appearance are described, drawing on Procopius. It is not indicated in Graves's diaries what iconographic material Graves consulted. However, he did acquire a

[10] Seymour (1995), 259. On the other hand, Seymour-Smith considered that the novel was 'improved' by the change. See also R. P. Graves (1990) 280; Christensen (2014).

[11] Seymour (1995), 131.

[12] In this it closely follows the gender relationships in Procopius's *Secret History*. See Kaldellis (2004), 142–50; Brubaker (2005).

coin of Justinian from the antiques dealer Georg Schwarz,[13] which he had made into a brooch.[14] There are no portraits of Belisarius or Antonina surviving from antiquity, but for Justinian and Theodora there are several representations. Discarding the numismatic evidence, the style of coins having become rather schematic by this period, the most important portraits are those surviving in the church of San Vitale at Ravenna, Italy. These appear on either side of the apse: left, the emperor with three male courtiers, the bishop Maximianus, and two other clergy, and five *protectores*; right, the empress with two male nobles and seven ladies.[15] These mosaics belong to the consecration of the church by Maximianus in 548. Church and mosaics exist precisely because of the reconquest of Italy from the Ostrogoths by Belisarius. Another Ravennate mosaic, this one in Sant'Apollinare Nuovo, is labelled with Justinian's name and appears to represent the emperor in old age (he died aged 82 in 565).[16] Amongst small art-works, the triumphal general on the 'Barberini Ivory' has been identified as Justinian.[17]

Unfortunately, there were other Justinianic monuments dedicated specifically to Belisarius's campaigns of reconquest in the west which have not survived, including figural mosaics in the Imperial Palace of Constantinople, a complex poorly known archaeologically and principally reconstructed through literary notices.[18] Procopius described them as follows:

> On either side is war and battle, and many cities are being captured, some in Italy, some in Libya; and the Emperor Justinian is winning victories through his General Belisarius, and the general is returning to the Emperor, with the whole army intact, and he gives him spoils, both kings and kingdoms and all things that are most prized among men. In the centre stand the Emperor and the Empress Theodora, both seeming to rejoice and to celebrate victories over both the King of the Vandals and the King of the Goths, who approach them as prisoners of war to be

[13] Diary entry for Friday, 31 Dec. 1937.

[14] Diary entries for Wednesday, 8 June; Monday, 13 June 1938.

[15] Barker (1966), pl. IV; Browning (1987), pls. 22–4; Paolucci (1971), 46–7; Moorhead (2001), pl. 7; Maas (2005), pls. III–IV.

[16] Barker (1966), pl. VI.

[17] Browning (1987), pl. 1; Cameron (1993), pl. 6; Maas (2005), pl. iii; Olovsdotter (2005), pl. 20; Mitchell (2007), pl. 5.5; Aillagon (2008), fig. 25.

[18] Much of the court intrigue of the novel took place within this palace. See Brett *et al.* (1947); Talbot Rice (1958); Müller-Wiener (1977), 229–37.

> led into bondage. Around them stand the Roman senate, all in festal mood. The spirit is expressed by the cubes of the mosaic, which by their colours depict exultation on their very countenances.[19]

Some idea of the appearance of the mosaics may be gained from the Ravenna churches, and suppliant fifth–sixth-century barbarians figure in both mosaic and marble sculpture,[20] conforming with the traditions of triumphal art as seen, for example, on the Arch of Galerius at Thessalonike.[21] A gold medallion of Justinian depicts the emperor mounted, his horse led by a winged Victory carrying a traditional trophy.[22]

Also lost is Justinian's Column, recorded in a Renaissance sketch as being topped by a massive equestrian statue of the emperor.[23] A helical, figural frieze depicting the wars may have been sculpted up the shaft in the manner of Trajan's Column in Rome, although this is not certain. From Graves's accurate and detailed description, it is clear that the sketch caught his eye during his research, and he used the detail to make a political point:

> In the Square of Augustus, opposite the Senate House, Justinian had placed a colossal equestrian statue of himself; it stands upon a very lofty pedestal plated with finest pale brass. He is shown there in armour of antique pattern and wearing a helmet with an immensely long plume. In his left hand is an orb surmounted by a cross. His right hand is raised in a gesture which is intended to mean: 'Begone, enemies!' But he carries no arms, not even a dagger, as if the gesture and the frown of his face were sufficient discouragement. And indeed in the latter part of his reign he treated his armies as if he had no further use for them.[24]

Justinian was described by Graves as 'a strange, round-faced, smiling, lecherous fellow',[25] and as 'a clever fellow, cowardly, vacillating,

[19] Procopius, *Buildings* 1.10.16–18.

[20] Paolucci (1971). Cf. Safran (1993), pl. 9. Three suppliant barbarians with offerings also appear embroidered on Theodora's robe in the San Vitale mosaic, but, curiously, not on Justinian's attire (Maas (2005), pl. III; Canepa (2009), fig. 25).

[21] Laubscher (1975).

[22] Barker (1966), pl. I; Browning (1987), pl. 12; Maas (2005), pls. i–ii; Cormack and Vassilaki (2008), no. 29.

[23] Becatti (1960), 90–4, pl. 81; Barker (1966), pl. X; Müller-Wiener (1977), 248–9, fig. 282; Raby (1987), fig. 1; Maas (2005), pl. iv. In general see MacCormack (1981); Canepa (2009). In any case this was most likely a reused statue of Theodosius I.

[24] Graves (1938) 395–6. Based directly on Procopius, *Buildings* 1.2.1–12.

[25] Graves (1938) 59.

manageable. The one difficulty with him is that he is religious, guiltily religious, and anxious, above all things, to keep his soul clear of any taint of heresy'.[26] Of the empress in earlier life: 'Theodora was small and sallow complexioned. She was not a particularly good dancer or instrumentalist or acrobat; in fact, she was rather below the average of excellence at all these things. But she possessed an extraordinarily quick wit and a complete freedom from sexual shame.' Antonina shared many of these traits, 'but she was not a physical fighter like Theodora, who went for her tormentors with nails and teeth. She took her revenge in other ways: chiefly—as she grew a little older—by frightening her enemies into imagining themselves the victims of her magical powers. She gradually came herself to believe in the magic.'[27] It is rather as though the two women bore aspects of Laura Riding, attributed to them by Graves whilst under her domination and deep into his White Goddess (ir)rationalizations. For surviving likenesses of Theodora there is only one certain instance, the San Vitale mosaic. A marble head at Milan, Italy, has been identified as depicting her, but out of context and without any inscribed label this is an insecure identification.[28] However, it is a significant indication of Theodora's dominance that, unlike other empresses, she should have been figured alongside the emperor in the surviving and lost mosaics.

In order to fill in the background of Theodora and Antonina it was necessary for Graves to explore the life of the underclass associated with the circus and the stage. He embroidered both the practicalities of presenting beast-fights and chariot-races, and endowed the people with a quasi-pagan religious culture which paid much honour to the old gods and dabbled heavily in magic. The chariot-races and the circus factions which dominated Late Roman and medieval Constantinople were painstakingly revealed.[29] The wild-beast displays which marked the intervals between races remained popular and appear prominently on some of the later ivory diptychs.[30] Graves was slightly off the mark in some elements. For example, the prolongation of gladiatorial fighting (that is, men against men, as opposed to men against wild animals) into the sixth century would not be supported

[26] Graves (1938), 95.
[27] Graves (1938), 55.
[28] Browning (1987), pl. 5.
[29] Cf. Cameron (1973), (1976).
[30] Browning (1987), pl. 3; Olovsdotter (2005), pls. 1, 5, 8–9, 11, 18–19; Cormack and Vassilaki (2008), nos. 14–15; Aillagon (2008), no. II.16; Dodge (2011), figs. 23–4.

by modern scholarship.[31] Conversely, the evocation of magical practices such as divination and formal cursing are now strikingly illustrated by a mass of curse tablets and 'voodoo' effigies found in association with circuses in particular.[32] The evidence of texts for love and vengeance spells comes mainly from Egypt, and Graves picked up on the strong tradition of Nilotic magic which permeated ancient views of 'popular' practices.[33] This was explored to give Theodora and Antonina a dark and mysterious context, but also the evincing of Egyptian sorcery chimed in well with Graves's own Egyptian experiences during the few months of his lectureship at Cairo University in 1926. Nocturnal fortune-telling beneath the Giza pyramids and visits to moonlit ruined temples may be cited here, against a background of the 'Tutmania' which was in full flow in the 1920s and 1930s, and the more general spiritualist taste which Graves overtly pandered to in *Goodbye to All That* (discussed later in this chapter).[34] This was also a realm in which Riding was dominant, claiming as she did the ability to cast fortunes and observe ill-omened spirits in domestic contexts.[35]

In truth, the achievement of Theodora in becoming empress was extraordinary, even more so than the *parvenu* emperors Justin and Justinian, who assumed imperial office in the face of aristocratic opposition and ambition. Theodora and Antonina married well through their natural talents and these marriages pulled them up from the very bottom to the very top of Late Roman society. This is clearly demonstrable by the relief on the south-east side of the base of the Obelisk of Theodosius I in the Constantinople Hippodrome (AD 390).[36] The scale of human figures depicted on it exactly reflects their social importance. The emperor stands in the imperial box holding a victor's wreath, the courtiers and guards around him barely coming up to his shoulders. On either side of the box stand senators of similar stature, with guards behind them. Below are two rows of smaller heads, the free Constantinopolitan viewing audience of *humiliores*, but even they dwarf the front rank of entertainers. Musicians play and

[31] Dodge (2011), 69–78.

[32] Cameron (1973), 173, 245; (1976), 61–2, 94; Gager (1999), 14–77, 121; Bagnall (1993), 273–5; Heintz (1998); Janowitz (2001), 86–96; Collins (2008), 64–103.

[33] Graves (1938), 49, 55–6.

[34] Graves (1957a), 335–55; Seymour (1995), 135–7. See Frayling (1992).

[35] R. P. Graves (1990), 80–2, 303, 307; Seymour (1995), 139.

[36] Müller-Wiener (1977), 65, figs. 42, 45–6; Safran (1993), pl. 8.

dancing girls gyrate at the equivalent of half the scale of the emperor, despite the fact that they are the nearest people to the viewer. The taint of *infamia* was still attached to all those who shamelessly paraded themselves before the public gaze, courting celebrity: actors, gladiators, trainers, prostitutes, pimps, and service staff in bars and restaurants.[37] Such activities also attracted the unlucky *fascinatio* of the 'evil eye' which, combined with the real physical dangers of *circenses* and *venationes*, fostered a world of sympathetic and black magic.[38] Imperial governments were always deeply suspicious of such magical practices, but to this was added the Christian moral condemnation of actors and harlots operating in an entertainment tradition which both harked back to a 'pagan' past and formed a lure away from the clerically controlled, 'proper' public congregation in churches.

Theodora and Antonina were presented as especially morally infamous by Procopius, Stanhope, and Graves, creating and perpetuating a tradition of lasciviousness which has persisted to the present.[39] Painting, opera, and theatre have projected the image through other media, with varying degrees of imperial stateliness, gender confusion, and abandoned evil.[40] Theodora was also sometimes fickle towards Belisarius, although Antonina, despite her extra-marital passions, always rose to the occasion to support her husband. She was a constant companion on campaign, even becoming adept in accurately shooting artillery pieces![41] Her military service is compared with Germanicus's wife, Agrippina the Elder, in a nice crossover with *I, Claudius*.[42]

A second area that Graves engaged with in *Count Belisarius* was the Christian culture of the sixth century. He was at pains to outline the essentials of different doctrines of the nature of Christ, but always the

[37] Edwards (1997); Potter (1999). [38] Johns (1982) 62–75.

[39] Procopius, *Secret History*; Mahon (2006), 24; Graves (1938), 56, 58, 222–3. This played particularly well in novels: Marmontel (1767); Graves (1938); Silverberg (1975). Bradshaw (1988) chose to project a more sympathetic picture. For a full list of novels relating to the Justinianic period see Christensen (2014), appendix (to which should be added Silverberg 1975; Duffy 2010).

[40] e.g. C. Busch, *Theodora, She-Bitch of Byzantium*, featuring Jef Valentine in the title role, which first played at the Limbo Lounge, New York, in 1984: <http://www.charlesbusch.com/Theodors, She-Bitch of Byzantium.htm>. For previous plays about Belisarius see Christensen (2014), appendix.

[41] Graves (1938), 255, 401.

[42] Graves (1938), 140. Cf. Graves (1934a), 229–30.

debate itself was presented in mocking terms. Christian dispute was seen as 'the disease of the age'. 'Wherever two or three are gathered together, in tavern, barracks, brothel, or anywhere else, they immediately begin discussing with every assumption of learning some difficult point of Christian doctrine.'[43] We see here Graves's equivocal reception of organized, church Christianity, which echoed the cynical amusement of the 'apostate' emperor Julian.[44] Graves also revealed something of his own intellectual snobbery and self-identification. While mocking the ignorance of classical literature displayed by a churchman, who confuses a reference to Aeneas the Trojan with the story of St Paul's Aeneas of Lydda, Graves could not resist commenting that:

> I have heard it argued that soldiers should not be educated, on the ground that among the most vigorous barbarian nations, such as the Goths and Franks, whose principal men are all soldiers by trade, book learning is despised. But the proverb 'a scholar made is a soldier spoiled' applies, in my opinion, only to private soldiers, not to any sort of officer![45]

The present essay is not the place for a detailed recounting of the campaigns of Justinian's wars.[46] It is sufficient to note that Belisarius commanded armies on various occasions facing the Sassanid Persians on the eastern front, and led armies west to reconquer North Africa and Italy, from Vandal and Ostrogoth 'usurpers' respectively. During all this it must be admitted that Graves's Belisarius was something of a character vacuum filled principally with ideals of generalship. His decisions were always inspired, but often thwarted by prickly and jealous subordinates, or the machinations of Justinian's other minions. His military reverses were always occasioned by the indiscipline and false confidence of the soldiery. 'Belisarius was everywhere, like lightning in a storm.'[47] 'Thus by the bravado of Peter, the treachery of King Harith, the credulousness of John the Epicure, the cowardice of these other generals, Belisarius was robbed of what might have been the greatest of his victories.'[48] Belisarius was always right when it came to military decisions, even winning victories at a distance

[43] Graves (1938), 16. [44] Amm. Marc. 22.5.4. Picked up in Vidal (1964).

[45] Graves (1938), 22.

[46] For which see Fauber (1990); Cameron *et al.* (2000), 73–6; Mahon (2006); Haldon (2000); Greatrex and Lieu (2002); Christie (2006); Dignas and Winter (2007); Hughes (2009); Jacobsen (2009).

[47] Graves (1938), 373. [48] Graves (1938), 323.

through his advice to the eunuch general Narses, given in Constantinople when the latter was appointed as commander in Italy.[49]

Much of Belisarius's generalship followed Procopius's account, which in turn conformed with literary ideals of skilled leadership. Belisarius led in the style of Julius Caesar. Like Caesar, reverses were attributed to the indiscipline and excess enthusiasm of the soldiery, forcing the commander to fight battles in circumstances against his better judgement. Lower-order soldiers could always be blamed for forcing the hand of a noble and gifted leader. Graves made the link in the foreword to *Count Belisarius*:

> Here is a Roman general whose victories are not less Roman, nor his strategical principles less classical, than Julius Caesar's. Yet the army has by now changed almost beyond recognition, the old infantry legion having at last disappeared, and Belisarius (one of the last Romans to have been awarded the dignity of the Consulship and the last to be awarded a triumph) is a Christian commander of mail-clad Household knights, nearly all of barbarian birth, whose individual feats rival those of King Arthur's heroes.[50]

Here Graves introduced several aspects which run through the book. The character Modestus opined that: 'It is long years since a soldier with true Roman blood in his veins led any of the armies of the Emperor. Nowadays all the high commands have somehow fallen into the hands of hired barbarians—Goths, Vandals, Gepids, Huns, Arabians—and the result is that the old military system, which once built up the greatest empire that the world has ever known, has lately degenerated beyond all recognition.'[51] Nevertheless, Belisarius carefully nurtured the courage of serving soldiers and improved discipline through stringent training. New recruits were not thrown directly into situations beyond their experience but deployed sensitively, perhaps echoing Graves's Great War experiences.[52]

Belisarius's generalship style was epitomized in Graves's description of preparations for the Battle of Dara(s).[53] The infantry was the weakest element of the army, with trained and raw formations, and Belisarius armed them according to a specific tactical role (for

[49] Graves (1938), 292–3.
[50] Graves (1938), 7. See also Graves and Liddell Hart (1963), II, 9.
[51] Graves (1938), 33–4.
[52] Graves (1957a), 94–5, 103, 167, 188–9, 195–6, 224, 246–7.
[53] Graves (1938), ch. 7.

example, with pikes to defend bridges over defensive ditches) and experience (new recruits with javelins for skirmishing). Large numbers of infantry were armed with bows to counteract the Persian massed archery. Defensive ditches were dug with bridges and re-entrants designed to channel the enemy attack, and cavalry were positioned on the wings. In particular, '600 Massagetic Huns were stationed inside each corner of the re-entrant, ready to bring a cross-fire of arrows against the enemy'.[54] Time and again, as can be seen from this passage, Roman defensive deployments, or raids into Barbaricum, were reminiscent of Graves's Western Front experiences.

Throughout the book Graves paid close attention to military equipment, contrasting the armaments of Romans, Goths, and Huns.[55] This perhaps reflected the detailed treatment in *Good-bye to All That* of weaponry which developed so specifically and rapidly for Great War trench combat.[56] From the start this was used to set up Belisarius as a military thinker, even as a youth. A discussion during 'The Banquet of Modestus' compared the traditional military arts of Old Rome with the state of play in a period of barbarian dominance.[57] The elderly host Modestus sang the praises of tradition—the infantry of the legions with short swords—and condemned the bow as cowardly by reference to Homeric archers. The Gothic cavalry officer in Roman employ, Bessas, advocated the qualities of Hunnic horse-archers and Gothic lance-armed cavalry:

> It was you Romans who first instructed us barbarians in the warfare by which we defeated you here at Adrianople. It was you who taught us to co-ordinate our military movements, and showed us the importance of defensive armour, and of fighting in regular formation. We merely applied your teaching to cavalry fighting. And although we were lucky enough to defeat your main army we did not destroy your empire.[58]

With the issues established, it only remained for the precocious young Belisarius to formulate the perfect contemporary solution:

[54] Graves (1938), 112.

[55] For the Roman army, opposing forces, and warfare in the sixth century see Jones (1964), 654–86; Bivar (1972); Coulston (1986); Ravegnani (1988); Haldon (2000); Cameron *et al.* (2000), 288–314; Halsall (2003); Syvänne (2004); Rance (2005); Lee (2005).

[56] Graves (1957a), 89–90, 97, 100, 115, 122, 137–9, 149, 159–60, 177, 200–2.

[57] Graves (1938), ch. 2. [58] Graves (1938), 39.

> I do not think that perfection in equipment and military tactics has been attained by the Gothic lancer. The Gothic lancer is a brave man, and his charge is terrible because of the weight of his horse, and because of the heavy armour he wears—cuirass, shield, helmet, greaves. But the Hun horseman is a brave man too, and he can let loose a rain of arrows while riding at full gallop; only his horse is too light to carry a fully armoured man. Thus the Hun has not attained perfection either. Yet, noble Bessas, was it not fear of the Huns that first drove you Goths over the Danube into our Thrace? For your foot-archers could not overtake them, nor could your lancers withstand their volleys of arrows. Now, suppose that one could combine Hun archer and Gothic lancer into a single fighting man and civilize him as a Roman, and put him under proper camp discipline—that, I think, would be to breed a soldier as near perfection as possible. And he would be a Roman both in name and spirit. I intend to command such troops one day.[59]

Of course this is set up early so that when Belisarius rose to high military command he could have a bodyguard formation, his 'cuirassiers', armed in this fashion, which then acted to instruct other troops, so spreading the general's incisive ideas. Thus chapter 4, 'An Improved Cavalry', runs predictably on. This neat construct was based directly on an early passage in Procopius's *Wars* in which the historian sought to explain to his cultured elite audience that archery had become dominant in contemporary conflicts. He cited the literary view of cowardly Homeric archers, but asserted that the new archers achieved notable deeds in the recent Persian wars:

> The bowmen of the present time go into battle wearing corselets and fitted out with greaves which extend up to the knee. From the right side hang their arrows, from the other the sword. And there are some who have a spear also attached to them and, at the shoulders, a sort of small shield without a grip, such as to cover the region of the face and neck. They are expert horsemen, and are able without difficulty to direct their bows to either side while riding at full speed, and to shoot an opponent whether in pursuit or in flight. They draw the bowstring along by the forehead about opposite the right ear, thereby charging the arrow with such an impetus as to kill whoever stands in the way, shield and corselet alike having no power to check its force.[60]

[59] Graves (1938), 40. [60] Procopius, *Wars* 1.1.12–4 (trans. Dewing 1914).

Now compare Graves's version:

> Belisarius, then, armed all his men with the lance, and a stiff bow that had a slow shooting rate but could drive an arrow through any corselet. He also gave them each a small handy shield, strapped to the arm, which acted as a receptacle for half a dozen sharp darts . . . As a final arm for use when even the lance failed they carried a heavy broadsword in a sheath on the left thigh. To control all these weapons, and the horse at the same time, needed many months of practice. A bow, for example, is a weapon that needs both hands: so Belisarius trained the men to manage their horses without the bridle, by pressure of the knee and heel. But he also introduced the novel device of steel stirrups, which were suspended by straps from the saddle as an aid in mounting and riding the very large horses that they favoured. Stirrups are now in general use throughout the army, though at first despised as womanish. Lastly he supplied his men with wide, well-stuffed saddles, in front of which were strapped, when not in use, their woollen cloaks for cold and rainy weather. They wore sleeveless mailshirts of thigh length, and tall rawhide boots. When not in use, the bow was slung behind the back: the arrows were contained in a quiver next to the broadsword; the lance was carried in a leather bucket on the right side.[61]

The interesting features are the points at which Graves misread or garbled Procopius, and where he embroidered the description with his own detailed inventions.[62] Graves did ride for pleasure, so was not entirely impractical. At Ewhurst and on Mallorca he also practised archery, shooting at sugared buns. One birthday he received the present of a bow and arrows, and Seymour made the direct connection between this and the prominence of archery in Graves's account of Belisarius's wars.[63] However, Graves evidently misunderstood the forms and uses of archery equipment of Late Roman (and other) period(s). Contradicting Procopius, Graves incorrectly placed the quiver on the rider's left side with the (correctly) positioned sword. Probably because Procopius was thinking of the bow in use, that writer made no mention of a bow-case, and Graves positioned the bow on the rider's back. In reality bows were placed, unstrung, in a bow-case on the rider's left side. Contemporary horsemen carried

[61] Graves (1938), 66–7.

[62] Six 'darts' inside the shield was a detail drawn directly from the fourth-century military writer Vegetius (*Epitoma rei militaris* 1.17).

[63] R. P. Graves (1990) 279, 284; Seymour (1995), 257. See also Seymour-Smith (1995), 293.

both bow-case and quiver suspended from their waist-belt.[64] There is actually very little Late Roman iconographic or artefactual evidence for Graves to have worked from (or at least little had been published by 1937). However, the high relief rider figure in the large grotto/*iwan* at Taq-i-Bustan in south-west Iran depicts the Sassanid *shahanshah* Chosroes II, the very king who was the main protagonist in Belisarius' Persian wars. It depicts lamellar armour in the head, neck and fore-quarters of the horse, and shows the rider with a steppe nomad form of quiver, suspended diagonally on his right side. On his left, just behind his back, the upper ear of his cased composite bow is visible.[65]

Throughout *Count Belisarius* bows were usually described as 'stiff'. 'Stiff' says nothing about the type of bow employed and today 'heavy' would be used of a weapon with a high draw-weight. The reader is repeatedly reminded that Belisarius's education included archery.[66] Indeed, Graves was obsessed with the power of bows, something he did pick up from Procopius's comparative descriptions of Roman and Persian performance.[67] Several times Belisarius performed prodigious feats of distance shooting, to the consternation of enemies, but these were actions more appropriate to Western Front snipers than to Roman generals.[68]

It should be noted that archery with composite bows was an indigenous cultural component of hunting and warfare in the Levantine-Iranian region from the Bronze Age onwards, and horse-archery was dominant from the Parthian period through into the Sassanid era, and up to the seventeenthth century. Sixth-century church mosaics from Jordan provide clear examples of the type of recurved, composite bows, with set-back handles, which were used throughout the Roman empire as a result of Levantine contacts.[69] The Chosroes relief and western literary sources also demonstrate that both the Late Roman and Sassanid Persian empires were heavily influenced by the weapons and tactics of their northern nomad neighbours. In the fourth century new nomad peoples appeared, generically referred to

[64] Coulston (1985), 270–5.
[65] Fukai and Horiuchi (1972), pls. XL–XLI, XLIV.
[66] e.g. Graves (1938), 11, 28. Cf. Procopius, *Wars* 5.22.5–6.
[67] Graves (1938), 37. Cf. Procopius, *Wars* 1.18.32–5.
[68] e.g. Graves (1938), 248, 376–7, 403. Cf. Procopius, *Wars* 5.23.9.
[69] Piccirillo (1992), 59, 154–5, 187, 191, 256.

as 'Huns', and their archery equipment marks their influence in the fifth century.[70] The archaeological distribution of 'Attila-Empire' period fittings from composite bows, principally bone ear and grip laths, extends west to a burial at Wien-Simmering (Austria).[71] The bone is generally all that survives from these weapons after the wood, horn, and sinew perish. An exception is provided by gold-foil covers of non-functional, presentation bows, wooden 1:1 models which seem to have been bestowed on vassals by Hunnic rulers. These have been found in fifth-century cemeteries in Hungary and Poland.[72]

Graves was clearly fascinated by the Asiatic steppe nomads designated as 'Huns'. This demonstrably came out of his reading of Ammianus and Procopius, the former's work paraphrased in his description of the AD 378 Battle of Adrianople.[73] Some of Ammianus's ethnographic detail is also ploughed into the exploration of Hunnic culture, but details are embroidered with some fanciful elements, such as the cuirasses armoured at the front but not on the back, 'because they consider this cowardly'.[74] There are also problems with Hunnic designations such as 'Massagetic' and 'Bulgarian' in *Count Belisarius*, both of which are anachronistic, whereas 'White' or 'Hephthalite' are correct usages for the sixth century.[75] This reflects the confusing tendency of the ancient sources, from Herodotus onwards, to refer to all steppe nomads as 'Scythians'.

Thus, Graves was quite correct to ascribe elements of Roman archery to Hunnic contacts, but he played down indigenous Roman and Persian archery for dramatic reasons. However, he was completely mistaken in ascribing the introduction of stirrups to Belisarius. There is no evidence of metal stirrups before the later sixth century, when they occur in Avar graves in Hungary and Lombard cemeteries in northern Italy.[76] The earliest actual

[70] Coulston (1985), 241–5, 273–5, 293; Bishop and Coulston (2006), 205–6, 249. In general see Mode and Tubach (2006).

[71] Polascheck (1932); Coulston (1985), 224, 242.

[72] Coulston (1985), 243; Aillagon (2008), 261.

[73] Graves (1938), 37–8. Cf. Ammianus Marcellinus 31.12–3.

[74] Graves (1938), 121–3. Cf. Ammianus Marcellinus 31.2. This is especially nonsensical for horse-archers, whose 'Parthian' shooting was practised while retiring away from an enemy!

[75] Graves (1938), 13, 111–12, 121, 139, 171, 403. See Bivar (2004).

[76] Daim (2003), 468, figs. 1.3, 3; Aillagon (2008), fig. 30.

appearance of stirrups in iconography is on a sculpted stone funerary panel from the tomb of the Chinese emperor T'ang Tai-tsung, dating to around AD 630.[77] Here a Turkish cavalryman holds the emperor's horse, which bears a saddle with a stirrup. The man himself has a quiver suspended from a waistbelt on his right, and a bow ear is visible behind his back, denoting a sheathed bow suspended on his left. Apart from the chronological mistake, why did Graves specify 'steel' stirrups, rather than iron or bronze ones? Indeed, wooden stirrups or even leather toe/foot-loops may have pre-dated metal stirrups, but would generally have been invisible in the artefactual record. This may have been because of Graves's own experience as a rider in the twentieth century and perhaps was a detail taken from First World War cavalry equipment. His very specific treatment of the horseman's lance supports the latter hypothesis. At rest, the butt of a British cavalryman's lance sat in a leather 'bucket' to ease carriage. The upright weapon was steadied by a shaft loop which could be slipped up the rider's forearm, thus leaving both hands free, which was clearly a concern for Graves.[78] Alternatively, lances are often seen in contemporary photographs of troops in transit slung diagonally across the men's backs.[79] Perhaps it was this detail which also made Graves erroneously describe the bow slung across the back. The lance was a great subject of technical debate within the British Army during the whole of the nineteenth and early twentieth centuries, but it enjoyed something of a renaissance shortly before the Great War, and all cavalry regiments on the Western Front carried them initially. Interestingly, this is not true of the Yeomanry and Commonwealth mounted troops deployed in Palestine, although Indian regiments were lance-armed.[80]

Graves was clearly fascinated by the combined bow and lance-armed cavalry of the Late Roman armies. During the period in which he was working on *Count Belisarius* he also wrote the four-stanza poem 'Cataphracts', later renamed 'The Cuirassiers of the Frontier'.[81] This presented a view of corrupt, metropolitan Christian society as

[77] Bivar (1972), fig. 27.
[78] Badsey (2008), 210–11, Pl. 5–6.
[79] Badsey (2008), pl. 1.
[80] Anglesey (1994), 223, pls. 8, 41; Carver (2003), pl. 49; Badsey (2008), pls. 1, 6.
[81] Graves and Ward (1997), 80–1, 311. Two drafts were recorded in the diary entry for 20 July 1937.

seen by the 'barbarian' soldiers on the frontiers, and it wove in many of the salient themes of the novel:

> Goths, Vandals, Huns, Isaurian mountaineers,
> Made Roman by our Roman sacrament,
> We can know little (as we care little)
> Of the Metropolis: her candled churches,
> Her white-gowned pederastic senators,
> The cut-throat factions of her Hippodrome,
> The eunuchs of her draped saloons.
>
> Here is the frontier, here our camp and place—
> Beans for the pot, fodder for horses,
> And Roman arms. Enough. He who among us
> At full gallop, the bowstring to his ear,
> Lets drive his heavy arrows, to sink
> Stinging through Persian corslets damascened,
> Then follows with the lance—he has our love.
>
> The Christ bade Holy Peter sheathe his sword,
> Being outnumbered by the Temple guard.
> And this was prudence, the cause not yet lost
> While Peter might persuade the crowd to rescue.
> Peter renegued, breaking his sacrament.
> With us the penalty is death by stoning,
> Not to be made a bishop.
>
> In Peter's Church there is no faith nor truth,
> Nor justice anywhere in palace or court.
> That we continue watchful on the rampart
> Concerns no priest. A gaping silken dragon,
> Puffed by the wind, suffices us for God.
> We, not the City, are the Empire's soul:
> A rotten tree lives only in its rind.

Reference to the drawing of bows (2.4) recalls attention to technical details of archery in the novel.[82] The 'gaping silken dragon' (4.4) was the *draco*, a standard consisting of a shaft topped by a metal head with a textile, 'wind-sock' body, which hissed and moved sinuously in a breeze.[83] It imitated the snake rather than some form of mythical

[82] Graves (1938), 37, 110–11, 263–4, 321.
[83] As described in Amm. Marc. 16.10.7.

dragon. Graves was quite right to think of Roman military standards as gods, and this type had originally been a second-century AD Roman adoption from steppe nomads across the Danube.[84] It is noteworthy that Graves dropped the more correct term for heavily armoured Late Roman cavalry (*catafracti*) and adopted the more modern, and imprecise, 'cuirassiers', a usage found throughout the novel.[85]

It is interesting that Graves was affected by cavalry practices in his own time. Cavalry are hardly mentioned in *Good-bye to All That*,[86] not surprising in the autobiography of an infantryman obsessed with his time in the trenches of the Western Front. The battlefield roles of horsed soldiers were contentious and endlessly debated in the run-up to the Great War. Indeed, the opportunities to deploy mounted troops in the western theatre only occasionally occurred, and dismounted cavalry were often sent into the line to make use of the manpower.[87] A supposed obsession with the panache of the charge and the effect of cold steel (the *arme blanche*) amongst British generals, some of whom, like Field Marshal Douglas Haig and General Edmund Allenby, had cavalry regimental backgrounds, has been used to lampoon such senior commanders since 1918. In reality it was men like these who were most in favour of the flexible use of cavalry, the only troops who could move across western battlefields with anything like speed (before the motorized infantry of World War II and thereafter), and who were, after all, armed with exactly the same Short Magazine Lee-Enfield (SMLE) rifle as all the British infantry.[88] Such officers were also the first and most in favour of the use of new weapons and tactics (machine guns, tanks, aeroplanes, and so on).[89]

Significantly, the theatre in which cavalry did fulfil their flexible role most effectively, combining sabre-charges and dismounted fire-power, was Palestine. Allenby's Egypt Expeditionary Force (EEF) defeated the Turks at the Third Battle of Gaza in 1917 through mobility, successfully charging entrenched infantry at Beersheba and artillery at Huj, and outflanking the Turkish main army by taking

[84] Coulston (1991); Töpfer (2011), 33–5.

[85] Graves (1938), 111, 129, 219, 252, 254, 321, 358, 377.

[86] Exceptionally Graves (1957a), 151, 180.

[87] This whole subject is explored by Badsey (2008), (2009), 55–105; Kenyon (2011).

[88] Badsey (2008), 247–9.

[89] Corrigan (2003), 189, 206, 289–94; Reid (2006), 304.

the eastern, desert route. Graves knew all about this, because it was the most important part of a campaign for which the Arab Revolt was the irregular element.[90] Graves had published his *Lawrence and the Arabs* in 1927. Lawrence's own *Seven Pillars of Wisdom* was first released in 1926, but Graves had already seen chapters in manuscript.[91] It was T. E. Lawrence who, in 1931, originally suggested that Graves should write a book about Count Belisarius.[92] Both men liked the comparison between Lawrence and Belisarius, the cavalry general who achieved so much with such slender resources.[93] Moreover, there was an Arthurian, knight-errant element to these perceptions of Lawrence, which also came through occasionally in *Count Belisarius*, for example in the naming of Eugenius's father, Geraint,[94] in the repeated use of 'tilting' in connection with Roman cavalry lances,[95] and in the overt comparison between Belisarius and Arthur.[96]

BELISARIUS IN GRAVES'S WORLD

Belisarius's personal story ended in penury and mendicancy as a paradigm of honourable sacrifice, unrecognized and unrewarded. This theme was largely responsible for the appearance of the general in western art, depicted in paintings in prison or begging in the streets of Constantinople, subjects found particularly appealing in the eighteenth and early nineteenth centuries.[97] The 'uplifting' element was the appreciation of his achievements shown by his loyal veterans and the population of the city who showered him with coins.[98]

90 Anglesey (1994), 125–87; Badsey (2008), 29–31, 283–8, 300–2. There has been a proliferation of literature devoted to this theatre in recent years: Bruce (2002); Carver (2003); Barr (2006); Woodward (2006); Grainger (2006); Ford (2009).

91 Graves (1957), 322; Seymour (1995), 96, 150–1.

92 Seymour (1995), 255.

93 Graves and Liddell Hart (1963), I. 152–3.

94 Graves (1938), 43–4.

95 Graves (1938), 111, 336–7.

96 Graves (1938), 7.

97 Notably paintings by François André Vincent (1776), Jean François Pierre Peyron (1779), Jacques-Louis David (1781), and François-Joseph Kinsoen (1817). There is also the sculpted bust (1791) of the elderly, blind Belisarius by Jean-Baptiste Stouf in the J. Paul Getty Museum, Malibu, USA.

98 Mahon (2006), 208–9; Graves (1938), 414–18.

Count Belisarius the novel did not meet with the same great success as the *Claudius* books, the main complaint being that the characterization of Belisarius was too idealized and perfectly virtuous. Perhaps such a model of loyalty and competent generalship was out of step in the cynical 1930s. Famously, Graves rebutted this criticism by treating it as a sad comment on the state of twentieth-century literary taste![99] However, he may be said to have already made a major contribution to this critical reaction through his other writings. Readers in the run-up to the Second World War had been subjected to a relentless 'industry' of war literature. Graves led with his published collections, alongside those of Owen, Sassoon, and Blunden in particular.[100] His *Good-bye to All That*, first published in 1929 and revised (excising Riding[101]) for republication in 1957, was even more influential, coming after Sassoon's *Memoirs of a Fox-Hunting Man* and Edmund Blunden's *Undertones of War*.[102] Avowedly written to meet a financial crisis, the book was successful in sales but ruffled feathers, in particular breaking the long-standing friendship with Sassoon. It is very revealing of Graves's attitudes towards war, command, and courage in general, and in particular it reveals specific wartime experiences which bear directly on the writing of *Count Belisarius*.

Graves composed *Count Belisarius* almost exactly twenty years after his last personal experience of Western Front combat. Axiomatically, he did not have a 'Good' war and was traumatized by his experiences for the rest of his days, like so many of his contemporaries. For the first ten years his nights were haunted by nightmares. Although never personally gassed, his dread of the possibility was heightened by the fact that not only were the early types of gas-mask primitive and improvised, but his badly reset nose and consequent

[99] R. P. Graves (1990), 279; Seymour (1995), 301–2; Christensen (2014). The novel was awarded the Prix Femina Vie Heureuse in 1939, which Graves received in person at the Institut Français in Paris; see R. P. Graves (1990), 299; Seymour (1995), 267.

[100] A situation nicely illustrated by the complaint made about the war by Captain Flash-heart: 'The blood, the noise, the endless poetry...!' (*Blackadder Goes Forth*, episode 4, 'Private Plane', BBC 1989).

[101] Riding's frontispiece poem was removed, as was the 'Dedicatory Epilogue to Laura Riding', Graves (1929), 445–8.

[102] Sassoon (1918); Blunden (1928). For recent treatments see Bond (2008); Madigan (2011) 1–11, 14, 19–21.

breathing problems prevented him from using even the redesigned respirators.[103] Interestingly, to make a very broad, related comparison with another trench-warfare veteran, it was Adolf Hitler's direct experience of being gassed that led to him completely forbidding gas attacks in the Battle of Britain and other military contexts (but not, of course, application in genocide). The Western Front was principally an artillery war, and it was a shrapnel wound during a bombardment which so nearly killed Graves.[104]

There are many points at which links between the military detail in *Count Belisarius* and the Great War are clear. Of course this should not be taken too far by ascribing everything to experience of the trenches. The very degree of detailed treatment of material culture in the book revealed Graves's wide reading, industry, and inventive imagination. Nevertheless, his approaches to and treatments of military material are revealing of the man, and of war on a 'human' level. One passage in *I, Claudius* is particularly striking: 'Soldiers really are an extraordinary race of men, as tough as shield-leather, as superstitious as Egyptians and as sentimental as Sabine grandmothers.'[105] As Miranda Seymour pointed out, 'Graves . . . was thinking of the men who served under him at the Front'.[106] This is undoubtedly correct. The 'superstitious' practices and beliefs of First World War Tommies are alluded to in *Good-bye to All That* on a number of occasions, involving the darkly humorous treatment of corpses and the fear of 'unlucky' pronouncements.[107] These have also been commented on by modern historians of the trench-warfare experience. For example, when steel helmets were first issued to replace peaked cloth caps, in some sectors troops exhibited marked reluctance to wear them due to the unlucky circumstance of sniper shots killing targets through their helmet.[108] The usual carrying of good-luck charms and talismans may be common for all soldiers through history, but Graves's reference to Egyptians picks up on the ancient period reception of Egyptian 'magic', and may again owe something to his own observation of Egyptian street life during the academic year spent teaching at Cairo University (1926–7).[109]

103 Graves (1957a), 97, 108, 157, 160, 163, 206.
104 Graves (1957a), 227–8; Seymour (1995), 53–4.
105 Graves (1934a), 231.
106 Seymour (1995), 216.
107 Graves (1957a), 95, 121–3, 205, 220, 223.
108 See Madigan (2011), 183–4, 187–8.
109 Graves (1957a), 135–55.

Sentimentality, Sabine or otherwise, was also a marked trait of Great War Tommy culture, but reference to hard shield-leather is off the mark with regard to the actual construction of Roman military shields of the first and second centuries.[110]

Of course, 'reception' of 'the Great War' has evolved over more recent decades, with new academic work (the so-called 'Two Western Fronts' debate),[111] the new practice of Conflict Archaeology on Great War sites,[112] and the war's presentation through documentaries, films, comedies, and school curricula.[113] For a minority of the veterans, and more significantly for post-First World War generations, the wave of poetry and prose which came out of the trenches was very influential, first in rarefied literary circles. This broadened out to nurture a view of the First World War in wholly negative terms through the 1930s, making major contributions to pacifism and appeasement. Since the Second World War the renaissance of war poets' work has enshrined a picture of the Great War as one of callous 'chateau generals', hidebound blimpish commanders, and senseless waste leading to an exhausted and indecisive peace. 'Lions led by Donkeys' became the popular phrase for the tragedy of the soldiers on the Western Front.[114] Serious modern scholars, on the other hand, have not really advocated this view. Sir Douglas Haig, commander of British forces from 1915 to 1918, and post-war rector and Chancellor of the University of St Andrews, is seldom named in *Good-bye to All That*.[115] However, a general atmosphere of suspicion exists therein about the competence of higher command, the planning of operations, and the prolongation of the war beyond 1917, continued principally in the interests of generals and politicians.[116] An alternative, dashing, mounted *exemplum* of Great War

[110] Bishop and Coulston (2006), 61–2, 91–4, 179–82, 217.

[111] e.g. Ferguson (1998); Sheffield (2001); Corrigan (2003); Todman (2005); Reid (2006), 10–18; Hart (2008); Badsey (2009).

[112] Superbly represented for the Western Front by Desfossés *et al.* (2008); Brown and Osgood (2009). For the Palestine and Transjordan theatre see <http://www.jordan1914-18archaeology.org/index.htm>.

[113] See Fussell (2000); Todman (2005).

[114] Epitomized by Alan Clark's polemical and amateurish *The Donkeys*, Clark (1961). For critiques see Sheffield (2001), 17; Corrigan (2003), 213; Todman (2005), 99–103; Reid (2006), 9–10.

[115] Graves (1957a), 267–8. For a balanced recent biography of Haig see Reid (2006).

[116] Graves (1957a), 108, 114, 150–2, 156, 226, 271.

generalship was presented by the career of Graves's friend T. E. Lawrence. This was the model taken forward to the Second World War by Basil Liddell Hart (Captain B. H. Liddell Hart, 1895–1970), another friend of Graves, and, with Graves, the other early biographer of Lawrence.[117] In film and television the 'chateau' command lived on in *Oh! What a Lovely War* (1963 stage play; 1969 film) and *Blackadder Goes Forth* (first broadcast 1989). There is no doubt of the personal courage of soldiers such as Graves and Sassoon, but it was used up in the gruelling and unceasing circumstances of front-line service. The theory ran that every man had a finite quantity of courage, some more than others, but that with every brave action and protracted period in a combat zone that courage was consumed, until the bravest of men cracked.[118] Being the most educated in British society, and to some extent the most sensitive from their upbringing and poetic nature, the 'war poets' were also the most articulate critics of the war and its direction, and especially of politicians and senior soldiers.[119] *Goodbye to All That* certainly played a major part in the formation of what can now be seen as a partial view of the Western Front, one manifested in the popular media by *Oh! What a Lovely War* and *Blackadder*.[120]

To return to *Count Belisarius*, and ending on a positive note, the last word may be left to Miranda Seymour:

> *Belisarius* is, nevertheless, one of Graves's finest novels. The intrigue which takes centre-stage in the *Claudius* novels is here moved into the shadows, while the light falls with remarkable clarity on the scenes of war in North Africa and Italy. Liddell Hart thought it a superb book; Winston Churchill read and studied it for helpful ideas during the Second World War. Belisarius himself is made too one-dimensional

[117] Graves (1927); Graves and Liddell Hart (1963); Liddell Hart (1934). There is a mass of Lawrence-related literature, and for the more recent contributions see James (1995); Barr (2006); Korda (2011).

[118] Graves (1957a), 178–9.

[119] Ferguson was especially critical of the 'war poets' stance: 'The memoirs of the 1920s and 1930s were disproportionately the work of public school and university-educated men with little pre-war experience of hardship, much less war. Their disillusionment was predicated on the illusions of privileged youth; whereas little of the discomfort they complained about was new to the "other ranks"' (Ferguson (1998), 451–2).

[120] Todman (2005), 116–18, 145–6; Badsey (2009), 37–54.

by his unfailing decency, but Graves defended his right to paint a truthful picture of a good man in a dirty world. At a time when the subject of leadership was being discussed in every journal and newspaper, *Belisarius* seemed to him an inspiring example.[121,122]

[121] Seymour (1995), 259. Churchill wrote to Graves (10 Sept. 1939) in praise of the book: 'I most heartily congratulate your brilliant piece of work. You have "rolled back the time curtain" in a magical way and made all this strange epoch young again. I daresay some of your readers will have felt that there was too much war, but the vivid accounts you give of those long-forgotten campaigns, in my mind, only enhance the value of the work' (quoted in Seymour-Smith (1995), 356).

[122] The writer is very grateful to a number of colleagues and friends who have been extremely helpful in the preparation of this paper, notably Alisdair Gibson, Edward Madigan, Roger Rees, and Sean Tougher. Dunstan Ward, editor of *Gravesiana*, very kindly made the text of Peter Christensen's posthumous paper available before publication. Hazel Dodge and Edward Madigan kindly read and commented on the manuscript to its great advantage, and suggested additional bibliography.

6

The Golden Ass and the Golden Warrior

Sonia Sabnis

Robert Graves's translation of Apuleius's *The Golden Ass*—published by Penguin Classics in the United Kingdom in 1950 and by Farrar, Straus & Young in the United States in 1951—remains widely available in English-speaking countries, both on the used-book market and in new printings. E. J. Kenney's translation (1998) has supplanted it in the Penguin Classics series, but its American publisher—now Farrar, Straus & Giroux—has reissued it periodically through various imprints, most recently in 2009.[1] In spite of the translation's mixed reviews, it continues to be important in the reception history of Apuleius among English readers, and especially those outside the university. In this essay I focus on the American printings of this translation and their marketing in order to show how Graves's literary celebrity and his connection to T. E. Lawrence contributed to the popular reception of Apuleius in the twentieth century. The continued importance of this translation is already bound up with Graves's literary fame, but the marketing of Graves's *The Golden Ass* in its American incarnation goes further in its evocation of twentieth-century celebrity. The blurb that appears on the inside dust-jacket (on the back of paperback editions) reads as follows:

[1] That Penguin did not retain the rights for the American edition was the subject of tense correspondence between Graves's agent and various Penguin representatives both several years before and after the translation appeared; both Allen Lane and Penguin's American representative noted with chagrin that it was the only translation in the Penguin Classics series not also distributed by Penguin in the United States. This correspondence is contained in file DM1107 in the Penguin Archives in Special Collections at the University of Bristol.

> In all literature there are few books with the vitality of *The Golden Ass*. Boccaccio borrowed freely from it, and later it served both to amuse and instruct Cervantes, Fielding, and Smollett. T. E. Lawrence carried it, in its original Latin, in his saddlebags with him all through the Arab Revolt, and it was Lawrence who first introduced the book to his friend Robert Graves.
>
> Mr. Graves has now freed the story from the archaic language with which it was encrusted, and at last the modern reader may, for the first time, appreciate for himself the lusty incident, curious adventure, and bawdy wit in which *The Golden Ass* abounds.
>
> The story is about Lucius Apuleius, a young man of good birth, who, while disporting himself in the cities and along the roads of Thessaly, encountered many diverting and strange adventures. Not the least of these was that Apuleius offended a priestess of the White Goddess, and for his offense suffered the indignity of being turned into an ass. How Apuleius supported his misfortune and how he contrived at last to appease the Goddess and resume his human form make up the body of the tale.
>
> Robert Graves has obviously enjoyed his labors on the story, for he writes: 'It is not strictly speaking the first modern novel, because Petronius' incomplete *Satyricon* antedates it by a century, but it is the most terrifying, and most sincere.'
>
> To which the publishers can only add, in the words of both Robert Graves and Apuleius, 'Now read on and enjoy yourselves.'

My aims in this essay are first to show that there is no evidence for the claim about *The Golden Ass* as companion to Lawrence during the Arab Revolt, then to contextualize the claim, speculating on how and why this myth has been perpetuated in the United States. The archaeological metaphor—'Mr. Graves has now freed the story from the archaic language with which it was encrusted'—hints at a comparison between Graves and his friend Lawrence in two distinct aspects familiar to Americans: the young archaeologist and the liberator of the Arabs from their Turkish oppressors.[2] Turning to the translation

[2] These are two facets of Lawrence that were repeatedly and sensationally emphasized by Lowell Thomas. For example, Thomas (1927), 364 and 365: 'He united the wandering tribes of the desert, restored the sacred places of Islam to the descendants of the Prophet, and drove the Turks from Arabia forever. Allenby liberated Palestine, the Holy Land of the Jews and Christians. Lawrence freed Arabia, the Holy Land of millions of Mohammedans.' 'After his rejection [by the Army Medical Board] Lawrence returned to his ancient ruins and toiled lovingly over inscriptions that unlocked the secrets of civilizations that flourished and crumbled to dust thousands of years ago.'

itself, I compare his translation strategies—which have never been in line with scholarship, aiming instead for a general audience—with the ways in which he wrote about his friend Lawrence in his biographical works. The similarity that is especially striking after decades of interest in and scholarship on both Lawrence and Apuleius is Graves's persistence in demystifying both a celebrity and a novel. Many scholars today would agree, I argue, that the timeless appeal of Lawrence and Apuleius lies in their continued inscrutability, their inconsistencies, their resistance to being solved or even summarized. Although the claim on the advertising of *The Golden Ass* is false, both Lawrence and Graves did read and enjoy Apuleius's novel. Lawrence praised the humour of *The Golden Ass*, while Graves firmly believed in its religious import. What is remarkable about these individual responses is that they adhere roughly to the comic-versus-serious contest that continues both to generate scholarly discussion, and perhaps more importantly, to dictate non-specialist reader responses to Apuleius' *The Golden Ass*. Ultimately, then, I hope to make a brief entry into reception studies of Apuleius in the last century. Two major works on the reception of *The Golden Ass* have appeared recently, but neither one goes as far as the twentieth century.[3] If an extended study were to be done, Robert Graves's translation would be an essential component.

Lawrence and Graves met at Oxford in 1920.[4] Lawrence was 31 and Graves 24. Their friendship does seem to have been established and fostered by literature: Lawrence admired Graves's poetry, and Graves wrote that Lawrence was one of the few whose close readings and criticisms he valued,[5] although later Lawrence was frank about his dislike of *I, Claudius* (Graves relied on Lawrence as a fact checker, an editorial relationship documented well by their curious correspondence).[6] The friendship seems also to have been strained by Graves's relationship with Laura Riding. Earlier, however, Lawrence aided Graves financially, both recommending him for a professorship in Cairo, which he held briefly, and giving him one of the private printings of his magnum opus *Seven Pillars of Wisdom*, with typically

[3] Carver (2007); Gaisser (2008).

[4] Graves wrote about their meeting in chapter 28 of *Good-bye to All That.*

[5] 'Lawrence was for years the only person to whom I could turn for practical criticism of my poems', Graves and Liddell Hart (1963), 10.

[6] Graves and Liddell Hart (1963), 174–8. For a good overview of the literary correspondence, see Orlans (1993), 23, 32, 41, 117, 126–7.

pragmatic instructions to read, then sell.[7] Graves's biography of Lawrence, *Lawrence and the Arabs*, was similarly sanctioned by its subject as a profitable enterprise for its author.[8] In *T. E. Lawrence to His Biographers*, Graves printed letters from Lawrence that demonstrate both their friendship and the detailed corrections Lawrence made to the biography. Of interest here are the particulars about Lawrence's campaign reading that he recorded in a letter written to Graves from Karachi in June 1927:

> As a bookman you may be amused to know that I carried with me during the desert war 1) a Morte d'Arthur, 2) Aristophanes, 3) Oxford Book of English Verse, and no other books. They say I carried Doughty [*Travels in Arabia Deserta*], but it's not true.[9]

Graves not only reproduced this list in his biography of Lawrence but also commented on it as somewhat revelatory concerning the character of his subject, as I shall discuss later. In reporting his campaign reading to D. G. Hogarth a year previously, Lawrence added the detail that he had read all of Aristophanes' *Peace*, 'very gratefully & without much technical trouble'.[10] There is no mention of Apuleius at all in this discussion of Lawrence's campaign reading materials, though Apuleius does appear in *Lawrence and the Arabs*. In the index he is listed erroneously as 'Apuleius, Marcus', and the reference is a footnote on Lawrence's correspondence with his friend Vyvyan Richards. This letter, which Lawrence wrote from Cairo (not the desert) in March 1916, appears more fully in Garnett's volume of Lawrence's letters (the date is listed incorrectly as 1915 several times in *Lawrence and the Arabs*); Lawrence is discussing the future possibilities for a joint enterprise in book printing:

[7] In *Good-bye to All That* Graves also notes that Lawrence saved him from debt. 'He gave me four chapters of *Seven Pillars of Wisdom*, his history of the Arab revolt, to sell for serial publication in the United States' (Graves (1957a), 236). These appeared in *The World's Work*.

[8] In Britain it was published as *Lawrence and the Arabs* (Jonathan Cape, 1927); in the United States as *Lawrence and the Arabian Adventure* (Doubleday, Doran & Co., 1928). This titling difference alone bespeaks the crusading version of Lawrence that Lowell Thomas vigorously presented to American audiences.

[9] The letter, dated 28 June 1927, is reprinted in several collections in addition to *T. E. Lawrence to His Biographers* (p. 55). The original is in the Houghton Library, Harvard University. Michael Korda's recent (2010) biography of Lawrence supports this account of Lawrence's 'camel-borne field library' (p. 401 n.).

[10] Garnett (1939), 512.

> If you can muster up the strength please write to me (via Oxford) and tell me how things look. I think we will have to do Apuleius, which is my present stand by.... The Kelmscott *Coleridge* however relieves me at high moments, and Apuleius ordinary times.[11]

From this letter it is clear that the blurb on Graves's translation has some basis in reality. Lawrence was reading Apuleius in Egypt, and sharing his pleasure with Richards at least; if Lawrence did not directly recommend Apuleius to his friend, Graves had access to his correspondence on it. However, these letters also indicate clearly that Apuleius was not Lawrence's companion in the desert.

Whether or not he was reading the original Latin, as the blurb implies, is also unclear. The references to Latin in his correspondence indicate a far less intimate relationship with the language. In a 1914 letter Lawrence described Latin as an awfully dull language:

> You know when you have after many years of tribulation learned it, you find out to your horror that there are only two or three little books in it worth the re-reading: and to think that with a little of that labour one might be proficient in Greek! The excuse made for Latin is that scientific books and philosophy demand a knowledge of it: but if I had my way I would build a causeway to America with all such productions.[12]

One would hope that Lawrence's reading of Apuleius in the ensuing years improved his opinion, but even in 1934 (a year before his death) he was complaining about Latin in another letter: 'My Latin wasn't ever much good, so that I have never enjoyed Catullus. I suppose that means that I have never justified the time I spent trying to learn the beastly language? There seem to be ten good Greek books to every Latin one.'[13]

The inventory of books at Lawrence's cottage in Dorset, Cloud's Hill, lists three editions of Adlington's Apuleius translation.[14] Only one of these contains the Latin text, the first Loeb edition, with Adlington's translation revised by Sir Stephen Gaselee; this came out in 1915, the year before Lawrence's letter to Richards. Thus, it seems likely to me that Lawrence was at best 'loebing' Apuleius,

[11] Garnett (1939), 201. The passage is quoted more fully later in this chapter.

[12] These and the following remarks on Latin are collected in Orlans (1993), 253–4.

[13] This letter (to C. Day Lewis) was written six months before his death. Lawrence also showed frustration with Greek while struggling with the *Odyssey* translation in 1930, Garnett (1939), 677: 'I wish Greek had never been invented.'

[14] Lawrence (1937), 446.

reading Adlington's revised translation and perhaps occasionally looking at the Latin on the facing pages.

What, then, are we to make of the highly suspicious comments that advertise the American printings of Graves's translation? Graves's own relationship with Apuleius is less well documented prior to his translation, but it is easy to disprove the claim that Lawrence was the one who introduced Apuleius to Graves. A 1917 letter to Robert Nichols from the Isle of Wight, where Graves was convalescing, indicates that Graves already had Apuleius some three years before he had even met Lawrence: 'I have here with me my Sorley, my Skelton, my Keats, and my ballad book; and also my dear Apuleius, so I'm not too badly off.'[15]

I have not found any evidence that Graves himself contributed to the blurb about Lawrence or reacted to it; in fact, despite their friendship, it seems highly unlikely that he would have given Lawrence credit for this important literary discovery.[16] More probably, however, both Graves on the Isle of Wight and Lawrence in Cairo were reading the newly printed first Loeb edition of Apuleius. Further research, especially in the unpublished letters of both men, may yield more incidental comments on *The Golden Ass*, but it is clear enough, even without all the available evidence, that the claims made in the American advertising are patently false. Lawrence did not have *The Golden Ass* in his saddlebags during the Arab Revolt, and he was not the one who introduced it to his friend Robert Graves. The two friends shared an appreciation for Apuleius, but it was one they reached independently, and in Lawrence's case in far less romantic circumstances than the blurb implies.[17]

[15] O'Prey (1982), 73. Graves writes about this time on the Isle of Wight in *Good-bye to All That*, Graves (1957a), 188–91. Graves's continued affection for the book is attested by a letter written by Beryl Graves to Betty Radice in 1984 (now preserved in the Penguin Archives), sanctioning the revision of the translation by Michael Grant: 'It was Robert's favourite book and I'm sure he'd like it to be given "a new lease on life".'

[16] The Farrar, Straus & Giroux Records in the Manuscripts and Archives Division of The New York Public Library indicate next to nothing about how this blurb was generated, but it is repeated in publicity as well as on the books themselves.

[17] An Apuleian connection between the two men is notably absent in Graves's own recollection, Graves and Liddell Hart (1963): 'At Oxford Lawrence forced two books on my attention in a way which I thought a little odd, and which made no sense to me for many years. The first was Maurice Hewlett's *Richard Yea-and-Nay*, a historical novel about the Crusades in which a Christian knight is passionately in love with a lady named Jehanne who has fallen into Saracen hands. The other was a collection of short naval stories by (I think) Henry Morley, called *Strange Cargoes*.'

Here is the version that appears on the most recent printing by Farrar, Straus & Giroux (2009):

> In all literature, there are few books with the vitality of *The Golden Ass.* Boccaccio borrowed freely from it, and later it served both to amuse and to instruct Cervantes, Fielding, and Smollett.
>
> T. E. Lawrence carried it—in its original Latin, of course—in his saddlebag throughout the period of the Arab Revolt, and it was Lawrence who first introduced the book to the poet Robert Graves. Graves himself became entranced by it—and the result is this translation, which, more than fifty years after its first publication, remains the most vibrant English-language version of Apuleius's raucous tale.
>
> The story is that of Lucius Apuleius, a young man of good birth who, while disporting himself in the cities and along the roads of Thessaly, encountered many diverting and strange adventures. Not the least of these was when Apuleius offended a priestess of the White Goddess—and for his offense suffered the indignity of being turned into an ass. How Apuleius deals with the misfortune and eventually managed to appease the goddess so that he could resume human form makes up the body of this tale, which Graves has conveyed in modern English infused with a timeless bawdy wit and sense of adventure.
>
> Robert Graves (1895–1985), born in London, was one of the most talented, colorful, and prolific men of letters of the twentieth century. He is best known for his historical novels *I, Claudius* and *Claudius the God.* He spent much of his life on the island of Majorca.

The changes from the 1951 are minor but striking: there is an added assumption of Lawrence's classical erudition hidden in the new punctuation and the additional phrase 'of course'. Do we even have to ask whether Lawrence could read Latin, whether he wanted to? The assumption of rigorous classical education not only coheres with fantasies about literary friendships forged at Oxford, but also follows in Lowell Thomas's well-trodden footsteps in lionizing Lawrence, the archaeologist, scholar, and freedom-fighter, for American audiences. 'Saddlebags' plural become a single saddlebag, perhaps to emphasize the paucity of Lawrence's impedimenta and thus to exalt *The Golden Ass* among them. And finally, 'the poet Robert Graves' has replaced 'his friend Robert Graves'. Graves's own literary fame is augmented slightly, but the added biographical information indicates that by 2009 Graves's celebrity has waned; the assertion of *poet* to a generation of readers who know him as the author of *I, Claudius* may also aid the general sense of poetic mysticism that the book promotes by maintaining the reference to the White Goddess, the product of

Graves's own idiosyncratic imagination. The editorial mimicking of Apuleius' own promise of pleasure in the Prologue from the earlier editions has been lost. Though the raucous wit of the novel is stressed, the more recent edition eliminates the language that casts the translator as the liberating archaeologist—Graves is no longer freeing the text from its encrustation of archaism but now encountering the text as the donkey Lucius encounters his saviour goddess. Graves takes on the more passive role of entrancement. Moreover, the retained prominence of the White Goddess preserves Graves's own reading of Apuleius, despite its incongruity with scholarly accounts of Isis and the final book of *The Golden Ass.*

The newest version of the advertisement implies that Lawrence has retained his celebrity longer than Graves. How has the fiction of their Apuleian intimacy been perpetuated? Perhaps someone with no Classics knowledge but astute marketing skills confused Apuleius and Aristophanes and used Lawrence's repeated references to the latter to construct this tantalizing history. Perhaps the influence of Belisarius, whom Lawrence did introduce to Graves, intruded into *The Golden Ass.*[18] Perhaps the two friends did discuss Apuleius to the extent that Graves condoned some exaggeration for the sake of book sales, for he knew first-hand of Lawrence's mystique in the United States.[19]

Regardless of its origin, this advertisement invites the reader to draw connections between the continued curiosities of Apuleius and the enduring enigma of Lawrence. In the next section I consider the effects of the advertising; in spite of the lies, the Graves–Apuleius–Lawrence connection offers at least two models of twentieth-century readership useful to understanding the novel's reception among popular and specialist audiences.

[18] Although this fact is well documented, it does not seem to have affected the advertisement of *Count Belisarius*. Perhaps the connection with Lawrence would improve sales!

[19] In *Good-bye to All That* ((1957a), 229) he records the following anecdote, the deep irony of which makes it worth reporting in full: '[In his rooms there were] two heavy leather chairs, simply acquired. "An American oil-financier had come in suddenly one day when I was visiting T. E. and said: I am here from the States, Colonel Lawrence, to ask you a single question. You are the only man who will answer it honestly. Do Middle-Eastern conditions justify my putting any money in South Arabian oil?" Lawrence, without rising, simply answered: "No." "That's all I wanted to know; it was worth coming for that. Thank you, and good day!" In his brief glance about the room he had found something missing; on his way home through London he chose the chairs and had them sent to Lawrence with his card.'

That his reading material would give insight into a person's character is a hypothesis that Graves himself would certainly support. In *Lawrence and the Arabs* he analyses Lawrence's choice of reading (Apuleius is conspicuously absent):

> to avoid becoming a second Don Quixote, Lawrence had to arm himself with a careful twentieth-century scepticism which he continually used in test of his behaviour; true mediaevalism was often cynical, never sceptical. It is, therefore, interesting to note that he carried three books with him throughout the Arabian campaign. The first was Malory's *Morte D'Arthur*; but the second was the comedies of Aristophanes, whose laughing scepticism, especially in his anti-militaristic *Lysistrata*, provides a fine antidote to false romanticism... The influence of the *Oxford Book of English Verse* on his feelings and actions during the campaign would be well worth studying.[20]

Let us return to Lawrence's letter to Vyvyan Richards concerning their printing (on a small hand-press) enterprise:[21]

> If you can muster up the strength please write to me (via Oxford) and tell me how things look. I think we will have to do Apuleius, which is my present stand by. *Cupid and Psyche*, and the wonderful end of the book, after the sheer humour of some of the beginning, are worthy of anything we can do. I'm afraid my entanglements are going to keep me in the Near East a certain part of each year: however an apprentice, or a working partner, should more than fill that part of the work. I only want a niche which will not take up too much time in getting into every visit. You know Coleridge's description of the heavenly bodies in the *Mariner*? 'Lords that are certainly expected' etc.... I don't want to be a lord or a heavenly body, but I think one end of the orbit should be in a printing shed.... It's a bad life this, banging about strange seas with a khaki crowd very intent on banker and parades and lunch. I am a total abstainer from each, and so a snob. The Kelmscott *Coleridge* however relieves me at high moments, and Apuleius ordinary times.[22]

His comments on *The Golden Ass* in the letter to Richards are brief but insightful: he pinpoints Cupid and Psyche, the ending, and the humour of the beginning—all elements that still stand out in any

[20] Graves (1991), 160–1. Some biographers and scholars have continued along these lines; see for instance Kaplan (1995) and her references.

[21] Richards wrote of this endeavour in an essay called 'Book Printing' in Lawrence (1937).

[22] Garnett (1939), 201.

reading or analysis of the novel. Furthermore, the contrast, however ephemeral, of Apuleius in 'ordinary times' and Coleridge 'at high moments' is another point of interest. One could draw a parallel between the military bureaucracy and leisure against which Lawrence rebelled and the social obligations and imperial pretensions from which Lucius, Apuleius' protagonist, seeks an escape. Looking forward to the campaigns described in the *Seven Pillars of Wisdom*, we could further compare Lawrence and Lucius: the degradation of their circumstances was balanced by the rhetoric of chivalry and heroism, yet never without a parodic element of play-acting, deceit of others as well as self-deceit. In recent years scholars have focused on the aspects of *The Golden Ass* that make vivid the experience of slavery, Lawrence's preferred metaphor for his own circumstances in the Arab Revolt:

> We had sold ourselves into its slavery, manacled ourselves together in its chain-gang, bowed ourselves to serve its holiness with all our good and ill content. The mentality of ordinary human slaves is terrible—they have lost the world—and we had surrendered, not body alone, but soul to the overmastering greed of victory. By our own act we were drained of morality, of volition, of responsibility, like dead leaves in the wind.[23]

Although their desires for debasement manifested themselves very differently, Lawrence shared with the protagonist of Apuleius' novel a recognition of the pleasures of slavery—an alternate translation of *serviles voluptates* ('falling a slave to pleasure' in Graves)—and a need to be beholden to a master (Feisal, Allenby, Fotis, Isis) while in other respects appearing as the champions of personal freedom and individual triumph.

Above all, though, Lawrence appreciated the 'sheer humour' of Apuleius, the way in which even the most solemn events can be made to look foolish and silly. Asininity is an element in the epigraph to Graves's biography of Lawrence, *Lawrence and the Arabs*:

> *Onager solitarius in desiderio animi sui attraxit ventum amoris.*
> Jeremiah [2.24]

The last words of Graves's *Lawrence and the Arabs* indicate his intention: 'Mr. Winston Churchill's short summary of Lawrence is

[23] Lawrence (1935), 29.

a very penetrating one: "A rare beast; will not breed in captivity."'[24] This assessment was reported with pride by Lawrence to Graves, and the latter dutifully used it as the conclusion to his Lawrence biography: 'It has suggested the text from the Vulgate, which I have made the motto to the book.'[25] Strangely, the text of the motto is not precisely the text the Vulgate, which reads more fully as follows:

> *onager adsuetus in solitudine in desiderio animae suae adtraxit ventum amoris sui nullus avertet eam omnes qui quaerunt eam non deficient in menstruis eius invenient eam . . .*[26]

Despite the gender of the subject, the passage in its context concerns a female wild ass in heat, an image that has been interpreted variously; in some critical editions of Jeremiah the reference to the wild ass is omitted completely.

I think it is fair to say that Graves probably did not mean to compare Lawrence to a she-ass in heat, but was attracted to the image of *onager solitarius* as a desert and deserted animal; indeed, the verse immediately preceding this one in Jeremiah uses the image of a female camel.[27] However damning the comparison is supposed to be in the words of the angry prophet, the image of the wild animal finding its satisfaction in spite of, or even because of, its solitude is an attractive one to align with Churchill's pithy remark. The degradation inherent in this comparison to an ass is, as I have argued, fitting for Lawrence's own view of his experiences and motivations. The change from Cairo bureaucrat to adventuring exploder of trains—the version of Lawrence Americans knew in the 1920s and 1930s from Thomas, and after 1962 from David Lean's epic film—both elevated Lawrence, in the romantic view, and degraded him. 'I liked the things underneath me and took my pleasures and adventures downward. There seemed a certainty in degradation, a final safety', Lawrence wrote.[28] Some of the best and most memorable writing in *Seven Pillars of Wisdom* comes in the descriptions of

[24] Graves (1991), 437.

[25] Graves (1991), 437. The inventory of Graves's library at Canellun includes a Sixto-Clementine Vulgate.

[26] In the KJV: 'a wild ass used to the wilderness, that snuffeth up the wind at her pleasure; in her occasion who can turn her away? All they that seek her will not weary themselves; in her month they shall find her.'

[27] Carter (1928) also picks up on the epigraph: 'This is but a prelude to a more leisurely analysis.'

[28] Lawrence (1935), 149–50.

Lawrence's physical endurance, and this is a trait his work shares with Apuleius's *The Golden Ass*: 'Generally I had been hungry; lately always cold: and frost and dirt had poisoned my hurts into a festering mass of sores.'[29] These words could easily be a paraphrase of Lucius' self-reflection as a donkey in *The Golden Ass*. In spite of my research showing that *The Golden Ass* was not Lawrence's companion during the Arab Revolt, the parallels between the novel and Lawrence's experiences are hard to resist; such a fanciful and romantic reading is, I suspect, exactly what the marketers of Graves's translation were hoping to achieve by using Lawrence to advertise it.

Graves himself strongly resisted the popular romantic version of his friend. His insistence on portraying Lawrence as simply as possible is comparable to his choice to use a simple and staid language in his translation of Apuleius. Graves was one of the few who spoke out with vehemence against the romantic image of Lawrence that has persisted to this day.[30] His intentions to demystify Lawrence, or at least to shut down certain areas of speculation, are especially clear in his publications after Lawrence's death (in 1935), but can also be seen throughout the biography *Lawrence and the Arabs*. At the same time, both Lawrence and Graves had no scruples about capitalizing on the legend that Lowell Thomas had perpetuated in the United States: Lawrence gave four excerpts of *Seven Pillars* to Graves to sell; these appeared in an American serial titled *The World's Work* in 1926 and 1927, accompanied by introductory notes taken from Thomas's book *With Lawrence in Arabia*. The same serial had already published a series of articles on the Arab campaign by Lawrence in 1921, and also printed four excerpts from *Lawrence and the Arabs* in 1928. Despite the antipathy between Lawrence and Thomas, and the clear way in which Graves's biography was meant to correct Thomas's sensational version, the appearance of all three names as bylines in this serial suggests complicity rather than competition.

Graves's biography of Lawrence carries with it the approbation that it was the only biography of Lawrence sanctioned and checked by the man himself; *The World's Work* introduces its series with the

[29] Lawrence (1935), 502; cf. Richards (1936), 212.

[30] Cf. Richards (1936), 211: 'Robert Graves and others have brought against Lawrence the charge that he was a romantic—Graves of course deploring it, but hero-worshipers savouring it and calling him Crusader, Elizabethan, Monk, and so forth....'

benediction: 'The author has had access to many of Lawrence's private papers.' These facts are true—Graves includes much of the correspondence between the two in *T. E. Lawrence to his Biographers*—but it is also noteworthy that Lawrence issued a backhanded compliment to the poet when he wrote to Graves about *Lawrence and the Arabs* in 1927: 'The whole of it does not carry so much meaning, to my judgement, as the single poem about Alexander in your collection.'[31] Graves would probably not disagree, for his introductory words in the biography seem oddly similar to his words about his Apuleius translation:

> I have tried to give a picture of an exasperatingly complex personality in the easiest possible terms. I have tried also to make a difficult story as clear as may be by a cutting-down of the characters that occur in it; mentioning by name only the outstanding ones . . . [32]

For some American reviewers, however, the result was an exasperating simplification and a project that would necessarily backfire.[33] The *New York Herald Tribune* reviewer, William McFee, pointed out that 'Robert Graves, in his attempt to prune away the absurd romancings and ballyhooings of Mr. Lowell Thomas, has only given us other equally fantastic tales that are pretty hard to swallow'.[34] McFee himself cannot shake off the Lowell Thomas influence, however, concluding: 'The disappointing thing about this book is that though its author is a writer of repute it somehow lacks that romantic glamour which makes a man like Lawrence credible to ordinary folk.'[35] John Carter, the *New York Times* reviewer, was less critical than McFee but saw Graves's project as doomed from the start—'the more one is told about Lawrence the less comprehensible does he become'—and also cited certain criteria of credibility: 'In appraising Lawrence we must forget the standards of common sense and humanity. Lawrence is a fabulous monster, a human hippogrif, a

[31] Orlans (1993), 279. [32] Graves (1991), 6.

[33] 'Exasperating' is the assessment of MacDonald (1928), 176.

[34] McFee (1928). The metaphor here is apt for my comparison with the Apuleius translation, since one of the basic premises of *The Golden Ass* is the credibility of fantastic tales, illustrated by a sword-swallower performing in Athens! McFee's incredulousness, however, concerns the implied claim in the biography that Lawrence devoured 150 books per week while at Oxford.

[35] McFee (1928).

military unicorn, who appeared like a portent in the Eastern War and who disappeared, when that war was over.'[36]

Hybrid bodies of fantastic origin and dubious existence are also key to Apuleius' *The Golden Ass*. The hybrid and mutable quality of individuals is not only key to the plot, but also reflects the language—a Greekish Milesian tale told in Latin—and Apuleius himself, a half-Numidian, half-Gaetulian imperial citizen, who intrudes his own biography only once (contrary to Graves's easy assimilation of author and protagonist) in the text.[37] In his translator's introduction Graves argues that Apuleius' lively diction is contrived, and states firmly: 'Paradoxically, the effect of oddness is best achieved in convulsed times like the present by writing in as easy and sedate an English as possible.' As we will see, this pronouncement has its proponents and detractors (perhaps depending on one's perception on the convulsed present). Along with the simple style, Graves also chose clarity over Apuleius' riddling obscurity: 'to avoid the nuisance of footnotes I have brought their substance up into the story itself whenever it reads obscurely.'[38] As in *Lawrence and the Arabs*, an attempt to obviate the reader's exasperation only exacerbates it.[39]

These are the two major reasons why Graves's translation of Apuleius has not found favour among audiences of scholars.[40] For instance, Graves's rendering of the Prologue cannot be easily forgiven. It is apparent that Apuleius means to build ambiguity and

[36] Carter (1928), 10. Compare also the highly favourable review in the *Nation*, Milton (1928): 'Mr. Graves's book really is a poet's book about another poet, for it is difficult to fasten a more satisfactory tag upon Lawrence.'

[37] *seminumidam et semigaetulum*, Apul. *Apol.* 24; *Madaurensem*, *Met.* 11.27. In his translation Graves interpolates Apuleius's hometown prior to this section as well as in the Prologue, Graves (1951a), 283: 'I had decided to go straight home to Madaura after my long absence.'

[38] Graves (1951a), 11. Still, Graves is the only modern translator to have retained a sense of the Greek title in his translation, the full title of which is *The Transformations of Lucius, Otherwise Known as the Golden Ass*. For the title, see Winkler (1985), 293–5. *Asinus Aureus*, the title attested by Augustine (*Civ. Dei* 18.18), gives the commonest English title, but most specialists prefer *Metamorphoses*.

[39] One of the major corrections that Michael Grant made in his revision, Grant (1990), xvii: 'This is *not* such good practice; in fact, in a modern translation it will not do. Moreover, Graves's insertions are not always justified and are sometimes merely expressions of personal opinion.'

[40] The contemporary reviews I discuss below are the most critical, but even reviewers of more recent translations have drawn attention to the weaknesses of Graves's translation, e.g. DeFilippo (1992) (see n. 44) and Smith (2001). For a different view of Graves's Apuleius translation, see Brittan-Ortiz (1999).

riddles into his text, both catering to the erudition of his readers and tying an insoluble knot of narrative authority, religious knowledge, and philosophical truth. The enigmatic Prologue establishes this programme, and thus Graves's uncomplicated assimilation of the Prologue's speaker to the author Apuleius, together with the gratuitous insertion of Apuleius's own biography, is indeed grievous:

> Open a copy of the old Penguin translation of Apuleius by Robert Graves and one finds, in place of the teasing play of *quis ille? paucis accipe*, a gross interpolation: 'Let me briefly introduce myself as Lucius Apuleius, a native of Madaura in North Africa, but of ancient Greek stock.' This may seem an egregious instance of *traduttore traditore!*, but it is sobering to recall that over the course of forty years and multiple impressions, hundreds of thousands of English 'general readers' approached and appreciated Apuleius through Graves's gateway, never suspecting that the Prologue posed any problem at all. For better or worse, Graves's version forms part of the *Wirkungsgeschichte*—the 'effective history'—of the text . . . Moreover, Graves is merely following a long line of readers in privileging the authorizing aspects of the Prologue over its generic signifiers.[41]

Graves's firm commitment to Apuleius as the speaker of the Prologue and the conflation of the details of the Prologue with Apuleius's own biography put him in irresolvable conflict with scholars of the last twenty years who have expended considerable effort in proposing alternative identities and taking pleasure in the elusiveness of the question *quis ille*? that encapsulates the conundrum of the Prologue.[42] Graves thought he had solved this problem. Likewise, Graves had no interest in the speculation regarding the identity of 'S.A.', the dedicatee of Lawrence's *Seven Pillars of Wisdom*.[43] Despite Graves's claims to know beyond any doubt of Lawrence's involvement with a woman, Lawrence scholars and enthusiasts have matched Apuleianists in speculating on the solution (or ultimate irresolution) of this riddle. Like *quis ille*, the S.A. enigma will never be solved, much to the frustration and delight of aficionados. Lawrence relished such enigmas, perpetuating his own mythology, whereas Graves exerted himself, both before and after Lawrence's death, to set down an indisputable record of his friend's life and character.

[41] Carver (2001), 168.
[42] Harrison (1990) and Kahane and Laird (2001).
[43] Graves (1963).

Many reviews of Graves's *The Golden Ass* were positive, citing especially its freshness and clarity; indeed, in 1950 its primary competitor was Adlington (1566).[44] Graves's reputation as a poet and as the author of *The White Goddess* also affected the reception of his Apuleius translation. For instance, the short review in the *New Yorker* concludes as follows:

> This rendering . . . is fresh and much more readable than the previous English translations. Mr. Graves was probably led to undertake it by his earlier researches into the worship of the White Goddess—the most ancient Occidental deity—to whom he devoted his book 'The White Goddess' (1948). The new work glows with the same vast scholarship that illumined the earlier one—a scholarship that Mr. Graves wears as easily as an old dressing gown.[45]

The simile here is ironic if read in conjunction with the less favourable review of D. S. Robertson, an eminent editor of the text of the *Metamorphoses*, that appeared in the *Classical Review*. Robertson begins: 'The merits of this spirited work are not those of exact scholarship.'[46] Still, he concedes that some of his subsequent criticisms, based on Graves's neglect of scholarship, are likely to be felt only by a certain group of specialists: 'In fairness, however, it must be admitted that most of this matters little enough to the ordinary reader.'[47] But Robertson also takes issue with Graves's theory of translation:

[44] This is not to say that other translations into English were not produced: see Pavlovskis-Petit (2000) for an overview. Jack Lindsay's translation, which is also still broadly read but, unlike Graves's translation, firmly committed to the liveliness of Apuleius's style, was originally published for the Limited Editions Club in 1932 (in a run of 1,500 copies) but was not published widely until 1962. Joseph DeFilippo's review of J. Arthur Hanson's 1989 Loeb translation concisely sets these three in relation to each other, DeFilippo (1992), 301: 'the ease of [Graves's] English too often and too thoroughly smooths over the dark irregularities of Apuleius' Latinity. The most recent and widely read translator of *The Golden Ass*, Jack Lindsay . . . made a concerted effort to render stylistic details of the novel into English that somehow reproduces the sound of Apuleius' Latin. But the results of this attempt, though sometimes remarkable, often purchase rhetorical effect at the price of meaning. The new translation by Hanson, neither as smooth as Graves, nor as flamboyant as Lindsay, is just right: it is enjoyable to read without sacrificing the precision that would enable one to understand the meaning of the original, insofar as this can be done with any translation.'

[45] Rovere (1951). [46] Robertson (1951), 241.

[47] Robertson (1951), 242.

> [T]here is something to be said for a simple style, but the loss is great. In the main run of the narrative the reader of this translation gets no inkling of one of the greatest charms of the original, its piquantly unsuitable magniloquence of description and discourse, and its splendid heroics, fantastically embroidered with every device of rhetoric, and then sent crashing to earth with an inimitable twist of final bathos.[48]

Robertson is in fact more charitable towards Graves than F. L. Lucas, who issues the following pronouncement in the *TLS*: 'A Roman Oscar Wilde should not be made to write as if he had been a Roman Defoe . . . The truth seems to be that Mr Graves preferred plain English (which he writes well) and so found this flimsy pretext [the sedate style].'[49]

Graves was riled enough by this review that he wrote a letter to the editor in response, citing the viciousness of Apuleius's African style. 'I could, of course, have translated it in a variety of eccentric modern styles, but the Milesian story-teller has long ago left the street-corner and is now sustained by the magazine public; *The Golden Ass* must, in fact, compete with the lucidly written pieces printed in the New Yorker or it top-of-the-market rivals.'[50] The magazine public was also the target audience of *Lawrence and the Arabs* twenty-odd years earlier, and the similarities between the criticisms of both works are striking: in essence, Graves seems to have sold himself short as a poet and prose stylist, misrepresenting both subjects despite his claims to intimacy therewith.

In this letter to the *TLS* Graves's defence says much regarding an aspect of literature that Apuleianists neglect but that Graves knew acutely, the market.[51] Marketing and marketability are especially

[48] Robertson (1951), 242.

[49] Lucas (1950), 336. For more on the translation style, see Burton's essay, Ch. 7 in this volume.

[50] Graves (1950b). Graves's citation of an American magazine in a letter to the *TLS* is particularly interesting, and perhaps reveals his own leanings towards the readership on the other side of the Atlantic where *The Golden Ass* had not yet been published. American reviews of the translation, including Rovere (1951) in the *New Yorker*, were by and large favourable, although brief.

[51] As was recognized by Horace Gregory in a 1961 article calling for a reappraisal of Graves in the United States, Gregory (1961), 1: 'The time is ripe for a revaluation of the writings of Robert Graves. In the United States he is best known as a writer of prose . . . His translation of Apuleius' "The Golden Ass" is another triumph, largely because it contains an inspired, yet clear-eyed version, far better than Walter Pater's, of the story of Cupid and Psyche. He has written as many other books in prose as a

important, not only as we approach the twentieth-century reception of Apuleius, but also because the American market proved bountiful for Lawrence and Graves. Because of their various enterprises directed towards American audiences, I suspect that Graves may have tacitly approved the fiction about Lawrence and *The Golden Ass* on his translation; it was simply an addendum to the work he had already done in representing Lawrence to Americans, earning a living from his fame with Lawrence's approval. This aspect of the translation is connected to Graves's portrayal of Apuleius as a competitive storyteller with a demanding audience, and this point, in my opinion, merits further consideration by scholars. For it is usual to think of Apuleius as peerless, without competition; it is unusual to think of Apuleius's literary emulations apart from an elite and educated perspective. The questions of Apuleius's intended, actual, and ideal audiences remain thorny, but perhaps Graves's concern with the literary market should be reconsidered, especially with a view to the valuations of rhetorical performance that form a key component of the Second Sophistic. Perhaps Apuleius's motives for writing the *Metamorphoses* were similar to those of Graves and Lawrence in the 1920s—more financial than literary.[52] Graves's assertion that Apuleius's elaborate style is primarily the result of competition with the Milesian storytelling methods of the age, and therefore not as unique, sophistic, or African as others would have it, may merit further consideration, but it is difficult to divorce this claim both from Graves's persistent identification of the novel's author with its protagonist and from the thesis that the religious message is his primary theme.

P. G. Walsh, the translator of the 1994 Oxford World's Classics edition, is the only recent translator to address at length Graves's

Victorian novelist, spurred (so I think) by a spirit of high courage, a contentious temperament—and the important need of earning a living.'

[52] One ms. of Apuleius, Vat. lat. 3384, contains the marginal note that the *Metamorphoses*, which follows the *Apology*, Apuleius's speech defending himself on charges of magic, in many manuscripts, was intended as a gift of gratitude to the magistrate (the proconsul Claudius Maximus) who acquitted him. Graves undertook the Lawrence biography to make money, and Lawrence took on the *Odyssey* for the same reason. Both projects capitalized on Lawrence's fame, just as the blurb about Lawrence on *The Golden Ass* seeks to do with a gesture towards Lawrence's myth. The quick success and eventual neglect, at least in scholarly circles, of Lawrence's *Odyssey* and Graves's *The Golden Ass* are somewhat comparable.

translation as a precedent (E. J. Kenney, who did the new translation for Penguin Classics published in 1998, mentions much older translations but curiously makes no mention of Graves, his immediate predecessor in the series).[53] This is Walsh's criticism, which aligns well with Carver's comments:

> The poet-craftsman's enviably supple use of the English language makes this translation attractive to read independently of the Latin, but it is by no means always faithful to the original, and in places seems merely to offer a paraphrase of Adlington. Of Graves a similar judgement can be passed as of Adlington; literary skill and versatility, not exact scholarship, is the primary requirement for the popular success of a translation. There is a disastrous exordium with 'Apuleius' address to the reader', in which the miniature biography which belongs to the hero Lucius is attached to the author; the translation misleads at some points and condenses at others. But the jocose spirit of the original is well captured, and one may confidently predict an extended life for this version.[54]

Indeed, Graves's translation of Apuleius is inextricable from the ways in which Apuleius has been read by English-speaking audiences since 1950. For instance, Salman Rushdie wrote an essay about *The Golden Ass* in the 1980s and alludes to it in one of his most celebrated novels, *Midnight's Children*: it is Robert Graves's translation that he read and cites.[55] Graves's *The Golden Ass* is not a significant source for mainstream teaching or hermeneutic purposes, but some classicists at least acknowledge his interpretations of the novel.[56] On a much smaller scale, the false Lawrence connection also seems to implicate itself in the way in which non-specialist audiences are thinking about Apuleius; internet searches show that the lie on the dust-cover of the American edition has been repeated often in references to Apuleius outside academic publications.[57]

My conclusions are as follows: the tantalizing blurb on American editions of Robert Graves's Apuleius translation, that Lawrence carried Apuleius's work in Latin during the Arab Revolt and that he introduced it to Graves, is false. Nevertheless, it is tempting to use this lie not only as a point of entry into the reception of Apuleius in the twentieth and twenty-first centuries, but also as a way of demarcating

[53] See, however, Grant (1987), (1990), and Hare (1995).
[54] Walsh (1994), xlix. [55] Rushdie (1991), 365.
[56] e.g. Winkler (1985), 14 and Krabbe (1989), 12, 25, and *passim*.
[57] e.g. <http://www.jnanam.net/golden-ass/>.

two major interpretive modes concerning Apuleius's *The Golden Ass*. Simply stated, I would put Graves in the serious camp, in which a message of religious import is privileged above the raucousness of the storytelling, whereas Lawrence, who cited the humour of the novel in his letter to Vyvyan Richards, would fall into the comic camp, not necessarily denying a serious religious or philosophical message, but unwilling to rank this lesson above the novel's indulgence and entertainment. Despite the lack of evidence for a significant connection between Lawrence and Graves's translation of Apuleius, Graves's treatment and understanding of both can be compared for their preference of simplicity and straightforwardness. However baseless, such speculation is exactly what the blurb on American editions of Graves's *The Golden Ass* encourages its (American) audience to perform, deepening the inscrutability of both Apuleius and Lawrence and thus perhaps working directly against Graves's own aims. Despite its flaws, Graves's translation of Apuleius continues to be important for popular audiences, and as long as this bit of misinformation is perpetuated, it will form a small but tantalizing component in the reception history of *The Golden Ass*.[58]

[58] I owe thanks to Ann Topjon, Philip O'Brien, Walter Englert, Rebecca Gordon, Laura Leibman, Celia Oney, McKenzie Funk, and Rosa Schneider for help in the preparation of this essay. I would also like to thank Alisdair Gibson and the other participants in the seminar at St Andrew's as well as the Special Collections staff of the University of Bristol Library and the Manuscripts and Archives Division of the New York Public Library. Support for research was provided by the Stillman Drake and Summer Research Funds of Reed College.

7

'Essentially a Moral Problem': Robert Graves and the Politics of the Plain Prose Translation

Philip Burton

INTRODUCTION

Familiarity with Robert Graves's classical translations can easily blind us to the apparent paradox of his undertaking translation in the first place. A handful of English authors, such as Marlowe, Dryden, Pope, and Cowper, are equally known for their classical versions as for their original works. Rather more have produced occasional translations. Often, however, translators are viewed as inglorious drudges, with no voice of their own. Certainly, few established authors have produced so much translation from the classical languages as Graves published between 1950, the year of his translation of Apuleius's *The Golden Ass*, and 1959, when his version of the *Iliad* appeared.

And yet this burst of translation follows immediately upon the publication of *The White Goddess* in 1948, in which Graves famously works out his theories of poetic inspiration and of the single-hearted dedication of all true poets to the Goddess. The picture of the inspired poet he paints in *The White Goddess* may not sit easily with our stereotype of the plodding, worthy translator. We might have expected him to dismiss his translations as mere potboilers, as he regularly did his *Claudius* novels. However, despite the commercial success of his classical translations—his agent even managed to sell the rights for the translation of his *The Golden Ass* into Swedish[1]—Graves seems not to have thought of his translations in this light.

Equally, we might have expected Graves, when rendering Greek and Latin verse into English, to have produced English verse, as a sort of extension of his own poetry. This had, after all, been the practice of such contemporary poets as Louis MacNeice, Cecil Day-Lewis, and Graves's own *bête noire*, Ezra Pound. Instead, as we will see, this is not the case.

This chapter is concerned with three recurrent themes in particular. First, there is Graves's insistent espousal of the plain prose style of translation, even in translating complex poetic texts. Second, there is his use of translation as a form of self-positioning vis à vis both the original authors, and other translators. Third, there is the question how far Graves's practice can be seen as reflecting a wider cultural *Zeitgeist* and how far it is a matter of personal idiosyncrasy. Overarching all three is a consideration of the concept of the 'morality' of translation, a key term in Graves's own discussion of his own approach. These themes are, of course, closely interlinked, and overlaps are inevitable.

First, some background. Graves published four translations of major classical works: *The Transformations of Lucius, otherwise known as The Golden Ass*, by Lucius Apuleius in 1950; the *Pharsalia. Dramatic Episodes of the Civil Wars of Lucan* in 1956; *The Twelve Caesars of Suetonius* in 1957; and *The Anger of Achilles* (i.e. the *Iliad*) in 1959. The first three of these were published in the Penguin Classics series, the last by Doubleday in America and Cassell's in Britain. There are also passages in his historical novels which are closely modelled on specific passages in ancient authors.[2] Similarly, his 1955 novel *Homer's Daughter* has much material based on identifiable passages of the Odyssey—on this more later.[3]

Our title phrase is taken from the introduction to his *The Golden Ass* translation, where Graves wonders aloud 'how much [the translator owes] to the letter, and how much to the spirit'. It is, he muses, 'essentially a moral problem'.[4] The choice of adjective was not lightly made. As early as 1946 he writes to the Penguin Classics editor

[1] 'Moral Principles in Translation', Graves (1965), 130.

[2] e.g. the speech of Saturninus in Josephus, *Jewish Antiquities* 19.2, reproduced at Graves, (1976) 68–9.

[3] A translation of Terence was planned, but abandoned in favour of an edition of the 1689 version by Lawrence Eachard, published in 1963.

[4] Graves (1950a), 10.

E. V. Rieu noting 'another moral point which crops up. Apuleius sometimes gets his sentences in the wrong order...'[5]—the 'moral question' being how far the translator should seek to reproduce what the author *meant* to say, rather than what he actually did say. The phrase recurs yet again in the title of his 1962 address to the Institute of Linguists, 'Moral Principles in Translation'. As to what Graves meant by it, we may, I suggest, best approach this indirectly, through a consideration of the three main issues set out above: his use of the plain prose style, the use of translation as self-positioning, and the relative importance of cultural *Zeitgeist* and individual choice. It is to these that we turn now.

THE PENGUINS AND THE PLAIN STYLE

> 'Did you like that story?' asked Crossley.
>
> 'Yes,' said I, busy scoring, 'a Milesian Tale of the best. Lucius Apuleius, I congratulate you'.[6]

So the anonymous narrator of Graves's famous short story 'The Shout' (1929) salutes the teller of his inset narrative. There is something distinctly Apuleian about this story; a tale of supernatural powers, lunacy, sex, and cricket, with fluid frontiers between the realms of fiction and reality. Particularly notable here is how Graves is already casting himself as an Apuleius figure, a master fabulist with unique religious insight. Some twenty years on, Graves would return to *The Golden Ass* repeatedly during his researches in comparative religion which led up to the publication of *The White Goddess*. The work is, as Graves tells it, the story of a man who makes the cardinal errors of meddling with magic and of trying to help those less fortunate than himself; who is redeemed only when he commits himself to the worship of the Goddess; all with a few side-swipes at Christianity thrown in along the way.

[5] Letter of E. V. Rieu to Graves, 1 Oct. 1946, quoted in Hare (1995), 196. Graves refers here to the internal organization of Apuleius' sentences rather than their sequence in relation to each other.

[6] 'The Shout', repr. in Graves (1951b), 77.

But how to translate Apuleius? *The Golden Ass* is notoriously written in a precious and overwrought Latin. Graves was well aware of this, quoting Elizabethan translator William Adlington's description of it: 'so dark and high a style, in so strange and absurd words and in such new invented phrases, as he seemed rather to set forth to show his magnificent prose than to participate his doings to others.' However, Graves tells us, Adlington is missing the point: rather

> Apuleius . . . was parodying the extravagant language which the 'Milesian' story-tellers used, like barkers at country fairs today, as a means of impressing simple-minded audiences. The professional story-teller is still found in the West of Ireland. I have heard one complimented as 'speaking such fine hard Irish that Devil two words of it together in it would any man understand'.[7]

But this hard Irish, Graves concludes, like Apuleius's hard Latin, is always genuinely archaic, not humorously coined for the occasion.

Notable here is Graves's identification of Apuleius's style with that of Irish storytellers. Graves could claim Irish descent from his father Alfred Perceval, son of the Anglican bishop of Limerick and himself a prominent man of Anglo-Irish letters. This Irish link is important to him; *The White Goddess* is, of course, his most famous exploration of Celtic myth, but is only one instance of his fascination with it. Graves's own (partial) Irishness allows him to claim special qualification to translate the 'Irish' style of Apuleius; and, by an implicit, if circular, argument, his success as a translator of Apuleius may bolster his own claim to Irishness.

However, the key question of *how* to translate Apuleius remains unanswered. For Graves ((1950a), 10), the answer was simple if paradoxical: 'The oddness of effect is best achieved in convulsed times like the present by writing in as easy and sedate an English as possible.' Granted this premise, Graves is, for the most part, as good as his word. Consider, for instance, this passage from Apuleius's *Metamorphoses* (3.29) along with its translation in his *The Golden Ass* ((1950), 94):

> sed tandem mihi inopinatam salutem Iuppiter ille tribuit. nam cum multas villulas et casas amplas praeterimus, hortulum quendam prospexi satis amoenum, in quo praeter ceteras gratas herbulas rosae virgines matutino rore florebant. his inhians et spe salutis alacer ac laetus proprius accessi, dumque iam labiis undantibus adfecto, consilium me subit longe

[7] Graves (1950a), 9.

salubrius, ne, si rursum asino remoto prodirem in Lucium, evidens exitium inter manus latronum offenderem uel artis magicae suspectione uel indicii futuri criminatione. tunc igitur a rosis et quidem necessario temperavi et casum praesentem tolerans in asini faciem frena rodebam.

At last Jupiter the Deliverer generously offered me a chance to escape. After we had passed several farm buildings and large country houses I saw a charming little garden full of many different sorts of flowers, among them budding roses still wet with the morning dew. I gasped for joy and quickened my pace, and had almost come up to the roses, my mouth watering hopefully, when at the last moment I thought better of my project. If I suddenly ceased to be an ass and became Lucius again, the bandits would be sure to kill me, either because they took me for a wizard or for fear that I might inform against them. For the present I must lay off roses and put up with my misery a little longer by champing my bit like the beast I was.

Claims to a 'plain style' are notoriously hard to substantiate, resting as they often do on the (notional) linguistic competence of an (often undefined) audience. While there is, as we will see, considerable contemporary debate of the value of 'plain English', most discussions characteristically point out what is foreign to it rather than what is essential. However, even if we are no longer the original target audience, this still seems—to this reader's instinct at least—to have a reasonable claim to be accessible to a fairly average mid-twentieth-century public. More importantly, Graves's contemporaries seem to have felt the same. Thus F. L. Lucas—himself a notable soldier, novelist, translator, scholar, and stylist—in the *Times Literary Supplement* of 2 June 1950, allowed that Graves had produced a version in 'clear and easy English', which, he adds archly, 'many who do not know Apuleius will heartily enjoy'.[8] Returning to his Apuleius translation in his 1962 lecture on 'Moral Principles in Translation', Graves essentially restates his earlier views: 'since [Apuleius's] stories need no rhetorical stiffening, I have translated them for the general public in the plainest possible English.'[9] While this is arguably good Edwardian paradox (one is sometimes reminded that Graves grew up in the literary England of Shaw, Chesterton, and Belloc), it is perhaps rather less than a developed argument.

[8] For a wider consideration of Lucas's and other responses, see Sabnis, Ch. 6 in this volume.

[9] Graves (1965), 130.

We turn now to Graves's translation of Lucan's *Pharsalia*. Here, despite—indeed, because of—the sheer obscurity of Lucan's style, Graves once again advocates a translation into 'simple English'. To illustrate his practice, he takes his version of *Pharsalia* 5.229–35. Appius Claudius has asked an oracle whether he can safely sit out the Civil War in Euboea. Graves translates:

> secreta tenebis litoris Euboici memorando condite busto,
> qua maris angustat fauces saxosa Carystos
> et, tumidis infesta colit quae numina Rhamnus,
> artatus rapido fervet qua gurgite pontus
> Euripusque trahit, cursum mutantibus undis,
> Chalcidicas puppes ad iniquam classibus Aulin.

> 'Appius, you are indeed fated to take your solitary ease in Euboea; by being buried in a sequestered but famous tomb near the quarries of Carystos. It will face across the narrow sea towards the town of Rhamnus in Attica, sacred to Nemesis, the goddess who punishes human ambition. In between lie the so-called Hollows of Euboea, where the sea is disturbed by the rapid, constantly-shifting current form the Straits of Euripus: a current which sets the ships of Chalcis adrift and swings them across to Aulis in Boeotia—that fatal shore where long ago Agamemnon's ships assembled before sailing to Troy.'

and goes on to observe:

> Since this is what the passage means, surely it should be so rendered? Why let sentences remain obscure, just because a few Latinists may nod appreciatively at the references to Agamemnon's marshalling of his naval forces against Troy; to the Goddess Nemesis' temple at Rhamnus; and to the asbestos quarries of Carystos?[10]

Again, considered as a specimen of simple English, Graves's version is certainly a success; another distinguished reviewer, Peter Green, in *Times Literary Supplement* of 11 February 1957, praised his 'vigorous, direct, crystalline prose', which 'purge[d] Lucan of his offensive turgidities'. However, we may still venture qualifications. Is Graves right, for instance, to assert (in a subordinate clause) that his translation not just represents, or approximates to, but really *is* 'what the passage means'? How, for instance, does one bring out the oracular *double entendre* of *condite* in line 230? Is Graves's solution—'buried',

[10] Graves (1965), 131–2, closely following Graves (1956), 21.

then 'sequestered'—just too prosaic? What about the antithesis between the divine and the mortal in Graves's reference to the 'goddess' who punishes 'human ambition'—is Graves here bringing out what is latent in the text, or importing his own theological concerns? How far should one go in cashing out allusions? Is the reference to Aulis, for instance, so recondite as to need Graves's rather clunky gloss on it? And if we allow the extraneous reference to Appius's 'fate' in the first line, is the translation improved by the hackneyed 'fatal shore' (*iniquam puppibus Aulin*) in the last? To what extent—to anticipate our argument—are such editorial intrusions desirable or necessary?

Graves's third Penguin, his 1957 version of Suetonius's *The Twelve Caesars*, continues the plain-prose approach; and here it is perhaps most justified. The nineteenth-century view, cited by Graves in his foreword, that '[Suetonius'] language is very brief and precise, sometimes obscure, without any affectation or ornament', is not obviously wrong. Nor indeed might we quarrel with Graves's own claim that 'the genius of Latin and the genius of English [are] so dissimilar that a literal rendering would be almost unreadable'.[11] Nonetheless, we may be uneasy at some of Graves's statements: in particular, his conclusion that, 'for English readers Suetonius' sentences, and sometimes whole groups of sentences, must often be turned inside out',[12] may sound worryingly cavalier. We shall return shortly to the question of what liberties Graves thought a translator might morally take with his original.

The Anger of Achilles

Graves's espousal of the plain-prose aesthetic in his Penguin translations may simply be seen as a feature of house style (though, as we will argue, that is hardly an adequate explanation). It is true that if we turn to Graves's non-Penguin translation, *The Anger of Achilles*, we do find Graves modifying this aesthetic somewhat. As he writes:

> before translating *The Golden Ass* from Apuleius' over-ornate Latin, I decided to give it a new lease of life by using a staid but simple English prose. I cannot quite do the same here, because Homer wrote in

[11] For a history, and critique, of such 'dynamic equivalence' in translation, see Venuti (1995), esp. 1–42.

[12] Graves (1957b), 7–8.

> hexameter verse, and . . . a solemn warning, a divine message, a dirge, or a country song disguised as a simile . . . all sound wrong when turned into English prose . . . I have therefore followed the example of the ancient Irish and Welsh bards by, as it were, taking up my harp and singing only where prose will not suffice.[13]

However, this is a modification rather than a repudiation of his earlier approach. Despite some short verse passages, *The Anger of Achilles* is predominantly a prose translation, and the level of the prose itself has, with due allowance for the subject matter, not changed much from the 'staid and simple' style adopted in *The Golden Ass*. Here, for instance, is Agamemnon addressing Achilles in the quarrel scene in Book 1.131–7:

> Do not argue with me, Achilles!' shouted Agamemnon. 'I refuse to be bullied. So I must surrender Chryseis, and expect no compensation – is that it? You, I suppose, are to keep your prize of honour and leave me chafing empty-handed? No, indeed! If the generous Greeks offer me some fair substitute, well and good. If not, I will choose my own prize of honour . . .[14]

Indeed, the text as revised for radio (see Wrigley, Chapter 16 in this volume) notably tones down the colloquialism at this point. But colloquialism is not the only continuity. As with Apuleius, a Celtic dimension is introduced, in reference to the 'Irish and Welsh bards'—Graves's Welsh connections being no less important to him than his Irish ones. The cases of Homer and Apuleius are not exactly similar; in Apuleius's case, it is the *author's* style which has the Celtic affinities, whereas in Homer's it is the *translator's*. In each case, however, it is a typically Gravesian twist that it is his knowledge of Celtic mythology which makes him specially qualified as an English translator of Greek and Latin.

FOOTNOTES, CUTS, AND EXPANSIONS

The plain prose style is thus central to Graves's practice as a translator; and an integral part of this is his attitude to footnotes, cuts, and expansions. For 'the nuisance of footnotes' he repeatedly professes his

[13] Graves (1960a). [14] Graves (1960a), 180.

dislike; these, he says, 'distract the eye and should, wherever possible, be brought up into the text' (Graves (1965), 132). This does not—we should note—mean simply that one should avoid relegating to footnotes material present in his source-text, as (for instance) S. A. Handford had done in his Penguin volume of Caesar's *The Conquest of Gaul.*[15] Rather, as Graves observes à propos of his Suetonius translation: 'Wherever his references are incomprehensible to anyone not closely familiar with the Roman scene, I have also brought up into the text a few words of explanation that would normally have appeared in a footnote.'[16]

His Lucan version, however, stands out as an exception to this no-footnote rule. If we open the first full spread of pages, we find (on p. 26) a full eight footnotes. Footnote 1 tells us simply: 'The whole passage is heavily satirical.' Page 27 has six more. Five of these begin as follows: 'Nero fancied himself as a charioteer . . . '; 'Nero had a noticeable squint'; 'Nero was grossly fat'; 'Nero was ashamed of his premature baldness'; and 'Nero's musical and poetic talents were a by-word at Rome'. Nor does it end there. Here are two further, random examples. In Book 4.313–18 Graves translates:

> Like beasts [the starving Pompeians] pulled at the udders of their slaughtered mares, and finding no milk in them sucked the corrupt blood instead; or they bruised grass and leaves, pressed juice from the green shoots and pith of trees, and collected dew drops from the branches.

—but notes: 'It would have been more sensible to dig under the trees for the water accumulated there during the flood which had caused the shoots to sprout.'[17] And on the page opposite, where Lucan refers to 'the broiling tropical island of Meroë . . . where the naked Garamantians plough their fields . . . ', Graves is again brisk:

> A geographical error. The Garamantians (now the Karamatse of the Niger Bend) were then living in the Fezzan Oasis of the Sahara, hundreds of miles nearer Spain than the people of Meroë in the Sudan, which lay seven degrees south of Fezzan.[18]

Indeed, Graves's attitude to his Lucan version as a whole led to a cooling-off of relations between him and E. V. Rieu. The Penguin

[15] Handford (1951), 26.
[16] Graves (1957b), 8.
[17] Graves (1956), 94.
[18] Graves (1956), 95.

Archives held at the University of Bristol reveal tantalizingly guarded expressions of concern at the time; thus, in July 1955 we find the Penguin editor A. S. B. Glover asking Rieu 'whether you feel it is desirable that I should ask him to modify some of his remarks, especially his attack on Virgil's private life'. More explicit is the observation of Rieu's successor Betty Radice in February 1977, that 'Old E.V.R. always said it was a blot on the series and he regretted "letting Graves get away with it"'.[19]

In mitigation, we may point to an element of principle here; for Graves consistently approves the principle of allowing the translator generous scope for expansions and cuts. Indeed, in his 'Moral Principles in Translation' he professes to have had 'only amicable feelings for the Finnish translator' who cut three chapters from *Count Belisarius*.[20] In the introduction to *The Anger of Achilles* he undertakes to cut not only those 'post-Homeric interpolations that spoil the narrative', but also certain of Homer's 'formal phrases of which one tires after awhile'.[21]

Conversely, a good translator (in Graves's view) may add material. One of his poetic heroes, the Tudor poet John Skelton, had produced a version of Diodorus Siculus, based on the Latin version of Poggio Bracciolini, in which he had done just this. In 'Moral Principles' Graves quotes a passage from Skelton's version as an example of the liberties a gifted translator might take. Here is Skelton's version, together with Poggio's Latin:

> But Hercules, having pity on the miserable depopulation and lamentable destruction of so noble a country, devised the means for to deliver them of this mischief. He animated himself to pourvey a redress, and by reason of this prudent policy he utterly destroyed all the wild beasts aforesaid and saved the country from all danger of the wild beasts aforesaid. And so all the coasts adjacent he set in quiet and made them convenable and commodious to be inhabited, in making the soil apt for to be sown with all manner of grain, to plant and graft all manner of trees bearing fruit, to order their vines and improve the ground with such economical feats of husbandry that the ground was encrassate and

[19] Both documents in Bristol University Library Penguin Archive file DM 1107/L66. I take this opportunity to thank the staff of the Library for their courtesy and assistance.

[20] Graves (1965), 129. We may in passing admire the ease with which Graves lets his readers know that even some of his less well-known works have been translated into Finnish.

[21] Graves (1965), 132–3.

> enfatted meetly for the fructuous increase of their oils. Thus Hercules destroyed all the wild beasts and worms and so enprospered the region of Libya, that it flourished in worldly felicity and prosperous wealth more than any other realm of our knowledge or experience.

> *Tum in Libya feris beluis plena nonnullas quas subegit oras ita domesticas reddidit, ut agrorum cultura, plantis fructiferis, vitibus, oleis, fertiles redderentur. Ita Libyam antea ob feras multiplices infestam ac desertam, adeo habitabilem cultamque praebuit, ut nulli alteri regioni cederet fertilitate.*

Skelton's version is delightful—but clearly not strictly Diodorus, nor even Poggio Bracciolini. Within Graves's own oeuvre this practice of supplementing the original may best be illustrated by his translation of Suetonius. We have noted his disarming observation that he has 'added a few words of explanation' where modern readers might find the original obscure. The extent of this is perhaps best illustrated from a memo drawn up for Penguin by John Bramble around 1970:

> More difficult is the question of Graves' supplements and explanatory glosses . . . For example, on p. 16, 'he pacified the province' gives rise to 'At any rate, on his arrival in Spain he rapidly subdued the Lusitanian mountaineers, captured Brigantium, the capital of Galicia, and returned to Rome . . . '. On p. 31, the mention of Aegisthus allows a conceit entirely of the translator's making . . . On p. 39, we hear of woodcutters, and the size of the cottage, on the basis of what can only be conjecture . . .

'Beyond a certain point,' Bramble concludes, feelingly, 'it becomes unacceptable.'[22] It does, however, illustrate how Graves is prepared to view translation as being more than a representation of the mere words of the original. All of which takes us back to the politics of the plain style.

THE POLITICS OF THE PLAIN STYLE

The choice or affectation of a plain prose style is not, of course, an abrogation of all stylistic choice. It something which calls for

[22] Penguin Archive DM 1107/L72. I quote this by kind permission of John Bramble.

discrimination, in the avoidance of extremes. In *The Reader Over Your Shoulder*, their 1943 guide to clear thought and expression in English, Graves and Alan Hodge single out for praise the 'all-purpose English prose . . . which avoided the excesses both of coarse familiarity and of ornate abstruseness', whose rise they trace to the seventeenth century. Such a style avoids the 'foppish rhetoric' of the Elizabethans John Lyly and Sir Philip Sidney, which Graves and Hodge blame on the fact they are both recent graduates. Among the better writers of the seventeenth century, they note, Ben Jonson had (somewhat anachronistically) 'served in the Army', and hence 'it was natural that his unambiguous moral judgements should be expressed in a firm and lucid style' (note here the link between style and morality). Likewise, John Bunyan 'had served as a common soldier under Cromwell', and hence 'the dialogue of *The Pilgrim's Progress* suggests, in its economy and picturesqueness, the verbatim report of a capable assize-clerk'.[23] The ideal plain prose stylist, then, should be educated, but not too much or too recently, and preferably should have an army career behind him—someone, in short, like Robert Graves.

The plain style, then, should avoid excesses of not only euphuism but also of colloquialism. This same aesthetic is naturally carried over into Graves's plain-prose translations. À propos of *The Golden Ass*, he writes to E. V. Rieu in 1946 professing himself 'appalled to find how difficult it is to be modern without falling in to US slang'.[24] Similarly, in his introduction to *The Anger of Achilles* he writes that, 'so primitive a setting forbids present-day colloquialisms, and I have kept the diction a little old-fashioned'. Over-colloquialism can, indeed, be practically a mark of moral turpitude. The villain of Graves's 1955 novel *Homer's Daughter*, Antinous, typically speaks in a very offhand and familiar way. Consider this account of his conversation with the Telemachus figure Clytoneus with the passage from *Odyssey* 2.301–5 on which it is based:

> Antinous sauntered up with a cheerful smile and clasped Clytoneus' hand. 'My dear Prince,' he cried, beaming, 'how glad I am that you have come to join us! You were seething and walloping like a stewpot, back there in the Temple of Poseidon . . . Well, well. Public speaking exhausts a man . . . and I dare say you are feeling peckish . . . '[25]

[23] Graves and Hodge (1943), 80–3. [24] In Hare (1995), 195–6.
[25] Graves (1955b) 84.

Ἀντίνοος δ᾽ ἰθὺς γελάσας κίε Τηλεμάχοιο·
ἔν τ᾽ ἄρα οἱ φῦ χειρὶ ἔπος τ᾽ ἔφατ᾽ ἔκ τ᾽ ὀνόμαζε·
'Τηλέμαχ᾽ ὑψαγόρη, μένος ἄσχετε, μή τί τοι ἄλλο
ἐν στήθεσσι κακὸν μελέτω ἔργον τε ἔπος τε,
ἀλλὰ μάλ᾽ ἐσθιέμεν καὶ πινέμεν, ὡς τὸ πάρος περ.'

Graves's own relationship with the colloquial seems peculiarly fraught. His novels, in which one would expect to find most colloquial dialogue, are set in a bewildering range of periods and milieus, as the titles reveal: *The Golden Fleece, King Jesus, I, Claudius, Count Belisarius, Wife to Mr Milton, Sergeant Lamb of the Ninth, Seven Days in New Crete.* Graves shows little interest in writing a typical 'realistic' novel; in other words, a novel where characters would be expected to speak in a range of contemporary styles. Indeed, the one apparent exception to this rule, his 1936 novel of stamp-collecting *Antigua, Penny, Puce*, has a narrative tricksily ending thirteen years after the date of publication.[26]

However, this avoidance of the contemporary itself raises another issue. How does the historical novelist navigate his way between the Scylla of pseudo-archaism and the Charybdis of anachronism? Certainly Graves is aware of this dilemma. The former problem is well illustrated by a passage from *Antigua, Penny, Puce*, where the conventional aspiring author Oliver is writing a historical novel, of which we read only a few lines:

> 'Nay,' cried the good bailiff of Hochschloss, 'all folk who journey through this bailiwick must first drink the health of my Lord the Duke: in mead, be they poor; in good Rhine wine, be they of the better sort.'[27]

As for the problem of anachronism, we may cite Graves's quotation of a (possibly apocryphal) novel by an unnamed twentieth-century writer, in which one Tudor lady 'remarks[s] brightly to her chivalrous hero, "I hate parties, don't you, darling?"'[28] We may tentatively suggest that Graves's frequent choice of *very* remote settings for his historical/fantasy novels is one way out of this bind; given that *any*

[26] Graves is not often viewed as a postmodern author, but *Antigua, Penny, Puce* has fair claims to that title, containing not only play with conventions of time-reference (and so also genre), but also with parody and pastiche (historical fiction, Victorian epistolography, broadsheet balladry, legal documents, and newspaper reports), authorial omniscience, and metafiction.

[27] Graves (1968), 120; parodied later in the same novel.

[28] Graves (1965), 120.

dialogue set in (say) second-millennium Colchis is *bound* to be anachronistic, the reader implicitly expects a lower degree of verisimilitude than s/he would in a novel of present-day life.

This is not, of course, to say that Graves could not write effective contemporary dialogue; *Good-bye to All That* is full of it, albeit presented as transcript from life rather than Graves's own composition. Even here, however, it is notable that there are few departures from broadly conventional English. These are usually for more or less comic relief; we may think of the 'proletarians' in the public fever-hospital in chapter 2 ('That young Matthew was a fair toff'), the obnoxious Carthusian slang of chapter 8 ('You'll get cocked-up for festivity'), or at best the comic-affectionate Wenglish of the Welsh soldier 'Dym Bacon' in chapter 25 ('Do you call this a bloody breakfast, man? Dym bacon, dym sausages, dym herrings, dym bloody anything!').[29] The better working-class characters speak a simple, dignified form of the standard language ('If we get half a platoon of Mons Angels, that's about all we will get'; 'Shouldn't take that, sir; it will bring you no luck').[30]

It is tempting here to suggest an implicit contrast between Graves's terse, spare style and the frivolous late-Victorian Oirishry of his father's verse; we may think of Alfred Perceval Graves's best-known work, the comic song 'Father O'Flynn' ('Powerfullest preacher, and | Tinderest teacher, and | Kindliest creature in ould Donegal'). Alfred Perceval's colloquialism dated rapidly; mounting tension in Ireland from the late Victorian era, the Easter Rising of 1916, and the establishment of the Free State in 1922 all helped dry up the market for such literary creations. Yet Alfred Perceval's verse possesses real technical virtuosity, of a W. S. Gilbertian variety (a factor which may have contributed to Robert's emphasis on the inadequacy of mere technique for true poetry). Moreover, it was genuinely popular in its day, and beyond; for much of the 1950s, while Robert was producing his translations, he was in part supported by royalties on this song.[31] Implicitly at least, his plain-prose translations, along with his insistence on their 'Irish' dimension, offer a reproach to Alfred Perceval's debased Hiberno-English pseudo-realism.[32]

[29] Graves (1957a), 19, 49, 219.

[30] References from Graves (1957a), 124, 100.

[31] Graves (1995), 206, 255.

[32] Graves's self-identification as Irish has been variously received in Ireland itself; see Ling (2011), 571. On the wider politics of translation in Ireland, see Cronin (1996).

TRANSLATION AND SELF-POSITIONING

We have just touched on Robert Graves's use of translation as a means of self-positioning vis à vis his father. We move on now to his self-positioning vis à vis other translators. All four of Graves's translatees had received classic English translations in the early modern period: Apuleius by Adlington in 1585, Suetonius by Holland in 1606, Lucan by Marlowe (published posthumously) in 1600, the *Iliad* by Chapman in 1598. About Adlington's Apuleius Graves is effusive: it is variously 'vigorous', 'extravagant', and even 'superb', and Adlington himself 'a pretty good scholar'. Clearly the man who can provide a modern English replacement for this version must claim to be a pretty good scholar and stylist himself.

In the case of Lucan, Graves is able to acknowledge the 'magnificence' of Marlowe's translation—but fortunately Marlowe had not got beyond the first book. Graves next turns to Rowe's version of 1718, quoting Samuel Johnson's description of it as 'one of the greatest productions of English poetry'. Graves is unimpressed; the language has here 'lost its exuberance' since Marlowe's day, and moreover, Rowe 'adds mistranslation to Lucan's obscurity'.[33] Thus Graves claims not only to be a superior translator to Rowe (perhaps not so great a claim), but also to be a better English critic (and Latinist) than Johnson.

Most notable, however, is Graves's introduction to Lucan, where the Roman poet is quite gratuitously identified with Ezra Pound, 'the most Lucan-like of the modernists', and as such appealing primarily to the 'young and disorientated'. As I have noted elsewhere, Graves believes that Lucan 'us[es] Caesar as a whipping-boy for Nero', just as his editor Housman used other editors as a whipping-boy for Lucan.[34] By the same token, it seems clear that Graves is using Lucan, with his literary preciosities, factual ignorance, and general psychological flakiness, as a whipping-boy for Pound. At the same time, it is worth remembering how Graves here disregards his own self-denying ordinance on the use of footnotes. Given the Lucan connection, it is tempting to suggest that this too is literary self-positioning; for Housman, the famous editor of Lucan *in usum editorum*, has more than anyone a claim to greatness as both classical scholar and as poet (being, indeed, one of relatively few contemporaries whom Graves

[33] Graves (1956), 21–2. [34] See Burton (1995), 191–218.

admired). Graves's annotations may at least plausibly be read as an exercise in Housmanesque waspishness and reductivism.

Graves's introduction to Suetonius is, following his *contretemps* with Rieu over the Lucan introduction, short to the point of curtness. However, *The Anger of Achilles* is a more complex case. Tactfully, Graves spends little time comparing his work with that of other translators, saying only that he approves of Lattimore's 1951 version—but only as a 'crib', as he fails adequately to 'remedy [Homer's] defects'.[35] However, two at least of the previous translators from Homer were figures of great importance in Graves's life. I have in mind Samuel Butler, whose plain-prose *Iliad* and *Odyssey* appeared in 1898 and 1900 respectively, and T. E. Lawrence, whose rather more ornate *Odyssey* translation came out in 1932.

The influence of Butler upon the young Graves is well known, and many aspects of his thought and general style Graves does not repudiate. Graves's attachment to the plain-prose style has its pre-echo in Butler's own manifesto as a translator of Homer:

> The genius of the language into which a translation is being made is the first thing to be considered; if the original was readable, the translation must be so also . . . It follows that a translation should depart hardly at all from the modes of speech current in the translator's own times . . . [36]

Graves's belief in the *Odyssey*'s female authorship goes straight back to Butler, and of course forms the basis for his 1955 novel *Homer's Daughter*.[37] His belief that the *Iliad* is an extended satire at the expense of the Dark Age chieftains is largely a development of Butler's views as set out in *The Humour of Homer* (1892). However, Graves must have been aware that his cult of the White Goddess would not have approved itself unreservedly to the sceptical atheist Butler. Against this background, we may see Graves's engagement with Butler in the 1950s as part of a somewhat uneasy process: both affirming his Butlerian heritage in writing *Homer's Daughter* and in his practice of the plain prose style, and moving away from it in his rejection of the *Odyssey*'s status as true poetry and his supplying a mixed poetry-and-prose version of the *Iliad* which supplied the element of poetic dignity absent from Butler's somewhat burlesque version.

[35] Graves (2001), 177. [36] See Butler (1898), v.
[37] See the essay by Murnaghan, Ch. 3 in this volume.

Graves's relation to T. E. Lawrence is, if anything, more intense and complex. Lawrence is to some extent Graves's *alter ego*. Both men had an Anglo-Irish-Welsh background, a love of scholarship (and of climbing), a distinguished war record; each had written a notorious war memoir. Indeed, Graves's 1927 biography of the man, *Lawrence and the Arabs*, repeatedly shows Graves using Lawrence to locate himself, both socially and intellectually.[38] The Acknowledgements alone are revealing:

> Mrs. Fontana, Mrs. Thomas Hardy, Mrs. Lawrence (his mother), Mrs. Kennington, Mrs. Bernard Shaw, Field-Marshall Viscount Allenby, Colonel John Buchan, Colonel R. V. Buxton, Colonel Alan Dawnay, Mr. E. M. Forster, Mr. Philip Graves, Sir Robert Graves, Dr. D. G. Hogarth, Mr. Cecil Jane, Mr. Eric Kennington, Mr Arnold Lawrence [a younger brother], Sir Henry MacMahon, Private Palmer of the Royal Tank Corps, Serjeant Pugh of the Royal Air Force, Mr. Vyvyan Richards, Lord Riddell, Mr. Siegfried Sassoon, Lord Stamfordham, the Dean of Winchester, Mr. C. Leonard Woolley, and others.

To be sure, Graves had impeccable *haut bourgeois* connections. Even so, this is still quite some parade: distinguished soldiers, novelists, poets, dons, archaeologists, and churchmen rubbing shoulders with aristocrats, mothers, younger brothers, and a few Other Ranks. The sense of self-positioning continues in the opening words of the account proper: 'I write of him as Lawrence since I first knew him by that name, though, with the rest of his friends, I now usually address him as "T.E.".'

But if Graves saw Lawrence in part as an *alter ego*, he was also his mirror image. Lawrence had served as a guerrilla leader, Graves as a regular infantry officer. Lawrence was fascinated by technology, Graves looked with suspicion even on a typewriter. Lawrence saw the future in the 'little man' and the corporate State, whereas Graves increasing cultivated the individual and the cosmopolitan. Most tellingly, the two men differed on literary stylistics. Graves wrote critically in *Good-bye to All That* of the 'furious keying-up style' in *The Seven Pillars of Wisdom*. Lawrence's *Odyssey* had been widely, and understandably, criticized for swerving between Charles Doughty-esque archaism on the one hand and Edwardian schoolboy slang on the other. Graves's plain-prose *Iliad* may be viewed in part as a riposte to

[38] Graves (1927).

Lawrence and his 'keyed-up' style of translation. Arguably, indeed, Graves's *Lawrence and the Arabs* is his first major translation: a plain-prose intra-lingual version of *The Seven Pillars of Wisdom*, analogous to his later plain-prose inter-lingual versions.

Not least important, perhaps, is the difference between the two men's views on the authorship of the *Odyssey*. Graves, as we have noted, remained in this regard a disciple of Butler. In 1945 we find him writing to E. V. Rieu about how the work 'suggest[ed] the hand of a predecessor of Aphra Behn, Anita Loos, Amanda Ros and who was it wrote *Gone with the Wind*?'[39] Ten years later, in *Homer's Daughter*, the heroine Nausicaa (closer to the Homeric Penelope and Telemachus than to her namesake), lying sleepless in Eumaeus's hut, discovers she has no difficulty composing 'beautiful, smooth-flowing hexameter verses'—these being the first draft of the *Odyssey*:

> 'To be a poet is easy,' I thought . . . Eumaeus, when I told him later about my experience, gave credit to the goddess Cerdo, who inspires poetry and oracular utterances . . . ; but I had the fleas to thank for keeping me awake . . .

The *Odyssey*, then, has the outward form of poetry, but Nausicaa herself knows it is not truly inspired by the goddess. Indeed, with his own religion of the White Goddess now fully developed, Graves has an ambivalent attitude to women as poets in general. As he notes, 'poetry should not be an affair of sex any more than, for example, surgery . . . Sex has no place in the operating-theatre. Poetry is a sort of operating-theatre'[40]—being, we assume, at once a peculiarly masculine affair and a peculiarly asexual one. True poetry, that is; and if the *Odyssey* is the work of an 'authoress', it cannot *a fortiori* be true poetry. Lawrence, on the other hand, had been clear that the *Odyssey* was the work of a man—'a bookworm, no longer young . . . married but not exclusively, a dog-lover, often hungry and thirsty, dark-haired'. His attitude towards women is one of 'infuriating male condescension . . . [Nausicaa] fades, unused', while Penelope is just a 'sly, cattish wife'. If Graves had hero-worshipped Lawrence before, he now takes the opportunity to distance himself from him on the Homeric question.

[39] Quoted in Hare (1995), 194.

[40] Graves (1951b), 98–9. '*-ESS*', Written in 1929, but apparently not published earlier.

CONCLUSIONS

Our main points should probably be clear. First, Graves's claims to be pursuing a plain-prose style in his classical translations are basically justified. It is, however, simplistic to accept this as being just a matter of making the texts accessible to the uninitiated. Moreover, such domesticization comes at a price. Modern scholars using his Suetonius may wince, for instance, at 'sergeant' for *centurio* or 'Regiment' for *legio*; surely 'centurion' and 'legion' are hardly abstruse in English. Underlying his practice, however, is his sense of human behaviour as constantly repeating the same basic tropes in different guises. Modern scholars of reception often point to the ways in which writing about the past can be a way of writing about the present. It is far from clear that Graves made a sharp distinction between the two.

Secondly, Graves's insistence on the plain style is crucial to his self-fashioning. A recurrent theme of his writings is the way in which the upper-middle-class, half-German boy from Wimbledon is able to communicate with the mass of his fellow-Britons. And indeed, this seems to be largely justified. Nonetheless, Graves's evident belief in his gift may reflect a need for reassurance that he had indeed transcended his origins. This need may have been heightened by his lifestyle in the late 1940s and beyond; with his return to Deyá after the Second World War, he was necessarily less in touch from day to day with ordinary speakers of English, and more with cosmopolitan and largely educated friends he gathered round him there, notwithstanding his friendships with the working-class Alan Sillitoe and (slightly later) Spike Milligan. Perhaps more problematic are Graves's claims to a sort of hypostatized Celticity which gives him special insight into the meaning of Greek and Latin texts and how they should be translated. Graves also uses his classical translations as a means locating himself as an author, both personally in respect to characters such as Lawrence or Pound, and also within the wider scheme of English literature.

As a corollary to these points, I may return to my earlier observation on the prevalence of plain-prose ideals in post-war English stylistics. George Orwell's celebrated essay 'Politics and the English Language' of 1946 was one manifestation of this; of course Orwell's 1948 novel *Nineteen Eighty-Four* is in large part an exploration of similar themes. The same year saw also the appearance of Ernest Gowers' *Plain Words* (followed in 1951 by *The ABC of Plain Words*). By the mid-1950s Graves could be seen, at least by some, as a representative or even a prophet of this new aesthetic. Consider the well-known leading article by J. D. Scott in the *Spectator* of 1 October 1954:

> Genuflections towards Dr Leavis and Professor Empson, admiration for people whom the Thirties by-passed, Orwell above all (and, for another example, Mr Robert Graves) are indeed signs by which you may recognize the Movement... The Movement, as well as being anti-phoney, is anti-wet; sceptical, robust, ironic...'

While we can only speculate what Graves would have felt being co-opted as a forerunner of Kingsley Amis, it is clear at least that it was precisely this quality of worldly-wise plain speaking which commended him to this new post-war audience.[41] We might also draw wider connections, and link the Penguin Classics project of the late 1940s–1950s to the politics of the Butskellite settlement generally. Certainly, Allen Lane did take pride in offering attractive editions of good literature at modest prices. We may note also that one of the key members of the Penguin editorial team, W. E. Williams, had during the Second World War run the Army Bureau of Current Affairs, a body often credited with spreading left-wing ideals among servicemen and servicewomen.[42] The difficulty here, however, lies in what we might call a remoteness problem. There is nothing in the correspondence between Graves and Rieu to suggest this was ever the intention of the versions. While the homely tone of Rieu's own prefaces certainly lend themselves to this interpretation, and while he and Graves concurred in the desirability of a sturdy, plain prose style, they seem to have done so for very different reasons. Moreover, as we have seen, the plain-prose aesthetic is not unique to the 1940s and 1950s. Apart from Butler's plain-prose *Iliad* and *Odyssey*, we might point to W. H. D. Rouse's *The Story of Odysseus* (1937), a far plainer version than either Butler's or Rieu's; an extract from the preface should give the flavour: [43]

> Those who like thrillers and detective novels will find excitement enough here... Those who like fairy tales will find nothing better than Polyphemus the Goggle-eye. Those who like psychology will find plenty to entertain them... they will find that Homer uses [the words] people did use in daily life and did not reject blunt words or even invented words.

[41] See further Morrison (1980), 218–21. For a different view from within the Movement, see the comments of Donald Davie (1952), 28: 'minor modern poets... have employed successfully for their limited ends a personal diction deliberately impure, eccentric and mannered. Robert Graves... [is] one example.'

[42] On whom see now Meredeen (2008).

[43] Rouse (1937), vii–ix.

Arguing that Graves's style of translation reflects a cultural *Zeitgeist* can, it seems, be achieved only if we define the period in question rather broadly, and do not question too deeply the ways in which the spirit moved. There is inevitably a sense of which Graves was a man of his time and background, for all his attempts to transcend them; to this extent his work clearly needs to be set in its context. But such contextualization in itself must be counterbalanced by consideration of the individual, the particular, and the downright eccentric.

What, then, in the last analysis, do we make of Graves's account of translations as a 'moral matter', an evaluation of 'how much [the translator owes] to the letter, and how much to the spirit'? Graves would have been mischievously aware of the biblical background to this saying—St Paul's words at 2 Corinthians 3: 6, that 'the letter killeth, but the spirit giveth life'. The obvious interpretation is that a literal translation takes the life out of a piece, and that we should prefer a freer version which captures the spirit of the thing. Graves would, I think, not have dissented from this. Indeed, he might also have wished to have applied to himself the words he used of Apuleius's gargantuan translation of the Greek *Lucius, or the Ass*: 'He has touched nothing . . . which he has not transformed.'

I began by pointing to the apparent paradox of the inspired devotee of the Muse being also the faithful translator. But if this is a paradox, it is one Graves himself recognized and addressed. Early in *The White Goddess* (p. 21), Graves advances the view that English *poetic* diction should be 'neither over-stylized nor vulgar'. In other words, poetry and prose share a similar aesthetic basis, even if poetry contains also a level of formalism not found in prose. Translation is essentially a moral matter partly because the translator is required to observe a basic level of integrity in his preservation of the essential meaning of the original, a meaning does not reside in the individual words but in the overall intention of the original author. The good interpreter is one who can discern and reproduce this essence faithfully, even if this involves a certain amount of addition to or subtraction from the original. This degree of integrity is comparable the moral imperative on the poet to use his special insight to report the world as his vocation demands. [44]

[44] I am indebted for suggestions to the anonymous OUP reader, to my colleagues at Birmingham who commented on a draft version, to Lorna Hardwick, and to those present when this material was first aired in St Andrews.

8

Robert Graves's *The Greek Myths* and Matriarchy

Sibylle Ihm

I first came to know of Robert Graves right at the beginning of my studies of classical philology at the University of Hamburg in the early eighties. One of my academic teachers spoke about Graves's book *The Greek Myths*. In his opinion this book provided a fresh view on the subject. It was some time later, when I was more advanced in my studies, that I began to wonder if the myths and commentaries on the myths written by Graves could be entirely correct. When I read other studies popular in Germany—such as the works of Karl Kerényi and Martin Nilsson—I wondered why they differed so much from Graves's approach.

Central to Graves's, so to speak, creative mishandling of the Greek myths is his idea that generally all myths deal with a universal female figure. She is seen as the goddess of a matriarchal cult, where all the male figures are sacred kings who are put to death after a brief reign. His interpretations may appear a bit far-fetched, and in order to illustrate his thoughts, some examples will be given. For example, in chapter 42d, Graves retells the myth of Phaethon:

> One morning Helius yielded to his son Phaethon who had been constantly plaguing him for permission to drive the sun-chariot. Phaethon wished to show his sisters Prote and Clymene what a fine fellow he was: and his fond mother Rhode (whose name is uncertain because she had been called by both her daughters' names and by that of Rhode) encouraged him. But, not being strong enough to check the career of the white horses, which his sisters had yoked for him, Phaethon drove them first so high above the earth that everyone shivered, and then so

> near the earth that he scorched the fields. Zeus, in a fit of rage, killed him with a thunderbolt, and he fell into the river Po. His grieving sisters were changed into poplar-trees on its banks, which weep amber tears; or, some say, into alder trees.

Graves gives the following explanation (42.2):

> [The story] has a mythic importance in its reference to the annual sacrifice of a royal prince, on the one day reckoned as belonging to the terrestrial, but not to the sidereal year, namely that which followed the shortest day. The sacred king pretended to die at sunset; the boy interrex was at once invested with his titles, dignities and sacred implements, married to the queen, and killed twenty-four hours later. In Thrace, torn to pieces by women disguised as horses, but at Corinth, and elsewhere, dragged at the tail of a sun-chariot drawn by maddened horses, until he was crushed to death . . . The myths of Glaucus,[1] Pelops[2] and Hippolytus[3] refer to this custom, which seems to have been taken to Babylon by the Hittites.[4]

I have searched a long time for the aforementioned ancient Thracian women dressed up like horses, but there weren't any. It's the same with Corinth. No maddened horses drawing a sun-chariot can be

[1] Glaucus (71a) was a Corinthian king. One version of the myth says that he was devoured by his mares, crazed from drinking the water of an enchanted spring. Another version records that his death was caused by the goddess Aphrodite, whose anger was provoked by the fact that Glaucus did not let his mares copulate, in order for them to run faster. So she angered his horses. In the end, the horses tore Glaucus's body apart.

[2] Pelops (109j) wanted to marry Hippodamia, the daughter of King Oenomaus of Pisa. Oenamaus had already killed thirteen suitors of Hippodamia after beating them in a chariot-race. Pelops (or alternatively, Hippodamia herself) convinced Oenomaus's charioteer to sabotage the linchpins attaching the wheels to the chariot. Oenomaus died in the race. Graves obviously confused the names of Pelops and Oenomaus.

[3] Hippolytus (101g) was a son of Theseus and either Antiope or Hippolyte. Hippolytus rejected the advances of Phaedra, his stepmother. Then Phaedra told Theseus that Hippolytus had raped her. Theseus believed her and cursed Hippolytus. Hippolytus's horses were frightened either by a sea monster or a wild bull, sent by Dionysus. The horses dragged Hippolytus to his death.

[4] The Hittites are an ancient people who established a kingdom in northern Turkey from the eighteenth century BC. In the fourteenth century BC the Hittite Kingdom was at its height, encompassing central Anatolia, north-western Syria, and upper Mesopotamia. After 1180 BC the kingdom disintegrated into several independent 'Neo-Hittite' city states, some of which survived until as late as the eighth century BC. The Old Hittite Kingdom managed to conquer Babylon at one point during the sixteenth century BC, but made no attempt to govern there. There is no evidence to show that the Hittites brought myths of any kind to Babylon.

found. The name Phaethon obviously means shining and this myth clearly belongs to the myths of stars. If Phaethon is the son of Eos, goddess of the dawn, Phaethon could be the impersonation of the morning-star.

Graves gives a similar explanation in the myth of the giant Diomedes (130b), king of Thrace. Diomedes owned four man-eating horses, the so-called Mares of Diomedes. Heracles had to steal the mares as his eighth labour. In the end Heracles fed Diomedes to his own horses. Heracles' friend Abderos, who was left in charge of them, was eaten too. Graves writes (130.1): 'Heracles . . . annulled the custom by which wild women in horse-masks used to chase and eat the sacred king at the end of his reign; instead he was killed in an organized chariot crash.' But again, no word of this story can be found in Herodotus.[5]

Graves comes to the following conclusion (71.1):

> The myth of Lycurgus . . . and Diomedes . . . suggest that the pre-Hellenic sacred king was torn in pieces at the close of his reign by women disguised as mares. In Hellenic times, this ritual was altered to death by being dragged at the tail of a four-horse chariot, as in the myth of Hippolytus . . . Laius . . . Oenomaus . . . Abderus . . . Hector . . . and others.

In his introduction Graves explains his theories further:

> A study of Greek mythology should begin with a consideration of what political and religious systems existed in Europe before the arrival of

[5] Graves gives Herodotus 1.168 as a source. This myth is widely preserved, but not in Herodotus. Graves thinks—wrongly—that two other heroes came to death by their horses. One of them is King Laius, father of the famous Oedipus. Oedipus was told by the Delphic Oracle that he would kill his father and marry his mother. Thinking that he was from Corinth, he set out toward Thebes to avoid this fate. On the road he met Laius. Oedipus refused to defer to the king, although Laius's attendants ordered him to. Being angered, Laius either rolled a chariot-wheel over his foot or hit him with his whip, and Oedipus killed Laius. No horses were involved. Graves describes the death as follows (105d): 'Oedipus . . . flinging Laius on the road entangled in the reins, and whipping up the team, he made them drag him to death.' His explanation (105.8) repeats his description: 'Oedipus confessed that he felt himself disgraced as having let chariot horses drag to death Laius.' The other one is Hector, the Trojan prince and one of the greatest fighters in the Trojan War, killed by the Greek hero Achilles. After he died, Achilles attached Hector's corpse to the chariot and dragged him around the walls of Troy. Graves writes (163.4): 'Hector was a title of the Theban sacred king before the Trojan War took place; and he suffered the same fate when his reign ended—which was to be dragged in the wreck of a circling chariot.' Again, his myths and commentaries are pure imagination.

> Aryan invaders from the distant North and East... The Great goddess was regarded as immortal, changeless, and omnipotent; and the concept of fatherhood had not been introduced into religious thought... Men feared, adored, and obeyed the matriarch.[6]

He then discusses the moon's three phases, which he refers to woman's three phases—maiden, nymph, and crone—and the queen's choosing of an annual lover and his (or his substitute's) death in midwinter as a symbol of fertility, the so-called sacred king. He relates the Greek myth to this conclusion: 'Early Greek mythology is concerned, above all else, with the changing relations between the queen and her lovers';[7] 'All early myths about the gods' seduction of nymphs refer apparently to marriages between Hellenic chieftains and local Moon-priestesses';[8] 'Achean invasions of the thirteenth century B.C. seriously weakened the matrilineal tradition... and when the Dorians arrived, towards the close of the second millennium, patrilineal succession became the rule.'[9] In Graves's opinion, the wave of immigrations to prehistoric Greece, at least the Achaians and the Dorians, replaced the original Pelasgian matriarchal social and religious institutions with patriarchal ones. Graves thinks further that the local myths were consciously or unconsciously altered to bring them into line with the invaders' beliefs. The invaders found illustrations of the myths and rituals, but were unwilling or unable to interpret them correctly. So they invented their own explanatory stories. Graves calls this distortion of sacred pictures 'iconotropy'.[10] His aim is to reconstruct the correct myths, or what he considers to be the correct versions, and to develop the underlying matriarchal myths.

Pharand has shown recently that Graves worked simultaneously on *The White Goddess* and *The Greek Myths*. He comes to the conclusion that 'Many of the explanations in *The Greek Myths* incorporate the thesis of *The White Goddess*: that ancient Moon-Goddess-worshipping matriarchies were subordinated by patriarchal forces who placed male divinities in positions of supremacy'.[11] Pharand points out that Graves had developed his theory of the goddess and the idea and term

[6] Graves (1955a), 13. The German translation *Griechische Mythologie* by Hugo Steinfeld is more direct: 'Ein Studium der griechischen Mythologie sollte, wie bereits Bachofen und Brieffault forderten, mit dem Kennenlernen des matriarchalischen und totemistischen Systems, das in Europa vor dem Erscheinen der patriarchalischen Eroberer aus Osten und Norden herrschte, beginnen.' Von Ranke-Graves (1987), 12.

[7] Graves (1955a), 16.

[8] Graves (1955a), 18.

[9] Graves (1955a), 19.

[10] Graves (1955a), 21.

[11] Pharand (2003), 182–91, 188.

'iconotropy' also in his earlier books *Historical Commentary to King Jesus* (1946) and *The Golden Fleece* (1944). By using his work *The White Goddess* as a source for *The Greek Myths*, Graves founds his interpretation on the thoughts of Graves. In this universe of self-referencing some of the wildest speculations can blossom, but unfortunately no scientific positions. Nevertheless his conceptions were more or less accepted in philological discussions for a long time.

Graves says that 'all detailed interpretations of particular legends are open to question until archaeologists can provide a more exact tabulation of tribal movements in Greece and their dates. Yet the historical and anthropological approach is the only reasonable one.'[12]

What does he mean? He himself explained 'historical' with 'successive stages, reflected in numerous myths'.[13] Graves tries to answer the unanswered question of historical research through the interpretation of the myths. His use of 'historical' is a special one. There is another reason why 'historical' isn't the right term: Graves interprets his sources in his own way and ignores everything that differs from his own view—although in the twentieth century the scientific handling of the sources had already been developed. Graves also calls his method 'anthropological', whatever this means. He says, 'the close analogues which E. Meyrowitz's Akan Cosmological Drama . . . offers to the religious and social changes are here presumed.'[14] Therefore Graves presumably had the tradition of the early evolutionists in mind.

'Pelasgians' was a term the ancient Greek writers used for the earlier Greek population. Pre-Hellenic Pelasgians, and especially the mother goddesses, are still poorly understood. Small, mostly corpulent, figurines are well known and are found in various regions originating from different epochs. These might have been created in order to represent goddesses. But it is not clear—even if several scholars support this opinion—whether the Pelasgians worshipped a great goddess, whether they were a matriarchal society, or whether the later goddess worship descended from it. And there is, of course, no evidence of sacred pictures illustrating myths in prehistoric

[12] Graves (1955a), 20; cf 22. [13] Graves (1955a), 19.

[14] Graves (1955a), 22. Cf pp. 22–3 for the Ghanian Akan religion which is theocentric and the cosmology refers to of the Akan relationship with the differing aspects the Supreme Being who is God, the Great Designer, Creator and Infinite. For Akan and Graves see Pharand (2003), 187; Pharand (2007), 67–8.

Greece. Graves himself was widely read, and it is therefore interesting to note which books he neither cited nor seemed to know: for example, Karl Kerényi's works on Greek religion, William Smith's *Dictionary of Greek and Roman Biography and Mythology* (1843–9), or Pierre Grimal's *Dictionnaire de la mythologie grecque et romaine* (1951).

The question remains: how did Graves come by the idea of a universal female figure and the existence of a matriarchy in prehistoric Greece? He found the idea of matriarchy and mother goddesses in several books written by Bachofen, Harrison, and Frazer. Kerényi especially opposed the approaches of Harrison and Frazer.

The idea of matriarchy was expounded by the Swiss anthropologist and sociologist Johann Jakob Bachofen (1815–87) in his book *Das Mutterrecht: Eine Untersuchung über die Gynaikokratie der alten Welt nach ihrer religiösen und rechtlichen Natur* (Mother-Right: An Investigation of the Religious and Juridical Character of Matriarchy in the Ancient World), published in 1861. Bachofen presents a radically new view of the role of women in a broad range of ancient societies. He assembled documentation demonstrating motherhood as the source of human society, religion, and morality. Bachofen proposes four phases of cultural evolution: he calls the first phase hetairism, where man lived in a state of sexual promiscuity. The second phase is the 'mother-right'. Promiscuity excludes any certainty of paternity, therefore the mothers were the only known parents of the younger generation. As a result they held a position of such high respect and honour that it became the foundation of a regular rule of women—they were worshipped as life-giving goddesses. The third phase was called the Dionysian, when patriarchy began to emerge. The fourth phase is the Apollonian, in which all traces of the matriarchal past were eradicated and modern civilization emerged.[15]

Mother-right and gynaecocracy or matriarchy often get mixed up.[16] Today some criteria are established which fit Bachofen's definition: Firstly, the wife does not leave her family and her old home, but stays with her children and her husband only visits her (matrilocal). Secondly, inheritance of name and of property is through the mother and not through the father (matrilineal). Such concepts have been

[15] For a recent evaluation of Bachofen's theory cf. Louis (2009), 44 ff.

[16] Cf. Rose (1911), 277–91.

rediscovered in the twentieth century. Matriarchy signifies a society in which woman rule. Bachofen most certainly thinks that women once had political and social control, which is now widely doubted.[17] Bachofen also thinks that women founded mystery religions and received all benevolence and devotion. He uses Greek myth as proof of his concept of mother-right, and is convinced that myth reflects the social realities of ancient life.[18]

Bachofen's theories on the development of culture led to a long scientific discussion, with classical philologists, in particular, arguing against them.[19] Ethnologists and psychologists, on the other hand, appreciated Bachofen's work. In 1924 Carl Albrecht Bernoulli values Bachofen highly, in his book *J. J. Bachofen und das Natursymbol* (Bachofen and the Symbolism of Nature). Another of his first defenders was the Munich psychologist Ludwig Klages in 1926. This started a lively discourse, in which Bachofen's theories were recognized as a method of going back to the earliest beginnings of culture as well as the origins of social and cultural anthropology. 'Myth and religion alike, at the end of the century, are viewed on the issues connected with the Mystery religions: sexuality, fertility, maternity, and the structure of the family.'[20]

Graves was familiar with Bachofen's work, and Bachofen has influenced scholars whom Graves used as sources for *The Greek Myths*.[21] Graves also knew of Robert Briffault (1876–1948), a French historian and social anthropologist whose mother came from Scotland. Briffault believed strongly in Bachofen's theories. He pursued the theory that early human society consisted of matriarchal 'queendoms' based on worship of the great goddess, and were characterized by pacifism and democracy. Another scholar, whom Graves mentions

[17] Briffault (1959), 83–4, whom Graves cites, comes to the following conclusion concerning the term matriarchy: 'It may, I think, be legitimately used in a relative sense, and in opposition to the term "patriarchal", when referring to a state of society in which the interests and sentiments that are directly connected with the instincts of women play a more important part than is the rule in the civilized societies with which we are most familiar.'

[18] Bachofen (1861), 79 and 73 ff.

[19] e.g. Toepffer in his book *Attische Genealogien*, published 1889, or Ernst Howald in 1926. Cf. Eugen Fehrle (1927), 43–62.

[20] Louis (2009), 49.

[21] Graves mentions Bachofen in the introduction of *Griechische Mythologie* (Von Ranke-Graves (1987), 12). The name does not appear in the English translation (p. 13).

in his introduction and even more often in his commentaries, is J. G. Frazer (1854–1941). The Scottish social anthropologist describes, in his book *The Golden Bough*, ancient and modern cults, rites, and myths and he too was affected by Bachofen's work.[22] Frazer tries to reconstitute the earliest social and religious forms of humanity. Proceeding from this point, Frazer distinguishes three steps in the evolution of man: magic, myth, and science. When man loses his belief in magic, he justifies his formerly magical rituals by declaring that they honour mythical beings. It was Frazer who originally developed the idea of the year-king's union with the goddess and his annual sacrifice.

> Such festivals [Saturnalias] seem to date from an early age in the history of agriculture, when people lived in small communities, each presided over by a sacred or divine king, whose primary duty was to secure the orderly succession of the seasons, the fertility of the earth, and the fecundity both of cattle and of women. Associated with him was his wife or other female consort, with whom he performed some of the necessary ceremonies, and who therefore shared his divine character. Originally his term of office appears to have been limited to a year, on the conclusion of which he was put to death; but in time he contrived by force or craft to extend his reign and sometimes to procure a substitute, who after a short and more or less nominal tenure of the crown was slain in his stead.[23]

Frazer broadened that theory by saying that all worship in Europe and the Aegean, which involved any kind of mother goddess, had originated in pre-Indo-European Neolithic matriarchies. But he never thought that this cult might lead to any form of gynaecocracy:

> But this social advance of women has never been carried so far as to place men as a whole in a position of political subordination to them... The theory of a gynaecocracy is in truth a dream of visionaries and pedants. And equally chimerical is the idea that the predominance of goddesses under a system of mother-kin... is a creation of the female

[22] His book was first published in 1890; then—this time in six volumes—in 1900; and again, now in twelve volumes, in 1907–15. Cf. vols. 1 and 2 of Frazer (1994).

[23] Frazer (1927), ch. 110, p. 278. Frazer was the first to analyse the relations between myths and rituals and claimed that myth emerges out of ritual during the natural process of religious evolution; cf. Frazer, *Man, God, Immortality*, *passim*, e.g. ch. 114: 'myth changes while custom remains constant; men continue to do what their fathers did before them, though the reasons on which their fathers acted have been long forgotten. The history of religion is a long attempt to reconcile old custom with new reason, to find a sound theory for an absurd practice.'

> mind. If women ever created gods, they would be more likely to give them masculine than feminine features . . . The theory that under a system of mother-kin the women rule the men and set up goddesses for them to worship is indeed so improbable in itself, and so contrary to experience, that it scarcely deserves the serious attention which it appears to have received.[24]

In Frazer's concept the mother is not the head of the family—this position was held by the senior male on her side. Frazer calls this *avunculi potestas*.[25] The cult of the great mother goddess, the *magna mater*, is part of it. Women enjoyed economic, social, and religious privileges but mother-right doesn't mean any preference given to women in general, and certainly not gynaecocracy. Graves adopts this concept: 'commander-in-chief (was) usually the queen's maternal uncle, or her brother, or the son of her maternal aunt.'[26]

Frazer's ideas, in this regard, have not stood the test of time. M. K. Louis values the new approach in Frazer's theory, but not the thesis itself: 'Frazer's innovation is to reframe a whole tradition of chthonian mythography in terms of primal anxieties about food and sex . . . What Frazer omits, of course, is the spiritual and emotional dimension in primitive religion.'[27]

Bronze Age antiquity is a field of extensive speculations. One approach maintains that first there was a native agricultural population who primarily worshipped goddesses associated with the fertility of the earth. Then, in about 2000 BC, the Greeks arrived, warriors and robbers with horses, and brought with them male deities. Afterwards resident females and incoming males were brought together in a single religious system. Of course, this hypothesis is an oversimplification and there is no evidence to prove it. The goddess or the great goddess is a primary type of female deity, but this doesn't mean that there was a single goddess who was identical across cultures. Rather, she was a concept common in many ancient cultures, existing in many countries and times, though not under the same name. However, there have also been male gods. The notion of a prehistoric mother goddess has been linked to the idea of matriarchy, or rule by

[24] Frazer (1927), ch. 56, pp. 127–9.

[25] Frazer (1910), 513; this book was originally published in Edinburgh 1881.

[26] Graves (1955a), 15. [27] Louis (2009), 22.

women. But although the evidence of the Minoan[28] and Mycenaean[29] cultures indeed show that women held a higher status than in classical Greece, there is no sign of mother-right or matriarchy. In fact, and unsatisfyingly for Graves's followers, there is no evidence to prove that matriarchy ever existed. 'Furthermore, it has recently been noted that the depiction of goddesses and similar figures might be evidence for contemporary male fantasy.'[30]

One of Frazer's and Bachofen's close disciples was Jane Ellen Harrison (1850–1928), whom Graves mentions in his introduction. She was a British classical scholar, linguist, and feminist. Harrison is one of the founders, together with Karl Kerényi and Walter Burkert, of modern studies in Greek mythology. In her book *Prolegomena to the Study of Greek Religion*, published in 1907, she tries to analyse the rites of ancient Greece and to explain the mythical thinking beneath them. She believes in Bachofen's theories,[31] and follows Frazer's concept of the matriarchal mother goddess (chapter 6), even if her

[28] Our knowledge of Minoan culture comes from pictorial material and archaeological evidence. There are several pictures and statues demonstrating worship of a goddess, and that has been regarded as evidence for matriarchy. Women seem to have had a high status as priestesses of goddesses and to have participated in the daily life of the palaces. But, as contemporary discussions show, the evidence of art can be interpreted in different ways. For example, there is little evidence that a single unified great mother or earth goddess existed. It is more likely that there were several female deities with varying functions. And as Rose (1911), 32 puts it, 'to draw sociological conclusions from religious beliefs and practises is always a hazardous course; it does not follow that, because a people chiefly worship a goddess, they treat mortal women with particular respect or reckon descent through them.' Rose sees no evidence for matriarchy; Hirvonen (1968/1992), 151 ff. accepts the view that the same material recognizes a more privileged position of women; Thomas (1973/1992), 195–219 considers the conditions of ownership and inheritance of property through the mother, the degree of freedom, and religious practices. He, on the contrary, thinks that in Minoan culture all three elements of a matriarchal society are visible.

[29] Our knowledge of Mycenaean Greek comes from four sources: the archaeological evidence; works of art; literary sources, especially Homer and Hesiod; and the Linear B tablets, contemporary documents. Billigmeier and Turner (1981) 10, 'suggest that women in Mycenaean Greece may have enjoyed a more equal socio-economic status than they did in Classical Hellas'.

[30] Culham (1987), 14; cf. Blundell (1995), 18: 'Many feminist scholars today, while accepting that some prehistoric societies were much more egalitarian than later historical ones, reject the notion of outright female dominance. As a feature of myth, rule by women . . . can best be understood, not as a memory of historical events, but as a narrative "providing justification for a present and perhaps permanent reality by giving an invented 'historical' explanation of how this reality was created". In other words, the myth explains why men and not women rule.'

[31] Harrison (1907), 261 and 283.

approach is a quite different one, with an emphasis on 'the spiritual and emotional dimension in primitive religion'.[32] Harrison, a respected historian of Greek religion, gave Frazer's popular work academic credibility.

Today mainstream anthropology has abandoned the nineteenth-century theories of primitive matriarchies in favour of discussions of matrilineality and matrilocality. Graves was well read, so we can assume that he followed the scientific discussion about matriarchy, mother goddesses, and mythological annual death. It is easy to see how Graves put together the ideas and theories found in his books. He didn't follow one opinion or one scholar, but selected those views from different sources which suited him. His ideas can be seen as a valid contribution in their historical context, despite their now obvious deviations from adequate scientific methods.

In *The Greek Myths* Graves follows a system of different steps introduced by Bachofen and Frazer: 'My method has been to assemble in harmonious narrative all the scattered elements of each myth, supported by little-known variants which may help to determine the meaning, and to answer all questions that arise, as best I can, in anthropological or historical terms.'[33] 'Yet myths, though difficult to reconcile with chronology, are always practical: they insist on some point of tradition, however distorted the meaning may have become in the telling.'[34] Whether proceeding 'step by step' with reference to Bachofen and Frazer really constitutes a scientific 'narrative' or, more likely, such a 'narrative' can be formed in this way with some hope that it will be *accepted* as a scientific one, is a question to be discussed. From today's vantage-point the answer seems to be obvious, but we have to give consideration to the argument that sometimes a strong narration, even without proper scientific background, may result in a scientific stimulus. To some extent, Graves seems to have been carried away by his concept of the great goddess and the sacred king, seeing it in seventy-one out of 171 myths.

Graves develops a kind of chronology (1.1): 'In this archaic religious system there were, as yet, neither gods nor priests, but only a universal goddess and her priestesses, woman being the dominant sex and man her frightened victim'.[35] In these archaic times cannibalism and religious murder were symbols of the uncivilized state. Also

[32] Louis (2009), 22.
[33] Graves (1955a), 22.
[34] Graves (1955a), 20.
[35] Graves (1955a), 28.

archaic is the conflict between the sacred king and his substitute (111.3). Both had had sexual intercourse with the goddess. As already mentioned, when their reigns came to an end the sacred kings were killed by women. 'The tribal Nymph, it seems, chose an annual lover from her entourage of young men, a king to be sacrificed when the year ended; making him a symbol of fertility, rather than the object of her erotic pleasure.'[36] Later, the 'Hellenic invasions of the early second millennium B.C.' changed things, and a 'male military aristocracy became reconciled to female theocracy'.[37] In the Mycenaean period, king and substitute ruled together, but not without friction. Afterwards, 'a new stage was reached, when animals came to be substituted for boys at the sacrificial altar'.[38]

Graves's premise that women were the dominant sex changes due to his interpretation of myth, first, through the use of a substitute and the prolonging of the king's reign, and through the king's refusal to die at the end of his lengthened reign. In the end, after society had become patriarchal, women were sacrificed. His other premise, that men were women's frightened victims, is verified by his interpretation of Greek myths.

It has been demonstrated that Graves constructs an imaginary world out of his interpretations of Greek myth. He considers the old stories as a source of information for prehistoric times, and the reason for his view can be found in the works of Bachofen, Frazer, Harrison, and others, who developed ideas of the matriarchy, great goddess, and sacred king. Graves sought proof for these theories in the Greek myths themselves.

Graves's works should not be underestimated. A longing for a deeper understanding had put him on a track leading away from academic methods, although his works were, and are still, a subject of discussion at universities. His ideas were more important and more influential (until today) in popular science and even esoteric circles. Naturally, his works became an inspiration for the women's liberation movement, especially during the so-called 'second-wave feminism', a period of feminist activity in the 1960s and 1970s. One of its pioneers was the American librarian Elizabeth Gould Davis, whose book *The First Sex* was published in 1971. Like Graves, Gould Davis wants to show that early human society consisted of matriarchal queendoms

[36] Graves (1955a), 14. [37] Graves (1955a), 18. [38] Graves (1955a), 19.

with the cult of the great goddess. Later, their pacifism and democracy were destroyed by the invasion of nomadic tribes who were warlike and destructive. Then the society changed, becoming based dominantly on property rights and worshipping a male deity. She argues that the replacement of the great goddess by a male deity is the theme of all surviving myth.

Another pioneer was Merlin Stone, Professor of Art and Art History at the State University of New York at Buffalo. She published her book *When God Was a Woman* in 1976.[39] Her two main sources were Margaret Murray (1863–1963)—a British anthropologist and Egyptologist, who mainly wrote about witchcraft and whose ideas were influenced by the ideas of Frazer and his sacred and sacrificed king—and Robert Graves himself. Like Graves, Stone postulates a prehistoric matriarchy which was destroyed by the patriarchal Indo-Europeans.

Women's studies in Germany were initiated by Heide Göttner-Abendroth (b. 1941). She was an activist in second-wave feminism from 1976 onwards and founded the 'Internationale Akademie für Moderne Matriarchatsforschung und Matriarchale Spiritualität' (HAGIA) in 1986.[40] Modern matriarchal studies stand in the tradition of second-wave feminism. Göttner-Abendroth focused her studies on matriarchal or matrilineal societies.[41] In her book *The Goddess and her Heros* she states that she first came to know *The Greek Myths* of Robert Graves as a student at the age of 21. She was deeply impressed by his view of history and his statements about matriarchy and the cult of the great goddess. Graves's ideas influenced her decision to pursue her research in this field.[42]

[39] First published in the UK with the title *The Paradise Papers*.

[40] The International Academy for Modern Matriarchal Studies and Matriarchal Spirituality.

[41] Göttner-Abendroth defines modern matriarchal studies as the 'investigation and presentation of non-patriarchal societies', and matriarchies as 'non-hierarchical, horizontal societies of matrilineal kinship'. In her view, matriarchy means 'non-patriarchic matrilineal societies' and a matriarchal society is an 'egalitarian and peaceful society'. She has continued to publish on feminist theories of matriarchy until recently. Among her publications are: *The Goddess and her Heros: Matriarchal Religion in Mythology, Fairy-Tales and Poetry* (1995); *Die Göttin und ihr Heros—a study in matriarchal religion* (1980); *The Dancing Goddess: Principles of a Matriarchal Aesthetic* (1991a); *Die tanzende Göttin*, (2001); and three volumes of *Das Matriarchat* dealing with contemporary matriarchal societies across the world.

[42] Göttner-Abendroth (1995), 5.

Of course, these works have been severely attacked. As previously stated, it was held against them that serious study of artefacts does not support the idea of a peaceful matriarchy, and that there is no evidence for a female monotheism.[43] The authors were academically skilled, but their scholarly standards fell short in not following the scientific discussion of Graves's books. There is no hint in their works that subsequent research following *The Greek Myths*' publication had concluded that his opinions cannot be proven. But that did not alter their enthusiastic reception. Sometimes wishful thinking overcomes the necessity to cross-check with reality, mostly with the hope of a self-fulfilling prophecy in mind.

One striking example is the book *The Great Cosmic Mother*, in which Monica Sjöö and Barbara Mor cite Graves extensively, even his so-called Pelasgian creation myth.[44] Already in 1956 Karl Kerényi (in his review of Graves's book) had pointed out that this myth is a complete invention by Graves.[45] When you check the references given by Graves you see, of course, that Kerényi is right—no trace of such a myth can be found in Greek literature. Nevertheless, nearly thirty years later in 1987, this myth reappears as a proof of the worship of the great mother goddess. This is a glaring example of how errors perpetuate themselves. The authors of *The Great Cosmic Mother* are not linked to the academic world; but a book, once it is published and can be bought, will be read, and, as long as its design makes it look like a scholarly work, there will be readers who believe in its content.

As a final example, the psychologists Jennifer Woolger and Dr Roger Woolger, an analyst and lecturer respectively, have written a book titled *The Goddess Within*.[46] Here, too, Graves is extensively cited. He serves as a valuable witness for a matriarchy in Crete,[47] and his interpretations of Athena and Medusa[48] are repeated: that is, that Medusa represents a rival matriarchal religion and Athena the great mother goddess.[49]

Graves's ideas about myth are not only cited in more-or-less scientific books—they have also inspired a kind of new religion.

[43] For examples of positions against Gould Davis: Ginette Castro (1990), 33; Philip G. Davis (1998); Eller (2000) argues that the archaeological evidence produced by Graves cannot prove a matriarchy; cf. Joan Marler (2006) 163–87.

[44] Sjöö and Mor (1987), 57; ch. 1.

[45] Kerényi (1956), 553.

[46] Woolger and Woolger (1990).

[47] Woolger and Woolger (1990), 25–6.

[48] Graves (1955a), 33.3–5.

[49] Woolger and Woolger (1990), 83–4.

Since 1970 a growing western movement of goddess spirituality has emerged.[50] Some, but not all, participants in the goddess movement consider themselves witches, Wiccans or Wiccens—'wicca' is the root from which the word witchcraft is said to derive. They believe that it is an old religion which was practised all over Europe until after the arrival of Christianity. It is practised in women-only groups. The goddess movement draws some inspiration from archeological and anthropological findings. Their supporters think that Neolithic and some later cultures were not based on patriarchal domination, and almost always included reverence for the divine embodied as female. Ancient myths are often used as a foundation. They do not understand these myths literally, but—as with Graves—figuratively or metaphorically. These myths are often rewritten or reinterpreted, because there is little written material from what is considered the pre-patriarchal period. Graves's work *The White Goddess* and his interpretations of Greek myths are regularly cited by Wiccans. It can be seen that they have adopted his model of the ritual year and the annual sacrifice of the king: the goddess gives birth to the god in midwinter; the god gains power until Easter, and the goddess returns to her maiden state; in May the goddess becomes pregnant by the god; in August the god's powers wane, and he dies at the end of the harvest. Some Wiccans mark the holiday by baking a figure of the god in bread and then symbolically sacrificing and eating it. Then he is once again born from the goddess. The goddess herself ages and rejuvenates with the seasons. This is exactly the model worked out in Graves's introduction to *The Greek Myths*.[51]

As in the works of the German-speaking psychoanalysts Sigmund Freud and, even more so, C. G. Jung, ideas which should explain a state of mind or being become a source and guideline to a movement which tries to transform or establish those texts in reality. Influenced by his time, but most likely by his German origins too, Graves was one of those scholars to whom a mixture of methodology and imagination was just right. Similar approaches can be seen in other German thinkers, like Rudolf Steiner or Georg Groddeck. All of them dealt with the hidden elements of human nature, all were skilled

[50] Cf. Christ (1979); Valiente (2000), a collection of poems, published posthumously; M. Murray (1921) and (1933); Adler (1979); Starhawk (1979); cf. the works of Zsuzsanna Budapest (1990), (1998), (1999).

[51] Graves (1955a), 13–14.

narrators, all lived in the late nineteenth and early twentieth centuries, and all are still influential. Their stimulus remains, although their methods and results do not (entirely) hold up.

Graves's approach to the Greek myths was inappropriate but, in his time, quite fashionable. Even today his prose style is recognized as admirable and his comments are interesting. He mixes fact and conjecture in such a convincing and barely detectable way that anyone unfamiliar with the subject has to believe that all his conjectures *are* facts. Graves has become famous with feminists and supporters of goddess spirituality, although I don't think that he could have had this kind of reputation in mind when he developed his theories. He wanted to be taken seriously by the scientific world, as his letter in the *Times Literary Supplement* shows. There he describes his work as 'a well-documented book of 350,000 words . . . written by a single hand on the whole corpus of Greek myth'.[52] But, as time went by, he became famous for it in quite another way.

[52] Robert Graves, 'The Greek Myths', *Times Literary Supplement*, 25 Mar. 1955 p. 18. This was in reply to a review of 4 Mar. 1955, p. 137; cf. rejoinder 29 Apr. 1955, p. 209.

9

Scholarly Mythopoesis

Robert Graves's The Greek Myths

Vanda Zajko

INTRODUCTION

Commissioned by E. V. Rieu for Penguin Classics and published in 1955, *The Greek Myths* quickly established itself as a modern handbook of myth for the educated reader and retains something of that status today, despite an avowedly idiosyncratic take on its subject matter. Within the scholarly community, however, its reception has been far less favourable, in part because it is so hard to categorize definitively, staking a claim as both reference work and a work of literature in its own right. This ambiguity was identified by reviewers from the start: as we shall see, several of Graves's contemporaries criticized the premises for his claims and his erratic use of sources whilst at the same time acknowledging the imaginative power of his work. The audacity of a project which on the one hand collates the stories of ancient Greece from the creation of the world to the return of Odysseus to Ithaca, an event which signifies for Graves the beginning of the end of the heroic age, and on the other offers interpretative essays purporting to explain why the stories take the form they do, does appear hubristic by today's standards of the criticism of myth, which tend to reject large-scale all-encompassing theories out of hand. But at the time Graves was writing, in the wake of Frazer and the Cambridge Ritualists, this was not quite so much the case, and giving due consideration to the intellectual context for his undertaking, the influences upon him, his attitudes to Englishness, to the past, and to the practices of traditional scholarship, helps to frame his achievement in a way that allows for its re-evaluation as a unique contribution to the twentieth century's imaginative engagement with the ancient world.

Graves wrote *The Greek Myths* between 1951 and 1953, and mentions its composition in his correspondence from that period, making scattered comments both about his method of working and about his ideological commitments, and from these comments and from the introduction to the published work itself it is possible to gain a sense of how Graves viewed his collection and how he thought it would be received. It is clear that from the outset he saw his role as providing a corrective to the conservative treatments of most other scholars, whom he regarded in the main as reducing the myths to fairy stories, the product of the childhood of Greece, and thus diminishing their seriousness and cultural importance. The task he set himself was to establish the historical basis of Greek mythology and religion and restore its centrality to the study of 'early European history, religion and sociology',[1] a task which he claimed had thus far been 'shirked by all but a very few independent-minded scholars';[2] he also worked with a theory of 'true myth',[3] which he aimed to distinguish from 'allegory, fable, decorated history, streetcorner anecdote and novelette',[4] and indeed the collection was originally entitled 'Greek Myths and Pseudo Myths' to make this principle clear.[5] For Graves, the processes of compiling, organizing, and interpreting the myths were entwined from the outset, and his instincts towards folding individual narratives into a bold and all-encompassing vision were grounded in his belief in a particular model of human development and its socio-religious entailments. For this reason the explanatory notes to each chapter were conceived of as an integral part of the work and not as scholarly accoutrements for the benefit of just a few.

The form of the published work, and in particular the relationship between the accounts of the myths themselves and the references and notes, has always been central to debates about its value. It is not clear that E. V. Rieu, who commissioned the work for Penguin, knew precisely what its emphases and scope would be at the outset, but

[1] Graves (2011a), 11. [2] O'Prey (1984), 109.
[3] Graves (2011a), 12. [4] O'Prey (1984), 104.
[5] It was eventually simplified at the request of Viking Press, which was originally going to publish the work in America.

shortly after its publication, in July 1955, a letter from Andreus Glover on behalf of the publisher demonstrates a realistic attitude towards its perceived strengths and weaknesses. In a response to criticism from a Lt.-Col. P.B.S., he writes:

> We realised of course when we first arranged the publication of the book with Mr Graves that we were not likely to get a piece of pure scholarship undiluted with the peculiar Gravesian opinions and were quite prepared to be shot at for producing something quite unlike Smith or The Oxford Companion to Classical Literature. However, the reception which the book has seems to show that a very large number of people are finding the classification and retelling of the myths themselves useful and discounting as much as they see fit the peculiar Gravesian approach.[6]

The idea that readers could enjoy the retellings of the myths themselves without necessarily subscribing to the 'meta-myth' that underpinned them might not have pleased Graves himself, but it did make it possible for different kinds of readers to engage with the text, even if they had no interest in his imaginative reconstructions of prehistorical religion. The distinction that is made here between what might be seen as the standard reference works of classical scholarship and the 'peculiar Gravesian approach' contributes to a sense that Graves defiantly set himself apart from the mainstream and had no regard for tradition, but this, as we shall see, oversimplifies his position. It was not, moreover, a consistent element in Penguin's marketing of Graves, as is evidenced by the blurb on the back of the first edition of *The Greek Myths* (Graves (1955a)), which endeavoured to establish a sense of continuity between Graves's work and one of its more conventional predecessors:

> Not for over a century, since Smiths's *Dictionary of Classical Mythology*, has the attempt been made to provide for the English reader a complete 'mythology' in the sense of a retelling in modern terms of the Greek tales of Gods and heroes. In the two volumes of this book, Robert Graves, whose combination of classical scholarship and anthropological competence has already been so brilliantly demonstrated in *The Golden Fleece*, *The White Goddess*, and his other novels, supplies the need.

[6] Letter from A. S. B. Glover of Penguin Books to a Lt.-Col. P.B.S, dated 11 July 1955, Penguin Archive, University of Bristol.

The ambivalent status of *The Greek Myths* is here robustly contextualized within Graves's oeuvre, with previously published works of fiction and theory suggested as the frames of reference needed to evaluate it properly. Certainly when it is evaluated in this way, it begins to appear less an oddity and more a significant landmark within a particular mythographical tradition.

GRAVES'S METHOD

Graves's preoccupation with myth was above all concerned with origins, and in this he was following a tradition which can be traced back through the Cambridge Ritualists and Sir James Frazer's *Golden Bough*, via the comparativism of Max Müller and his protracted debates with Andrew Lang, to Herder's *Volk* beyond. He had encountered the works of Frazer and Jane Harrison whilst at Oxford, and mentions Harrison's *Prolegomena to the Study of Greek Religion* in the introduction to *The Greek Myths*, but his fascination with the prehistorical derived as much from his own reading as from his formal education. Immersed in the Irish culture beloved by his father from an early age, and drawn to the pagan traditions of his adopted homeland of Wales, the ancient world of the Greeks did not occupy an especially privileged place in his mental landscape, and he did not regard it as the domain only of classical scholars. For Graves, the problem of origins was broader than its manifestation within one particular culture, and local and temporal differences were far less significant than the underlying psycho-social structures which he viewed as universal and as responsible for the mythopoetic activity in all prehistoric societies. His approach was to view the narrative details of individual myths as clues to their earliest meaning, often relying on the etymological significance he found in the names of protagonists to lead him to their ritual basis. Graves's methodology thus involved a figuration of the texts of the past as puzzles to be solved, an attitude he also displayed in selecting the topics for his novels, several of which aimed to put the record straight about figures from the historical archive. His emphasis on the linguistic skills needed to pursue his project owed much to the German philologists of the preceding century, who had asserted the interrelatedness of all the languages derived from Indo-European in order to intervene in large-scale debates about the trajectory of history. Robert Ackerman has described this intervention as follows:

> The movement from Latinity to Hellenism reached its culmination in the German philological movement of the early nineteenth century. The philologists, moreover, were another expression of the deep interest in language as a phenomenon that was part of historicism. Language was felt to be the repository of the earliest, and therefore the deepest and most important, intuitions and emotions of the *Volk*; preserved in so much linguistic amber was not only what the *Urmensch* saw but also how he saw it and what he felt about it. Therefore, in this last pre-archaeological, pre-ethnographic period, philology seemed to offer the best hope for deciphering the riddle of the past in the sense that it permitted moderns to feel their way into ancient modes of consciousness.

Graves shared the view that linguistic traces held the key to unlocking the mysteries of the prehistoric *mentalité* but, working in a later period, he supplemented the evidence he gleaned from this source with the archaeological material he found so irresistible. He placed great emphasis on artistic representations, believing that the form a story eventually took could often be explained by what he called 'iconotropy', a process by which a mythographer had 'accidentally or deliberately misinterpreted a sacred picture or dramatic rite',[7] resulting in undue distortion and complexity; by correcting this process of distortion, the critic could arrive at a more authentic version of a myth. For Graves, very many of the Greek myths in their most well-known form did not constitute 'true myth' according to his criteria, and the most crucial factor in deciding whether a particular story should be granted that status was whether it could be stripped back in such a way as to highlight its correspondence with the narrative structure, derived from ritual mime, in which its origin lay. He outlines his views in the following passage from the introduction:

> Yet genuine mythic elements may be found embedded in the least promising stories, and the fullest or most illuminating version of a given myth is seldom supplied by any one author; nor, when searching for its original form, should one assume that the more ancient the written source, the more authoritative it must be. Often, for instance,

[7] Graves (2011a), 21.

> the playful Alexandrian Callimachus, or the frivolous Augustan Ovid, or the dry-as-dust late-Byzantine Tzetzes, gives an obviously earlier version of a myth than do Hesiod or the Greek tragedians; and the thirteenth-century *Excidium Troiae*, is in parts, mythically sounder than the *Iliad*. When making prose sense of a mythological or pseudo-mythological narrative, one should always pay careful attention to the names, tribal origin, and fates of the characters concerned; and then restore it to the form of dramatic ritual, whereupon its incidental elements will sometimes suggest an analogy with another myth which has been given a wholly different anecdotal twist, and shed light on both.[8]

This passage makes clear the unorthodoxy of Graves's position in so far as the ancient material is concerned: whilst a large-scale sense of history is central to his interpretative vision, his sense of 'mythical soundness' is not dependent on whether an individual source counts as 'early' or 'late', nor is he concerned with the context within which a story is told. In fact, the unacknowledged origin of Graves's list of references to primary texts which follow each passage of narrative in *The Greek Myths* was William Smith's 1844 *Dictionary of Greek and Roman Biography and Mythology*, and the extent to which he can be shown to have drawn upon it unreflectively suggests that the whole question of the validation of sources was not one that interested him very much at all per se. The key to determining whether a narrative detail is significant is not to be found in the specific relationship between a story and the circumstances of its telling, but rather in the relationship between one story and another in so far as a similarity of underlying structure can be detected. In order to understand this more fully, we must turn to an earlier work of Graves's, *The White Goddess*, and to the 'one story and one story only'[9] that he considered worth the telling.

The Greek Myths and *The White Goddess*

It was in *The White Goddess* that Graves's ideas about the universal prehistory of humankind first took shape in discursive form, although

[8] Graves (2011a), 12–13.

[9] This truncated line comes from Graves's poem 'To Juan at the Winter Solstice', first published in the collection *Poems 1938–1945* and often used as a metonym for the set of ideas associated with the Great Goddess.

its startlingly rapid process of composition intimates that the material emerged, Athene-like, in a more-or-less complete state, and traces of its patterns of thought can indeed be discerned in earlier essays and poems.[10] The main argument comprises both a theory of societal evolution which focuses on the putative transition from matriarchy to patriarchy and an account of the development of myth that emphasizes its origins in a common language. Graves sets out his wares early on in the introduction:

> My thesis is that the language of poetic myth anciently current in the Mediterranean and Northern Europe was a magical language bound up with popular religious ceremonies in honour of the Moon-goddess, or Muse, some of them dating from the Old Stone Age, and that this remains the language of true poetry—'true' in the nostalgic modern sense of 'the unimprovable original, not a synthetic substitute'. The language was tampered with in late Minoan times when invaders from Central Asia began to substitute patrilinear for matrilinear institutions and remodel or falsify the myths to justify the social changes. Then came the early Greek philosophers who were strongly opposed to magical poetry as threatening their new religion of logic, and under their influence a rational poetic language (now called the Classical) was elaborated in honour of their patron Apollo and imposed on the world as the last word in spiritual illumination: a view that has prevailed practically ever since in European schools and universities, where myths are now studied only as quaint relics of the nursery age of mankind.[11]

The focus of this passage is Greece, and the opposition of magical poetry to rationality is heavily reminiscent of Nietzsche's lapsarian narrative in *The Birth of Tragedy out of the Spirit of Music*, although for Graves the point of decline comes very much earlier, so that everything we now recognize as ancient Greek culture is tainted. But the book (originally entitled 'The Roebuck in the Thicket') also covers a vast array of Celtic material as well as data from western Europe and the ancient Middle East, and treats all of it in the same way, synoptically, giving priority to no particular culture or period. The central idea is that myth derives from ritual dramatization of the

[10] Graves recounted the process of writing *The White Goddess* in a talk he gave at the YMHA in New York on 9 February, 1957: the first draft of the whole book was written over a period of just three weeks in 1944.

[11] Graves (1999b), 6.

worship of the Great Goddess in one of her three aspects of maiden, nymph, and crone, and it permeates the volume; but myth is just one of the cultural forms examined, along with literary texts, cultic practices, and archaeological remains, and the different kinds of evidence are synthesized to form a complex, kaleidoscopic image both of a prehistorical past and of the processes that brought about its demise.

If the overall approach of *The White Goddess* is broadly anthropological and often compared to *The Golden Bough*,[12] its claims about myth are rather more straightforwardly Euhemerist than those of its predecessor. Whereas Frazer moves at different periods between various positions on what we might describe as a ritualist–Euhemerist continuum,[13] Graves asserts strongly that all myths are evidence of historical events and can be demonstrated as such once the interpretative work of identifying later accretions and distortions has been accomplished.[14] His claims are bold, and he knows full well they will be disparaged by many. In the following passage (one of several such) he offers up the evidence as he sees it for evaluation by potential critics:

> Since the close connexion here suggested between ancient British, Greek, and Hebrew religion will not be easily accepted, I wish to make it immediately clear that I am not a British Israelite or anything of that sort. My reading of the case is that at different periods in the second millennium BC a confederacy of mercantile tribes, called in Egypt 'the People of the Sea', were displaced from the Aegean area by invaders from the north-east and south-east; that some of these wandered north, along already established trade-routes, some elements reaching Ireland by way of North Africa and Spain. Still others invaded

[12] So, for example, in his introduction to the latest edition of *The White Goddess* (1999b), Grevel Lindop compares them thus: in a sense, Graves's work rests on a brilliantly simple transformation of Frazer's theory. *The Golden Bough* had demonstrated that a wide range of primitive religions centred on a divine king, a man who represented a dying god of vegetable fertility and who either killed his predecessor, reigning until killed in his turn, or else was sacrificed at the end of a year's kingship. Graves's contribution was to supply the missing female part in this drama: to suggest that originally the god-king was important not for his own sake, but because he married the goddess-queen; and that whilst kings might come and go, the queen or goddess endured (p. xi).

[13] See the discussion in Ackerman (2002), 57–9.

[14] e.g. Graves (1999b), 9: 'they are all grave record of ancient religious customs or events, and reliable enough as history once their language is understood and allowance has been made for errors in transcription, misunderstandings of obsolete ritual, and deliberate changes introduced for moral or political reasons'.

> Syria and Canaan, among them the Philistines, who captured the shrine of Hebron in southern Judaea from the Edomite clan of Caleb; but the Calebites ('Dog-men'), allies of the Israelite tribe of Judah, recovered it about two hundred years later and took over a great part of the Philistine religion at the same time. These borrowings were eventually harmonized in the Pentateuch with a body of Semitic, Indo-European and Asianic myth which composed the religious traditions of the mixed Israelite confederacy. The connexion, then, between the early myths of the Hebrews, the Greeks and the Celts is that all three races were civilised by the same Aegean people whom they conquered and absorbed.[15]

No attempt is made in *The White Goddess* to cite authorities for this kind of account of prehistorical tribal movements; it is enough for Graves to assert that there is a reason for the similarity of cultural expression he has uncovered which differentiates his explanations from those dependent on the psychological.[16] A similar strategy is adopted in *The Greek Myths*, where the passages of explanation following each section of narrative stand alone without references to any kind of source in a way that has provoked a considerable amount of scholarly derision.[17] For Graves, however, the need to replicate

[15] Graves (1999b), 56.

[16] Despite having read both Freud and Jung, Graves was very hostile to any suggestion that his work might testify to the existence of any kind of collective unconscious. The terms in which he attacks this notion are themselves interpretable in a way that is revealing of his own psychology: 'Freud, indeed, never realized to his dying day that he was projecting a private fantasy on the world, and then making it stick by insisting that his disciples must undergo prolonged psycho-analytic treatment until they surrendered and saw the light. Much the same goes for Jung. My world picture is not a psychological one, nor do I indulge in idle myth-making and award diplomas to my converts. It is enough for me to quote the myths and give them historical sense: tracing a certain ancient faith through its vicissitudes—from when it was paramount, to when it has been driven underground and preserved by witches, travelling minstrels, remote country folk, and a few secret heretics to the newly established religion. Particularly by the endowed Irish poets and their humble colleagues, the Welsh travelling minstrels—descendants of the poets expelled by the Christian Cymry, and preservers of the pre-Christian *Mabinogion* myths.' This passage is taken from A Talk for the Y.M.H.A. Centre, New York, 9 February 1957, given as Appendix B in Lindop's edition of *The White Goddess* (Graves (1999b), 496).

[17] So, for example, Nick Lowe in a review in the *TLS* (23 Dec. 2005), entitled 'Killing Graves', of Nigel Spivey's book *Songs on Bronze: The Greek Myths Made Real*: 'Nuttier still are the astounding pseudo-scholarly interpretative commentaries on each section, which historicize everything in terms of Graves's personal mythology of the White Goddess, under which nasty patriarchal Dorians displace matriarchal Pelasgians worshipping Graves's triple goddess, and commemorate it all in dying-god

scholarly paraphernalia is quite simply less pressing than the obligation to disseminate his vision of the Great Goddess, whose potency cannot be reduced to, or contained by, the impoverished rhetoric of reality.

The following extended passage demonstrates clearly how the force of Graves's meta-myth shapes his interpretation of the content of individual myths. It begins with an imagined conversation between the poet and the goddess:

> One question I should myself like to ask her is a personal one: whether she ever offered herself as a human sacrifice to herself. I think her only answer would be a smiling shake of her head, meaning 'not really', for instances of the ritual murder of women are rare in European myth and most of them apparently refer to the desecration of the Goddess's shrines by the Achaean invaders. That there were bloody massacres and rapes of priestesses is shown in the Tirynthian Hercules's battles with the Amazons, with Hera herself (he wounded her in the breast), and with the nine-headed Hydra, a beast portrayed on Greek vases as a giant squid with heads at the end of each tentacle. As often as he cut off the Hydra's heads they grew again, until he used fire to sear the stumps: in other words, Achaean attacks on the shrines, each of the armed orgiastic priestesses, were ineffective until the sacred groves were burned down. *Hydrias* means a water priestess with a *hydria*, or ritual water-pot; and the squid was a fish which appears in works of art dedicated to the Goddess not only in Minoan Crete but in Breton sculptures of the Bronze Age.
>
> Tales of princesses sacrificed for religious reasons, like Iphigeneia or Jephthah's daughter, refer to the subsequent patriarchal era; and the fate supposedly intended for Andromeda, Hesionë, and all the other princesses rescued by heroes in the nick of time, is probably due to iconotropic error. The princess is not the intended victim of the sea-serpent or wild beast; she is chained to the sea cliff by Bel, Marduk, Perseus or Heracles after he has overcome the monster which is her emanation.

Here the overarching idea and dominant belief is that myths containing the detail of the sacrifice of women cannot refer to the actual sacrifice of women because in the prehistoric past, the time that is reflected in myth, men were sacrificed in order to propitiate the Goddess, but women were not. Narratives which include depictions

rituals which encode the truth *Da Vinci*-style for scholarly cryptographers to decipher. Unlike the narrative portions, none of this stuff is even cosmetically source-referenced—for good reason, as Graves has made it up from whole cloth.'

of this activity must then be regarded as deriving from the later, patriarchal period during which women *were* killed brutally, usually because they were priestesses of the Goddess who were murdered defending her shrines: this is one of those instances where the stories that survive represent the mythmaking of those who overthrew the Goddess. In the second paragraph, the principle of iconotropy is evoked to explain the kinds of myths from a variety of cultures which depict women being killed by some sort of monstrous being: the error here is that the mythographers who have interpreted the visual representations of this type of scene construe the image literally, whereas in fact the monsters depicted are symbols of the power of the Goddess and not her potential destroyers. If we compare this exegesis from *The White Goddess* with the treatment of the myth of Iphigeneia in *The Greek Myths*, the potent intertextual relationship between the two works is thrown into sharp relief, and the nexus of ideas that dominate the earlier work can clearly be demonstrated to have affected the way the account is given in the latter.

Graves divides the story into two sections: the first (116.d) forms part of the broader narrative of the descendants of the House of Pelops and the immediate context is Orestes's voyage to Tauris to steal the statue of Artemis; the second (161.d–e) belongs to a series of chapters about the foundation and fate of Troy, and here the sacrifice of Iphigeneia by Agamemnon is related in detail. In the first instance, the narrative passage dealing with Iphigeneia is short:

> Now, Iphigeneia had been rescued from sacrifice at Aulis by Artemis, wrapped in a cloud and wafted to the Tauric Chersonese, where she was at once appointed Chief priestess and granted the sole right of handling the sacred image.[18]

The explanatory notes, where Graves articulates his position on the meaning of the myth, are much longer:

> 1. The mythographers' anxiety to conceal certain barbarous traditions appears plainly in this story and its variants. Among the suppressed elements are Artemis's vengeance on Agamemnon for the murder of Iphigeneia, and Oeax's vengeance, also on Agamemnon, for the murder of his brother Palamedes. Originally the myth seems to have run somewhat as follows: Agamemnon was prevailed upon, by his fellow chieftains, to execute his daughter Iphigeneia as a witch when the Greek

[18] Graves (2011a), 436.

expedition against Aulis lay windbound at Aulis. Artemis, whom Iphigeneia had served as priestess, made Agamemnon pay for this insult to her: she helped Aegisthus to supplant and murder him on his return . . . [19]

2. Patriarchal Greeks of a later era will have disliked this myth—a version of which, making Menelaus, not Orestes, the object of Artemis's vengeance, has been preserved by Photius. They exculpated Agamemnon of murder, and Artemis of opposing the will of Zeus, by saying that she doubtless rescued Iphigeneia, and carried her away to be a sacrificial priestess—not at Brauron, but among the savage Taurians, for whose actions they disclaimed responsibility. And that she certainly did not kill Orestes (or, for the matter of that, any Greek victim) but, on the contrary, helped him to take the Tauric image to Greece at Apollo's orders.[20]

In the second instance, the narrative passage is quite extensive and the attendant note considerably shorter and, some might argue, rather inconsequential:

When the Greek fleet assembled for the second time at Aulis, but was windbound there for many days, Calchas prophesied that they would be unable to sail unless Agamemnon sacrificed the most beautiful of his daughters to Artemis. Why Artemis should have been vexed is disputed. Some say that, on shooting a stag at long range, Agamemnon had boasted: 'Artemis herself could not have done better!'; or had killed her sacred goat; or had vowed to offer her the most beautiful creature born that year in his kingdom, which happened to be Iphigeneia; or that his father Atreus had withheld a golden lamb which was her due. At any rate, Agamemnon refused to do as he was expected, saying that Clytaemnestra would never let Iphigeneia go. But when the Greeks swore: 'We shall transfer our allegiance to Palamedes if he continues obdurate,' and when Odysseus, feigning anger, prepared to sail home, Menelaus came forward as peace-maker. He suggested that Odysseus and Talthybius should fetch Iphigeneia to Aulis, on the pretext of marrying her to Achilles as a reward for his daring feats in Mysia. To this ruse Agamemnon agreed, and though he at once sent a secret message, warning Clytaemnestra not to believe Odysseus, Menelaus intercepted this, and she was tricked into bringing Iphigeneia to Aulis.

When Achilles found that his name had been misused, he undertook to protect Iphigeneia from injury; but she nobly consented to die for the glory of Greece, and offered her neck to the sacrificial axe without a word of complaint. Some say that, in the nick of time, Artemis carried her off to the land of the Taurians, substituting a hind at the altar; or a

[19] Graves (2011a), 440. [20] Graves (2011a), 440 n.2.

> she-bear; or an old woman. Others, that a peal of thunder was heard and that, at Artemis's order and Clytaemnestra's plea, Achilles intervened, saved Iphigeneia, and sent her to Scythia; or that he married her, and that she, and not Deidameia, bore him Neoptolemus.[21]
>
> A version of the 'Jephthah's daughter' myth (see 169.5) seems to have been confused with Agamemnon's sacrifice of a priestess at Aulis, on a charge of raising contrary winds by witchcraft; Sir Francis Drake once hanged one of his sailors, a spy in Cecil's pay, on the same charge. Agamemnon's high-handed action, it seems, offended conservative opinion at home, women being traditionally exempt from sacrifice. The Taurians to whom Iphigeneia was said to have been sent by Artemis, lived in the Crimea and worshipped Artemis as a man-slayer; Agamemnon's son Orestes fell into their clutches (see 116.e).[22]

In her analysis of these passages, Sheila Murnaghan argues that Graves 'retells Iphigeneia's killing by Agamemnon in a way that removes the element of sacrifice and turns it into an assault on female power',[23] and it is true that he does seem rather to despise the later Greeks for shying away from the more brutal aspects of the story to which he himself returns. But what is interesting methodologically speaking is that he performs this corrective operation in the notes and not in the narrative section; that is to say, it is in the explanatory notes that the 'true myth' is told, and this reconstructed version itself comes to life more fully when read alongside the 'theoretical' accounts of prehistorical culture to be found in *The White Goddess.*

There are some places, however, where far from crowding the reader with tantalizing detail and forging potential connections with a range of other texts, *The Greek Myths* presents a tale in such a stripped-back version that it disappoints. Consider, for example, the following account of 'the myth of Daphne' from the section on Apollo's nature and deeds (21.1), and the accompanying passage of explanation:

> Apollo was not invariably successful in love. On one occasion he tried to steal Marpessa from Idas, but she remained true to her husband. On another, he pursued Daphne, the mountain nymph, a priestess of Mother Earth, daughter of the river Peneius in Thessaly; but when he overtook her, she cried out to Mother Earth who, in the nick of time, spirited her away to Crete, where she became known as Pasiphaë.

21 Graves (2011a), 653.

22 Graves (2011a), 656.

23 Murnaghan (2009), 88.

> Mother Earth left a laurel-tree in her place, and from its leaves Apollo made a wreath to console himself.
>
> His pursuit of Daphne the Mountain-nymph, daughter of the river Peneius, and priestess of Mother Earth, refers apparently to the Hellenic capture of Tempe, where the goddess Daphoene ('bloody one') was worshipped by a college of orgiastic laurel-chewing Maenads (see 46.2 and 51.2). After suppressing the college,—Plutarch's account suggests that the priestess fled to Crete, where the Moon-goddess was called Pasiphaë (see 88.e)—Apollo took over the laurel which, afterwards, only the Pythoness might chew. Daphoene will have been mareheaded at Tempe, as at Phigalia (see 16.5); Leucippus ('white horse') was the sacred king of the local horse cult, annually torn in pieces by the wild women, who bathed after his murder to purify themselves, not before (see 22.1 and 150.1).

To anyone familiar with Ovid, these rather stilted and bald few lines lack the sensuality, verve, and pathos of his version of the myth, a version which, after all, has inspired numerous other artists and poets, and the notes seem pedantic and obfuscatory. What is even more surprising is that Ovid is not mentioned as a source for the story—the only two references that are given are Apollodorus's *Library* and a rather obscure text of Plutarch.[24] Whether it was some sense of an 'anxiety of influence' that led Graves to cut Ovid out, or whether it was because the Ovidian version, with its strong emphasis on sexual desire, did not cohere easily with the Gravesian perspective, there is little doubt that here the intrusion of the meta-myth detracts from the attractiveness of the individual tale.

From a traditional scholarly perspective, it has been easy enough to decry the lack of rigour in Graves's main thesis and to point both to errors and to flights of fancy. In one of the first reviews of *The Greek Myths*, H. J. Rose, whose *Handbook of Greek Mythology* was standard issue at the time, did both, referring to the 'series of tangled narratives, difficult and tedious to read and made none the better by sundry evidences of their author's defective scholarship', and criticizing the 'fantastic picture of a culture such as never existed in Europe or out of it', before finally concluding that 'if anything in the book were to be taken seriously, it might be worthwhile to list a few of the sheer "howlers" which stud it; but it is not'.[25] But criticism of this kind rather begs the question of what kind of project Graves was

[24] Apollodorus 1.7.9; Plutarch, *Agis* 9. [25] Rose (1955), 208–9.

concerned with in these two works which are so closely connected to each other, and how it relates to the more conventional mythographical endeavours normally preferred by the academy. Grevel Lindop describes *The White Goddess* thus, suggesting that its relationship to academic scholarship is predominantly one of satire:

> the kind of work Northrop Frye has usefully called an 'anatomy': a book . . . packed with learning and catalogues of strange facts, mixing verse, prose and dialogue to analyse its subject exhaustively and at the same time satirise contemporary society and academic scholarship. Such books are written with their author's lifeblood and take a lifetime to comprehend, though they may be read the first time with intense excitement.[26]

This kind of analysis, one which attributes to Graves a complex and knowing engagement with the practices of the academy and a polemical attitude towards the world around him, seems both more plausible and more rewarding than the kind which simply focuses on the things he 'got wrong'. He was, after all, a highly literate man, a poet, novelist, and prodigious essayist, and if the White Goddess had become a 'personal mythology'[27], it also underpinned an engagement with the ancient world that was to become one of the most popular of the twentieth century.

GRAVES'S MYTHOPOIESIS

Graves was thoroughly aware of the controversy that the interpretative passages in *The Greek Myths* were likely to engender, and discussed the matter on several occasions in correspondence with his publishers. When the intended length of his volume became obvious, there was some discussion of whether the accounts of the myths themselves should be separated from the notes,[28] but having discussed the matter with the editorial board at Penguin,

[26] Graves (2011a), x.

[27] This phrase is used by Nick Lowe in the review cited in n. 17.

[28] In a letter to A. S. B. Glover at Penguin, the commissioning editor E. V. Rieu asks whether they are 'even tacitly committed to the notes', and whether it wouldn't be better to make one 150,000-word volume of the stories. At a meeting between the three of them in 1950 there was talk of keeping the notes only for the Viking Press publication in America.

A. S. B. Glover wrote to Graves on 13 May 1952 that, 'in view of the special public for whom we issue our books—and I note from a remark of your own that you are conscious that it is a special public—we feel that the separation of the context from the notes would, all things considered, be very unfortunate'. It was nonetheless the case that Graves took deliberate steps to mitigate the extravagance of his arguments, asking Glover to 'tell Alan Lane I am pulling my punches in the explanation with many more perhaps's and it seems and the introduction is now a model of tentativeness and discretion'.[29] He also sought to reassure his publishers and his readers as to the validity of his anthropological credentials by suggesting that the title of Fellow of the Royal Anthropological Institute might be put after his name on the title-page (he had been elected to this position in 1954).[30] Although on some occasions Graves showed a kind of sensitivity towards the values of the academic establishment, on others he was far more bullish: in a letter to Selwyn Jepson, at the time when Viking Press pulled out of publishing a hardback edition of *The Greek Myths* in America on the recommendation of its scholarly readers, he referred scathingly to these latter as 'Professors Tush and Bosh'. In a letter to Ava Gardner he was somewhat more measured in evaluating his work, but accurately predicted the kind of reception it would receive when he wrote: 'I am not a Greek scholar or an archaeologist or an anthropologist or a comparative mythologist, but I have a good nose and a sense of touch, and think I have connected a lot of mythical patterns which were not connected before, Classical faculties will hate me, and I will get a lot of sniffy reviews.'[31]

As we have seen, H. J. Rose was indeed sniffy when he reviewed the book for the *Classical Review* in 1955, and attacked Graves in particular for his assumption that there must be 'some general hypothesis to guide the study of myth'. He was prepared to allow a mythologist his 'pet theories', but only if he gave the facts 'correctly and conveniently', which, he was clear, Graves did not:

[29] This comment is included in an undated letter from the Penguin Archive, University of Bristol.

[30] Letter from Graves to Allen Lane dated 10 Dec. 1954, Penguin Archive, University of Bristol.

[31] Both these citations come from the third volume of Richard Graves's biography of his uncle: R. P. Graves (1995), 235–6.

> He tells indeed one myth, or saga, or *märchen*, after another, arranging them in an order for which I cannot find much justification, and is at pains to include every detail he can lay hands on, from any sort of authority from good epic and dramatic tradition down to the latest and obscurest scribblers, concerning whom he never asks where they got their information, what its age and value may be, and how much of what they tell us is due to their own fancy or that of some minor poet or local chronicler.[32]

Reviewing the work in the following year, Kevin Herbert picks up on the same phrase of Graves's and coins the rather witty term 'leuko-theistic' to describe his particular take on the kind of grand theory which to his mind has given students of myth a bad name:

> The author's basic mistake then is his assumption that there must be some 'general hypothesis' to guide the study of myth. This is the very notion which was so long the bane of these studies and which is now generally avoided. The allegorical, the rationalistic, the euhemeristic, the psycho-analytic, and many other comprehensive theories have been advanced in the past, and now we have still another—the leuko-theistic.[33]

The main criticisms of Graves's work by academic reviewers at the time of its publication were, then, his propagation of a new, large-scale theory to explain all myth and his cavalier and idiosyncratic treatment of sources. Both these strands have also been picked up more recently by Nick Lowe in a review of *Songs on Bronze: The Greek Myths Made Real*, by Nigel Spivey. In a piece which is overtly hostile to Graves throughout,[34] Lowe argues that Graves masked what was in fact a work of fiction under the rhetoric of scholarship, whereas Spivey 'cloaks his own scholarship in the rhetoric of fiction'.[35] This formulation appears to subscribe to the idea of a clean separation between the categories of fiction and scholarship and to reprove Graves for perpetuating an act of deceit on his audience. But, as we have seen, there is no attempt at such separation throughout Graves's oeuvre. What is more, as Bruce Lincoln has pertinently reminded us, 'students of myth seem particularly given to producing mythic, that is, ideological narratives,

[32] Rose (1955), 208. [33] Herbert (1956), 192.

[34] So, for example, this description of *The Greek Myths* as 'a sourcebook that for 50 years has peddled this kind of drivelling fakery to generations of the gullible, while perversely managing to cling to the status of a minor English classic'.

[35] Lowe (2005), 7.

perhaps because the stories they tell about storytelling reflect back on them as storytellers themselves'.[36] He argues that 'the prehistorical' particularly attracts the kind of scholarly mythopoesis to which Graves was prone:

> All of these exercises in scholarship (= myth + footnotes) suffer from the same problem. They attempt to reach so far back into prehistory that no textual sources are available to control the inquiry, but where archaeology offers a plethora of data. In practice, all the remains found throughout Eurasia for a period of several millennia can be constituted as evidence from which to craft the final narrative, but it is often the researchers' desires that determine their principles of selection. When neither the data nor the criticism of one's colleagues inhibits desire-driven invention, the situation is ripe for scholarship as myth. Prehistory here becomes 'pre-' in a radical sense: a terrain of frustration and opportunity where historians-cum-mythographers can offer origin accounts—complete with heroes, adventures, great voyages, and a primordial paradise lost—all of which reflect and advance the interests of those who tell them. Ideology in narrative form.[37]

The point here is not so much that these sorts of accounts are in some way invalid or to be avoided, but rather that their status as a kind of myth-making activity should be recognized as part of their intellectual and imaginative engagement with the past.

Even those who did not like *The Greek Myths* when it appeared appreciated, for the most part, that it possessed some literary quality.[38] But for Rose it was precisely this quality that distracted from the serious purpose for which such a work was intended, and he attacked Graves's supplements to the ancient texts as 'legitimate enough in a work of the imagination, but quite out of place in a handbook of mythology, where a story should be told as the authorities tell it, or epitomized from their account'.[39] It may be that Rose was comparing Graves's collection unfavourably with the ancient mythographer Apollodorus, whose work may seem to offer an unadorned and economical account of the whole range of Greek mythological stories,[40] or indeed with his

[36] Lincoln (1999), 209. [37] Lincoln (1999), 215.

[38] So, for example, Kevin Herbert: 'If one is looking for the colorful and the imaginative, then Graves' peculiar mixture of myth and his own metamyth is the place to seek it. The result is not a dull show, whatever else it may be': (1956), 191.

[39] Rose (1955), 208.

[40] But so little is known about Apollodorus that there is an element of fantasy here too. Is the following imagined description of his work-process so different from that of

own, in which he is careful to differentiate himself from the extravagances of over-inventive analysis.[41] But even those who see themselves as compiling rather than deciphering myth have interpretative decisions to make, and it is not at all clear a priori that those who adopt a cautious approach to this activity produce a more enduring work, one that succeeds in capturing the imagination of generations of readers.[42] It seems highly likely that Graves himself would regard *both* of the following texts as instances of his own particular brand of a kind of modern scholarly mythopoesis:

> The Amazon Queen Penthesileia, daughter of Otrere and Ares, had sought refuge in Troy from the Erinnyes of her sister Hippolyte (also called Glauce, or Melanippe), whom she had accidentally shot, either while out hunting or, according to the Athenians, in the fight which followed Theseus's wedding with Phaedra. Purified by Priam, she greatly distinguished herself in battle, accounting for many Greeks, among them (it is said) Machaon, though the commoner account makes him fall by the hand of Eurypylus, son of Telephus. She drove Achilles from the field on several occasions—some even claim that she killed him and that Zeus, at the plea of Thetis, restored him to life but at last he ran her through, fell in love with her dead body, and committed necrophily upon it there and then. When he later called for volunteers to bury Penthesileia, Thersites, a son of Aetolian Agrius, and the ugliest Greek at Troy, who had gouged out her eyes with his spear as she lay

Graves? 'At one extreme we can form a picture of an industrious Apollodorus with access to an excellent library containing everything he might want. He read widely in literary and mythographic sources of all ages, including ones rarely read in his day, taking copious notes on the origins of various myths, tracking their variations among different authors and compiling an original account', Scott Smith and Trzaskoma (2007), xxxvii.

[41] See Rose (1928), 9: 'The failure of so many theories may well make us hesitate before adopting another; and indeed, the best modern mythologists are as a rule none too eager to put forward a complete theory of the origin and primary meaning of any myth.'

[42] The editor of a collection of essays about modern mythography in the *Classical Bulletin*, 84/1 (2009), 57 has recently warned against too 'sniffy' an attitude towards compilers from a perspective of reception: 'Classicists need to pay attention to the modern handbooks, anthologies, and compilations through which knowledge of mythology is transmitted. These works play a large role in shaping the views of the classical world held by our students and by the wider educated public, and it is important to consider both their form and their intended audience. While handbooks and anthologies may seem like neutral repositories of information, the project of collecting, selecting, and retelling myths involves choices driven by the author's ideas about the classical past and about the current value of classical learning.'

dying, jeeringly accused Achilles of filthy and unnatural lust. Achilles turned and struck Thersites so hard that he broke every tooth in his head and sent his ghost scurrying down to Tartarus.[43]

Penthesileia, dead of profuse wounds,
Was despoiled of her arms by Prince Achilles
Who, for love of that fierce white naked corpse,
Necrophily on her committed
In the public view.

Some gasped, some groaned, some bawled their indignation,
Achilles nothing cared, distraught by grief,
But suddenly caught Thersites' obscene snigger
And with one vengeful buffet to the jaw
Dashed out his life.

This was a fury few might understand,
Yet Penthesileia, hailed by Prince Achilles
On the Elysian plain, pauses to thank him
For avenging her insulted womanhood
With sacrifice.[44]

[43] Graves (2011a), 675.
[44] Graves (2003), 461 (originally published in *Collected Poems 1955*).

10

Freedom to Invent

Graves's Iconoclastic Approach to Antiquity

Isobel Hurst

In *The White Goddess: A Historical Grammar of Poetic Myth*, Robert Graves begins his investigation into the mysterious nature of poetic inspiration by reflecting on the fundamental importance of poetry in his own literary endeavours and personal affairs:

> Since the age of fifteen poetry has been my ruling passion and I have never intentionally undertaken any task or formed any relationship that seemed inconsistent with poetic principles; which has sometimes won me the reputation of an eccentric. Prose has been my livelihood, but I have used it as a means of sharpening my sense of the altogether different nature of poetry, and the themes that I choose are always linked in my mind with outstanding poetic problems.[1]

Despite this 'passion' for poetry as a way of life, Graves claims that he was saved from a falsely reverential attitude for poets by growing up with a poet for a father, one whose 'light-hearted early work' included 'The Invention of Wine'.[2] He describes Alfred Graves as 'a dear old fellow who in young and vinous days used to write with some spirit and very pleasantly', and was 'hand in glove with Tennyson and Ruskin and that lot' (other friends included the Pre-Raphaelite poets Dante Gabriel Rossetti and William Morris).[3] Robert Graves may define himself as an 'eccentric', an outsider, yet his account of his early life repeatedly emphasizes literary connections. Even in a

[1] Graves (1999b), 13. [2] Graves (1960b), 15. [3] O'Prey (1982), 30.

description of childhood walks, Graves self-consciously creates a suitably eccentric chain of literary connections, linking him to Swinburne, Walter Savage Landor, and Dr Johnson.[4] In regarding poetry as a 'passion' and prose merely as a 'livelihood', a lesser although financially rewarding art, Graves echoes a writer he particularly admired. Thomas Hardy, distinguished first as a Victorian novelist and later as an innovative poet in the early decades of the twentieth century, was a potent influence on Graves's early writing. Hardy told Graves that he prized the poetry that 'came to him by accident' more highly than the novels he could make himself write 'by a time-table'.[5]

Graves has little confidence in the poetic canon and a very personal sense of what makes a true poet: Virgil, Pope, Milton, and Dryden attract his censure, although Romantic poets such as Keats, Blake, and Coleridge are favourably received; some other touchstones include Skelton, Apuleius, and Homer.[6] He records in *The Common Asphodel* that he was often told that he would be carried away by Swinburne's 'melodious' opening chorus in *Atalanta in Calydon*, but found it lacking in 'technical competence', an opinion confirmed by Robert Bridges.[7] His opinions about contemporary poets are similarly dogmatic, and personal connections do not inhibit Graves's uncompromising judgements. While acknowledging (somewhat reluctantly) to T. S. Eliot that he is 'obviously and ungainsayably a poet', Graves writes that he has 'consistently denied' the title of poet to Eliot's friend Ezra Pound, arguing that he could not find 'a single line or stanza' that was 'true or beautiful'.[8] In the Clark Lectures, delivered at Cambridge in 1954–5, Graves attacks poetic 'idols' such as Yeats, Pound, Eliot, Auden, and Dylan Thomas and their academic acolytes, complaining that the 'living poet-hero is a modernism';[9] his praise is reserved for Laura Riding, Robert Frost, e. e. cummings, Alun Lewis,

[4] Graves (1960b), 9.

[5] Graves (1960b), 249. Graves might be said to have followed the example of Sir Walter Scott, a poet who wrote himself out of debt with a series of historical novels.

[6] Graves describes himself as reading Keats and Blake in the trenches while other soldiers read military texts or rubbishy novels, and 'some of the poems in *Over the Brazier* were written in the Everyman edition of Keats's poetry given to Graves by his father.' Kersnowski (2002), 31.

[7] Graves (1949), 9.

[8] O'Prey (1982), 342. Graves's antipathy for Pound was anticipated by T. E. Lawrence, who introduced them by saying that they would dislike each other: Kersnowski (1989), 39.

[9] McGuinness (1999), 46, 53.

and Siegfried Sassoon. However, while Graves isolated himself from modernist revolutions in poetry, his stimulating effect on younger poets was intense: Ted Hughes received a copy of *The White Goddess* as a present from his English teacher, and found that the text confirmed his idea of poetry as 'a bardic, prophetic, shamanic calling';[10] Seamus Heaney also experienced a 'profoundly felt' influence.[11] Miranda Seymour remarks that Graves received many 'letters from young poets in the Sixties and Seventies who had chosen him for their mentor and exemplar'.[12]

In a letter following the publication of *Claudius the God*, Graves recalls that he 'was never a Classical scholar of any accuracy or distinction and stopped dead off when the war broke out'.[13] As Frank N. Kersnowski observes, 'Graves had the classical education of his class; but he never accepted its confines, though he would never completely leave it.'[14] It was a classical education on a Victorian model that was already much criticized. Graves's father selected Charterhouse, a public school with no entrance paper in Greek grammar, so that Graves was able to secure the top scholarship of his year.[15] Graves does not seem to have had a high opinion of the school's classical teaching, and quotes a disparaging comment made by a contemporary who was to accompany him from school to St John's College, Oxford, to study *Literae Humaniores* or 'Greats': 'we have spent fourteen years of our lives principally at Latin and Greek, not even competently taught, and now we're going to start another three years of the same thing.'[16] Graves takes pride in the family talent for 'writing graceful Latin verses', a pursuit for which his father had rigorously trained him, with Virgil and Ovid as the prescribed models of metrical correctness; this aptitude is listed not as evidence of poetic inclinations but as one of a set of skills that includes taking examinations, solving puzzles, and filling in forms.[17] In a school where other boys were less skilled at the production of verses, Graves had access to a valued currency: in 'Alcaics Addressed to my Study Fauna' (1913), published in the school magazine, the *Carthusian*, he describes one of the ornaments in his study at school as 'Bought for a couple of Greek

[10] Sagar (2009), 2–3.
[11] Brearton (2008), 73.
[12] Seymour (1995), xviii.
[13] O'Prey (1982), 240.
[14] Kersnowski (2002), 42.
[15] Seymour (1995), 19.
[16] Graves (1960b), 37.
[17] Graves (1960b), 16.

Iambics'.[18] Miranda Seymour observes that such composition gave Graves 'a lasting distaste for virtuosity as opposed to inspiration', and as a critic he is dismissive about the kind of poems that were inspired by the '*gradus ad parnassum* spirit', the odes and pastoral poems of eighteenth-century Augustanism.[19] Nevertheless, he did publish a few Latin poems later in his career.[20] It is worth noting that he found it 'easy' to compose 'mock-heroic satires' about his teachers, 'from sheer boredom with the literary epic'.[21] An aversion to Virgil and an inclination towards satire and parodic forms persist throughout Graves's career.

Graves describes Homer as a bard, 'chanting his epic to the sound of his lyre', affecting his listeners as profoundly as the music and dance of the tragic chorus: 'the poet and his listeners fall under the spell; and whether the mood is love, terror, or a sudden deep understanding of the past or future, the experience is always something that no so-called "prose poetry" can achieve.'[22] Virgil, on the other hand, represents Apollonian 'literary or academic poetry', in which the poet only pretends to be entranced by the Muse: Graves condemns him as 'a literary pretender to poetry'.[23] In 'Virgil the Sorcerer', Graves justifies his aversion to the 'suave hexametrist', 'glib, bald-pated | Self-laurelled Maro', by condemning the 'golden and lick-spittle tongue' that served 'Caesar's most un-Roman tyrannies' (pp. 270–2). Virgil abandoned pastoral poetry in favour of epic, establishing a formula for a successful poetic career that Graves saw as a disastrous influence on Western literature.[24] In *The White Goddess* he dismisses the

[18] Graves (2000a), 730. Further references to this edition are given parenthetically in the text.

[19] Seymour (1995), 23. The *Gradus ad Parnassum* was a dictionary that gave the quantities which would enable the student to select a Latin word which would fit the allocated metre, and also suggested synonyms.

[20] One brief example is 'Jugum Improbum': 'Pyrrha, jugo tandem vitulum junges-ne leoni? | Sit tibi dilectus, num stricto verbere debet | Compelli pavitans medium moriturus in ignem?' Graves (2000a, 610).

[21] Quoted in Seymour (1995), 23.

[22] Graves (1972), 2.

[23] Graves (1972), 2. Graves was elected Professor of Poetry at Oxford, 1961–6: recent predecessors included Maurice Bowra, Cecil Day-Lewis, and W. H. Auden, and Graves was followed by Edmund Blunden. He lectured on Virgil, the 'Anti-Poet', whose two thousand years of unmerited influence over Western culture were, Graves argued, based on the cowardly subservience that endeared him to 'government circles'. For Graves, Virgil was unoriginal, lacking a sense of humour and 'animal spirits'. Quoted in Griffin (1992), 141–2.

[24] See Davis (1999), 209–19.

Aeneid, 'designed to dazzle and overpower', and offers faint praise of Virgil's 'musical and rhetorical skill, the fine-sounding periphrases, and the rolling periods'. Virgil and Horace (a witty and affable 'elegant verse-writer', not a poet) are contrasted unfavourably with the 'fearlessness, originality and emotional sensitivity' and the 'sincere love of women' that Graves finds in Catullus.[25]

Charterhouse proved crucial to Graves's poetic development because of his friendship with George Mallory, who introduced him to Eddie Marsh, a friend of Rupert Brooke and one of the editors of the anthology *Georgian Poetry*. Marsh praised Graves's poems, but pointed out that his diction was outdated: readers of poetry in 1913 might not be receptive to 'the fashions of 1863'.[26] Graves responds that 'it would be most extraordinary if my technique wasn't obsolete': his style had been formed by his 'reading, the immense preponderance of the "classical" over the modern', and the Victorian literary tradition embodied by his father. Nevertheless, Graves pledges, 'when this ridiculous war is over', 'I will write Chapter II at the top of the new sheet and . . . try to root out more effectively the obnoxious survivals of Victorianism'.[27]

Mallory encouraged Graves to read modern authors such as George Bernard Shaw, Rupert Brooke, H. G. Wells, John Masefield, and, crucially, Samuel Butler. In *The Humour of Homer* (1892), Butler seeks to present the *Iliad* and the *Odyssey* to a new readership in an unconventional and un-intimidating manner. The domestic comedy he finds in Homer often features female characters, in line with his theory that the 'authoress of the *Odyssey*' was more novelist than epic poet. His idiosyncratic interpretations provoked readers such as the classical scholar Jane Harrison, whom Butler suspected of having written a scathing anonymous review titled 'How to Vulgarize Homer'.[28] His rapid paraphrases pile up mundane details in a gossipy tone that anticipates James Joyce's treatment of the Nausicaa and Penelope figures in *Ulysses* (1922): 'First [Juno] bolted herself inside her own room on the top of Mount Ida and had a thorough good wash. Then she scented herself, brushed her golden hair, put on her very best dress and all her jewels. When she had done this, she went to Venus and besought her for the loan of her charms.'[29] Like Joyce, Graves appreciated and imitated Butler's good-humoured assaults on

[25] Graves (1999b), 383. [26] Graves (1960b), 48. [27] O'Prey (1982), 30.
[28] Robinson (2002), 115. [29] Butler (1913), 70.

the dignity of Homer. The idea that Homer was a 'deadpan' joker, an entertainer who knew what the public liked, is one that Graves keeps returning to, excavating the real Homer from the dusty platitudes of centuries of schoolmasters and classical scholars: 'The point missed by dreary generations of dull dogs, says Mr. Graves, is Homer's caustic humour.' Graves's Homer was a satirist rather than a tragedian, 'an iconoclast with a deep sense of irony who had to wrap up his jokes about the gods and his lampooning of the ancient heroes to get them by his stuffy public'.[30]

The ease with which classically educated officers such as Rupert Brooke, Charles Hamilton Sorley, and Robert Graves translated their wartime experiences into Homeric terms has been explored in scholarship on the literature of the Great War.[31] Officers who were barely out of school or university read Homer in the trenches, but discovered the ideal of epic heroism to be impossible to reconcile with the conflict in which they found themselves. Rupert Brooke died of blood-poisoning on the Greek island of Skyros before he ever reached the Dardanelles, where he had hoped to fight on 'the plains of Troy'.[32] In a letter to Eddie Marsh, Graves undercuts his father's sentimental image of the poet as a Greek hero: 'my Father (dear old man!) said that this was a fitting end for Rupert, killed by the arrows of jealous Musagetes [Apollo] in his own Greek islands; but fine words won't help.'[33] Romanticized allusions to fallen heroes and Georgian lyricism in the style of Brooke proved untenable as Graves became increasingly cynical about the war; Siegfried Sassoon, who said that war should not be written about in 'a realistic way', had not yet experienced trench warfare.[34]

In 1916 Graves was reading Charles Hamilton Sorley, 'a brilliant young poet' killed in action in 1915, who had been awarded a classical scholarship in Graves's first year at Oxford.[35] In an early example of

[30] Quoted in Kersnowski (1989), 69–70. Graves gives a similar justification of his enjoyment of Apuleius: '*The Golden Ass* is a very much better book than I had suspected and the queer Latin is a deliberate joke, a parody of the high-faluting style of the popular story teller who liked to impress audiences at fairs and street corners.' O'Prey (1984), 47.

[31] See Vandiver (1999), 432–55, and (2010).

[32] 'Do you think *perhaps*... they'll make a sortie and meet us on the plains of Troy? It seems to me strategically so possible.... Will the sea be polyphloisbic and wine-dark and unvintageable?' Brooke (1968), 662.

[33] O'Prey (1982), 31.

[34] Graves (1960b).

[35] O'Prey (1982), 39.

his habit of rewriting other poets' texts to produce versions that he considered superior, Graves writes in 1916 to Siegfried Sassoon, saying that he would 'love' to suggest some emendations to Sorley's 'When You See Millions of the Mouthless Dead' and what Graves calls the 'Odyssey poem'.[36] This last is a verse letter addressed to the 'bard' of Marlborough (the public school at which Sorley was a pupil), beginning: 'I have not brought my Odyssey | With me here across the sea . . . ' The poet is confident that his reader will 'remember' the Homeric poems, and can therefore mingle recollections of Greek epic with the diction of twentieth-century warfare and a wistful stanza about the pastoral delights of the England the poet is fighting for, before briefly alluding to the realities of the 'battered trenches'. However, given Graves's admiration of the poem (the emendation he suggests is a minor one), it is worth noting that Sorley treats Homer's characters with the conversational irreverence that Graves appreciates in Samuel Butler and emulates in many of his own poems:

> The honey-sweet converse of men,
> The splendid bath, the change of dress,
> Then—oh the grandeur of their Mess,
> The henchmen, the prim stewardess!
> And oh the breaking of old ground,
> The tales, after the port went round!
> (The wondrous wiles of old Odysseus,
> Old Agamemnon and his misuse
> Of his command, and that young chit
> Paris—who didn't care a bit
> For Helen . . .)[37]

Sorley's poem reflects a distrust of military commanders, but an appreciation of the camaraderie of the army. Graves was increasingly cynical about the purpose of the war, which he saw as a trade rivalry carried on for profit, but considered the idea of belonging to a regiment as a beneficial one for men.[38] He does not represent war in terms of heroic deeds or national glory but as a mundane existence. In 'The Legion', a Roman centurion who has survived battles with Belgian and Gallic tribes grumbles about the new recruits who have

[36] O'Prey (1982), 48. For Graves's revisions of Milton, Wordsworth, and other poets as 'powerful misreadings', see Bennett (1999), 19–35.

[37] Sorley (1916), 74. [38] Kersnowski (2002), 43–6.

replaced his dead comrades, describing them as 'Unsoldierlike, slovenly, bent on loot'. He is rebuked by his companion, who reminds him, 'The Legion is the Legion while Rome stands' and predicts a victory over Gaul. Graves, like other writers at the time, is responding to the invasion of Belgium and France by the Germans, suggesting a parallel to Roman incursions, yet the 'Roman' soldiers have much in common with British troops. Elizabeth Vandiver remarks that in the poem Rome is an important and ambivalent 'symbolic equivalent' for Britain, and Graves invites different readings of the relationship.[39] In 'The Cuirassiers of the Frontier' the speaker describes a camp full of soldiers, 'Goths, Vandals, Huns, Isaurian mountaineers', who are fighting for Rome, a metropolitan civilization they do not belong to, and who are loyal only because they receive food, arms, and the opportunity to fight. Graves often chooses to speak from the point of view of an outsider rather than a central figure: in the prose poem 'As It Were Poems', the speaker claims to have been present at the events recorded in a variety of legends, including those of Reynard the Fox, Robin Hood, Isis, and Apuleius' *Metamorphoses.* In most of these legends he does not identify with the hero—like T. S. Eliot's Prufrock, who sees himself not as Prince Hamlet but an 'attendant lord', 'almost ridiculous— | Almost, at times, the Fool'.[40] Graves often takes on the perspective of hurt, sick, or dying men: in the legend of the Trojan War, he is Ajax, the son of Telamon, whom Odysseus cheats of the dead Achilles' armour. The speaker goes on to accuse Odysseus of setting him up to be seen as a 'madman' by replacing the Trojans he had killed with 'slaughtered sheep' (p. 334).[41]

Even in contemplating his own nearness to death, Graves adopts a tone of humorous detachment. Seriously wounded at the Battle of the Somme in 1916, he was thought to have died. Although he survived and was taken to hospital, his death had already been reported in *The Times.* In 'Escape' (p. 27), Graves depicts his experience as a temporary death, a journey to the underworld followed by a return to life. His underworld is a mythical realm inhabited by figures from Greek and Roman literature. Unlike Virgil's Aeneas and Dante in the *Inferno*, he

[39] Vandiver (2010), 21–7.

[40] 'The Love Song of J. Alfred Prufrock', in Eliot (1954), 7.

[41] In Sophocles's *Ajax*, when the hero experiences a fit of madness sent upon him by Athene, he attacks a flock of sheep in the belief that he is killing the Greek kings who cheated him of Achilles' arms, and then commits suicide when he realizes that he has brought shame on himself.

does not have to pass Cerberus, as he is already 'half-way along the road to Lethe' when he becomes conscious. Proserpine, the queen of the underworld who remains connected to the earth and returns there every spring, decides that he is not really dead and sends him back along the road he unconsciously travelled. He is pursued by comically indignant groups of 'demons, heroes, and policeman-ghosts', and at first thinks he can get past Cerberus by threatening him with his revolver, before realizing that he has no weapons. He succeeds in escaping by addressing the three-headed beast like a pet, and pacifying him with a drugged morsel based on army rations:

> Not even a honeyed sop . . .
> Nothing . . . . Good Cerberus! . . . Good dog! . . . but stop!
> Stay! . . . A great luminous thought . . . I do believe
> There's still some morphia that I bought on leave.
> Then swiftly Cerberus' wide mouths I cram
> With army biscuit smeared with ration jam;
> And sleep lurks in the luscious plum and apple.
> He crunches, swallows, stiffens, seems to grapple
> With the all-powerful poppy . . . then a snore,
> A crash; the beast blocks up the corridor
> With monstrous hairy carcase, red and dun—
> Too late! for I've sped through.
> O Life! O Sun!

The pathos of untimely death is forgotten as the soldier dodges the unconscious monster and sprints back to earth. Elizabeth Vandiver notes that while there is an obvious reference to the Sibyl in the *Aeneid* overcoming Cerberus with a similar honeyed sop, the 'comic touch' with which the scene is handled recalls another *katabasis*, that of Dionysus in Aristophanes's *Frogs*.[42]

Nietzsche was one of a small number of authors (including Keats, Homer, and Samuel Butler) whose works Graves had with him during the war: these books had a powerful influence over his development of theories of poetry.[43] *The Birth of Tragedy* (1872) identifies a struggle between Apollonian and Dionysian elements, two irreconcilable aspects of human experience, as the central theme of Greek literature and myth. The Delphic god Apollo is associated with civilization, intelligence, and technical skill in art; Dionysus with

[42] Vandiver (2010), 317–18. [43] Seymour (1995), 44.

wine, festivals, music, and instinct. Graves emphasizes the Dionysian origins of poetry in religious ritual and in dance. He wants poets and critics to accept his theory that Apollo (the sun god) had usurped the position of a female lunar deity, the White Goddess, just as he later took control of the Delphic Oracle from its priestess. Where Nietzsche saw the balancing of Apollonian and Dionysian elements in Athenian tragedy as the ideal form of art, Graves condemns Apollonian classicism as harmful to poetry. For Graves, genuine poetry is invariably concerned with 'the relations of man and woman, rather than those of man and man'. He criticizes 'Apollonian Classicists', who attempt to be independent of women and 'fall into sentimental homosexuality'.[44] In 'Apollo of the Physiologists' (p. 408), his detestation of the 'Victorian-Hellenistic' 'academic god' even extends to his role as healer. Poetry, Graves asserts, must deal with love and death: 'a true poem is necessarily an invocation of the White Goddess, the Muse, the Mother of all Living, the ancient power of fright and lust . . . whose embrace is death'. He finds classical poetry unsatisfactory because Apollonian poets, influenced by philosophers like Socrates, value logic and decorum too highly and do not acknowledge the authority of the White Goddess, 'a lovely, slender woman with a hooked nose, deathly pale face, lips red as rowan-berries, startlingly blue eyes and long fair hair; she will suddenly transform herself into sow, mare, bitch, vixen, she-ass, weasel, serpent, owl, she-wolf, tigress, mermaid or loathsome hag'.[45] Graves first found a version of the muse who embodies love and death in a poem by Keats, 'La Belle Dame Sans Merci',[46] and although he criticizes Romantic writers for their mental and physical weaknesses, he acknowledges that they can achieve a properly 'fatalistic regard for the Goddess'.[47] Grevel Lindop argues that the White Goddess owes something to the later nineteenth century in the idea of the 'eternal feminine', a divine female power that possesses the mortal women who inspire artists and poets.[48]

[44] Graves (1999b), 437–8. Graves describes here a conversation in which one of his Oxford tutors will only admit that Sappho is 'very, very good' once he is sure that his confession will not be overheard. In asserting Sappho's 'unique authority', Graves also refutes the 'malevolent lies of the Attic comedians who caricature her as an insatiable Lesbian'.

[45] Graves (1999b), 20.

[46] R. P. Graves (2003), 22.

[47] Graves (1999b), 21.

[48] The *femmes fatales* Lindop invokes as a comparison include Pater's 'Gioconda' from *The Renaissance* (1873), Swinburne's Proserpine, and the triple figures of the 'Well-Beloved' in Thomas Hardy's novel. 'Introduction', in Graves (1999a), xi.

On returning to Oxford after the war, Graves decided to study English instead of Classics (as did Edmund Blunden, also a war poet and friend of Siegfried Sassoon, although he only stayed for one term). However, this change of degree did not involve a complete rejection of the classical tradition: Graves valued St John's for the college's association with A. E. Housman, who had become a distinguished poet and classical scholar despite his disastrous results in Greats. Living in a house rented from the poet John Masefield, in an area nicknamed Parnassus (Boars Hill), Graves was surrounded by poets and scholars who were immersed in Greek and Latin literature and whose own work renewed those classical texts for a twentieth-century readership, such as the Poet Laureate Robert Bridges and the classical scholar and translator Gilbert Murray.

At this time Graves was also influenced by the psychologist and anthropologist W. H. R. Rivers, an expert in shell shock whose patients had included Siegfried Sassoon and Wilfred Owen. Rivers helped Graves to explore the connection between the unconscious and creativity, persuading him that writing about pain and then analysing the poems he produced would be more effective than attempting to repress his war experiences.[49] Graves remained sceptical about Freud, as the poem 'Hippopotamus's Address to the Freudians' suggests.[50] Rivers also introduced Graves to Sir James Frazer's *The Golden Bough* (1890), a work of comparative mythology that proposed a new understanding of primitive religions and influenced T. S. Eliot's *The Waste Land* (1922).[51] Grevel Lindop argues that Frazer's work was 'probably the one book most fundamental to the methods and conclusions of *The White Goddess*'. Frazer contended that ancient religions centred on the death of a god-king who killed his predecessor and reigned until he was either killed by his successor or sacrificed at the end of the year. Graves's 'brilliantly simple transformation' of Frazer's theory suggested that the god-king was only important because he married the immortal goddess-queen

[49] Seymour (1995), 106.

[50] Responding to Plutarch's *Of Isis And Osiris*, the poem represents the hippopotamus indignantly claiming that Oedipus has been improperly credited for what should be the Hippopotamus complex: 'I slew my sire, | I forced my dam. ... Free from repression | Or urge to confession, | Freud's little lamb.'

[51] Shalom Goldman describes Graves's *The White Goddess* as 'a kind of displacement and rearrangement of the central themes of *The Golden Bough*, ... radically different' from Eliot's response: Goldman (2003), 43.

whom Graves called the White Goddess.[52] Miranda Seymour comments that the synthesis of 'magical and dangerous' maenads and muses in Jane Harrison's *Prolegomena to the Study of Greek Religion* (1903) is a vital addition to Frazer in Graves's developing idea of the White Goddess. Harrison's writing on matriarchy influenced his theory (first explored in 1944 in *The Golden Fleece*) that the Greeks had defeated an earlier matriarchal civilization and challenged the supremacy of the Triple Goddess (bride, mother, and crone), replacing her with Zeus and the Olympian pantheon.[53]

Graves's friend T. S. Matthews describes his approach as the creative restoration of an original myth:

> To Robert the orthodox version of the Greek myths was an attempt to cover up or give a false interpretation to the older myths that lay behind them, and he set himself the task of peeling off the top layer of the palimpsest and restoring the faint traces of the original. Pure scholarship would have been unequal to this job, since too much evidence was lacking. Robert undertook to supply the missing evidence, either by setting the scholars at naught and reinterpreting what they had misunderstood or by imagining the nature or even the form of the missing facts.[54]

Graves himself repeatedly distinguishes his own 'heterodox' approach from that of university scholars, who must take care not to get out of step with their colleagues.[55] In some notes on his approach to history in *I, Claudius*, Graves comments: 'wherever authors have disagreed, or there has been a gap or confusion or mystery or they were obviously lying I have felt free to invent.'[56] In his treatment of myth, whether in poetry, fiction (*The Golden Fleece*), or non-fictional prose (*The Greek Myths*), Graves appears to operate on similar principles, taking liberties that a classical scholar could not. Much of his work on myth depends on the assumption that the Greek myths have a basis in historical fact, and in particular on changes in religious belief and ritual. In *The Golden Fleece*, a priestess of the matriarchal moon goddess in the sacred orange grove at Deya (near Graves's home in Majorca) is seen as resisting the influence of Ancaeus, the last surviving Argonaut, and ordering her followers to kill him. She is

[52] Lindop (2003), 30.
[53] Seymour (1995), 306–8. See also R. P. Graves (2003), 16–18.
[54] Kersnowski (1989), 20.
[55] Graves (1999b), 235.
[56] O'Prey (1982), 349.

horrified by his tales of Greek society, in which a man is the head of the household and they despise the Triple Goddess:

> The Nymph wondered whether she had misheard the words. She asked, 'Who may the *Father God* be? How can any tribe worship a *Father*? . . . The woman, not the man, is the agent, he the tool always. She gives the orders, he obeys. Is it not the woman who chooses the man, and overcomes him by the sweetness of her perfumed presence and . . . takes her pleasure of him, and when she has done, leaves him lying like a dead man?'[57]

Ancaeus explains the Greek system by which a father chooses a woman to be the mother of his children, and then has the power to reject her and send her back to her father's house if he wishes. It is significant that Graves chooses to locate the last surviving outpost of matriarchy so close to home, as the balance of power between man and woman, or the masculine and the feminine, is a constant preoccupation in his poetry and criticism. If a poet must love his muse, who is an incarnation of the White Goddess, his relationship to her will be closer to that described by the Nymph than to the patriarchal system Ancaeus defends.

In the surprisingly brief account of Pygmalion and Galatea which Graves gives in *The Greek Myths*, Pygmalion falls in love with Aphrodite and, 'because she would not lie with him, made an ivory image of her and laid it in his bed, praying to her for pity. Entering into this image, Aphrodite brought it to life as Galatea.'[58] Graves wrote two poems based on the myth: 'Pygmalion to Galatea' (1926) and 'Galatea and Pygmalion' (1938). In the first of these the sculptor addresses the woman he designed for himself, describing the qualities he wishes her to possess. She is to be his ideal woman: 'lovely', 'merciful', 'constant', yet 'various'. As he elaborates on these attributes, he begins conventionally with her beauty, then asks for a mercy that 'abstain[s] from pity', desiring her to prize her 'self-honour' and allow him to preserve his. When he asks for constancy, he wants her not to 'mask' the beauty he created, but to keep their love 'aloof and strange, | Keep it from gluttonous eyes, from stairway gossip'. She must be 'various' enough to keep the relationship interesting inside the confines of their

[57] Graves (2011b), 8–9.

[58] Graves (1960b) 65; Graves cites Apollodorus, Ovid and Arnobius as sources of the myth, and explains the statue as 'the goddess's white cult-image', which Aphrodite's priest kept in his bed; Graves (1960c), 212.

'fair-paved garden', graceful, 'witty, kind, enduring, unsubjected' (pp. 272–3). As Simon Brittan notes, Galatea is no longer a statue but not yet fully human: to reach Pygmalion she must step down from her pedestal and be debased, in order to comply with a 'sequence of demands and conditions so stringent that they would be more suitably addressed to Galatea as statue than as human'.[59] This domineering Pygmalion wants to mould Galatea as a lover, just as he shaped the beautiful limbs that he admires at the start of the poem.

In 'Galatea and Pygmalion' (pp. 353–4) the sculptor is no longer happy with his creation. The artist who 'enchanted' her from marble with his 'furious chisel' then sees his 'longings' fulfilled when she descends from her pedestal to his bed. He is 'lubricious' and drunken, she a 'woman monster' who 'Enroyalled his body with her demon blood'. Patrick Quinn interprets the poem in relation to Graves's life, as an 'allegory of a fading relationship' that reflects his increasingly intense artistic and personal conflicts with Laura Riding, who forced Graves to remain celibate.[60] Pygmalion's monstrous creation is also an artistic rival, as she attracts the attention of 'schools of eager connoisseurs' and, despite his jealousy, asserts her independence. She seeks fame for herself, not for him. Essaka Joshua argues that this poem is part of a 'revolution in viewpoint' in interpretations of the myth that 'concentrate keenly on Galatea's rights, her choices and her reaction to being created by Pygmalion'.[61] However, Graves is more concerned with the suffering of the artist whose cruel muse has sapped his artistic and sexual energies. Another poem from this period is 'Leda' (pp. 356–7), in which the 'Heart' develops a lecherous fantasy about Leda's 'horror' at being raped by Zeus in the guise of a swan, which becomes a dismayed depiction of her enjoyment:

> Then soon your mad religious smile
> Made taut the belly, arched the breast,
> And there beneath your god awhile
> You strained and gulped your beastliest.

Quinn argues that this stanza is a concession to Riding's belief in celibacy: 'by surrendering to sensual pleasure, the human is reduced to the status of a dumb beast, reminiscent of the Circe myth perhaps.'[62] Douglas Day compares Graves's depiction of an 'ugly

[59] Brittan (1999), 88.
[60] Quinn (1999), 101–2.
[61] Joshua (2001), 137.
[62] Joshua (2001), 98–9.

occurrence', a 'terrifying and sordid exhibition of lust', with that of Yeats in 'Leda and the Swan' (1923), 'primarily a mystical or religious experience' that leads to the founding of a new civilization.[63] The final stanza of Graves's poem is filled with a disgust that extends beyond the critique of Leda's lustful response to Zeus and reminds the reader that the conception of Helen led to 'bawdry, murder and deceit'.

In 'Judgement of Paris' (p. 536), Graves ponders how different Greek myth would have been if Paris had not chosen to give the apple to Aphrodite, but had instead 'favoured buxom Hera, | Divine defendress of the marriage couch'. Then Helen would have stayed with Menelaus, Hector might have died 'unhonoured in his bed', and the poets would have had to celebrate 'a meaner siege'. Graves argues in a lecture that the 'theme of complementary love does not occur in Classical literature, even by Homer'. Paris and Helen are drawn together by physical attraction, but Helen blames herself for having deserted Menelaus. Graves suggests that the 'domestic affection between Hector and his wife Andromache' is an enduring love, ended only by the masculine code of honour that sends him to his death, 'but the blind overwhelming power which took Helen to Troy has been sanctified in poetry at the expense of all other emotions, despite the eventual defeat of both lovers'.[64] The speaker of 'New Legends' (pp. 316–17) affirms the satisfaction of domestic contentment with an undemanding mistress. She is the opposite of a number of mythic heroines: a serene Andromeda, 'Chained to no cliff, | Asking no rescue of me', a Niobe with no children, an Atalanta who does not challenge him to race with her. D. N. G. Carter describes this poem (originally titled 'The Age of Uncertainty'), dating from an early and harmonious phase of Graves's relationship with Laura Riding, as a celebration of freedom from traditional gender roles, so that a man who recognizes a woman as an individual is enabled to 'cast off the burdensome prejudices of his patriarchal conditioning.'[65] In 'Anchises to Aphrodite' (p. 506), Anchises happily accepts his subservient position and marvels that the goddess has deigned to warm his couch. He is happy to take his place as one of thousands of lovers, even though he is aware that those who preceded him are 'gone as if they had not been'. This 'man-lion' adopts the kind of

[63] Day (1963), 135. [64] Graves (1995), 475. [65] Carter (1989), 230.

submissive tone that Graves's Pygmalion wants to hear from Galatea: 'Enroyalled I await your pleasure | And starve if you would have it so.'

Another poem that questions whether the patriarchal model of love can work is 'Ovid in Defeat' (1925). Graves imagines the poet in exile, still teaching the arts of love. Theodore Ziolkowski cites this poem as evidence that efforts to rehabilitate Ovid's reputation in the recent '*annus mirabilis Ovidianus*' (1922) had not been 'widely successful'. He describes Graves's 'bitter' poem as betraying 'an almost personal animosity towards Ovid . . . and toward the love code of his *Ars amatoria*'.[66] The last two lines of the first stanza describe Ovid's outlandish appearance in 'bearskin breeches', and are based on a line from Ovid's *Tristia* that Graves cites in a footnote: '*pellibus et sutis arcent mala frigora braccis.*'[67] Some of the precepts attributed to Ovid in this poem allude to the *Ars Amatoria*, although others have no obvious parallel. Genevieve Liveley describes Graves's poem as 'a neat synthesis of Ovid's erotic teachings', with a 'parodic abbreviation' of Ovid's own parodic farming imagery:[68]

> Let man be ploughshare,
> Woman his field;
> Flatter, beguile, assault,
> And she must yield.

As Liveley observes, while flattery, deceitful promises, and some degree of force are all part of the strategies Ovid suggests a lover will need to employ, Graves's rendering makes the 'aggressive power play' explicit and threatening. Graves reverses the Ovidian image, in which the persistent lover is like the field that gradually wears down the ploughshare.[69] The seriousness of Graves's pseudo-Ovidian proposition is called into question by the chiming of 'field' and 'yield'; the comic use of rhyme in this poem is best exemplified by the Byronic 'gist is' and '*tristis*':

> Follows his conclusion
> Of which the gist is

66 Ziolkowski (2005), 73.

67 *Tristia* 3.10.19. 'They keep off the dreadful cold with trousers of sewn skins.'

68 Liveley (2005), 41–4.

69 *Ars Amatoria* 1.474: *interit adsidua vomer aduncus humo*—'a curved ploughshare crumbles with constant ploughing of the ground'.

The cold 'post coitum
Homo tristis'.[70]

Graves then tries out another version of the image of the field and the ploughshare to characterize a 'newer vision', a simple reversal of gender roles so that man is the field ploughed by a woman. He develops the theme by further describing the man with a traditionally feminine metaphor, as a 'plucked flower' lying in the mire, seduced and abandoned by a woman who no longer desires him. Graves appears to argue that men are either vulnerable or already defeated by their cruel mistresses, the 'unfair fair'. However, this is not the conclusion of the poem—he goes on to establish that the reader (addressed by the poet as 'My amorous brother') must progress beyond such ideas of conflict and domination to an understanding that women are men's equals, 'Neither more nor less'. 'Plough then salutes plough', the final stanza begins, without attempting to explain how this symbolic parity might work. This is not the bitterly personal rejection of Ovidian precepts that Ziolkowski suggests, although Graves does disapprove of the Roman poet's 'erotic gamesmanship'.[71] In the end, the poet mockingly triumphs over the wretched Ovid, who stamps off through the snow with a 'toothache' inflicted on him by Graves.

Illicit longings underlying quiet domestic affection are the theme of 'An Idyll of Old Age' (pp. 140–2), in which Graves revises an episode from Book 8 of Ovid's *Metamorphoses*, the story of the aged couple Baucis and Philemon. Like Ovid, Graves expands on an element of the original myth and treats it from a comically unexpected point of view. Zeus and Hermes visit these poor but virtuous rustics and consume their simple food and drink. Then, as the gods lie 'shivering' in the spare bedroom, they eavesdrop on their hosts' conversation. The theme of their dialogue is love: Philemon celebrates married love as the merging of souls, and goes on to question the significance of the

[70] In 'Ovid and the Libertines', a review of Guy Lee's 1968 translation of the *Amores*, Graves takes up this phrase again, claiming that 'Ovid's generalization *post coitum homo tristis* ("after coition a man feels sad") is no longer challenged because simple, affectionate, trustful love-making has gone out of fashion. Nor has any convincing solution to the problem of how to reconcile marital with romantic love yet been offered.' He contends that modern life has blighted marital romance, especially for couples with children. Graves (1972), 133.

[71] Graves (1972), 135.

boyish 'ideal friendship' that he had experienced before marriage. Such affection is innocent and holy, when the lover is afraid even to touch the beloved. For a reader who is familiar with the Ovidian account of the devoted couple, Baucis's response is unexpected. She expresses affection for her husband, but also longs to be set free: she confesses that her eye is drawn to younger men, like the guest (Hermes), whose 'body brings my heart hotter romance | Than your dear face could ever spark within me'. Philemon is not shocked, but prepared to consider whether 'adulterous licence' might make them happy, whether the pure of soul would lose anything by experiencing 'the body's rapture | With a body not its mate'. He goes on to grant Baucis permission to go her own way and find love, and she offers him the same freedom. Zeus, despite his own multiple infidelities, is 'struck dumb at this unholy compact', but Hermes assumes that their faithful marital love will prove greater than the lust they talk about. The joke, in this poem, is on the gods, who are taken in by an invented dilemma, one that acts as entertainment for a couple who are physically beyond the infidelities they enjoy contemplating:

> Eternal Gods deny the sense of humour
> That well might prejudice their infallible power,
> So Hermes and King Zeus not once considered,
> In treating of this idyll overheard,
> That love rehearses after life's defeat.
> Baucis, kind soul, was palsied, withered and bent,
> Philemon, too, was ten years impotent.

Past love is also the subject of 'Theseus and Ariadne', in which Graves again tells the story from an unexpected perspective. While many poets and artists had depicted the sufferings of the deserted Ariadne, or her dramatic rescue by Dionysus, Graves focuses on Theseus's lonely old age. He dreams of the lost Ariadne, although he had once 'wearied of her constancy'. She, meanwhile, plays the queen 'to nobler company' (p. 404). Graves represents the aged Theseus once more at a disadvantage in 'Heroes in their Prime'. This poem highlights the discreditable stories that counter more commendable exploits in the lives of several Greek heroes: Theseus is mocked as the 'old, bald King of Athens', 'forced into self-banishment' by his own folly, before he is praised as the 'tall youth who laid low Procrustes' and killed the Minotaur. Similarly, Bellerophon is seen as the undignified 'tattered outcast' 'pitched into a thorn-bush' by Pegasus, before he is applauded for his victory over the fiery Chimaera. The apex of Jason's career is the capture of the Golden Fleece, contrasting with his miserable end as a 'chap-fallen beggar' in Corinth. The last two stanzas reveal Graves's twist on these extremes of heroic experience: while Theseus, Bellerophon, and Jason were distinguished as young men and later betrayed their early promise, there is a hero who achieved his prime as an old man. This hero is Nestor, who as a 'young braggart' hid from the Calydonian boar by climbing a tree, but in old age is revered by the heroes of Troy (p. 489). Graves brings out the untold stories and lampoons the ancient heroes, exposing them to a bracing realism that reveals their comic potential. It is no surprise that Ovid should have inspired such mocking treatment of gods and heroes, and Graves's aversion to Virgil, his resistance to academic poetry, and his fascination with the arts of love suggest that he might see himself as an Ovidian artist. As in his retelling of the Greek myths and the legends of the White Goddess, Graves's appetite for narrative, his appeal to multitudinous sources, and his unorthodox scholarship combine to create an interpretation of the classics that is distinctive and engaging. His love of Homer, the 'true poet' who casts a spell over his audience, pervades Graves's poetry, and his description of Homer might well apply to Graves himself as an interpreter of the classics: 'an iconoclast with a deep sense of irony.'

11

Restoring Narcissus

The Love Poems of Robert Graves

John Burnside

On 31 October 1917 T. S. Eliot wrote to Ezra Pound: 'I have been invited . . . to contribute to a reading of poets: big wigs, OSWALD and EDITH Shitwell [*sic*], Graves (query, George?), Nichols, and OTHERS.'

I imagine, had Robert Graves been in a position to read this letter, he would have found it amusing; his attitude towards the self—of the *named*, or social self that is—is always robust (indeed, we might say that it is more so than Eliot's was, at around this time), and his sense of *his* self remained, in most circumstances, more or less solid, throughout his career, as illustrated by the poem, 'My Name and I', which begins:

> The impartial Law enrolled a name
>   For my especial use:
> My rights in it would rest the same
> Whether I puffed it into fame
>   Or sank it in abuse.[1]

and later, continuing to make a distinction between the social self 'forced on me by fate' and the 'I' that 'was always I | Illegal and unknown' (one cannot help but recall, here, Jesus of Nazareth's dictum: 'Before Abraham was, I am'), insists that, while the speaker cannot repudiate 'This noun, this natal star | This gentlemanly self',

[1] 'My Name and I', Graves (1975), 143.

he is not identical with that socially conditioned being, created by 'Time and the registrar', saying:

> Yet, understand, I am not he
> Either in mind or limb;
> My name will take less thought for me,
> In worlds of men I cannot see,
> Than ever I for him.[2]

It is a sound and healthy distinction that Graves makes here, one from which we can fairly conclude that he had no intention of allowing himself (his 'truer' self, so to speak) to be perturbed by the competitiveness, or the contempt, of other poets, or indeed by the social world generally. What he did understand, however—and what his love poetry repeatedly explores throughout his career—is the very real threat to selfhood occasioned by sexual and/or romantic love in its debased forms, which might be described as varieties of 'needy attachment'. Again and again, especially in the earlier work, he returns to the theme of the potential loss of self—the loss of integrity, of reason, of independence—to the beloved and, while the statement of this problem was often glossed with irony or (often somewhat dark) humour,[3] we cannot help but feel that it was a very real one for someone of his passionate and idealistic temperament.

Indeed, what makes Graves such a fascinating love poet, is the fact that, over a lifetime, he is such a careful anatomist of those passionate and idealistic tendencies, a writer who is always unflinchingly honest about sexual craving and about the irrational impulses, such as jealousy, needy attachment, or the existential fear of being consumed or overwhelmed by the object of his desire, that haunt him. And even when it seems that he has entered into a just and equal partnership with the loved one, and is able to surrender his panic, the pleasure is marred by his own, and by the Beloved's, perfectionism—a strange yet familiar scruple of those for whom the marriage of two minds is alternately supreme fulfilment and painful test:

> Interalienation of their hearts
> It was not, though both played resentful parts

[2] Graves (1975), 143.

[3] One thinks of the squib, 'I'd Die For You' here: 'I'd die for you, or you for me, | So furious is our jealousy— | And if you doubt this to be true | Kill me outright, lest I kill you.' Graves (1975), 33.

In proud unwillingness to share
One house, one pillow, the same fare.
It was perfectionism, they confess,
To know the truth and ask for nothing less.

Their fire-eyed guardians watched from overhead:
'These two alone have learned to love,' they said,
'But neither can forget
They are not worthy of each other yet.'[4]

That this perfectionism is constantly compromised by the basest desires—the lust of 'Down, Wanton, Down', say, or the neediness of the loved one whose own sense of self depends too much upon acceptance by the (or perhaps *any*) other (a condition described in 'Prison Walls')—should come as no surprise, but rational love is also threatened by something that, although less easily recognized, contains its own very real dangers. By which I mean the desire to detach the self from the irrational and destructive force of romantic love and move on, alone, into the apparent perfection of isolation, as in the beautiful, if rather too deliberated, 'A Former Attachment':

And glad to find, on again looking at it,
It meant even less to me than I had thought—
You know the ship is moving when you see
The boxes on the quayside slide away
And become smaller—and feel a calm delight
When the port's cleared and the coast is out of sight,
And ships are few, each on its proper course,
With no occasion for approach or discourse.[5]

What could be more tempting, to the passionate soul, than this easy detachment? It seems almost perverse to point out that the poem begins, not with a renunciation of the desired object—surely the spiritual ideal in any meaningful discipline of detachment—but with a looking back upon what has been taken away. The fox who has lost his tail will, inevitably, seek to persuade himself, and others, that tails are less desirable or needful than they once seemed. Yet this is by no means the whole story, as a close reading of any number of poems makes clear. For Graves knows that there is a fundamental

[4] 'Perfectionists', Graves (1975), 343.
[5] 'A Former Attachment', Graves (1975), 79.

flaw in the conventions of romantic love and, afflicted with the romantic temperament as he is, he rediscovers, and reminds us of that flaw every time he falls. Like Ulysses, 'never done | With woman whether gowned as wife or whore', he found himself 'bound fast | Hand and foot helpless to the vessel's mast, | Yet would not stop his ears', and even though he sometimes 'loathed the fraud', again and again he finds himself unable to 'bed alone', or, indeed, to succumb to the temptation of emotional withdrawal.

'I'm a romantic', says F. Scott Fitzgerald, and he continues: 'A sentimental person thinks things will last, a romantic person hopes against hope that they won't.'[6] This condition—what we might call *terminal* perfectionism—is the defining characteristic of the romantic, the means by which he or she manages to have their cake and eat it too. We might see this condition as merely pathological—by demanding the impossible and so making of failure an inevitability, the romantic avoids being consumed by what Graves calls 'the harsh pride of need'[7]—but it seems to me that there is more to it than that. One might even argue that romanticism is a spiritual discipline—or at least, that it resembles one—in which the non-contingent self, the integrity of the 'I that was always I | Illegal and Unknown', is preserved and so dedicated to some nobler or more just pursuit than the self-validation of another romance. It might be argued, indeed, that this integrity is the subject of Graves's late, and remarkably serene, poem 'Singleness in Love':

> And the magic law long governing our lives
> As poets, how should it be rightly phrased?
> Not as injunction, not as interdiction,
> But as true power of singleness in love
> (The self-same power guarding the fifth dimension
> In which we live and move
> Perfect in time gone by and time foreknown)
> Our endless glory to be bound in love,
> Nor ever lost by cheating circumstance.[8]

This romantic's commitment to the original self naturally prompts in Graves a mistrust of the Freudians, whom he sees as

[6] Fitzgerald (1920), bk. 2, ch. 1.
[7] 'The Green Woods of Unrest', Graves (1975), 551.
[8] 'Singleness in Love', Graves (1975), 539.

unnaturally preoccupied with the crude and nasty elements of human desire:

> Freud's position is briefly this,' he says, 'that every dream is expressing some sort of desire which the dreamer in his waking life has not been able to attain and, more than that, has not even dared to consider, because somehow horrible, or unnatural or very strongly disapproved of... These wishes are centred in the passions and in order to account for children dreaming, Freud has been forced to say that even very small children are subject to the same inclinations and passions as grown persons; it is this theory that has given Freud most ill-fame and frightened away the common-sense man more than ever from the subject, particularly as the Freudian theory soon attracted to Vienna a number of students who liked nastiness for its own sake.[9]

Thus the Freudians, in their abandonment of 'common-sense' scruples, are disdained by Graves, who always fiercely opposes reductionism, just as they are by the Scottish psychoanalyst Ian D. Suttie, whose work—radical and illuminating in its critique of the cruder aspects of Freudian theory, and not perhaps as widely known today as it ought to be—I will come to in the final section of this essay. First, though, I would like to propose a review of our ideas of selfhood and the nature of love by way of a rather unexpected figure, one upon whom Graves touches only briefly, in *The Greek Myths*, but who seems to me not only to be one of the most misunderstood figures in myth, but also a leading player in the creation of a new—by which I mean old—understanding of what we mean by ideas like 'romantic love' and 'the integrity of the self'. This character is also, I think, an informing energy in Graves's view of the self, and of his understanding of love—both of its transforming grace and its impossibility—and for that reason, if for no other, Narcissus has to be a central, if somewhat shadowy, presence in any analysis of the love poems.

> NARCISSUS was a Thespian, the son of the blue Nymph Leiriope, whom the River-god Cephisus had once encircled with the wings of his streams, and ravished. The seer Teiresias told Leiriope, the first person ever to consult him: 'Narcissus will live to a ripe old age, provided that he never knows himself.' Anyone might excusably have fallen in love with Narcissus, even as a child, and when he reached the age of sixteen, his path was strewn with heartlessly rejected lovers of both sexes; for he had a stubborn pride in his own beauty. Among these

[9] Graves (1925).

> lovers was the nymph Echo, who could no longer use her voice, except in foolish repetition of another's shout: a punishment for having kept Hera entertained with long stories while Zeus's concubines, the mountain nymphs, evaded her jealous eye and made good their escape. One day when Narcissus went out to net stags, Echo stealthily followed him through the pathless forest, longing to address him, but unable to speak first. At last Narcissus, finding that he had strayed from his companions, shouted: 'Is anyone here?' 'Here!' Echo answered, which surprised Narcissus, since no one was in sight. 'Come!' 'Come!' 'Why do you avoid me?' 'Why do you avoid me?' 'Let us come together here!' 'Let us come together here!' repeated Echo, and joyfully rushed from her hiding place to embrace Narcissus. Yet he shook her off roughly, and ran away. 'I will die before you ever lie with me!' he cried. 'Lie with me!' Echo pleaded. But Narcissus had gone, and she spent the rest of her life in lonely glens, pining away for love and mortification, until only her voice remained. One day, Narcissus sent a sword to Ameinius, his most insistent suitor, after whom the river Ameinius is named; it is a tributary of the river Helisson, which flows into the Alpheius. Ameinius killed himself on Narcissus's threshold, calling on the gods to avenge his death. Artemis heard the plea, and made Narcissus fall in love, though denying him love's consummation. At Donacon in Thespiae he came upon a spring, clear as silver, and never yet disturbed by cattle, birds, wild beasts, or even by branches dropping off the trees that shaded it; and as he cast himself down, exhausted, on the grassy verge to slake his thirst, he fell in love with his reflection. At first he tried to embrace and kiss the beautiful boy who confronted him, but *presently recognised himself*, and lay gazing enraptured into the pool, hour after hour. *How could he endure both to possess and yet not to possess? Grief was destroying him, yet he rejoiced in his torments; knowing at least that his other self would remain true to him, whatever happened.*[10]

Several interesting features in this account stand out, but perhaps the most significant, for my present purpose, is the question: 'How could he endure both to possess and yet not to possess?', followed by the assertion that Narcissus 'rejoiced in his torments; knowing at least that his other self would remain true to him, whatever happened'. The first point, that relating to possession, is one that Ann Carson explores in wonderful detail in *Eros the Bittersweet*, a book characterized by Meghan O'Rourke as

[10] Graves (1960c), 85a–e, 286–8; my italics.

> a wittily epigrammatic analysis of the role of Eros in Greek culture. Carson marshals examples from Sappho, Plato, and lesser-known Greek poets, deftly explicating their vision of erotic love as temporary, contingent, and characterized by a thrilling sensation of lack. (As Emily Dickinson pithily put it, centuries later, 'So I found/that hunger was a way/of persons outside windows/that entering takes away.') Well-received among classicists, Eros quickly percolated into the living rooms of literary essayists—perhaps in part because it offers a plausible and pleasingly intellectual framework for a post-marriage society.[11]

The detail of Carson's argument is too complex to go into here, but it should be noted that it revolves around the ancient paradox that if I want (that is, lack) something, and if I then take possession of what I want, then I will, by definition, no longer want it. In short, the pleasure of romantic—or erotic—love is in the *wanting*, not the having, and any satisfaction leads to indifference. Thus, the only way to perpetuate such love is to be forever *on the point* of possession, simultaneously to possess and yet not possess. Assuming this argument holds, (and for the romantic it seems to be the only escape from the terror that 'things will last'), Narcissus can be said to have found in his image the perfect Beloved, one he can never possess yet can also never lose; while, because this image represents his true, 'illegal' self, he knows that he will always retain his integrity and not be overwhelmed by the neediness, or by the refusal, of the beloved other.

Yet another interesting detail of this myth—drawn from later, apocryphal material—is the suggestion that Narcissus was the original painter. The notion is discussed by the Renaissance architect and theorist Leon Battista Alberti in his *De Pictura*, where he tells his interlocutor, 'the true inventor of painting was Narcissus, that youth who, according to the poets, was transformed into a flower. And, since painting is the flower of all the arts, this story of Narcissus is most apt. For what is painting, if not an attempt, *through the discipline of art*, to embrace the surface of the pool in which we are reflected?'[12] Taking this notion, and the story of Narcissus as set out in *The Greek Myths*, it is difficult not to think that Freud and his followers make a significant error in reducing the role of Narcissus to that of a mere emblem for infantile 'self-love', a developmental phase that, if it is not overcome on the road to normalized adult

[11] O'Rourke (2004). [12] Alberti (1991); my italics.

relations, will flower into a psychopathology. Indeed, this diagnosis is not only an error but—given the significance of the Narcissus figure in the discipline of art—it can also be seen as a missed opportunity.

So who is Narcissus, and what is his business here? An alternative to the commonly accepted reading might run as follows: when Narcissus sees the beautiful youth in the pool he does not *know*, at first, that it is his reflection. (Ovid, for example, goes to some lengths to explain that he didn't know it was himself that he was seeing to begin with, and Graves echoes this in the phrase 'but presently recognised himself'). In that first glimpse he loves what he sees; only *later* does he understand that what he loves is actually himself. He sees himself in the pool, along with all the other things (the sky, the trees, the world all about him) and he finds this vision beautiful—and *this* is the cause of his initial delight. Having believed himself to be alone, looking at a world that was separate from him, he all of a sudden sees that he is *in* that world. He is as *real* and mysterious and beautiful as that world is —and yet he is also a separate, potentially knowable being. This is what he has been waiting for all along; this is why he rejected Echo, because she did nothing but repeat back to him what he had only just that moment said (thus confirming him in his original solipsism). Echo was insufficient to his desires because she agreed with him all the time (one might argue that she is therefore the ideal partner for a Freudian narcissist, that is, someone who is merely 'in love' with himself), and he was always waiting for something else. He wanted to see himself as a knowable object in a given world, a separate creature, both in and of the world around him, and, in rejecting Echo, he had rejected the world as mere reflection of his own wishes and needs (doing, in fact, the very opposite of what a Freudian narcissist would do). Yet, when he falls in love with his own image —the image of himself in a world that is neither echo nor reflection— he is suddenly surrounded by the unexpected and the unpredictable. Now everything is surprising, and now, of course, he is mortal. If he had not recognized himself in this world he could have lived forever in his solipsistic state. That was what the gods had promised at his birth—and that, in a sense, is exactly what he does not want. What he *does* want is a world in which the discipline of real love is possible— real love, not the gratification offered by Echo's unquestioning regard —and the beginning of that discipline is to know, and to be able to love, oneself. This will seem, no doubt, an idiosyncratic interpretation of the myth-story, but I do not think it far-fetched and, represented in this way, the story of Narcissus can be seen, not as one of self-absorption and hunger for crude gratification (Freudian 'narcissism') but as a parable of the first moment in which the emerging person knows him or herself as a singular, vulnerable, attentive creature, in a world shared by others, ready to move beyond 'the harsh pride of need' into the 'true power of singleness in love'.

In 1935, in the same year that he died, Ian D. Suttie's one major publication, a critique of Freudian analysis entitled *The Origins of Love and Hate*, was published by Kegan Paul.[13] It is a fascinating and, at times, inspiring book, one that is complex and far-reaching in its scrutiny of the Freudians' insistence on 'nastiness for its own sake' (positing, in its place, an investigation, and dismantling of what Suttie calls 'the taboo on tenderness'); nevertheless, some carefully selected excerpts might serve to set out those features of the argument that could be considered relevant here.[14] As with Graves, Suttie's main difference with the Freudians arises over their insistence on infant sexuality, to the exclusion of other concerns; against this he posits a notion of 'shared interest' which leads, not to neurotic and jealous possessiveness of the mother, but to an increased tenderness towards her and a growing sense of connection and attentiveness to their shared world, manifested, as the child grows, in a desire to make and share a culture and to enter into egalitarian love-friendships.

> We have now to consider whether this attachment-to-mother is merely the sum of the infantile bodily needs and satisfactions which refer to her, or whether the *need for a mother is primarily presented to the child's mind as a need for company and as a discomfort in isolation*. I can see no way of settling this question conclusively, but the fact is indisputable that a need for company, moral encouragement, attention, protectiveness, leadership, etc. remains after all the sensory gratifications connected with the mother's body have become superfluous and have been surrendered. In my view this is a direct development of the primal attachment-to-mother, and, further, I think that play, cooperation, competition, and culture-interests generally are substitutes for the mutually caressing relationship of child and mother. *By these substitutes*

[13] Suttie (1935).

[14] Similarities between Graves' and Suttie's views, mostly revolving around their common Matrist perspective, have been identified before now; in this essay I would like to emphasize another aspect of Suttie's work, however—that is, the emphasis on the idea of shared interest and friendship—which, to my knowledge, has not been much explored.

> *we put the whole social environment in the place once occupied by mother*—maintaining with it a mental or cultural rapport in lieu of the bodily relationship of caresses etc. formerly enjoyed with the mother. A joint interest in *things* has replaced the reciprocal interest in *persons*; *friendship* has developed out of love. True, the personal love and sympathy is preserved in friendship; but this differs from love in so far as it comes about by the *direction of attention upon the same things* (rather than upon each other), or by *the pursuit of the same activities even if these are not intrinsically useful* and gratifying, as is the case with much ritual, dance, etc. The interest is intensified even if it is not entirely created (artificial) by being *shared*; while the fact of sharing interest deepens the appreciation of the other person's presence even while it deprives it of sensual (or better of sensorial) qualities.[15]

This, then, is Suttie's view of 'the process of sublimation', and it differs from the Freudians' analysis in two important ways: first, it dispenses with the need to 'define all pleasure or satisfaction as sexual', and second, it brings to the fore the power of shared interest, leading to creative and appreciative play and so to culture. In this analysis 'necessity [or need] is not the mother of invention; play is', and pathological attachment to the other, or the 'dread of loneliness', predicated (as is so often the case, in Graves's early work in particular) on the unpredictability and wilfulness of that other, is transformed into a companionable state that allows for both the preservation of self's, and respect for the other's, integrity.

> Originally, the Baby–Mother bond is vaguely and intuitively appreciated by the former as mutual absorption. By degrees the baby's expanding activities and sense-impressions change the character of this bond. A service rendered to the baby's body and a caress are originally indistinguishable by it, but the baby's perceptions of and interest in its own body and its immediate surroundings grow rapidly under the influence of the mother's ministrations. In this way it develops Interest-in-Itself, the process Freud misconceives as Narcissism. It is of course arbitrary to say at what point the *companionship of love* becomes the *companionship of interest*, but there is no doubt that the feeling-relationship of the companions does change *as attention ceases to be absorbed wholly and reciprocally each in the other and becomes directed convergently to the same things*. Cooperative activities, identical or complementary attitudes to outside happenings, build up a world of

[15] Suttie (1935), 16, italics in the original.

> *common meanings* which marks a differentiation from simple love wherein 'the world' of each is the other person. The simple direct bond has become a triangular relationship wherein external objects form the *medium of play*.[16]

This world of common meanings, with its playful use of external objects to extend and redefine the nature of mutual play is, of course, the natural habitat of the mature love poem, and is the very opposite of the needy, manipulative, vampiristic lover of Graves's early nightmares. For the mature poet, however, the search for this world takes some interesting twists and turns—from the doctrinaire stance of 'Man Does, Woman Is', to the meditation on 'love's impossibility' of 'To Put It Simply'; but it is the poem 'At First Sight' that seems to me most interesting in the light of Suttie's remarks. I quote it here, in full:

> 'Love at first sight', some say, misnaming
> Discovery of twinned helplessness
> Against the huge tug of procreation.
>
> But friendship at first sight? This also
> Catches fiercely at the surprised heart
> So the cheek blanches and then blushes.[17]

This, I think, is one of Graves's finest short love poems, transcending as it does both his fear of the irrationality that love (or sex) imposes and the natural, true (that is, non-pathologized) narcissist's dread of losing his integrity in commitment to, and possible dependence upon or absorption into, the other. Yet it is not simply a question of replacing the difficult and painful matter of romantic love with some kind of 'Platonic' friendship that is being explored here; what arises is, in fact, altogether more challenging and, at the same time, more satisfying than the scenario proposed by the traditional love poem. What one admires most in Graves's love poetry is, perhaps, his honest determination not to use the occasions of love dishonourably, a crime for which he indicts no less a figure than Dante:

> He, a grave poet, fell in love with her.
> She, a mere child, fell deep in love with love
> And, being a child, illumined his whole heart.

[16] Suttie (1935), 32, italics in the original. [17] Graves (1975), 77.

From her clear conspect rose a whispering
With no hard words in innocency held back—
Until the day that she became woman,

Frowning to find her love imposed upon:
A new world beaten out in her own image—
For his own deathless glory.[18]

That deathless glory is not something Graves covets; instead, he recognizes that, while love is indeed impossible, the probably temporary, usually provisional, but genuinely *shared* attention of lovers-as-friends may well be the only means by which we are able to make sense of an impossible world:

When the immense drugged universe explodes
In a cascade of unendurable colour
And leaves us gasping naked,
This is no more than ecstasy of chaos:
Hold fast, with both hands, to that royal love
Which alone, as we both know certainly, restores
Fragmentation into true being.[19]

In the end, then, we can only see the full value of Graves's love poetry by taking it as a whole, as a lifelong investigation into the pitfalls and possibilities of romantic love and love-friendship. The younger Graves—a pre-Freudian (one might even say, pre-Socratic) Narcissus—was haunted both by a horror of love's irrationality and by the will to resist absorption by a needy other. These may seem unworthy or ugly concerns—mere neuroses, perhaps—but they are real, and Graves's researches into these regions are honest and uncompromising. So much so that, later, the mature poet emerges with a new vision of romantic love (the vision of a considered, non-possessive, and egalitarian love-friendship) that is both formed by, and capable of transcending, the careful lover's original 'narcissism'. The great achievement of his work in the love poem is that, at the end, Graves discovers what he had hoped for from the first: that, far from losing themselves in one another, true lovers discover a world in love, and make of it a unity and an order that is more than merely rational, for the time being at least.

[18] 'Beatrice and Dante', Graves (1975), 485.
[19] 'Ecstasy of Chaos', Graves (1975), 329.

12

Robert Graves at Troy, Marathon, and the End of Sandy Road

War Poems at a Classical Distance?

Tom Palaima

In 1941 Robert Graves was asked, 'as a "poet of the last war"', to comment on the poetry that was being written during World War II.[1] Graves rightly pointed out that the terms 'war poet' and 'war poetry' were 'first used in World War I and perhaps peculiar to it'; he then spent almost his entire essay explaining how war poems came to be 'published by the thousand' during World War I and why, when he was publishing his own *Collected Poems* in 1938, he 'could not conscientiously reprint any of my "war poems"—they were too obviously written in the war-poetry boom'.[2] This choice by Graves has made his war poetry less well known. The editor of a recent anthology of the 'essential' poetry of World War I with contextualizing commentary considers it a significant achievement 'to include some of the war poetry of Robert Graves which he suppressed for over half a century'.[3]

Graves may have been truthful in 1941, but it is only a partial truth. His 'suppression' of his war poetry and his limited original publication of it[4] also reflect an ambivalence on his part about how well his war poems convey his own experiences of war and his attitudes

[1] Graves (1995) 79–83, originally appearing as 'War Poets in This War', *Listener*, 26 (23 Oct. 1941), 566–7.

[2] Graves (1995), 79. [3] Roberts (1996), 11.

[4] On the publication history of his poems about war, see Graves (1988), 80–92.

towards the war in which he fought, was wounded, and even, for a time, was listed as killed, and his thinking about war as a human social phenomenon.

Graves was also a well-trained classicist, and a few of his war poems have clear classical themes. Of these, 'Escape', a *katabasis*, first privately printed in 1916, inspired by Graves's own death experience, and 'The Legion', first printed in 1917, have drawn the fullest recent critical attention.[5] A key quality of both poems that we shall see in other of Graves's war poems is the distance Graves intentionally puts between what other soldiers and he himself experienced during World War I and the subject matter and themes of individual poems. What Vandiver says about 'The Legion' is true about many of Graves's war poems: 'the poem does not specify any equivalencies and invites different readings.'[6] It is worth considering why Graves writes this way about the trauma of war.

We might also wonder why a prodigious scholar and writer who did so much work in the Classics (a dense handbook of mythology, historical novels, translations of vivid war epics: Homer's *Iliad* and Lucan's *Pharsalia*) used classical themes in his war poetry so rarely. In all of his collected writing on poetry Graves never mentions the standard Greek war poets Tyrtaeus, Callinus, and Archilochus, even though Archilochus has attitudes towards war that Graves could well have viewed with sympathy and Tyrtaeus and Callinus proffer values that Graves could have taken apart with critical ease. Graves as a critic takes up the supreme war poet Homer sparely and tangentially, most prominently in his essay on Virgil, whom he dismisses as a timorous, inoffensive 'anti-poet' who 'bartered his talent for social security', had 'little to say of personal value', and wrote using 'tricks and evasions'.[7]

For the last twenty years at the University of Texas at Austin I have taught a regular seminar focused on human creative responses to experiences of war and violence from the ancient Greeks to the present. I discuss here the war poems of Robert Graves from this perspective. Let me first explain my reasons for being concerned about what Graves is doing as a war writer. He has peculiar qualities

[5] Vandiver (2010), 26–8, 314–21.

[6] Vandiver (2010), 27, and see n. 82 for the few particular references in the poem, in three lines only, to the weaponry and provisions of World War I. Without them the poem would have no modern reference points.

[7] Graves (1995), 321–35, esp. 322–3.

as a war poet—we have already mentioned one—that can best be understood in relation to other writers of 'war myths', ancient and modern.[8]

Of the famous triad of World War I soldier poets associated directly or indirectly with Craiglockhart War Hospital and the Freudian ideas of Dr W. H. R. Rivers, Siegfried Sassoon, Wilfred Owen, and Robert Graves,[9] Graves strikes me as both the easiest to pigeonhole, as Paul Fussell has,[10] and the hardest to place in the right pigeonholes. If Graves is to be understood as a war poet, he also has to be understood in relationship to his memoir *Good-bye to All That*. Fussell considers *Good-bye to All That* a work of fiction. Fussell's reading of Graves's memoir brings up the thorny problem of truth in war writing, which we shall discuss below. We must also figure out the state of mind, spirit, and temperament Graves was in when he wrote his war poems, and when he produced *Good-bye to All That* in a remarkable, furious eight-week frenzy.[11]

I think that the rhetorical stance Graves adopts in some of his war poems relates to symptoms of post-traumatic stress (PTS) that he developed throughout a childhood that was strict, unnurturing, unplayful, and lacking strong parental or other humanly vital attachments.[12] They were intensified by the shocks of war.

This explains in part the characteristics of his war writing. Graves takes up the same subjects that other writers about war, particularly Greek authors of the archaic and classical periods, poets and non-poets, deal with directly, seriously, and with palpable, often intense feeling. By contrast, Graves uses rhetorical strategies that put him, and us as readers, at a distance from the strong emotions war evokes. His narrative voice in his war poems strikes us readers as detached and unemotional, but it helps us take in traumatic scenes and events without being too troubled or disturbed. This may be partly because

[8] See for an overview of twentieth- and now twenty-first-century war literature: Palaima and Tritle (2013).

[9] On Graves's intellectual relationship with Dr Rivers, which Graves insists was, unlike Sassoon's and Owen's, not for psychiatric treatment, see R. P. Graves (1995), 1–2, 468 n. 1.

[10] Fussell (1975), 203–20 *et alibi*.

[11] Fussell (1975), 208.

[12] See Ehrhart (1994) regarding what we might ruthlessly call the 'GIGO' or 'garbage in, garbage out' effect on individuals who go to war. According to it, reactions to events in war by specific soldiers are dependent on their psychological histories, states, and outlooks before they experienced combat trauma.

we are not among the group of individuals whom trench warfare caused to be, as Graves later puts it, 'bound to one another by a suicidal sacrament'.[13] Graves also writes his war poems in a clean and spare style that the experiences of war impose on other classic war writers, like Ernest Hemingway, Tim O'Brien, and George Orwell.[14] Their efforts thereby to capture what is concrete and real can make non-initiates feel left out.[15]

Athenian tragedians use myths in their plays to obtain an equal distancing effect. Think especially of what Euripides does in the *Trojan Women*, written and performed at the time of the massacre and enslavement of the population of the island city state of Melos.[16] Because the enormous human suffering in Euripides' play was represented in the Theatre of Dionysus as occurring to non-Greeks in the distant past after the fall of Troy, the Athenian veteran soldiers who made up Euripides' audience absorbed the right dosage of the trauma of the women and children they had enslaved on the island of Melos, whose adult male husbands, fathers, brothers, and sons they had killed—and killed in large numbers, probably about 500 adult males, up close and personally, with swords or spears.[17]

Yet, as we have mentioned, Graves largely eschews using classical themes in this way. 'Escape' is the chief exception that proves the rule. In it Graves takes up the harrowing topic of his literally coming back from the dead, and treats this morbid topic light-heartedly as a getaway from Cerberus and other legendary figures of Hades. One can imagine what he describes in the poem being rendered as an entertaining cartoon movie.

Graves's definition of his poetic audience is also very restricted. Graves as a war poet keeps his own feelings at a remove. This is very

[13] Graves (1995), 467.

[14] Reinforcing the habits of writing acquired, according to Graves (1957a), 20, from a headmaster who taught him to write 'eliminating all phrases that could be done without, and using verbs and nouns instead of adjectives wherever possible'. See Palaima (2002) and Hynes (1997), xv, on T. E. Lawrence's appraisal of 'sane, low-toned' war writing.

[15] Broyles (1984), 61 remarks that at some level the purpose of a war story 'is not to enlighten but to exclude; its message is not its content but putting the listener in his place. I suffered, I was there. You were not. Only those facts matter. Everything else is beyond words to tell. As was said after the worst tragedies in Vietnam: "Don't mean nothin'". Which meant, "It means everything, it means too much".'

[16] See Tritle (2000), 89–92; Green (1999), 103–8.

[17] Renfrew and Wagstaff (1982), 140–1.

different from what Sassoon and Owen are doing in their classic poems. And Graves's stance in his war poems is different from his own unremittingly and rather pig-headedly satirical take on Homer's *Iliad* as put forward in the introduction to his translation *The Anger of Achilles: Homer's Iliad* (1959).[18]

In my seminars we look at the following topics, which will help explain my interests in and perspectives on Graves's war poems: (1) how human beings respond, individually and communally, to experiences of war and violence; (2) how and why they use 'myths', defined, in the ancient Greek sense, to encompass all kinds of 'communication': diaries, memoirs, poetry, short stories, novels, journalistic accounts, popular or traditional songs, government reports, narratives within psychiatric sessions, histories, oral histories, biography, autobiography, letters, films (documentary and fictional), plays, and graphic arts, and now emails, blogs, text messages, and video clips; (3) how these accounts are received and interpreted by target and non-target audiences, both societies at large and different subgroups and individuals within societies; (4) what characteristics such 'myths' have; (5) how such 'myths' relate to moral questions.

More specific areas of concern are (a) universals and particulars in 'myths' of the experience of war at different times and places; (b) how elites control the information about war that non-combatants in societies receive; (c) the nature of 'truth' in such 'myths', specifically attitudes towards 'truth' and the boundaries between fact and fiction in authors of 'myths' as diverse as Wallace Terry and Joan Morrison (oral history), Tim O'Brien and Tobias Wolff (short stories and novels), Charles Patterson, Bill Ehrhart, and Rolando Hinojosa Smith (poetry), Chris Hedges, John Burnett, Gordon Dillow, and Seymour Hersh (journalism[19]), Jesse Odom, E. B. Sledge, Robert Graves, and Xenophon (war memoirs), Werner Herzog, Nancy Schiesari, Ricardo Ainslie, and Bernard Edelman (documentary film and its basis), Bill Broyles (scriptwriting and memoir), Larry Tritle, Paul Cartledge, James Tatum, Donald Kagan, and Graves himself (ancient historians and classicists[20]), and playwrights (both ancient

[18] Graves (1959), 13–35. [19] See Katovsky and Carlson (2004).

[20] In processing and analysing the messages of Graves's war poems, it is important to keep in mind that he is also a mythographer and one of the most influential, if highly idiosyncratic, interpreters of Greek and related myths in the twentieth century. The intelligent criticism of Graves's theories on myth by Kevin Herbert, a classicist

and modern), and, of course, in the audiences for these diverse creators of 'myths'; (d) the ways 'myths' affect how and why different societies engage in war and violence, that is, how 'myths' are constructed to encourage active participation in and support of socially sanctioned uses of violence or to oppose specific wars and what happens to soldiers fighting them; (e) the 'disillusionment', as Freud termed it in his 1915 essay, that occurs in times of war in modern European societies because of the irreconcilable differences in the social values promoted by 'myths' during times of peace and times of war; (f) taboos about what can and cannot be conveyed about war and death (especially from World War I onward) during times of war;[21] (g) target audiences for 'myths', why those targets are chosen by the authors of 'myths', and what happens when non-target individuals and groups receive the 'myths'; (h) difficulties in interpreting 'myths' of war across cultures. Of these (c), (e), (f), and (g) most concern us here with Graves.

I have also consulted over time, and even team-taught with, mental-health practitioners like Jonathan Shay, Aphrodite Matsakis, Ricardo Ainslie, Stephen Sonnenberg, and Lesley Martin, and have had war veterans, journalists, oral historians, authors, film-makers, writers, and musicians into my seminars. I taught at the United States Military Academy at West Point in October 2003 on unit cohesion and the ideology and morality of war in ancient Greece. The Academy professor who invited me there, Col. Ted Westhusing, died outside of Baghdad on 5 June 2005, a likely suicide victim of our congressionally authorized presidential use of pre-emptive force and of the contractor corruption that is prevalent within it. He was a former student, in intensive Greek, a scholarly collaborator and good friend.[22] So I find it impossible to write about even the war poetry of Robert Graves in a purely academic way. Another way of putting it is that I marvel at Graves's own self-willed detachment.

War is a constant in human history.[23] Warfare is a unique form of social activity that reveals the best and worst of what it is to be

and World War II Pacific theatre veteran, is still worth reading: Herbert (1956), 191–2.

[21] Palaima (2007), 18–28.

[22] Palaima (2007), 9 and nn. 2–3. See also 'Ted's Ghost: The Death of Ted Westhusing Leaves a Widening Circle of Sorrow', *Austin Chronicle*, 27 Apr. 2007: <http://www.austinchronicle.com/news/2007-04-27/469144/> (last accessed 08/06/12).

[23] Palaima (2005).

human. Reduced to its essence, as Paul Fussell notes,[24] war is ironic. And Graves is a poster child for what Fussell sees as irony. But Graves uses irony in a different way than Fussell does.

Owen and Sassoon reach the point of extreme anger in trying to get readers on the home front to feel what they and their fellow-soldiers have gone through, mostly for senseless reasons. Sassoon is angry with civilians on the home front who do not share in, or even acknowledge, the suffering of soldiers in the field, and who furthermore support, passively or actively, the governmental decisions that cause deaths and wounding, physical and psychological, on a scale that had never been seen before. The list of types that deserve to be satirized and psychologically wounded that Sassoon portrays in his poems is long:[25] smug and comfortable gentlemen, vicars and bishops, veterans of earlier wars, mothers, sisters, wives, young women, Members of Parliament, jingoistic newspaper men, cheering crowds, egotistical generals, even tombstone makers and monument builders.

Theirs is one approach to writing war poems. Sassoon and Owen use irony in order to inflict wounds. They present graphic portraits that are intended to cause trauma. They want to make readers suffer, not necessarily to feel what the soldiers themselves have suffered, not *sympathetic* suffering, not the 'pity and fear' of tragedy, just suffering itself. Graves generally veers away from such irony and such descriptions of violence, and not just because of his neurasthenia or PTS.[26] I think he grasps the danger in casting pearls of trauma before swine. For the same reason, Graves was horrified at what Sassoon was doing with his *non serviam*, and took steps to rescue him from what he, Graves, saw as a kind of pointless social or political suicide. The staff officers at headquarters and the people back home, as Fussell and many war writers and veterans have documented, were not ever going to 'get it'.

Despite clear and available facts, modern societies can and will deny the obvious. The statistics for World War I are morally inexplicable: over 65 million soldiers mobilized, over 8½ million killed

[24] Fussell (1975), 7 and 18.

[25] 'They', 'The Choral Union', 'The Tombstone-Maker', 'The General', 'Fight to a Finish', 'Editorial Impressions', 'Suicide in the Trenches', 'Glory of Women', 'Their Frailty', and 'On Passing the New Menin Gate', in Sassoon (1947), 23, 24–5, 27, 75, 77–9, 188.

[26] On Graves's self-admitted neurasthenic state, see Graves (1995), 1–4.

and died, over 21 million wounded. They make the words written on the British campaign medals given to every soldier who served seem like the words of a monster or a madman: 'For Civilization.'[27]

Graves believed firmly in the futility of trying to get the realities of war experience across to those who have not been through them.[28] So even in his occasional anti-war preaching Graves lacks conviction. A poem like 'The Next War' lacks intensity, zeal, and belief, even in its punch-lines.[29] We might compare Wilfred Owen's 'Dulce Et Decorum Est' with Graves's poem.

Owen's famous plea not to inspire impressionable and emotional young men to desire the false glory of war is addressed directly to his adult readers. He gives us what he calls in a letter to his mother from April 1918 an almost 'photographic representation' of what would otherwise be unimaginable conditions and sufferings.[30] Owen's vivid images immerse us in the horror of 'men cursing through sludge'. Most of these men, before going to war, were in their physical prime. They now are 'knock-kneed', 'coughing like hags', 'limping', 'blood-shod'. All of them Owen asserts with anaphora are 'blind' and 'lame'. One unfortunate soldier is 'guttering', 'choking', and 'drowning' in what looks to other soldiers through the eye-covers of their masks like a 'green sea' of gas.

In contrast, Graves's poem is addressed to the young children themselves (as if they can understand what he is getting at). He offers a general description of 'Kaisers and Czars' tritely strutting the stage and 'young friskies' jumping and fighting with 'bows and arrows and wooden spears' while 'playing at Royal Welch Fusiliers':

> You young friskies who today
> Jump and fight in Father's hay
> With bows and arrows and wooden spears,
> Playing at Royal Welch Fusiliers,
> Happy though these hours you spend,
> Have they warned you how games end?

[27] On European attitudes about the First World War, before and after it was fought, see generally Palaima (2005), 129, and Palaima and Tritle (2013), 728–31.

[28] Despite his belief, expounded in Graves (1995) 6, in poetry as an act of faith and that poems could 'move mountains' short distances.

[29] Graves (1988), 43–4.

[30] The letter (no. 609) contains a first draft of 'A Terre (being the philosophy of many soldiers)'. Owen (1967), 545. The original is in the Humanities Research Center of the University of Texas at Austin.

Boys, from the first time you prod
And thrust with spears of curtain-rod,
From the first time you tear and slash
Your long-bows from the garden ash,
Or fit your shaft with a blue jay feather,
Binding the split tops together,
From that same hour by fate you're bound
As champions of this stony ground,
Loyal and true in everything,
To serve your Army and your King,
Prepared to starve and sweat and die
Under some fierce foreign sky,
If only to keep safe those joys
That belong to British boys,
To keep young Prussians from the soft
Scented hay of father's loft,
And stop young Slavs from cutting bows
And bendy spears from Welsh hedgerows.
   Another War soon gets begun,
A dirtier, a more glorious one;
Then, boys, you'll have to play, all in;
It's the cruellest team will win.
So hold your nose against the stink
And never stop too long to think.
Wars don't change except in name;
The next one must go just the same,
And new foul tricks unguessed before
Will win and justify this War.
Kaisers and Czars will strut the stage
Once more with pomp and greed and rage;
Courtly ministers will stop
At home and fight to the last drop;
By the million men will die
In some new horrible agony;
And children here will thrust and poke,
Shoot and die, and laugh at the joke,
With bows and arrows and wooden spears,
Playing at Royal Welch Fusiliers.

'The Next War' shows flashes of Graves's below-the-surface Sassoonian anger at government ministers who 'fight to the last drop' of the blood of other men while themselves living comfortably at home.[31] His adult anger also is felt when he tells the boys that notions of fair play will not prevail when 'you'll have to play, all in; | It's the cruellest team will win'. But Graves does not put us in his scenes. Nor does he give us a narrator who can personalize observations. And his most graphic words are tame when compared to Owen's horrific vocabulary: 'starve', 'sweat', 'die' (three times), 'stink'. Graves as writer of 'The Next War' lacks the kind of literal enthusiasm that Graves as a well-trained scholar of Greek and Latin deeply believed was necessary to create good poetry. Still, we should acknowledge that Graves's poem is true to his conceit. His narrator speaks kindly words to young children. His language, observations, images, lessons, and warnings all merit a G-rating. In this way, too, the poem is non-classical.[32]

I think Graves saw that depictions of trauma and ironic twists, if embedded in poetic content that conveyed too much genuine human feeling and if described in vivid and beautiful language, could be used as a kind of entertainment by the audience and that sincere emotions would be misused in a philistine way, that is, desecrated. And I think he knew and felt this deeply well before he set foot in France.[33]

[31] Graves was certainly aware of the extravagant parody of Athenian ambassadors to the Persian court and to the court of Sitalces, king of the Odrysians in Thrace, in Aristophanes's war comedy *Acharnians*, produced six years into the Peloponnesian War. The ambassadors recount their sybaritic 'sufferings'. They have been forced to live for long periods in the midst of foreign luxuries and survive on ample *per diem* salaries, while Athenian soldiers and common civilians at war back home suffer and die.

[32] According to the Motion Picture Association of America, a G-rated movie 'contains nothing in theme, language, nudity, sex, violence or other matters that, in the view of the Rating Board, would offend parents whose younger children view the motion picture'.

[33] See King (2009), 10–28 for details of Graves's childhood. If we read Graves's own description attentively and with human sympathy, we can see that his childhood was not happy or nurturing. Graves felt anger and dislike toward, and distance from, his father Alfred, a schools inspector. Alfred, father of ten children by two wives, was absorbed in his own educational reform work (having to do in part with sports that his son Robert detested) and had no time or inclination to take Graves's youthful writing seriously. Afflicted with an almost James-O'Neill-like obsession with money, Alfred also placed Robert in a succession of preparatory schools that were below his level of intellectual attainment. These schools were not suited to Robert's temperament and spirit. Robert's lack of pocket money, ready-made clothes, and disinclination to participate in the sports that his father's reforms promoted marked him out. At home Robert lived in an atmosphere of extreme discipline, austerity, strict rules of moral conduct—King (pp. 17–19) says Graves lived in 'moral terror', coldness of

Tim O'Brien identifies this trap in 'How to Tell a True War Story'. An old lady, typical of many sentimental but essentially unsympathetic civilians, hears a sincere soldier's story. She feels a maudlin pity for the baby water buffalo that one young soldier Rat Kiley shoots to death part by part after the death of a fellow-soldier. She is incapable of understanding that he does this in a paroxysm of grief for the soldier friend he has lost:

> Now and then, when I tell this story, someone will come up to me afterward and say she liked it. It's always a woman. Usually it's an older woman of kindly temperament and humane politics. She'll explain that as a rule she hates war stories; she can't understand why people want to wallow in all the blood and gore. But this one she likes. The poor baby water buffalo, it made her sad. Sometimes, even, there are little tears. What I should do, she'll say, is put it all behind me. Find new stories to tell.
>
> I won't say it but I'll think it.
>
> I'll picture Rat Kiley's face, his grief, and I'll think, *you dumb cooze.*
>
> Because she wasn't listening.
>
> It *wasn't* a war story. It was a *love* story.[34]

In the same way, staff officers may feel a self-serving sadness over the men they send out to ghastly forms of death. It is one of the reasons behind Harrison Starr's advice to Kurt Vonnegut in *Slaughterhouse Five*. Might as well write an anti-glacier book as an anti-war book.[35]

Graves permits himself the use of irony also in his poem 'The Persian Version', published in *Poems 1938–1945*. It is another exception that proves the rule, as he sees it.[36] The poem operates within the sphere of central, even civilian command. It never gets to the actual suffering of the many Persian soldiers who lost their lives on the

disposition, rigid class separation, lack of companionship, Puritanism, prudery, and emotional repression. Graves (1957a), 12–43, describes his parents, home life, the several schools before Charterhouse that his father placed him in, and his years at Charterhouse where 'from my first moment . . . I suffered an oppression of spirit that I hesitate to recall in its full intensity'. Graves says that as the eighth of ten children he related to his mother and father as if they were grandparents—they were 40 and 49 years of age when he was born: 'We had a nurse, and one another, and found that companionship sufficient.' Moreover, at the age of 4½ Graves was sent off to a public fever hospital, where he first began to grasp the implications of class distinctions.

34 O'Brien (1990), 84–5.

35 Vonnegut (1969), 3.

36 Graves (1946), 46. It is the exception, too, in not being included in the posthumous 1988 collection of Graves's poems about war.

plains of Marathon. In fact, Graves classifies the poem not as a poem, but among what he calls his satires and grotesques. And I think we must take literally the short clarification that he writes in the foreword to *Poems 1938–1945*: 'I write poems for poets and satires and grotesques for wits. For people in general I write prose, and I am content that they should be unaware that I do anything else. To write poems for other than poets is wasteful.'[37] Graves has a nearly infinite capacity to be coy, but this statement, at least as it applies to his war writing, strikes me as meant to be taken straight. And it is telling.

> Truth-loving Persians do not dwell upon
> The trivial skirmish fought near Marathon.
> As for the Greek theatrical tradition
> Which represents that summer's expedition
> Not as a mere reconnaissance in force
> By three brigades of foot and one of horse
> (Their left flank covered by some obsolete
> Light craft detached from the main Persian fleet)
> But as a grandiose, ill-starred attempt
> To conquer Greece—they treat it with contempt;
> And only incidentally refute
> Major Greek claims, by stressing what repute
> The Persian monarch and the Persian nation
> Won by this salutary demonstration:
> Despite a strong defence and adverse weather
> All arms combined magnificently together.

'The Persian Version' appeals to intellects that are refined enough to appreciate pure irony, not irony in the service of social causes, least of all social reform. Its witticism is not even designed to bring home an intellectual point. True wits already see the lies, charade, and cruel misfortunes many suffer in life and surely suffer in war. They take delight when one of their kind points out another instance in a good literary style. But they do not feel any obligation to do anything about human behaviours that have been manifest in the western tradition, as Graves with his deep knowledge of classical texts would be well aware, ever since the god-sanctioned suffering brought on by Agamemnon's high-command egotism and poor strategizing in *Iliad*, Books 1 and 2.

[37] Graves (1946), no page number.

In his introduction to *The Anger of Achilles* Graves attributes the severe defeat that the Greeks are suffering by Book 9 to Agamemnon's 'own stupidity', and he describes Agamemnon's famous test of the troops in Book 2 as 'a fiasco' caused by his overacting to the point of convincing himself of the defeatism that was intended to be part of the ploy. In Book 4 Graves sees that Homer has made Agamemnon 'superbly ridiculous', 'self-pitying', and 'defeatist'.

Paul Fussell, in his many critical studies of war, comes close to sharing Graves's attitude and perspectives. But like Sassoon and Owen, Fussell has a different set of sensibilities. They think what they write can make some difference. Graves does not. Most telling is that Graves says he writes his poems for poets, because, essentially, it is stupid to do otherwise. This implies that his poems do not have the general political, communal, or social aims we associate with the Greek lyric war poets, the Greek tragedians, and the Homeric poems. Graves writes poems for special people and special people only. Readers like me, and perhaps you, are uninvited guests at a very special party.

According to Cormac McCarthy—and an implication of Weil (1939)—knowing and understanding the reality of war gives a profound insight into the human condition.[38] It is when such insight is falsified or not widely shared within an individual's defining larger and smaller culture groups that psychological wounding, disillusionment, and feelings of alienation and betrayal arise that can explain many of the distinctive symptoms of PTS.[39]

O'Brien also gives us some advice on how to tell whether a war story is true or not:[40]

> A true war story is never moral. It does not instruct, nor encourage virtue, nor suggest models of proper human behavior, nor restrain men from doing the things men have always done. If a story seems moral, do not believe it. If at the end of a war story you feel uplifted, or if you feel that some small bit of rectitude has been salvaged from the larger waste, then you have been made the victim of a very old and terrible lie. There is no rectitude whatsoever. There is no virtue. As a first rule of thumb, therefore, you can tell a true war story by its absolute and

[38] See the speech of Judge Holden in McCarthy (1985), 331. See also Knox (1990), 29.

[39] Bradley (2000); O'Brien (1990), 155–73: 'Speaking of Courage', and 73–91: 'How to Tell a True War Story'; Sassoon (1937), *passim*.

[40] O'Brien (1990), 68.

> uncompromising allegiance to obscenity and evil. Listen to Rat Kiley. Cooze, he says. He does not say bitch. He certainly does not say woman, or girl. He says cooze. Then he spits and stares. He's nineteen years old—it's too much for him—so he looks at you with those big sad gentle killer eyes and says cooze, because his friend is dead, and because it's so incredibly sad and true . . .

In these quoted words O'Brien is pushing into the territory explored, mapped out, sketched, and painted by Cormac McCarthy:[41] 'Only that man who has offered up himself entire to the blood of war, who has been to the floor of the pit and seen the horror in the round and learned at last that it speaks to his inmost heart, only that man can dance.' O'Brien's narrator is swearing allegiance to obscenity and evil in the same way that Owen in 'Dulce Et Decorum Est' runs a word-camera over the face of the soldier exposed to gas, 'a devil's sick of sin'. Graves never wants to go where they go, even in his poems.

The poem 'The Persian Version', which in its way is both a satire and a grotesque, and Graves as its author both rely on our understanding, from Herodotus's description of Thermopylae and the Persian empire in general, that there was one free person among all those human beings of all those different ethnicities and cultures over whom King Darius and later King Xerxes held sway. The poem also relies on our knowing Herodotus's description of what Xerxes saw sitting remotely on his ridge-top throne that overlooked the island of Salamis. From that human Olympus, watching Queen Artemisia in the naval combat, Xerxes sees what he wants to see. No one can make him the wiser. No one will tell the Great King that the queen of Herodotus's hometown of Halicarnassus rammed a ship in the Persian naval force and thereby sent to their deaths sailors who were Persian allies. Xerxes thinks she has acted with manly bravery for the Persian cause. Fussell himself singles out the two ironic concluding lines of 'The Persian Version' as characteristic of Graves's 'unsoftened views of the Staff and institutions like it':

> Despite a strong defense and adverse weather
> All arms combined magnificently together.[42]

They are in fact, in my opinion, characteristic of a different kind of irony, irony that is only used when Graves can be sure that it will have

[41] McCarthy (1985), 331. [42] Fussell (1975), 85.

the effect that he intends. Graves is acknowledging for those with wit that power-figures throughout history see the world and the consequences of their own decisions as they want to see them. The writing of a soldier poet will not change matters.

Here the effect is worked on wits who can appreciate that Darius, back in what we now call Iran (whether Persepolis or Susa), will accept the distant battle at Marathon, a small strip of beach and plain in the very north-east limits of Attica, a battle that we view as a turning-point in western history, as a minor skirmish in which the officers on the spot report that the troops acquitted themselves well. The mild sarcasm here also cuts into the flesh of western intellectuals who make more of the Battle of Marathon than it can bear.

We may compare here Graves's 1916 poem 'The Adventure',[43] about false reports from the field processed on the front by fighting soldiers and field officers. There, as in the companion 1916 poem 'The First Funeral',[44] Graves taps into nursery memories as he explores experiences that require close observation of the grotesque. In 'The Adventure', a fearsome tiger killed in a child's imagination becomes a German wire party that British machine-gunners said they wiped out. Inspection of the terrain, impressing what horrors on the soldiers' imagination Graves does not say, reveals no corpses. But if we want a corpse, Graves has already given us one.

In 'The First Funeral', a bloated corpse decaying on barbed wire in No Man's Land calls to mind a dead dog that Graves and his older sister came upon in 1899, when he was 4 years old, at the end of Sandy Road where it crosses the golf links. *She* prods it with a stick. *She* takes charge of its burial, sprinkling it with wild mint. Graves finds the mint. *They* give it a burial. Graves and his reader are on the safer terrain of memory in which he can and does take the action he cannot take in France. In France, at the front, he has no older sister to tell him what to do or to do it for him. The soldier is hung up on the German wire and couldn't be buried, Graves writes. He never tells us whether the soldier is British or German. The young brother and sister of Graves's memory declaim a short, matter-of-fact funeral prayer: 'Poor dog, Amen!' It is the kind of short, no-nonsense prayer that soldiers standing exposed to danger in No Man's Land could take time to utter.

[43] Graves (1988), 19. [44] Graves (1988), 18.

Randall Jarrell does take Graves at his word. For Jarrell, Graves is 'first and last a poet: in between he is a Graves'.[45] But even as a poet, Graves is *sui generis* Graves.

Soldiers will self-censor and keep to themselves what they know others cannot grasp without distortion or trivialization. Their self-imposed silence has a cost. Graves, I think, does this too. There are some examples: the suicide in the trenches that he reports matter-of-factly in *Good-Bye to All That*[46] and his vision of a dead enemy soldier in 'A Dead Boche'[47] are different strategies of indirection than he uses in 'The First Funeral'. The genuine indifference and incomprehension of non-combatants can be emotionally traumatizing. This leads some soldiers to keep inside those things they consider most personally meaningful, so that others will not be able to commit sacrilege upon their sacred knowledge.

Michael Herr and Bill Broyles both illustrate this added rule of war stories, namely that war stories can be told, not to communicate but to exclude. O'Brien's 'How to Tell a True War Story' contains elements of this. Sometimes soldiers themselves cannot interpret clearly the mysteries of events. Therefore, two of the most meaningful commentaries on anything that has happened or been experienced in war are three syllables and four syllables: 'there it is' and 'don't mean nuthin''. Compare Kurt Vonnegut's often repeated 'And so it goes' in *Slaughterhouse Five.*

This is the tone Graves strikes in 1915 in 'A Dead Boche'.

> To you who'd read my songs of War
>   And only hear of blood and fame,
> I'll say (you've heard it said before)
>   'War's Hell!' and if you doubt the same,
> To-day I found in Mametz Wood
> A certain cure for lust of blood:
> Where, propped against a shattered trunk,
>   In a great mess of things unclean,
> Sat a dead Boche; he scowled and stunk
>   With clothes and face a sodden green,
> Big-bellied, spectacled, crop-haired,
> Dribbling black blood from nose and beard.
>
> 13 July 1915

45 Jarrell (1969), 78.
46 Graves (1957a), 103.
47 Graves (1988), 30.

Here Graves the poet seems ready to preach that war is truly hell, but his heart is not in it. Graves cannot be Owen or Sassoon, O'Brien or McCarthy, or Homer as we see Homer. He checks up. He leaves off. He never drives any moral home. He leaves the German corpse 'Dribbling black blood from nose and beard'. He forces us to walk away from the scene of this single accident, just as he had to. As happens when we rubberneck as we drive by an auto accident, we never learn who this dead German is. Graves does not speculate like O'Brien in 'The Man I Killed',[48] or finally investigate like Paul Bäumer in Remarque's *All Quiet on the Western Front*.[49] The German corpse remains 'A Dead Boche'. He is not Graves's dead German. He is not ours. And Graves doesn't even fantasize or tap into nursery memories of performing shorthand rites. He cannot bring himself to write something like: 'Poor Boche, Amen!' because he never uttered the words 'Poor dog, Amen!' His sister did. Four syllables that might be set alongside 'there it is' and 'don't mean nuthin'', and 'and so it goes' are not even spoken in prayer here. Graves does not give us the moral horror of a gruesome combat death in Homer or emphasize the ghastly state of the decomposing corpse. He does not make his readers feel the revulsion caused by a human countenance transformed into 'a devil's sick of sin' or by obscenity that is like 'vile, incurable sore on innocent tongues'. If Graves did not tell us the German soldier was dead, we could, from how Graves describes him, think the soldier is sleeping off the effects of a nighttime pub-crawl.

'There it is' and 'don't mean nuthin'' mean *haec lacrimae rerum*, but both also have the thousand-yard pitying stare of the grunt who tells Herr this story:[50]

> 'Patrol went up the mountain. One man came back. He died before he could tell us what happened.' I waited for the rest of the story, but it seemed not to be that kind of story; when I asked him what had happened he just looked like he felt sorry for me, fucked if he'd waste time telling stories to anyone dumb as I was.

This story explains why soldiers engaged in the actual fighting can feel stronger ties with enemy soldiers than with their rear command or their populations back home. Tim O'Brien, in 'The Man I Killed', imagines an entire personal life history for an 'almost dainty young

[48] O'Brien (1990), 124–30. [49] Remarque (1929), 216–29.
[50] Broyles (1984), 61.

man of about twenty', a Vietcong soldier he was forced to shoot along a trail, where the enemy's head lay 'not quite facing . . . small blue flowers shaped like bells'.

Michael Herr gives us a story of group feeling for an unseen enemy. His nickname was Luke the Gook,[51] a North Vietnamese Army sniper ensconced in a cave in a cliff-face, harassing a unit of soldiers like a deadly mosquito with random, untimed single shots—obviously to conserve his scarce ammunition. The American army unit radios for an air-strike of napalm that nearly obliterates the cliff itself and 'galvanize[s] clean of every living thing' the ground around Luke the Gook's 'spider hole'. When, about twenty minutes later, another single shot is fired upon them, the unit erupts in wild cheers, celebrating that the single enemy who is trying his best to kill them has survived ungodly American firepower. In contrast, we can see that Graves's 'A Dead Boche' and 'The First Funeral' are Graves poems, singular within the genre of soldiers, of whatever literary talent, expressing their thoughts on a single enemy dead.

It is important for us as humanists and human beings to think about how our soldiers have responded for 3,500 years now to experiences of war, and how we have tried to deal with the ironies of war through our individual and collective voices. In this I am following a good old classical tradition.

I mean this in two senses. In the first sense, one can trace the tradition of 'myths' of war from the earliest masterpiece about war in western literature, Homer's *Iliad.* Here again, Graves has his own reading of the *Iliad.* His version of it, *The Anger of Achilles,* is to me unsettling. It is what gets Fussell to characterize Graves as a *farceur* who has never met a lie he didn't like and wouldn't tell.[52]

But this may simply prove that I am really an old lady, or I haven't fully absorbed O'Brien's definition of a 'true war story'. A true war story has no point. Truth does not exist in factual reality. Truth does not even lie in what seems to be a verbatim description of a dead corpse. Truth lies in what is unforgettable, Greek *a-lēthēs.* And what is unforgettable about a dead soldier on a wire may be that you

[51] Herr (1977), 125–6.

[52] Fussell (1975), 203–6, argues soundly from Graves's own commentary on his writing of *Good-bye to All That* that Graves is a 'tongue-in-cheek neurasthenic farceur whose material is "facts"' and who 'eschewed tragedy and melodrama in favor of farce and comedy'.

wanted to do what your sister helped you to do for a dead dog sixteen years in the past. And perhaps Graves's devastating takes on all the heroes in the *Iliad* and his championing of Thersites get across what war means: the *Iliad* as *Catch-22*.

Why not? Other Greek city states must have had what Athens had: an Aristophanes to make them laugh at horror. And Joseph Heller himself has said that he was obsessed with the *Iliad* when young, and that Achilles was his constant model for his central character, Yossarian.[53]

Recall that Aeschylus, the grandest Greek tragedian and himself a veteran of the Battle of Marathon—a fact he declared proudly in the funerary epigram he wrote for his own tombstone, making no mention of his achievements as a playwright—claimed that all of his tragedies were 'mere scraps from the banquet of Homer'. He was right. We can also go and touch each and every individual name on the wall that is the Vietnam Veterans Memorial on the plaza in Washington, DC. They will all tell us a story. They will all tell us certain universal truths.

This brings me to a second meaning of classical tradition, the now-extinct classical tradition of education. One of the great figures in the study of classical Greek epigraphy, A. G. Woodhead, writes about the classical education in Latin that was the basis of most educational systems for schoolboys through to the Second World War:[54]

> When the beginner in Latin has surmounted the first hurdles of basic grammar and made-up sentences, he moves on to tackle his first prose author. And this is usually the absorbing account, by no less a character than Julius Caesar himself, of how he and his Roman legions slaughtered large numbers of Gauls or, alternatively, how he and his legions slaughtered large numbers of fellow Romans. With this as his springboard, the student then proceeds to tackle Livy, where he reads how the Romans killed off large numbers of Carthaginians or vice versa—if not how they killed off more Gauls, or Samnites, or Aequi, or Volsci. I myself began Latin at the age of eight.

The well-spring of all western literature talks about war with brutal honesty. Schoolboys in western Europe and the United States until the 1960s were immersed pedagogically in the carnage, bloodshed, and treachery of ancient warfare. They learned about war as the Greeks themselves did in Homer and in Athenian tragedy, in a safe,

[53] Reilly (1998), 518–19. [54] Woodhead (1990), 1.

historically far off, never-never land. But they still learned hard and real lessons. After the Second World War, however, American schoolboys learned John Wayne movie fairy-tales and history made nice. During the Vietnam War, the only anti-war film that Hollywood produced was *M.A.S.H.* (1970), set during the Korean War.

There are consequences when we ignore war as we do now, when we transform violence into a game and pretend that, by dropping 'smart bombs' or using drone missiles, we can accomplish the necessary evil of war with no harm done to us who are the good guys. The fifth-century Athenians, in Pericles's vision, according to Thucydides, willed themselves to believe that they were the good guys. They pretended that in their imperial expansion they had created *kharis*, or favourable and obligatory good-will, wherever they had brought other Greek city states into effective subjugation. Their self-deception is patent. Graves saw it repeated in World War I. I think he knew he could do nothing about it except write for those who also grasped it.

In my view, Graves's reading of the *Iliad* is a modern reading that does not accept what one sort of ancient reading might have been. To me there is a simple answer to the question of why Homer is so graphically accurate about combat deaths and about the whole experience of war. He had to be. His audience knew what war was. They lived war. John Wayne would not do. John Wayne, Shane, Humphrey Bogart, Plato, and the extracted glories of Homer eventually didn't do for Tim O'Brien either.

In coming to terms, over a twenty-five-year period, with the meaning of war, O'Brien gradually discards the high-flown philosophical discussions of courage and honour that run through his first, immediately post-Vietnam novel, *If I Die in a Combat Zone.*[55] He gets rid of all traditionally heroic figures. In *The Things They Carried* he concentrates on the men in what he claims is his fictional platoon. He concentrates on the shit that he says is essential to the telling of a true war story, and on 'small blue flowers shaped like bells.' Paul Bäumer, in *All Quiet on the Western Front*, notices delicate butterflies while he is with his fellow-soldiers in a rare peaceful moment behind the lines, sitting out in the open taking an unhurried shit. This, for them, is the height of civilized luxury. He also notices a butterfly flitting among the skulls, bones, and decaying corpses in the region of all things dead

[55] See Palaima (2000), 8–10, 20–2.

that is ironically known as No Man's Land, but is really everyman's worst nightmare.

The Homeric poems served as acculturating instruments, in the same way that Remarque's *All Quiet on the Western Front* and O'Brien's *Things They Carried* are now used in schools. They have become something Graves did not want his works to become. Graves knew that the truths of such accounts would be stripped of their emotional force, and ultimately they could educate young men and now women to serve modern Agamemnons.

The *Iliad* gives an honest picture of almost all aspects of warfare. The catalogue includes betrayal of what is right; high command disregard for the common troops; REMF (or Rear Echelon Mother Fucker) screw-ups; the tragedy of war for the civilian population of a city under siege; combat rage; soldierly sympathies for the enemy; war fought for ignoble purposes; betrayal by the gods and piety serving no purpose; the deep pleasure men derive from the violence and hardships of war; cowardice and courage; death and destruction; blind luck and bad luck; and bad decision-making.

That Graves can go through the contents of the *Iliad* as I just have and put a satirical spin on every item is the equivalent of what Tim O'Brien and other war writers call 'heating up the story'. Graves is doing what a Thersites instinctively has to do, but, unlike Thersites, Graves aims at producing bitter and intellectualized laughter. Graves's translation of the *Iliad* is a hybrid, part prose, like *Good-Bye to All That*, written for 'the rest' of us, and part poetry, written for 'wits' who could savour the joke.

War stories and 'true' war stories reveal truths about our very natures as individuals and about the formative and driving principles of our culture. We ignore these truths only at our peril. Graves, I believe, knew that these crucial truths were being ignored, and decided—who can argue that he did so wrongly?—that these truths would always be ignored, or at least have no significant effect.

The ancient Greeks were not in danger of losing sight of the brutal realities of life or divorcing themselves from those realities. The *Iliad*, the *Odyssey*, Hesiod's account of divine conflict in the *Theogony* and the daily grind in the *Works and Days*, and later in fifth-century Athens, the many tragic and comic plays on military themes[56]

[56] Tritle (2000), 103–18.

(Aeschylus's *Agamemnon, Persians, Seven Against Thebes*; Sophocles's *Antigone, Ajax, Philoctetes*; Euripides's *Trojan Women, Iphigeneia at Aulis, Hecuba*; Aristophanes's *Peace, Birds, Acharnians, Lysistrata*) made it impossible for any young Athenian to be deluded into imagining the world was a nice place, that war was what John Wayne represented it to be,[57] that war could be made 'pleasant and honourable',[58] that human beings had advanced to such a stage that war among high civilized cultures was unthinkable, or that authority figures would act in the best interests of the community at large or of the soldiers in their charge. Nor did they believe in the Christian notion of love for their fellow-human beings that produces the internal psychological disturbance of the narrator in O'Brien's 'The Man I Killed', of Remarque's hero Paul Bäumer as he watches close up a French soldier die slowly in a shell-hole with him, or of the American GI whose thoughts are recorded in Studs Terkel's oral history:[59]

> It was sunshine and quiet. We were passing the Germans we killed. Looking at the individual German dead, each took on a personality. These were no longer an abstraction. They were no longer the Germans of the brutish faces and the helmets we saw in the newsreels. They were exactly our age. These boys were like us.

Graves uses rhetorical distancing everywhere in his war poems. It is a classical technique in so far as it removes us from having intense human emotional responses to what Graves is describing. It is nonclassical in that we readers are placed so deeply *in illo tempore* that we feel no true horror. Graves never puts us on the field of battle. We never confront a dead body with him. He presents us with what his first sight of a corpse called forth: the childhood memories of the dead dog his sister and he came across on a walk and the make-believe funeral rites they enacted. Even children know you bury all dead people, Graves says. It is time-honoured custom, a fact we have known since the last line of the *Iliad*, as rendered by Graves: 'So ended the funeral rites of Hector the Horse-Tamer.' But Graves makes us feel little *pathos* for the dead of war, buried or unburied, or for the soldiers and veterans who lived on.[60]

[57] Bourke (1999), 15–17; O'Brien (1973); Kovic (1976).

[58] Wells (1928), 139.

[59] Terkel (1997), 5.

[60] A preliminary version of this chapter focusing on Robert Graves' war poetry per se appeared in William Roger Louis (ed.), *Irrepressible Adventures with Britannia: Personalities, Politics and Culture in Britain* (I. B. Tauris: London, 2013), 137–50.

13

'Con *beffarda irriverenza*'

Graves's Augustus in Mussolini's Italy

Jonathan Perry

I, Claudius (1934) was famously and repeatedly—if also with a hint of ersatz self-deprecation—described by its author as a mere potboiler and 'literary conjuring trick', whose sole purpose was to materialize into solid cash. In letters from the time and in subsequent reminiscences he stressed the pleasing financial results of the *Claudius* books, as well as his pressing needs during their composition. In a letter dated 10 February 1935 he protested that, 'Neither of them is of any real worth: how can the revivifying of anyone as dead as Claudius be justified except as a literary conjuring trick? (But certainly Claudius has been very helpful in the money way. I am now able to support my children.)'[1] In May of that year Graves specified the necessity under which he had laboured (a £4,000 debt into which an ill-advised business venture had landed him), and he later observed that the books had 'bloody well got to' bring in heaps of money.[2] More appositely, Graves drew on a Latin phrase to describe the books, in a letter to John Buchan (to be explored in detail below), as '*manus manum lavat*'.[3]

[1] O'Prey (1982), 242, letter to Julie and Tom Matthews.

[2] O'Prey (1982), 245, letter to Edward Marsh; Seymour-Smith (1982), 228.

[3] Unpublished correspondence, dated 27 Mar. 1935, from Robert Graves to John Buchan, held in the John Buchan Archive, Queen's University, Kingston, Ontario. The full sentence reads, 'Claudius has been a very good friend to me ("manus manum lavat") and has got me free of a crushing debt that I expected to be on my neck for years.' The stationery upon which this letter was written is, incidentally, embossed with, 'Laura Riding'.

Nevertheless, Graves took unmistakeable pride in the favourable reviews and book prizes he garnered as a result of *I, Claudius* and *Claudius the God* (1934). A diary entry from 28 March 1935 contains the first notice of the books' jointly being awarded the 'James Tait Black Memorial Prize'. The full, rather ponderous, title is listed, together with the quickly added observation that the solicitor 'will remit money if I accept. Accepted.'[4] In the letter to Buchan, he wryly commented that this was 'My first prize since my preparatory school days',[5] but in the letter to Edward Marsh, on 12 May, he provided more ample—and more material—details about this honour: 'The other prize was the James Tait Black Memorial Award, given by the defunct relict of a Scottish publisher named Black, the judges being the Rector of Edinburgh University and the Professor of Rhetoric at Glasgow (I think). It is worth £116 5s. 3½d. and no ceremony is involved.'[6] Despite his dismissive claims of their intrinsic worth, Graves seems to have collected press notices and reviews of the *Claudius* books. Indeed, his pride in the more favourable clippings yielded one of the myriad stories of Laura Riding's jealousy, 'for returning one afternoon from his customary swim he discovered that they had been torn up and scattered about the floor'.[7]

Not every reviewer was so well disposed to the books, and some hewed closer to Riding's pronouncement that they were 'boring'.[8] However, one of the most negative reviews did not originate in the Anglophone world, but rather as a result of the books' translation and dissemination in Fascist Italy. Little attention has been paid to the international reception of the *Claudius* books, and yet this was much on Graves's mind, if only for financial reasons. Foreign editions of the books continued to generate revenue for several years, and, despite

[4] University of Victoria online collection, 'Diary of Robert Graves 1935–39 and ancillary material', accessed at: <http://graves.uvic.ca/index.xml>.

[5] Graves to Buchan, 27 Mar. 1935.

[6] O'Prey (1982), 245. Black was a partner in A. & C. Black, Edinburgh; he was involved in producing the 9th edition of the *Encyclopaedia Britannica* and mass-market editions of Scott's Waverley novels. James Black attended the Moravian School in Neuwied, and later the Royal High School under Dr. Carson who had preferred the Rectorship of the school to the Greek Chair at the University of St Andrews.

[7] Seymour-Smith (1982), 232.

[8] Seymour (1995), 213: 'But she [Riding] detested the *Claudius* books from the moment that she first looked at the typescripts; they were said to be boring and unreadable. They could not be mentioned in her presence; reviews had to be hidden from sight.'

growing international tensions in the 1930s, readers in Europe, and even those under the Fascist and Nazi dictatorships, also wished to experience Graves's vision of ancient Rome. For one example, Riding was particularly determined, according to Seymour-Smith, 'to get her hands on the large sum of marks [*sic*] (in April 1935 16,800 marks were due) which had accumulated in Germany on sales of *Ich, Claudius*'.[9]

An Italian edition, translated by Carlo Coardi, appeared in 1936, under the full title *Io, Claudio: dall'autobiografia dell'Imperatore Claudio, Imperatore dei Romani, nato nel 10 A.C., ucciso e deificato nel 54 D.C.* The book, composed of 493 pages and listed for sale at 12 lire, was published by Valentino Bompiani in Milan, and it was accompanied, also in 1936, by a translation of *Claudius the God*, published as *Il divo Claudio*. Thus, the books were not, as claimed in a recent article, 'banned [by Mussolini] for their unfavourable representation of imperial Rome'.[10] In fact, Bompiani seems, in many ways, to have been a daring publishing house, making available to Italian readers a wide range of literature from British and, more often, American authors. Among Bompiani's offerings in the 1930s were several translations, most of them furnished by Coardi, of John Steinbeck novels, George Santayana's essays, Marjorie Kinnan Rawlings's *The Yearling*, and even a collection of President Franklin Roosevelt's speeches entitled *La nostra strada (On our Way)*, published in 1934.[11]

Nevertheless, Bompiani's editions of the *Claudius* novels drew a dismissive, and then a minatory, reaction from a prominent classics scholar in the 'Nuova Italia' created by Fascism. This brief (137-word) review, by Professor Roberto Paribeni, appeared in the 1937 volume of the journal *Roma*, the official organ of the Istituto di Studi Romani (Institute of Roman Studies). The journal followed the convention of dating according to Fascist years, and thus this volume of *Roma* was XV, appropriately produced in '1937–XV'. In his review, Paribeni does not address the specific scenes and characters of the novels, nor Graves's individual style and craftsmanship. Instead, he focuses upon

[9] Seymour-Smith (1982), 249–50. The money—minus commission—was eventually obtained through the good offices of British literary agents.

[10] Burton (1995), 199.

[11] Titles included G. Santayana, *Il pensiero americano e altri saggi* (1939); J. Steinbeck, *Furore* (1940); M. K. Rawlings, *Il cucciolo* (1945); and several books by H. R. Knickerbocker, including *Ci sarà la guerra in Europa?* (1934).

the 'English' qualities of the work, and the insult 'they' have given 'us Italians' with this work of 'decadence'. The first paragraph reads:[12]

> *Che gli Inglesi, i quali erano alcuni decenni fa coloro che meglio comprendevano l'Impero romano, scrivano ora libri come questi, mi fa piacere, perchè ci vedo un altro segno della loro innegabile decadenza, per la quale, dopo quello che ci hanno fatto, non pretenderanno che noi Italiani vestiamo le gramaglie.*
>
> That the English, who were some decades ago the very ones who best understood the Roman Empire, have now written books such as these, pleases me, because I see here another sign of their undeniable decadence, which is fine—after this thing they have done here, they may not claim that we Italians are clad in rags.

The second paragraph names what does not please Paribeni, and here the warning seems directed squarely at the Milan offices of Bompiani:

> *Che un editore italiano li faccia tradurre e li stampi, e che gli Italiani li leggano e persino li lodino, mi fa dispiacere, perchè mi prova che essi non considerano ancora loro patrimonio l'Impero di Roma, e tollerano che ne siano trattati i personaggi (anche il festeggiato divo Augusto) e le istituzioni con beffarda irriverenza. Oltre a tutto, trovo anche abbastanza insulsi i due libri, accanto ai quali il Quo vadis? di Sienkiewicz e forse anche lo Spartaco di Raffaello Giovagnoli diventano grandissimi capolavori.*
>
> That an Italian publisher would countenance translating and printing them, and that Italians would read them and, even, praise them, does *not* please me, because it proves to me that they do not yet consider the Empire of Rome their own patrimony, and that they suffer its personages (even the [currently] celebrated *divus Augustus*) and its institutions to be handled with mocking irreverence. In addition to all of this, I even find the two books insipid enough that, alongside them, Sienkiewicz's *Quo vadis?* and perhaps even Giovagnoli's *Spartacus* appear the greatest masterpieces.

Paribeni, who in 1937 was Direttore generale of the Museo Nazionale Romano and of Antichità e Belle Arti, could speak with considerable authority on the personages and institutions of ancient Rome, having written books on Trajan, Hadrian, and the 'capolavori' of Roman art preserved in several Roman museums.[13] However, his

[12] Paribeni (1937), 148.

[13] Among his pre-war works were *Optimus Princeps: saggio sulla storia e sui tempi dell'imperatore Traiano* (G. Principato: Messina, 1927); *Le terme di Diocleziano e il*

pronouncements on the 'festeggiato divo Augusto' reveal the specific *mise-en-scène* of this review—and illuminate the chilly reception he gave to the 'irreverent' portrayal of this particular emperor.

The twenty-third of September 1937 marked the two-thousandth anniversary of the birthday of Caius Octavius, who would become the adopted heir of Julius Caesar, then Triumvir, and then, renamed Augustus, unrivaled master of the Roman Empire. In Augustus's honour Mussolini's government planned and oversaw a series of commemorative events to mark a year devoted to the subject between 1937 and 1938 (Fascist Years XV and XVI). The culminating event of this veritable *Wunderjahr* was the *Mostra Augustea della Romanità*, or 'Augustan Exhibit of Romanness', a display visited by over 100,000 Italians—and also by Adolf Hitler, on his state visit to Rome in May 1938. I am engaged in writing a monograph that will assess how Augustus was viewed in the 1930s, by scholars and by the larger public, not only in Fascist Italy but also in Nazi Germany, Third-Republic (and then Vichy) France, the United Kingdom, Canada, and the United States. My goal is to explain how the planners of the Augustan Bimillenary were able to draw upon an existing international appreciation of this significant historical figure, one which was consistent across cultures and overwhelmingly positive.

Paribeni was a prominent contributor to these commemorative efforts, and his position on these matters is best encapsulated in a lecture he gave to the Accademia d'Italia on 20 April 1938, as part of the celebrations of Rome's foundation during this special Bimillenary year. The highlights of this lively address will demonstrate its intended effect, as well as the contemporary resonances intended for those living under Mussolini's ascendant regime.[14] A sketch of the chaotic situation into which Octavian was thrust as a very young man is provided. Despite these considerable obstacles and his relative youth, Octavian won the loyalty of his father's troops, marched on Rome, and became, with universal consent, 'il capo dello Stato'. Through an 'exquisitely revolutionary' action, he gained legal office as triumvir and was applauded by a grateful people. He avenged his father (apparently single-handedly), eliminated decadent rivals like

Museo nazionale romano (La Libreria dello stato: Rome, 1932); *Il ritratto nell'arte antica* (Treves: Milan, 1934); and *L'Italia imperiale da Ottaviano a Teodosio* (Mondadori: Milan, 1938).

[14] Paribeni (1938).

Antony, took absolute power, and created peace, security, and universal tranquility. But then he faced a challenge: how could he keep and hold monarchic power, when Roman culture was marked by anti-monarchic prejudice? His brilliant solution to the dilemma was to become merely 'the superior among other men', that is, a *princeps*. As his work unfolded, Augustus, according to Paribeni, experienced a string of military successes (the disaster in the Teutoburg Forest is not mentioned), he renovated a decaying culture and restored old-fashioned morals, and, best of all, paved the way for the birth of a child in an obscure oriental town who would become the Redeemer of the world. As he died, Augustus could not know the full effect of his work, of course, but later generations would profit from the peace and the Prince of Peace generated during his reign.

Such was the fairly typical approach to Augustus by Italian academics in these commemorative years. However, I wish here to analyse two questions suggested by Paribeni's review. First, was Paribeni correct in concluding that Augustus is handled 'with mocking irreverence' in *I, Claudius*? If so, can it be said that Graves was deliberately downgrading Augustus in his character sketch, perhaps to undermine the emperor's standing in the Fascists' eyes? Second, is his portrait of Augustus recognizably 'English'? In other words, is the Augustus of *I, Claudius* remarkably different from those sketched by other British men of letters among his contemporaries? In this respect, at least, there is one of Graves's acquaintances near to hand: John Buchan, Governor-General of Canada after 1935 and author of a biography of *Augustus* in 1937. By comparing the reception of both authors—even in the pages of *Roma*—we can assess Italian expectations regarding 'their' Augustus in the years just prior to Ronald Syme's monumental portrait of 'Pax et Princeps' in *The Roman Revolution* (1939).

Despite Graves's protestation that, 'I identify myself with him [Claudius] historically, but merely historically',[15] the biographers have consistently interpreted the *Claudius* books as, in good measure, a wry commentary on his own domestic situation. By this reading, Claudius, like his creator, is beset by domineering women, preserving a modicum of self-respect by eluding their demands and making his own plans under their noses. As Miranda Seymour and many others

[15] Seymour-Smith (1982), 256, from a letter sent in December 1933.

have claimed, Livia, in particular, appears to be a stand-in for Laura Riding: 'As an empress who seeks deification to escape punishment by the gods for her crimes, Livia is hard to admire. In her daily life, she bears a striking resemblance to Riding at her most imperious.'[16] The dramatic possibilities of Livia, in particular, would continue to fascinate Graves, even after he had fashioned one of the great villainesses of 1930s fiction. In an Introduction to the *Lives of the Roman Empresses* (1935), he comments upon 'the terrible Livia, Augustus's wife, with whom rests the main responsibility for the conversion of the Republic into an Empire. Her rule lasted for an extraordinarily long time.'[17]

Even a cursory reading of *I, Claudius* would reinforce the conclusion that whatever buffoonery there is in the sketch of Augustus results from excessive uxoriousness on his part, in contrast to the truly demonic force in the piece, his consort. Throughout the novel, the wilful Livia is contrasted with the weak and malleable Augustus, through whom she works her plans. Very early in the novel, Claudius, Livia's grandson, avers: 'Augustus ruled the world, but Livia ruled Augustus . . . The only reasonable explanation is that Augustus was, at bottom, a pious man, though cruelty and even ill-faith had been forced on him by the dangers that followed his grand-uncle Julius Caesar's assassination.'[18] A few pages later,[19] Claudius again (though one wonders how he was so well informed on this point) claims: 'By following her [Livia's] advice he gradually concentrated in his single person all the important Republican dignities.'

The most remarkable instance of this dynamic at work in the imperial couple concerns Drusus's letter, which has gone astray and mistakenly fallen into the hands of his mother and stepfather. As this complex and intricately plotted scene unfolds, Augustus's true feelings are revealed:[20]

> [Augustus] read [Drusus's] letter, but it seemed to call for disapproval rather as something which had outraged my grandmother than as something written against himself. Indeed, except for the ugly word 'compel', he secretly approved of the sentiments expressed in the letter, even though the insult to my grandmother reflected on himself, as

[16] Seymour (1995), 213 and 216. [17] Graves (2000c), 136.
[18] Graves (1934a), 19.
[19] Graves (1934a), 24, with similar details on pp. 25 and 26.
[20] Graves (1934a), 43–4.

> having been persuaded by her against his better judgement . . . He [Augustus] disliked the situation as much as my father, and it was true that as long ago as before the defeat and death of Antony he had publicly promised to retire when no public enemy remained in the field against him . . . He was weary now of perpetual State business and perpetual honours: he wanted a rest and anonymity.

Livia, however, nips her husband's nascent republicanism in the bud. As Claudius observes: 'But my grandmother would never allow him to give up: she would always say that his task was not half accomplished yet, that nothing but civil disorder could be expected if he retired now. Yes, he worked hard, she owned, but she worked still harder and with no direct public reward. . . . He accepted his monarchial privileges in instalments.'

Furthermore, Graves implies that it was Livia, without the direct knowledge or overt complicity of Augustus, who had Drusus and his dangerous ideas eliminated. A terrible consequence indeed, but, to her mind, a necessary one, in the furtherance of her husband's—and her own—vital work. The scene in which Augustus asserts his independence, attempting to reinstate his own legitimate grandson Agrippa Postumus (chapter 13), is also crucial, as it determines Livia to remove her husband before he can endanger the system *she* has laboured so hard to construct. Thus, at every point it is Livia, and not Augustus, who is irreverently treated—and Augustus is even given a chance (chapter 14) to redeem himself, by begging Claudius's forgiveness for any unkind word or action flung his way.

Through his analysis of Augustus, then, Graves may have been attempting to absolve himself, while casting Riding as the grey eminence in the piece. Nevertheless, Graves claimed that his character sketches could possess a wider and more universal application. In the same letter in which he connected himself 'historically' with Claudius, Graves complained: 'You read it looking for things that I had no intention of putting into it.' One of the reasons he chose Claudius, he claims, was 'because he lived in an age in which every moral safeguard of a religious or patriotic or social sort had gone West—things were just disintegrating. He realised this and found it impossible to reintegrate them.'[21] Accordingly, one might ask whether this character sketch of the Julio-Claudians, including Augustus, was informed by

[21] Seymour-Smith (1982), 256.

the world situation of the 1930s. Could the general sense of disintegration that characterized the period have shaped his portrait? More directly, did the Fascist identification with Augustus factor into Graves's 'decadent' (according to Paribeni) sketch of the emperor's character?

While some have endeavoured to find anti-Fascist sentiments in Graves's writing in the early 1930s, it would be more reasonable to conclude that Fascism only rose to the surface in his work after he and Riding had been driven into exile from Mallorca. Even by July 1936, according to Richard Perceval Graves, 'the trouble seemed utterly remote'; by the end of that month it became clear that events were going to impose themselves even upon Deyá. Nevertheless, Graves was still reporting on the sinister demonstrations of Fascist power and the sufferings of its local victims with a curiously detached air. Graves saw a woman 'out of her mind with terror, rush shrieking down the road', and yet he could speak scornfully of the young Fascists in Palma, 'lounging about. Growing beards already . . . '.[22]

Even after their exile had begun, Graves referred to Fascism in passing, and sometimes managed to find the humour in Fascist pomposity. Volumes III and IV of *Epilogue: A Critical Summary*, the journal he and (mostly) Riding had begun in Mallorca, turned increasingly to international affairs, but still seen through the lens of literature and the proper reaction of poets committed to their art. In a joint essay entitled 'Politics and Poetry', composed by Riding, Graves, and others in their circle, the questions posed by Fascism seem incidental to the overall developments of literature in the current environment. Graves's contribution stands out, naturally, for its trenchant quality, but also for its wit, as he assesses the impact of Fascism on poetry:[23]

> Fascism, though like Communism attempting to arouse feelings of guilt in the poet toward his immediate physical world, does not issue invitations or make any promises to him . . . In Germany the given physical properties comprise the ideal of human self-sufficiency; in Italy, the authority for caprice of action. The Fascist poet is not invited to elevate and purify, he is merely permitted to cheer. This forbidding attitude to poetry on the Fascist side accounts for the extremely small number of

[22] R. P. Graves (1990), 238–41.

[23] Graves and Riding (1937), 28. Thanks are gratefully offered to the Houghton Library at Harvard University, for making available all four volumes of the journal.

> poets professing Fascist sympathies and for the rush of poetry-nervous poets to the Communist ranks.

In the midst of his essay, though, Graves added an ironic footnote concerning (of course) the funds that Stanley Baldwin had, in a speech in July 1936, promised to make available to poets:[24]

> But the Chancellor of the Exchequer had recently declined to accept a motion for increasing the Civil List pensions in art, science, literature and learning from £1,200 a year (the figure at which it has stood for 100 years) to £4,000 . . . That a poet was a research worker and to be endowed would never occur to any representative of democratic opinion. Mr Baldwin was not really serious in his plea for more poets: what he really meant to assert was the need for more politicians.

By contrast, Mussolini appears only very rarely in Graves's printed and private writing. His diary entry for 7 March 1937 begins with a note that he was working on the film-script for *Claudius* all day, and yet, on the way home from dinner in Lugano, he heard a drunken man shouting [in imperfect Italian]: '"Mussolini." Brutto uomo senza cuore! Ecco! La difficultà [*sic*] della ciutà [civiltà] . . . Noi altri . . . '.[25] In August 1937 Graves, together with Harry Kemp and Laura Riding, sent a letter to the *Daily Telegraph* protesting a comparison the paper had drawn between Mussolini and Augustus.[26] The writers note the 'ingenuity' of the parallel drawn between 'the Emperor Augustus and Signor Mussolini', but they claim that 'superficial resemblances can be found between any Monmouth and its Macedon.' The 'true historical parallel', in their opinion, is between Mussolini and 'the nationalist princeling Cymbeline of Britain, who in Augustan days played the Little Caesar on the borders of the Roman Empire, and was justly praised by contemporary critics for his energy in knitting together a backward and factious people'. Within two month of this editorial's appearance the Fascists had inaugurated the year-long

[24] Graves and Riding (1936), 49 n. 12.

[25] University of Victoria online collection. A copy of the original handwritten page is included on the webpage, and it appears that Graves has written a 'v' above 'ciutà' (as an abbreviation?).

[26] A copy of the *Daily Telegraph* clipping is included in the University of Victoria online entry for 29 August 1937. It is entitled 'History's Parallels: Caesar, Il Duce and Cymbeline', and is credited to H. V. Kemp alone. However, Graves has added, in handwriting below the clipping, 'Harry and I did this together'.

celebration of Augustus, whom they clearly considered more than a 'princeling' on the fringes of Empire.

Accordingly, it would seem clear that Graves was not inspired by Mussolini as he composed his portrait of Augustus, nor did he seem to have taken Augustus as seriously as certain of his contemporaries would have liked. Paribeni's reaction, or over-reaction, seems more the result of the specific demands of the Augustan year, and the changed circumstances of 1937, as opposed to those of 1934.

But what should we make of the claim concerning 'English decadence' in Graves's rendering of the Augustan Age? In precisely this period another British author, with whom Graves was on warm personal terms, addressed the character and achievements of the 'festeggiato' Augustus, and the enthusiastic reception of his work in Fascist Italy makes a telling contrast to the outrage that greeted *Io, Claudio*. In October 1937, shortly after the Augustan year had been inaugurated in Rome, John Buchan, the newly created Lord Tweedsmuir, published a substantial (350-page) biography entitled *Augustus*.[27]

Best known today for his Richard Hannay stories and novels, including *The Thirty-Nine Steps* (1914) and *Greenmantle* (1916),[28] Buchan was a prominent man of letters in the early twentieth century, who moved in influential intellectual and political circles and was renowned for incorporating his public service into his literary output. Drawing on his experiences in the Ministry of Information during the Great War, Buchan virtually created the spy-thriller genre (self-described 'shockers'), adding a dose of realism to these seemingly preposterous tales of adventure and intrigue. However, his war work also enhanced his substantial non-fiction and historical writing, which included a multi-volume and, for the period, definitive history of the war in 1921–2, as well as a series of biographies of great men of the past. These men were generally public figures who had taken on political roles in wartime, such as Cromwell, Lord Montrose, Sir Walter Raleigh, General Gordon, and several Scots heroes.[29] In this vein he composed a biography of Julius Caesar in 1932 and, at least at

[27] Buchan (1937).

[28] As a marker of Buchan's prescience, a BBC radio broadcast of *Greenmantle*, which centres upon wartime espionage in the Middle East, was postponed in the wake of the terrorist bombings in London in July 2005.

[29] See Lownie (1995), esp. ch. 11, 'Biographer and Historian'.

the beginning of *Augustus*, he claimed he had always wished to complete a biography of this figure.[30]

Nevertheless, the late 1930s would appear an odd moment for Buchan to have taken on a project of this sort. In 1935 he had been tapped by George V to represent the Crown as his Governor-General in Canada.[31] The position was a prestigious one, and his appointment broke tradition, as he was the first commoner to have been so honoured (the title 'Lord Tweedsmuir' was crafted to normalize the situation). Buchan went on to become one of Canada's most energetic and most admired Governors-General, as well as a pivotal character in Canada's development as a Dominion with an independent foreign policy. He encouraged this movement from the normal vantage-points of his official residences in Ottawa and Montreal, but also during his extensive travels to remote corners of the Northwest Territories. Buchan took the proofs of *Augustus* with him into the Arctic Circle, and his vigourous—despite being in his sixties and frequently in ill health at the time—celebration of the wide expanses of, especially, Western Canada set another example of public service. Buchan's tenure in the position, ended by his death in Montreal in 1940, was also, of course, full of daunting challenges. He weathered the abdication crisis, organized a highly successful royal tour of the new King George VI and Queen Elizabeth, and developed close connections with US President Franklin Roosevelt and Prime Minister Mackenzie King, to whom he dedicated his Augustus biography.[32] After his death Buchan's papers and personal library remained in Canada, and they are today housed at Queen's University in Kingston, Ontario.

[30] Despite a late start in Latin and Greek, Buchan was fortunate to study under Gilbert Murray at Glasgow, who became a lifelong friend and continued to correspond with Buchan concerning his Canadian appointment and the quality of his *Augustus*.

[31] George V was celebrated by Buchan in *The King's Grace, 1910–1935*, published by Hodder & Stoughton in April 1935.

[32] Buchan forwarded a copy of *Augustus* to President Roosevelt, who acknowledged it on 23 November 1937, in breezy, upper-class American: 'I am perfectly delighted to have "Augustus". I have glanced at it rather casually while I have spent these few days in my room with a bad tooth. I am looking forward with pleasure to reading it on my fishing trip. Thank you ever so much for sending it to me.' (Unpublished handwritten letter in the Buchan Archive, Queen's University, Ontario.)

Among the letters he received during his tenure as Governor-General was a congratulatory note handwritten by Robert Graves and dated 27 March 1935.[33] The letter is mentioned in Graves's diary entry for 28 March, and another letter is mentioned as having been sent in October 1937, but Graves and Buchan had been in epistolary contact since at least the mid-1920s.[34] Their mutual friend T. E. Lawrence played an important role in creating and cementing this relationship, but Graves also (perhaps unexpectedly?) praised the literary merits of Buchan's work, despite the profound differences between their accustomed genres and compositional styles. Graves described Buchan's 1924 poetry collection *The Northern Muse: An Anthology of Scots Vernacular Poetry* in effusive terms for *The Nation & Athenaeum*, proclaiming Buchan 'the first man to make a comprehensive Anthology of Scottish and Northern English poetry which Southerners can read with real pleasure'.[35]

It was, however, Buchan's capacity for friendship that most attracted Graves, who benefited at specific important moments from their association, and observed: 'It is impossible to do justice to John Buchan's warmth, modesty, generosity.'[36] Lawrence had introduced Graves to Buchan, and Buchan both lauded Graves' *Lawrence and the Arabs* (1927) and shared in the grief over Lawrence's death in 1935. Shortly before that point Buchan had helped Lawrence return to the RAF, while also helping Graves secure his professorship in Cairo.[37] Learning from his negotiations over the filming of Hitchcock's *The Thirty-Nine Steps*, Buchan also gave Graves shrewd advice in his negotiations with Alexander Korda

[33] He was also the recipient of a (characteristically bizarre) set of letters from Ezra Pound, typed on handmade stationery, embossed with Pound's portrait, and printed in Rapallo. This correspondence attempted to draw Buchan's attentions to the malicious intentions of 'Jewish' financial interests, and insisted that Buchan use his connections in the British Parliament to 'do something' about the current economic crisis.

[34] Two letters from Buchan, dated 8 Aug. 1925 and 8 Nov. 1927, are held in the Graves Manuscript collection at Southern Illinois University: Presley (1976), 172.

[35] As quoted in Lownie (1995), 191.

[36] As quoted in Adam Smith (1985), 350.

[37] Adam Smith (1985), 224 and 341. Graves mentioned this service in his 1965 BBC interview, citing the agency of three friends, Lawrence, Arnold Bennett, and Buchan. The film may be found online at: <http://www.bbc.co.uk/archive/writers/12243.shtml>.

over the film rights to *I, Claudius*.[38] Graves alludes to this service in his letter of congratulation to Buchan on his recent appointment:[39]

> Dear John,
> This evening I got a contract from Eliot for my Claudius film: he mentioned that you have approved it and I was on the point of writing to thank you when I found in the local Spanish paper a telegram saying that you would probably be made the next Governor-General of Canada, so that it is a great pleasure (if the telegram is true) to be able to combine thanks and congratulations. I think that it is a very good thing for Canada. I have been following the Canadian situation in the American press . . .

In my own research on Augustus in the 1930s I am setting Buchan's opinions against the backdrop of the extensive private and official correspondence contained in the Buchan Archive. For present purposes it is probably sufficient to comment that Graves would likely have been shocked by certain of Buchan's frank reactions, particularly those regarding the Spanish Civil War. In letters to the Canadian Prime Minister, who was negotiating at the League of Nations in Geneva in September 1936, Buchan upheld the primacy of Canada's, and Britain's, true international interests, in the midst of 'the wrangling of ambitious mob-leaders', the main cause of violent explosions on the Continent. While expressing confidence in the Prime Minister's abilities, Buchan acknowledged to his mother-in-law, on 16 September 1936, that 'This miserable Spanish business has hideously complicated matters'.[40] One wonders what Graves would have made of this characterization, as a recent refugee from this 'miserable' conflict?

As Buchan had drawn attention to Mackenzie King's 'cool, independent judgement' in a letter to Geneva dated 29 September 1936, he saw in Augustus the same qualities of rational, calm, and considered decision-making that were badly needed in the unsettled contemporary world of 'unnecessary European squabbles'.[41] Buchan addresses this directly in his preface to *Augustus*, admitting: 'I am conscious

[38] Lownie (1995), 241.

[39] Letter from Graves to Buchan, unpublished manuscript in the Buchan Archive.

[40] Letter from John Buchan to Caroline ('Tin') Grosvenor, 16 Sept. 1936, unpublished copy in the Buchan Archive.

[41] Letter from Buchan to William Lyon Mackenzie King, Prime Minister of Canada, 29 Sept. 1936, unpublished copy in the Buchan Archive.

that my interpretation of Augustus is a personal thing, coloured insensibly by my own beliefs. But, since the historian is most at home in an age which resembles his own, I hope that the convulsions of our time may give an insight into the problems of the early Roman empire which was perhaps unattainable by scholars who lived in easier days.'[42]

The present-day implications of Buchan's level-headed statesman are profound—and his point of view accords with that advocated by prominent academics in Britain and elsewhere in the 1930s.[43] His approach to the triumviral proscriptions is especially illuminating, since he took the opportunity at this point in the narrative to comment on this 'darkest stain upon Octavian's record' in sympathetic terms. Motivated both by revenge for his adopted father's murder and 'rational' self-interest, Octavian concluded that: 'The state should be re-made at whatever cost, and only violence could curb violence. To this task he brought both the stony-heartedness of self-absorbed youth, and the moral opportunism of the fanatic. His view was that of Horace Walpole: "No great country was ever saved by good men, because good men will not go the lengths that may be necessary."'[44] One might compare Stalin's famous dictum that 'No one makes a revolution in silk gloves'.

Regardless of its disturbing application in the 1930s, Buchan's approach to Augustus was typical of its era, as I am attempting to demonstrate in my study of the period.[45] This is an important factor to consider, especially when evaluating the fundamental departure in the literature that is Syme's *The Roman Revolution*. In his preface to that work, dated 1 June 1939, Syme famously acknowledged Hugh Last's assistance, 'though there will be much here that will make him raise his eyebrows'. More starkly, Syme posited a choice that existed

[42] Buchan (1937), 9.

[43] In an eight-page handwritten note, dated 24 November 1937, Hugh Macilwain Last, Camden Professor at Brasenose College, Oxford, made a lengthy series of corrections and suggestions for further reading. Buchan should not take umbrage at this, he insists, since 'I have treated your book as what it is—a work of the highest scholarship [underlined in the text]; and, if I seem at times hypercritical, the reason is that I am dealing with it just as I should with a work by Mommsen himself [underlined].' Unpublished manuscript letter, John Buchan Archive.

[44] Buchan (1937), 70–1.

[45] The most recent treatment of Buchan and the classics, Haslett and Haslett (2009), adds little to this discussion, and it mistakenly describes 'Alan Last' and garbles his interpretation of the Augustan age.

for Romans in Augustus' day—and perhaps even in the late 1930s: 'Liberty or stable government: that was the question confronting the Romans themselves, and I have tried to answer it precisely in their fashion . . .'[46] Early in the book Syme characterized the errors that had been generated by an overly sympathetic approach to Augustus in the past:[47]

> If despotism was the price, it was not too high: to a patriotic Roman of Republican sentiments even submission to absolute rule was a lesser evil than war between citizens . . . The happy outcome of the Principate might be held to justify, or at least to palliate, the horrors of the Roman Revolution: hence the danger of an indulgent estimate of the person and acts of Augustus.

'Indulgence' was, at the very least, what was expected for the celebrated Augustus in Italy, and while commentators in other countries were generally not as garrulous on the point, this estimate predominated in scholarship of the period, in every other national context. When Buchan's biography came to be evaluated in Fascist Italy, however, this national context was again held against its author. A review of his book appeared in the 1940 volume of *Roma*, in the context of a larger article surveying recent books on Augustus from around the world. The reviewer on this occasion was Massimo Pallottino, the University of Rome Etruscologist who went on to an eminent career after the Second World War. His assessment of *Augustus* is generally positive, beginning with a characterization of Buchan as a man of the world and a man of affairs, rather than as a professional historian *sensu strictissimo*:

> *L'opera Augustus di John Buchan (Lord Tweedsmuir: una delle figure più eminenti della vita politica inglese contemporanea), tradotta in italiano da B. Maffi (Milano, Corticelli, 1939) è senza dubbio un libro singolare, libro di un conoscitore di uomini e di un vigoroso scrittore ancor più che di uno storico nel senso professionale. . . .*
>
> The work *Augustus* of John Buchan (Lord Tweedsmuir: one of the most eminent figures in contemporary English political life), translated into Italian by B. Maffi . . . is without doubt a singular book, a book by one who understands men and of a vigorous writer rather than by a historian in the professional sense.

[46] Syme (1939), viii–ix. [47] Syme (1939), 2.

Pallottino proceeds to emphasize the skill with which Buchan presents the major players of the period, and he draws attention to the 'wise sketch of the psychological transitions of Augustus in the successive phases of his career' and the lucid judgements applied to governmental arrangements under Caesar, the Triumvirs, and the Principate.

Nevertheless, to his mind, the book was marred by a few defects, which resulted from the context in which it had been produced:

> *Ma non mancano gl'indizi di un concetto e di una visione ormai sorpassati della storia dell'Impero di Roma: di questi il più evidente è la condanna apodittica e globale degli immediati successori di Augusto, come uomini e come principi. Nella traduzione del Maffi è soppressa una curiosa allusione finale, di esplicito sapore antitotalitario, non giustificata dalle promesse, ma coerente con la nazionalità e l'ambiente dell'autore.*
>
> But there are not lacking some indications of a conception and of a vision already *passé*, concerning the history of the Roman Empire . . . In Maffi's translation there has been suppressed a curious final allusion, of explicitly anti-totalitarian flavour, not justified by the premises, but consistent with the nationality and milieu of the author.

This 'anti-totalitarian'[48] final allusion is probably a passage that is embedded in Buchan's speculation concerning what Augustus would have thought of the 1930s, were he to be resurrected and asked his opinion:[49]

> But chiefly, I think, he would be perplexed by the modern passion for regimentation and the assumed contradiction between law and liberty. To bring order out of anarchy he had been forced to emphasize the first, but he had laboured also to preserve the second . . . He would sadly admit that the machine which he had created had been too strong for Roman liberties, and that in its grip the Roman character had lost its salt and iron . . . And when this expert in mechanism observed the craving of great peoples to enslave themselves and to exult hysterically in their bonds, bewilderment would harden in his masterful eyes.

In his final autobiographical evaluation, *Memory Hold-the-Door*, published shortly after his death in 1940, Buchan comments directly

[48] The term 'totalitarian' was, of course, a creation of the Fascist regime, appearing first in Giovanni Gentile's entry on 'Fascismo' for the *Enciclopedia italiana* in 1932.

[49] Buchan (1937), 346–7.

on what he meant by this 'craving of great peoples', observing, 'Augustus seemed to me to embody all the virtues of a dictator, when a dictator was needed, and to have tried valiantly to provide against the perils. The book was kindly received by scholars in Britain, America and on the Continent, though my Italian friends jibbed at some of my political deductions.'[50]

While we in the twenty-first century might also 'jib' at the concepts of 'needed dictators' and 'dictatorial virtues', it is clear, from Buchan's correspondence at the time of composing the biography, that he was thinking of the real-world applications of his character sketch of the first *princeps*. Writing to the recently retired British Prime Minister Stanley Baldwin in October 1937, Buchan hoped *Augustus* would meet with Baldwin's approval, 'for it is a study of a very great practical statesman. One American College President who read the proofs, informs me that I have just not made Augustus the inventor of the British constitution! I wish to goodness his mantle had descended upon the present ridiculous Dictator of Italy!'[51]

Augustus was, in Buchan's estimation, 'the only dictator in history who kept his head',[52] and it was apparently this quality of calm and clear-eyed rationalism that Buchan believed would enable present-day statesmen to weather global crises. But how far did he expect British or Canadian Prime Ministers, or even American Presidents or European 'mob-leaders', to overrule the will of the people? Pallottino would probably have thought this incompatible with 'Anglo-Saxon sensibilities', and in another remarkable review of English opinion, he attributed this inability to face reality to the fundamental weakness of the European democracies.

Attacking an English writer called Percy U. Robinson, who had composed an article for *Ce soir* in April 1937, Pallottino pointed to a 'spiritual barrier' that divided 'official European "intelligence"' from '*la rinascente romanità dell'Italia nuova*'.[53] Robinson had suggested that Cato the Younger, if he were somehow resurrected and invited to attend the Roman birthday celebrations in Mussolini's Italy, would not recognize the ancient Roman spirit among his modern

[50] Buchan (1940), 199.

[51] Unpublished letter from John Buchan to Stanley Baldwin, former Prime Minister of the United Kingdom, 11 Oct. 1937, John Buchan Archive.

[52] This appears repeatedly in his descriptions of the book to friends and colleagues in letters from late 1937.

[53] Pallottino (1937), 179–80.

descendants. Faulting him for not understanding the truly Roman spirit that was operative in the modern Italian, Pallottino identifies the 'acute Anglo-Saxon sensibilities' that had coloured Robinson's perception. His failure to understand modern Italy is, nevertheless, symptomatic of the rottenness of all the European democracies, who, in a remarkably elegant phrase, advocate '*il culto del frammento; la valorizzazione del piccolo, ai danni delle cose grandi*' ('the cult of the fragment; the inflation of the petty, to the detriment of great matters').

Graves, naturally, interpreted this situation differently, claiming that, as noted above, the Fascist poet—a rare breed to begin with—was 'merely permitted to cheer', elevating and purifying in bombastic terms, beyond the humble level of daily life. Perhaps it is only by glorying in the 'small' that a poet can achieve true understanding. Shortly after finishing work on *Claudius the God*, Graves composed a poem entitled 'To Bring the Dead to Life'. As he had 'revivified' Claudius and his family, he was aware of the common destiny that awaits all humans, no matter how 'great':[54]

> So grant him life, but reckon
> That the grave which housed him
> May not be empty now:
> You in his spotted garments
> Shall yourself lie wrapped.

[54] As quoted in Seymour (1995), 215.

14

Josef von Sternberg and the Cinematizing of *I, Claudius*

A. G. G. Gibson

For a few weeks in 1937 Robert Graves's emperor Claudius flickered into life on the big screen. The extant rushes can be seen in *The Epic that Never Was*, Bill Duncalf's documentary about the making of Sir Alexander Korda's doomed film of *I, Claudius*.[1] Left as a fragile centrepiece is a critically acclaimed performance by Charles Laughton as Claudius delivering a masterful speech to the Senate.[2]

This essay will examine two main factors in the gestation of the screenplay based on Graves's *Claudius* novels: the emotional content of the script, and the experiences the scriptwriters brought to the 'transition' of Graves's Claudius from page to screen. The emotional content embedded in the screenplay takes three distinct forms; firstly, the relationships, sexual or otherwise, between Graves's Claudius and Messalina, which is an echo of Graves and Laura Riding, and has elements of Somerset Maugham's Philip Carey and Mildred. The second is the idea of a personal emotional battle as a consequence of disability. Both Graves and Somerset Maugham wrote about the experience, or the perception of the experience, of disability through biography and this motif was subsequently embodied through Laughton's performance. On screen Claudius was a combination of the

[1] This type of documentary is echoed by Keith Fulton's and Louis Pepe's film, *Lost in La Mancha* (2002), that chronicled Terry Gilliam's ill-fated attempt to film *Don Quixote*.

[2] There is much praise for Laughton: 'There is more than enough of Claudius in these rushes to see the blueprint of a great performance', Felix Barker 'The Epic That Never Was', *London Evening News*, 16 Dec. 1965 and *Liverpool Echo*, 18 Dec. 1965.

historical figure in the sources, the 'voice' of Graves in the novels, the 'voice' of the fictional creation (see Chapter 1 and 2 in this volume, by Bennett and Kennedy and O'Gorman),[3] all filtered through the screenwriters' experiences to create a Claudius who was an iconographic representation that combined disability and power. Thirdly, the filmmakers and Graves added a post-war dimension to the political sensibilities of the script that was embedded in their experiences of the Great War.

In 2014 it will be eighty years since the publication of *I, Claudius* and *Claudius the God*, which were such a success that within two years a film version was under way. The concept of filming the books has attracted the highest calibre of Hollywood players, but a completed movie has not yet made it to the big screen. This essay will also consider the chequered history of two film projects since 1937.[4]

KORDA'S PROJECT FOR *I, CLAUDIUS* (1937)

Robert Graves's first screen treatment, 'The Fool of Rome' (1936), opens in AD 15 with a description which faithfully, and unquestioningly, reproduces the accounts in the Suetonius and Dio Cassius: 'Claudius aged 25, with a rather fat, puzzled but not unintelligent face; constantly twitching with his hands; nervous tick of his neck ...'[5] Graves moves from a first-person narrator of the novel to a narrative driven by the visual nature of movie-making. There is not room for a full analysis here, but in the script Graves insists on reproducing every stutter by means of initial letter repetition, and later will use the stutter as a means for humour with comic word-play and slapstick.[6]

Graves is reported as using an 'analeptic writing technique', which Geoffrey Ashe explains is how an author is momentarily able to inhabit the world of the subject—it works as 'an intuitive recovery

[3] Cf. Furbank (2004), 94–114.

[4] I am grateful to Jonathan Perry, Amanda Wrigley, and Elisabetta Girelli who provided valuable comment on this essay, but any errors are entirely of my own making. I also thank the Librarians at St John's College Library, Oxford for their invaluable assistance with regard to access to materials in the Robert Graves Archive.

[5] Suet. *Claud.* 30; Dio Cass. 60.1–7; Sen. *Apoc.* 1.11, 5.1–2, 6.13.

[6] 'The Fool of Rome', manuscript RG: CC005-001.

of forgotten events by a deliberate suspension of time'.[7] Graves tried to get into Claudius's mind and used him to give perspective to events in first-century Rome. 'The supposed author of the story . . . has much the same function as the carefully costumed figure placed in the foreground of an architectural drawing to correct misapprehensions about its size, date and geographical position.'[8] Claudius gives us the standpoint to survey his world. Ashe suggests this projection of consciousness has artistic, if not scientific, value:

> Claudius cannot speak like Claudius if Graves does not think like Claudius. But it is suggested that it has scientific value; which is not so obvious. It is suggested that Claudius-Graves can possess special insight into the Claudius world, can, in fact, discover truths about it which are denied to plain Robert Graves. There is no warrant here for the gibe of 'mysticism'.[9]

However much Graves had insight into the dynamics of life and death in the Rome of the first century, he cannot re-enact Claudius' fractured speech, nor his emotional bearing as a result of enduring years of dysfluency.[10] But John Richardson proposed that the character of Graves is interleaved with that of the fictional Claudius (see Bennett in Chapter 1). *I, Claudius* was so vivid because for Graves it was semi-autobiographical—he was an educated man, but a misfit who had lived on the fringes of society, whose life was controlled by dominant female characters, while the early years of poverty resulted in a pared-down, simple life.[11]

For the screen, even with Graves's input, there were difficulties in meshing *I, Claudius* and *Claudius the God*, and several notable screenwriters would attempt the task in vain. Notwithstanding the problems with the screenplay, Korda and Graves communicated frequently about the proposed novelization of the film, to be titled 'The Fool of Rome'.[12]

[7] Ashe (1947); also cf. (1995). [8] Ashe (1947). [9] Ashe (1947).

[10] Dysfluency is characterized by syllable, sound or word repetitions; or it can be sound prolongations; or blocks, when no sound is emitted, see <http://www.asha.org/public/speech/disorders/stuttering.htm>.

[11] J. S. Richardson's unpublished paper *Robert Graves: the Novelist as Historian*.

[12] The diary of Robert Graves 1935–39 (RGC) and ancillary material, University of Victoria, notes script problems at 25 Apr., 13 June, 19 Oct. 1935; 8 Jan., 19 Feb., 1/Mar., 10 Sept. 1936.

By January of 1937 the pre-production was in further trouble as the script stalled, and Graves wrote, 'Biró had stewed a month making it cinematizable' and 'June Head having made 1/2 a Biró translation was now making a v.S translation'.[13] The film scenario was still in a transitional phase because Lajos Biró, Korda's original screenwriter, became ill and Josef von Sternberg had taken over as director from William Menzies, so Korda drafted in Carl Zuckmayer and Lester Cohen to bolster the writing team.[14]

This team brought a Central European (and latent Weimar) influence to *I, Claudius* through the work experiences of Korda, Biró, and Zuckmayer. Biró had left Budapest after the Hungarian rising led to the Hungarian Soviet Republic under Bela Kun in 1919.[15] He had worked on scripts for Korda in Vienna, such as adapting Mark Twain's *The Prince and the Pauper* (*Prinz und Bettelknabe*, 1920) at Sascha-Film, and later moved with Korda to the Berlin-based Deutsche Vereins-Film. Korda's political credentials were revealed by his support of the Hungarian Soviet, set up after the collapse of the Austro-Hungarian Empire.[16] Carl Zuckmayer provided a discriminating political awareness to the venture; he had left Austria because of his anti-National Socialist views, and his plays were banned in 1933.[17] He had written screenplays for silent films, including *Qualen der Nacht* (1926) and *Schinderhannes* (1928) in Weimar Berlin, from his own play, and *Der Hauptmann von Köpenick* (1926 and 1931) from his novel of the same name, before working with Korda and Laughton on *Rembrandt* (1936).[18] Von Sternberg had returned from Hollywood to make *Der blaue Engel* (1930) with Marlene Dietrich and Emil Jannings for Universum Film (UFA), which was a mainstay of Weimar cinema. UFA would later distribute

[13] RGC 8 Jan. 1937; Lajos Biró was an experienced writer (scenario, dialogue, screenplay) on many films prior to this, including *The Scarlet Pimpernel* (1934), *The Private Life of Henry VIII* (1933), *The Way of All Flesh* (1927), and Arnold Ridley's *The Ghost Train* (1931). Carl Zuckmayer was writer of von Sternberg's *Der blaue Engel* (1930), and along with June Head was writer alongside Biró on Korda's *Rembrandt* (1936).

[14] RGC, 8 Jan. 1937. Some sources also cite Arthur Wimperis, the lyricist and writer who previously collaborated with Korda and Biró on *The Private Life of Henry VIII* and *The Four Feathers*; he won a screenplay Oscar for William Wyler's *Mrs Miniver* and was nominated for *Random Harvest*.

[15] Lendvai (2002), 366–72.

[16] Tokes (1970), 732–4.

[17] 'Zuckmayer, Carl', in Hartnoll and Found (1996). Cf. Denman (2003), 369–80.

[18] Hesling (2007), 76–109.

Riefenstahl's documentaries *Der Sieg des Glaubens* (1933) and *Triumph des Willens* (1935) and the short *Tag der Freiheit: Unsere Wehrmacht* (1935).

In Lugano, February 1937, Graves's work on the 'laborious' novelization of the film was being held up by the lack of Korda's script. This still lay unfinished two days before filming started in March. Graves's diary hints at changes made to his version, 'Letter from Cunningham that he is sending 15,000 *lire* and enclosing Claudius scenario: different from all previous versions, drawing more on *I, Claudius*, but spoiling the assassination & accession series', and continues: 'Read the Claudius script which is more & more dreary as it goes on.'[19] Von Sternberg was now in a bind between Zuckmayer's and Graves's scenario,[20] even though Zuckmayer was probably guilty of some howlers—one example being Caligula giving his horse, Incitatus, a sugar-lump.[21] Presley suggests that von Sternberg combined the Zuckmayer and Graves scripts to produce his detailed shooting scripts 'CLAUDIUS: Combined Script', because they removed Zuckmayer's anachronisms,[22] but the further 'hybridisation' of the script through the accumulation of twentieth-century sensibilities left Graves at a loss. Graves is scathing: 'The Claudius scenario is a great joke: its permutations in and out of German, Hungarian and English as various big-shots take turns at it would make you laugh. I don't care personally. Von Sternberg has it in hand now.'[23] This entry does not marry up with the strenuous efforts Graves had made to keep the scenario close to his line of thinking. In October 1936 he had written, 'Reading script: absolutely cheap nonsense strung on historical absurdities'. Graves had seen Korda and 'Told him how awful it was. Persuaded him to recast entirely.'[24] Graves worked on the scenario over the next few days (19–23 October) and noted that at least the typists liked his work. After dinner with Korda and Biró he noted: 'They went through stuff, pronounced it a useful second stage. Will [Biró] stew over it for 10 days.'[25]

19 RGC 3, 4 Mar. 1937. Seymour (1995), 250.

20 Seymour-Smith (1982), 273–4.

21 Presley (1999), 167–72.

22 Presley (1999), 171. Seymour (1995), 248.

23 Letter to Julie Matthews, 18 Jan. 1937, in O'Prey (1982), 275.

24 RGC 16, 18 Oct. 1936.

25 RGC 23 Oct. 1936; Graves sent them a note on the scenario on 25th, and on the 30th Korda phoned to say they would not have the scenario fixed until the middle of the week.

The merits of the Korda production were scrutinized by the potential script editor Ian A. Richmond (University of Durham), who wrote to Graves:

> I simply do not understand why they can't use the actual materials that history gives them (as you have done so well) and make play with them. To turn Narcissus into a rich and rather silly corn-merchant instead of one of the great palace-figures, is just bilge and nonsense. Still worse the bringing of Incitatus into the Senate: no one ever says he was more the consul destinatus.[26]

And later Richmond complains of further confusion of events, concluding:

> Altogether, they just make hay of the whole thing: and I am now very doubtful whether I want to have anything to do with it, unless it can be got to run better, though I feel very keen on the possibilities. There are some splendid opportunities for them, to show Claudius the fool (under Gaius); Claudius the practical, in Britain and at Ostia harbour; Claudius the *cocu*.[27]

Nevertheless, Graves had written a scenario that mixed comedy and tragedy together, and believed 'the force of the picture will be secured by borrowing Mark Twain's method in *Huckleberry Finn*: namely, to alternate scenes of real horror, cruelty and tragedy with high comic sequences, so that each heightens the effect of the other'.[28] Von Sternberg was already familiar with Twain's model and had used it in *Shanghai Express* (1932), which interwove intrigue and comic scenes against the political backdrop of a civil war. This stratagem was reused by Herbert Wise in the *I,Claudius* television series.[29]

The Julio-Claudian political predicament in first-century Rome is reflected in the sense of crisis, real or otherwise, between the protagonists in 1937—Korda, Laughton, von Sternberg, and Graves. There

[26] Correspondence between Ian Richmond and Graves, 15 Oct. 1936, GB 473 RG/J/Richmond/1–5; Richmond would withdraw (4 Nov. 1936) because the studio would not pay his fee: £20 per scene, and he estimated there were twenty-six important scenes. The university did not want their name connected with the project but allowed Richmond to be involved.

[27] Correspondence between Ian Richmond and Graves, 15 Oct. 1936, GB 473 RG/J/Richmond/1–5.

[28] Typescript for an outline of the film *I, Claudius*, ref. RG/D/IC/8. The 1957 ms RG/D/IC/11 with Boland has the handwritten title of 'Claudius the Fool'.

[29] Interview on film by Vanezis (2002).

is little doubt that Laughton and von Sternberg had become incompatible on set, and their relationship careered from one-time friendship into alienation and despair. Simon Callow defends Laughton from an actor's perspective, expounding on the elusive nature of portraying a character. However, the director's autobiographical and contrary view is equally as reasoned.[30] In 1936 a debilitated von Sternberg had been recovering from an operation in London when he received a visit from Alexander Korda, who brought a copy of *I, Claudius* and 'a hastily written manuscript based on the two volumes . . . ' which is likely to be a treatment Graves produced.[31] Korda warned him of the problems he faced with his star (as through bitter experience Korda would now only produce, but no longer direct, the troublesome Laughton). Although Laughton visited the next day and professed his admiration for the director, von Sternberg writes somewhat ambiguously: 'The devil himself visited me on the following morning, bringing a bag of black grapes and a history of the Roman Empire . . . '.[32] While Laughton's biographer soundly defends him against artistic slights and accusations of being 'a prima-donna' and of hijacking the production, the director writes of his own failings as well as professing his difficulty in being able to quantify the ingredients that make up a man's talents.

Laughton had struggled to catch the essence of Claudius's character, but hit upon listening to the restrained and emotional abdication speech of Edward VIII in 1936. The abdication, an accession in reverse, resulted in the king passing to an inferior social and political status. But while there was loss, there was also triumph by his claiming love and reconciling this with his rejection and exile. Although nothing of Edward's 'regal' nature is extant in the film's Senate scene, there is real emotion in Laughton's delivery, his sense of isolation, abandonment, and, as Edward was no longer a royal, the notion of 'Otherness'. Laughton captured the emotional hardship of Claudius's years of rejection, and drama critic Harold Hobson wrote that he would have gone on to give one of his greatest performances had the film been finished.[33]

30 Callow (1987), 111–21; von Sternberg (1965), 172–89.

31 Graves wrote a scenario for the film in 1935, but it is not clear if this is the treatment for the 'Fool of Rome' (1936) in St John's, Oxford.

32 Von Sternberg (1965), 172.

33 RGA: Harold Hobson (1965).

Acting alongside Gary Cooper in *Devil and the Deep* (1932) had been a seminal moment in Laughton's development—'he immediately recognised in Gary Cooper something that was essential to film acting. "He gets at it from the inside, from his own clear way of looking at life"', and Callow concludes: 'His [Laughton's] great achievement as an actor was to journey to the farthest reaches of his temperament and somehow make of the section of himself he was exploring, the whole man.'[34] It is this creative journey which baffled von Sternberg, but it was ultimately necessary if Laughton was to fully realize Graves's creation. Laughton suffered greatly in finding Claudius, including prevaricating over which to foot to drag—he had not decided even while filming was going on. Von Sternberg questioned if it was a form of masochism. The cat-and-mouse game played between director and actor as each tried to wrest artistic control from the other would eventually result in von Sternberg calling in Korda for help: 'My peculiar type of wizardry, if such it be, had come to an end.'[35] While he recognized that Laughton was talented, the roots of their difficulties may, ironically, lie in their friendship, a friendship cultivated by Laughton in Hollywood. This was completely at odds with von Sternberg's preferred mode of operation—to mould unknown, unquestioning, and new actors.[36]

Graves's friend T. E.Lawrence had been critical about the novel *I, Claudius* (although he liked *Claudius the God*), but noted: 'You have made the scenes your own, and there is little parade of research: the tone is deliberately modern, and I like that.'[37] Lawrence wrote about the grim nature of the 'unrelieved crime and horror' in the book, and comments on the predicament of Claudius in the same breath as the marriage of Siegfried Sassoon: 'If any of my generation has earned a harbour after a storm, it is S.S. and I am hoping for him. Good wishes for poor Claudius, he deserved a harbour, too, but got Messalina instead, I fancy.'[38] The reference implies that Lawrence thought of Claudius as being three-dimensional, and signals Graves's skill in

[34] Callow (1987), 49. [35] Von Sternberg (1965), 189.

[36] Von Sternberg and Laughton met when the latter worked on *Devil and the Deep* (1932); 'at that time he was known as a so-called character actor, and he was in a film that dealt with a submarine and Tallulah Bankhead', von Sternberg (1965), 178.

[37] Letter, 12 Nov. 1933, in Graves and Liddell Hart (1963), 174–5. Lawrence writes of *Claudius the God* on 13 Jan. 1935.

[38] Letter, 17 Dec. 1933 to RG, in Graves and Liddell Hart (1963), 175–6.

creating a believable character. Later Callow would write about the physicality of Laughton becoming Claudius:

> The physical gesture of the performance is enormous: the stutters and the tics are nearly incapacitating, and the limp is one of utmost deformity, like a man walking along with one foot in a trench. The point is not that people do have just such terrible distortions in life, which they certainly do, but that behind them, inside them, is a quite different person, not a loon or a cripple, but a gentle, wise, and humorous man, a scholar and a poet, who has remained untarnished by his physical disadvantages and people's crass and cruel reaction to them. It is this gap which creates the scale of the performance—the huge obstacles surmounted by a witty and shrewd sprit, and which makes the climactic speech in which Claudius finally takes command in the Senate such an overpoweringly emotional experience . . . We see the spirit totally overcome the flesh.[39]

This touches on the essence of the Claudius of Graves and of Suetonius. The notion that Graves was writing a semi-autobiographical piece (much as Maugham would do with *Of Human Bondage*), with Claudius as a self-reference, points to an underlying perception.[40] Graves suffered enormously as a result of the war and, combined with subservient relationships with his partners, he seemingly found it hard to express his true feelings. Perry, in Chapter 13 of this volume, shows Graves identifying himself with Claudius, but intriguingly argues for Graves employing an Augustus/Livia axis rather than Claudius and Messalina as he exorcised his difficult sexual relationship with Laura Riding. If the Claudius novels were just 'potboilers' written for money in Graves's eyes, then they also served another purpose—Claudius's triumph in the Senate mirrored Graves's popular success with his books.

[39] Callow (1987), 117–18: 'The actuality of Laughton's performance remains shocking today.' Elsa Lanchester writes that in 1936 Laughton had been journeying to Rome 'to do some research on Claudius with Vincent Korda', and she tried cable her husband with the news that his great friend the producer Irving Thalberg had died. Thalberg had promised stability in Laughton's future with the offer of producing, but this prospect was now removed: Lanchester (1938), 184–5. Cf. Isabel Quigly in the *Spectator*, 24 Dec. 1965, a review of *The Epic That Never Was* and *The War Lord* directed by Franklin Schaffner. Laughton would later play the physically deformed Quasimodo in *The Hunchback of Notre Dame* (1939).

[40] Hastings (2009), 13–17, 161–8.

Sexual relationships of Byzantine intricacy formed a tangled thread running through the production—Riding/Graves, Oberon/Korda, Dietrich/von Sternberg, and Messalina/Claudius—but the final act would rest with Merle Oberon as Messalina, when she was involved in a car crash. The results of the crash brought the production to a standstill.[41] Korda and Oberon were soon to be married, and he had wanted a film, and a director, to securely establish her career, much as Marlene Dietrich's had been established by her series of films with von Sternberg in Berlin. There is a suspicion that the injuries were not as dramatic as first reported, and Roger Greenspun wrote of 'the mystery of Merle Oberon's seamless face';[42] but the crash became enough of a reason for von Sternberg to gratefully abandon shooting.[43]

The extant film version of Claudius's speech to the Senate was a numinous confluence of many literary talents, and one tributary was the work of Somerset Maugham. On 10 November Biró had fallen ill and was replaced by Carl Zuckmayer and the American Lester Cohen, who had written the screenplay for *Of Human Bondage* (1934).[44] Somerset Maugham had based the character of the club-footed anti-hero Philip Carey on himself, and drawing on his unpublished work, *The Artistic Temperament of Stephen Carey*, Maugham changed the original disability from a stutter to a limp. This was personal, because Maugham himself had a severe stutter; however, Gore Vidal was to comment: 'Maugham's self-pity, which was to come to a full rather ghastly flowering in *Of Human Bondage*, is mysterious in origin'.[45] Cohen had turned the novel into a screenplay, and he would be completely immersed in themes similar to those in *I, Claudius*: a restricted independence caused by personal circumstance (for example, how to fit into a society when you are an outsider); the experience of powerful emotional relationships through women, love, and sexuality; and the narrative's shifting relationship to reality and fiction.[46]

[41] Lanchester (1938); von Sternberg (1965); Callow (1987). See the essays of Tougher (Ch. 4) and Coulston (Ch. 5) for further discussion of the relationship between Graves and Laura Riding.

[42] Greenspun (1965). [43] Von Sternberg (1965), 189.

[44] Von Sternberg (1965), 175. The scriptwriters would be aware of D. W. Griffiths's conventional biopic, *Abraham Lincoln* (1930), which contains only one major political speech, and even in that omits certain phrases.

[45] Cf.Vidal (1999), ii; also Hastings (2009), 17–8, 49–50.

[46] Coincidentally, like Graves, Maugham also served in France at the Battle of Ypres in 1914. He returned as an ambulance-driver for the Red Cross and corrected the proofs for *Of Human Bondage* in St Malo in 1915: Cordell (1969), 89. Cf. Robert Calder's lucid introduction to Penguin's *Of Human Bondage*.

In *Of Human Bondage* Maugham adapted the model of the nineteenth-century German *Bildungsroman*, charting a journey to adulthood through the trials set before the main character, who is changed by these experiences, and has become a better person at the end. Calder refers to these as novels of all-round development and self-culture.[47] For Maugham, writing the book was cathartic; 'It's not an autobiography . . . but an autobiographical novel; fact and fiction are inextricably mingled; the emotions are my own but not all incidents are related as they happened and some of them are transferred to my hero not from my own life but from that of persons with whom I was intimate.'[48] There are similarities to Graves and *Good-bye to All That*, where Graves blurred the line between fact and fiction; while in *I, Claudius* he would, through his imagination, retell the account found in classical sources to the extent that one is uncertain how much is Claudius (from the sources), and how much is Graves. Richardson's critique leans towards Graves's self-identification with Claudius, and Bennett's essay (Chapter 1, this volume) examines these issues further. Like an archaeological paradigm, unpacking the 'true' Claudius really depends upon interpretation of the extant material.

On 20 April 1946 Maugham donated the manuscript of *Of Human Bondage* to the Library of Congress, and his address in the Coolidge Auditorium shows that his previous sentiments about Stephen Carey did not desert him: 'Certain of my recollections were so insistent that, waking and sleeping, I could not escape from them. My memories would not let me be.'[49] There are well-charted biographical similarities between Maugham's early life and the fictional record of Carey's.[50] Morgan concludes that in *Of Human Bondage*:

> Here was the painful reality of the cripple, who carried through life a feeling of apartness, friendless and longing for friends, but perversely compounding his alienation by his own aloofness. Here was the true condition of life, not success or invitations to the right homes or scores of admirers, but bondage. Philip Carey is in bondage to his physical defect, to his upbringing, and to the woman who mistreats him.[51]

[47] Calder (1972), 78.

[48] W. Somerset Maugham, from *The Art of Fiction*, in Morgan (1980), 194. Also see Calder (1972), 78–130; Curtis (1974), 76–90.

[49] Maugham in Cordell (1961), 70. See <http://www.loc.gov/resource/mff.003035/#seq-1> for details of Maugham's donation. Cf.hastings (2009), 484–5.

[50] See Hastings (2009), 13–30, 161–4.

[51] Morgan (1980), 195.

Maugham used Spinoza's idea of 'human bondage', but in a literary form that states that when feelings take control of people's lives it is these which make them into slaves. There are echoes of Graves's life in Morgan's appraisal, yet *Of Human Bondage* concerns Carey's struggle over time to 'free himself', although in reality Maugham never broke free from his chains. Was it the same for Graves?

In von Sternberg's film, Claudius was able to overcome years of isolation and ridicule to take control in the Senate, and he would later escape from the deceits of Messalina. Was it through articulation and speech that Claudius overcome the pastoral and somewhat idyllic isolation he found on his farm outside Rome, or was it his meteoric rise to prominence in the city that provided the ingredients for the self-expression that had been denied to him? Probably the latter. Maugham's work was part of a succession of autobiographical chronicle novels from the early twentieth century, like those of Compton Mackenzie, D. H. Lawrence, and James Joyce, but 'what Maugham contributed to the genre were the physical defect to explain the character's alienation and a sadomasochistic view of love'.[52] Philip Carey had chosen Mildred because she would humiliate him, and he would have to endure being in bondage to the woman he despised. Morgan highlights the influence of Leopold von Sacher-Masoch on Maugham regarding the torment a man endures when subjected to physical and mental ill-treatment by the woman he loves.[53] Although tied up with negative perceptions regarding imperial women in Rome, Suetonius, Tacitus, and Dio show how Claudius too had endured humiliation and repression until he unhappily extricated himself from Messalina, only to fall into the clutches of Agrippina. Graves did nothing to dispel the accusations of the sources, and it seems he himself would also fit this sadomasochistic model of love, in view of his tempestuous relationships with Nancy Nicholson and then Laura Riding.[54]

It is the emotional investment that makes the cinematic rhetoric work—if one has any doubts about the personal nature of the themes of alienation and degradation then one need look no further than Maugham. He gave a reading of the first chapter from *Of Human*

[52] Morgan (1980), 96.

[53] Morgan (1980), 96 discusses Maugham's *A Writer's Notebook*. Cf. Hastings (2009), 28, 50, 67, 70–1.

[54] Seymour-Smith (1982), 70–6, 88–90 (Nancy Nicholson), 107–8, 214–15, 233–41, 314–15 (Laura Riding); Seymour on relations with Nancy, pp. 79–83 *passim*, on Graves depiction of Laura Riding as Messalina, pp. 214–17.

Bondage to be recorded for the blind in 1946: 'I did not make a very good record of it because I was moved, not because the chapter was particularly moving but because it recalled a pain that the passage of more than sixty years ago had not dispelled.'[55] The emotional investment was amply demonstrated when Maugham broke down and cried during the recording of the reading.

THE POST-1937 SCREEN ADAPTATIONS OF *I, CLAUDIUS*

Since 1937 there have been several attempts to film *I, Claudius*, but these have all met with failure. The next venture was initiated by Vincent Korda (the younger brother of Alexander) in 1956, and he wanted Alec Guinness to star and Graves to write the script. Graves wrote to Guinness, 'so when he [Korda] gives the all clear I'll do it with an eye to your particular talents, giving Claudius a dry, comic but generous wit . . .'.[56]

On meeting Vincent Korda in Rome, Jenny Nicholson, Graves's eldest daughter with Nancy Nicholson, wrote: 'He was sweet, dear old philosophical Middle-European—you know him—"I only speak to people I like and even those with whom I do business I do not speak if I do not like – this is sad for them!"'.[57] In the same letter Nicholson summarized the positive start: Guinness wanted to do it, Anna Magnani wanted to do it, and that 'Film people here [Italy] say combination of Guinness & Magnani would bring backers and film distributors swarming. The triangle could only entice'.[58] However, Vincent Korda was held in such low esteem by Hollywood that when producer Bob Goldstein was in Rome he would not even answer the phone to Korda, and Nicholson doubted if he actually had the rights after all. The same year Ingrid Bergman had shown interest in obtaining the film rights to Graves's *Homer's Daughter*.[59] Nicholson wrote that Bergman was all set to play Nausicaa, and 'She wants you

[55] Maugham in Cordell (1969), 89. Hastings (2009), 484–5.

[56] Letter from RG to Alec Guinness, May 1956, in Seymour-Smith (1982), 473.

[57] Letter from Jenny Nicholson to RG, 15 Jan. 1956.

[58] Jenny Nicholson to RG, 15 Jan. 1956.

[59] RGA: letter from Bill Price to Robert and Beryl Graves, 18 July 1956, corroborates this ('what about Homers' (*sic*) Dought. (*sic*)'), with Bergman due to return the USA in the autumn of 1956. See Seymour-Smith (1982), 471–2.

to come over and write (with Roberto technically advising) the script . . .'.[60] But the trail went cold and the project was shelved. By December Nicholson had confirmed that Magnani wanted to play Messalina, could start shooting by early 1958, and Alec Guinness would make '*un Claudio perfetto*'.[61]

The trials of attracting Alec Guinness to play Claudius are hinted at by Graves in a letter to Will Price. He explains that Guinness wanted to avoid lavish American productions and concentrate on playing on a smaller scale in England. 'He feels just the same about Claudius—doesn't want that *Ben Hur* or *Quo Vadis* stuff, just the domestic palace drama. And why not?'[62] Graves's and Beryl's guess was it would not take much to scare the actor away from the project.

Guinness requested that Peter Glenville direct and that Graves write the script with Bridget Boland.[63] Seymour-Smith suggests this was due not so much to a lack of confidence in Graves, but because Guinness wanted to surround himself with known quantities that had produced a screen success.[64] Boland had worked with King Vidor adapting *War and Peace* (1956) for the big screen, so was no stranger to condensing a sweep of history, which was valuable experience, as Magnani had requested that the two *Claudius* novels be combined so she could have a death scene.

Nicholson also implored Graves to make certain that Guinness reassured Magnani that he was pleased that she would play Messalina, and also to refer to Glenville as 'a choice for director' (Glenville

[60] Letter from Jenny Nicholson to RG, 3 July 1955, see RG/J/NicholsonJ/1-147, in Seymour-Smith (1982), 472. 'Roberto' refers to the director Rossellini. See W. Graves (2001), 119–20.

[61] Magnani wrote to RG from Rome: 'Penso anche io, che Alec Guinnes sarà il perfetto Claudio, che voi avete creato. Perciò insuperabile!'; 7 Dec. 1956, RG/J/Magnani/1. This was written in the wake of *Demetrius and the Gladiator* (1954), with Barry Jones as Claudius and Susan Hayward as a histrionic Messalina.

[62] RGA: letter from RG to Will Price, 14 June 1956. Graves highlights his need of money, unlike Guinness, who has no interest in high earnings mainly because of punitive taxes. Writing from Mississippi, Price agrees with Guinness's distaste for sword-and-sandal Hollywood epics and adds: 'Did you hear the foul canard that *Quo Vadis* was billed in my native Southland as "Where yawl Goin?"' Letter from Will Price to Robert and Beryl Graves, 26 June 1956, RG/J/PriceW/50–3, also 58–61.

[63] There would be Oscar nominations for Glenville for *Beckett* (1964, Director), and Boland for *Anne of the Thousand Days* (1969, Adapted Screenplay). Guinness had worked with them on *The Prisoner* (1955).

[64] Seymour-Smith (1995), 474–5, 478, 483–5.

was Guinness's best friend and therefore might be biased as to who got most screen-time). Nicholson cautions: 'Tact—tact, sweet (even sickly) tact with these Empresses of the Cinema who were not born to purple!'[65] Jenny Nicholson also suggested two European directors who might be in the frame, Federico Fellini and Roberto Rossellini, although Rossellini had just left Magnani for Ingrid Bergman, so that was really a non-starter. As time passed the production drifted, and one backer after another dropped out, Boland fell out of favour, and Glenville directed *Hotel Paradiso* on Broadway instead, leaving Graves (and therefore Claudius) rather unemployed.[66]

In 1971 John Mortimer wrote a new screenplay for the director Tony Richardson, one of the British 'New Wave' directors. Richardson had won two Oscars for *Tom Jones* (1964); had directed the groundbreaking *Look Back in Anger* (1956) at the Royal Court; and had filmed the 'kitchen-sink dramas', *A Taste of Honey* (1961) and *The Loneliness of the Long Distance Runner* (1962), all of which should have been perfect experience for directing *I, Claudius*.[67] Notwithstanding, Graves rails against this new production, in a letter which also throws light on his relationship with Claudius:[68]

> Dear Sir:
> I was most interested in your news item of July 30th, which (mails being as they are in tourist-ridden Spain) has reached me only Friday: that Tony Richardson is filming *I, Claudius* in Italy next month.
>
> Although an authority on the period, Alexander Korda admitted such when I was allowed to vet and enlarge the script back in 1934, I have not been privileged to view Richardson's version, nor will my name appear (except perhaps as author) on the screen credits.
>
> It must not be forgotten that Claudius was deified and still officially retains his divine prerogatives; and the failure of anyone so far to complete a film of *I, Claudius*—though I have always hitherto profited from my rights in the work—seems to have been consistently due to the Emperor's objection to having his unfortunate physical disabilities

65 RGA: letter from Jenny Nicholson to RG, 16 Dec. 1956; the proposed contract shows Price as producer and the film rights belonging to the estate of Sir Alexander Korda.

66 Seymour-Smith (1982) 484–5.

67 RGA: 'Claudius the Play', *Evening Standard*, 29 Mar. 1972; by 22 May 1972 the *Evening Standard* was able to report that David Warner would play Claudius; Sally Kestelman, Messalina; Warren Clarke, Caligula; Freda Jackson, Livia; and Charles Lloyd Pack, Augustus. It opened at the Queen's Theatre, London, on 11 July 1972.

68 RGA: letter to *Evening Standard* (?), 18 Aug. 1971, RG/G/E/29.

paraded on the screen. His mind was sound as a bell but he had suffered from Little's Disease, a physical handicap which made his fellow-countrymen misjudge him as a mere fool or clown. I sincerely hope that Tony Richardson's version will not once more draw down Claudius' divine anger, and much regret that my advice on this matter has not been asked.

I should like the film public to know how the matter stands. I disassociate myself completely from the production—unless of course my help is ultimately invited and suitably rewarded.

Yours faithfully
Robert Graves

Richardson countered Graves's letter, explaining that even with attempts at a script by Edward Bond, Christopher Isherwood, and himself he could not raise the funds.[69] Later he considered casting Alec Guinness as Tiberius, but by March 1972 John Mortimer had produced a new script for the stage.[70] Reviews of the play ranged from hostile to lukewarm, with most opprobrium reserved for the banal script which reduces the grand ironies of Graves's original 'to slimy nudges and sly winks', due to the weak (Jack Tinker called it 'eunuch') direction of Tony Richardson. There are accolades for David Warner's performance as Claudius, where he balances disability with humility and intelligence—it is interesting that Warner's portrayal of Claudius's stutter, which is obvious at first, fades into the background and becomes non-existent, as it would for those who know a stutterer:

> David Warner's Claudius, passing from slobbering youth to deified maturity, changes surprisingly little apart from his loss of a stammer. Drawing his shoulders up to his ears and hobbling unsteadily from vulnerability to power, he conveys the blend of guile, weakness, virtue, and bottomless scepticism which makes one wish Brecht had turned his attention to Claudius.[71]

[69] RGA: letter from Tony Richardson to RG, 26 Aug. 1971, RG/J/RichardsonT/1.

[70] RGA: letter from Tony Richardson to RG, 14 Sept. 1971, RG/J/RichardsonT/2.

[71] RGA: Wardle, 12/07/1972; also see Eric Shorter 'Claudius crowded out by underlings', *Sunday Times*, 9 July 1972; Felix Barker, 'I, Claudius; Queen's Theatre', *London Evening News*, 12 July 1972; Jack Tinker, 'Oh, what a terrible accident!', *Daily Mail*, 12 July 1972; while Michael Billington feels 'I, Claudius' has little contemporary relevance—it shows how Claudius's 'initial benevolent idealism was subtly eroded by the powers of office until he too becomes a God. All power corrupts; and dictatorial power, however beneficently wielded, corrupts absolutely': 'I, Claudius', *Guardian* 12 July 1972. Jeremy Kingston, 'Theatre', *Punch*, 12 July 1972 harpoons the production, but amongst the numerous hostile reviews there is praise for David Warner. *The*

By comparison, Eric Harding writes of the Claudian metamorphosis from feigning stupidity in order to survive the calumnies of the court to becoming emperor—'scarcely perceptibly, his face gains more dignity as the man becomes more important, the shoulders less hunched, the stutter disappears'.[72] Numerous reviews pick up on the notion that power corrupts, but Harold Hobson questions whether, rather than corrupting those who hold power, 'it corrupt[s] those upon whom it is exercised, especially—and this is the fine and melancholy heart of the play—when it is exercised for their own good'.[73] The transition from stammering fool to clear spoken powerful ruler says a great deal about us. Would it make sense to have the powerful emperor as a stuttering fool—what is believable about that? The differences in the reviewers' versions of Warner's transformation agree on only one thing—that the stutter disappears. In spite of reviewers' comments, Graves said he was well pleased with John Mortimer's adaptation of *I, Claudius*, and 'occasionally I recognised my own language. Of course, there are technical deficiencies to be ironed out'.[74]

The potential presented by a 'Claudius' film has continued to attract successful producers and Oscar-winners. It was evident that not only was there kudos but money to be made for everyone as 'sales of *I, Claudius* and *Anna Karenina* boomed when they were linked with the television programs'.[75] Subsequent to the much-fêted 1976 BBC/Masterpiece Theatre TV series adapted by Jack Pulman,[76] the movie rights were held by Jim Sheridan, who had received Oscar nominations for *In the Name of the Father* (1993) and *My Left Foot* (1989), the latter about the life of the author and artist Christy Brown, who suffered from cerebral palsy.[77] Nothing came of this planned production. Scott Rudin, producer of *No Country for Old Men* (2007) and *There Will be Blood* (2007), bought the film rights for *I, Claudius*

Birmingham Post's J. C.Trewin sums it all up with: 'My only safe position is in mid-fence—and with a cushion.'

72 RGA: Harding, 15 July 1972.

73 RGA: Hobson, 16 July 72.

74 RGA: Robert Graves interview, in Foster (1972).

75 Stanton (1978), 27–40. Also see <http://catdir.loc.gov/catdir/toc/becites/cfb/78023543.html>.

76 See Joshel (2001).

77 One form of cerebral palsy is spastic diplegia, once known as Little's Disease—see Graves's letter to *Evening Standard*, 18 Aug. 1971. For a discussion of 'the problem of Claudius' see Osgood (2011), 9–28.

in 2007 for a reported $2 million, with Leonardo DiCaprio initially slated to star as Claudius and William Monahan as writer.[78] However, after a rights dispute with Sheridan, Rudin turned his attention to filming Stacy Schiff's book *Cleopatra: A Life*, to star Angelina Jolie, and in 2008 it was announced that Relativity Media had now acquired the film rights for *I, Claudius*, which was to be directed by Jim Sheridan.[79] Even if the big-screen movie remains dormant, though, the small screen retains its allure. In 2002 Paul Vanezis directed a documentary on the making of the 1976 series, *I, Claudius, A Television Epic* which is a neat reversal of Duncalf's *The Epic That Never Was*.[80]

CONCLUSION

If one accepts that the 'voice' of Claudius in the novels is a combination of Graves himself, Graves's imagination, and the man depicted by Suetonius, Tacitus, Cassius Dio, and a myriad of sources (see Chapter 2 in this volume, by Kennedy and O'Gorman), then the basis of the screen versions contain at least part of Graves and his creation. Graves fashioned a credible portrait of a disabled man, an incomplete man, struggling to survive in a difficult world, where his political and domestic relationships had parallels with Graves's own time. Perry, in Chapter 13, shows how the political landscape was shaped in the Rome of the mid-thirties, and filming started against the backdrop of the Spanish Civil War. Although not a catalyst for the novels, the parallels with current politics and Fascist imagery would not be lost on the film-makers.

Graves may have co-opted the *Bildungsroman* model utilized by Maugham to explore his relationship with Laura Riding through Claudius's subservient relationship with Messalina. *I, Claudius* and *Claudius the God* were analogous to the metaphor of disability and

[78] *Variety*, 5 Sept. 2007.

[79] Sheridan would co-write, with Nye Heron, *Hollywood Reporter*, 12 Sept. 2008; also nominated for *In America* (2002).

[80] In 2011 HBO and the BBC signed a deal to shoot a television mini-series based on both *Claudius* novels for 2013. The reboot will be under the control of Jane Tranter and Anne Thomopoulos, who produced HBO's *Rome* mini-series. Cf. <http://www.deadline.com/2011/06/hbo-bbc2-new-make-deal-to-turn-robert-graves-novel-i-claudius-into-epic-miniseries/#more-138836> (accessed 28/05/2012).

adversity that shaped Maugham and Philip Carey and the real and fictional Claudius suffered the double hardship. Maugham had shown how to use this paradigm within an autobiographical and complex story, and Lester Cohen probably instinctively understood the stylistic and structural correspondence between *Good-bye to All That* and *Of Human Bondage* —this would add the emotional depth to Zuckmayer's political sensibilities.

The von Sternberg film remains a fading beacon to what might have been. Through Laughton's performance there are glimpses of a distilled, humane Claudius, a survivor of Caligula's reign, whose metamorphosis from subject to emperor is played out against the backdrop of von Sternberg's and Vincent Korda's vision of the imperial city. This Rome reflected the monumental Fascist architecture of the thirties, which had in turn been inspired by ancient Rome. Leni Reifenstahl's *Triumph des Willens* (1935) documents the 1934 *Reichsparteitag der Einheit und Stärke* ('Reich Party Day of Unity and Strength') in Nuremberg, where the Reich Party Congress was staged as a carefully choreographed spectacle:

> In the motorcade sequence of Riefenstahl's film, Hitler's triumphal procession features his body—primarily stationary—in the rigid pose of a devotional statue or mythological figure, this rigidity playing a vital role in the film's myth-making program, While the motorcade and traveling camera contribute to the illusion of a moving body, the camera favors shots of Hitler erect in an open car, gliding immobile through the cheering crowd. In *Triumph of the Will*, Hitler-as-icon signifies politically—propagandistically—just as the statuary and *tableaux* of Venetian *trionfi* did.[81]

Von Sternberg offered a contrary political tableau in the scene where Claudius limped through the unruly jeering mob that lined Vincent Korda's monumental set of the Forum. It was a commentary on the gross distortion of the relationship between a ruling dynasty and its subjects and corresponds to Zuckmayer's political outlook as a refugee from a Weimar republic usurped by National Socialism.

I, Claudius was conceived in a post-war Europe, and imbued with republican sympathies by an author still reeling from the horrific amalgam of war and imperialism. For post-war Germany (and Graves's German relatives) the revolution of 1919 and the break-up of European

[81] Peucker (2004), 281–2.

empires was followed by the promise of new world, and many involved in *I, Claudius* were shaped by a middle Europe struggling with the harsh economic and social realities of peacetime.

Laughton's speech to the Senate also draws on themes in the speeches of Abraham Lincoln. The First Inaugural highlighted that it is the citizens who can amend or reject the constitution; we can look at this in stark contrast to the assassination of Caligula that would only benefit the few. But the screenplay's rhetoric looks to Lincoln's Second Inaugural, delivered near the end of the Civil War in 1865 and promoting Lincoln's plan for peace and reconciliation to heal a divided nation.[82] It seems reasonable to suggest that this sentiment would also resonate with a Europe denuded of a generation by war. The end of Laughton's speech follows the account found in Josephus, *Antiquities of the Jews* 19.4.5–6 as Claudius restores the rule of law. He dispenses an appropriate sentence, avoiding the excessive retribution of executing all the conspirators—only the murderers Chaerea and Lupus were killed. Claudius's act of mercy towards their families seems to be a twentieth-century reaction to senseless and unjust killing in wars, and points again to resolution and renewal.

The *Claudius* novels had sold well, and that made them an attractive proposition for film; big-screen adaptation of historical novels and plays would eventually prove successful at the Academy, with *Ben Hur* (1959) at the zenith with eleven gold statues.[83] Similar palace intrigue to that found in Graves's novels characterize such Oscar-winning adapted screenplays as Jean Anouilh's *Becket* (1964), Robert Bolt's *A Man for All Seasons* (1966), and James Goldman's *The Lion in Winter* (1968).

As if to confirm its publishing longevity and popularity, *I, Claudius* is the inspiration for Nelle Davy's well-received debut novel, *The Legacy of Eden* (2012), which charts the rise and fall of an Iowa family.[84] Nevertheless, regardless of the magnetism of the novels the near-mystical confluence of talent of 1937 has not reappeared

[82] McPherson (1990), 99–103.

[83] However, *Spartacus* (1960) only received Oscars for Set, Cinematography, and Costumes, and *Quo Vadis* (1951) received eight nominations but no awards. Even Cecil B. DeMille won only 'minor' awards for historical films, with *Cleopatra* (1934, Cinematography), *Samson and Delilah* (1949, Set and Costumes), and *The Ten Commandments* (1956, Visual Effects).

[84] *I, Claudius* was No.14 on the Modern Library Top 100 Best Novels of the twentieth century, <http://www.modernlibrary.com/top-100/100-best-novels> (accessed /30/05/2012), and one of *Time* magazine's All-Time 100 Novels.

on the big screen. The immense legacy of *I, Claudius* lies with the small screen, and is summed up by Mary McNamara:

> Although it still seems quite singular, the sandal prints of 'I, Claudius' are everywhere, in every TV dynasty or depraved power figure, in every hero whose physical limitations and tragic past bring about increased insight, in any story line crisscrossing the political and the personal. Now television is littered with humanized monsters, broken sages and 'real politics'; they are the hallmark of some of our best television, on cable and the networks.[85]

Claudius becomes a man for our times—a man from the inter-war years of *The Long Weekend* (by Graves and Alan Hodge)—and in each generation the best film-makers and writers have been attracted to making their version of Graves's story. Whether it is because of the Fates or, as Graves believed, the deified Claudius, Hollywood remains spurned. However, it is through different media that Claudius inhabits modern life; Graves's accomplishment is that, probably more than any other Roman emperor, Claudius has the most intimate relationship with an audience, not only through the historical novels but by appearing directly in peoples' living-rooms on radio and on television.

85 McNamara (2012).

15

Broadcasting the Common Asphodel

Robert Graves and the Mass Media

Mick Morris

> Here I sit in a sound-proof room, at a table bare but for my papers, a pencil and a glass of water. I am supposed to be addressing my public . . . An awkward situation. The chances are that not more than one person in every hundred has read my poems even by mistake . . . The chances are equally against any immediate increase in the number of my readers because of this broadcast.[1]

It *is* very hard to resist a writer who published a book on the future of swearing, counted among his muses Ava Gardner and Sophia Loren, once 'helped the police with their inquiries' into what seemed to be an attempted murder, and had come face to face with the angry ghost of Milton.[2] Most readers respond to what Robert Lowell, a great admirer of Graves, called his 'wonderfully nervous and ever exercised mind'.[3]

The aim of this chapter to say a little about Classics and the BBC, but to concentrate principally on the recordings, scripts, and letters that have survived which throw some light on Graves's methods, beliefs, and prejudices as a broadcaster on classical themes. The BBC from its earliest years included classicists and Classics in

[1] R. Graves 'The Poet and His Public: A Home Service Broadcast' (BBC Home Service, Oct. 1954) = Graves (1955c).

[2] John Cheever described Graves as 'a kind of prince, scourge, god and war-memorial', Bailey (2009), 427.

[3] Lowell (2005), 292.

its programming: in Scotland the first classicist to be heard over the airwaves was Sir George MacDonald, numismatist and author of the *Roman Wall in Scotland* (1911), who in December 1924, two years after the foundation of the British Broadcasting Company,[4] gave a broadcast to the Edinburgh area on 'The Romans in Scotland'. A month later John Harrower, Professor of Greek at Aberdeen, spoke on 'The Importance of Classics in School Education' to the Aberdeen region as part of the Schools Education slot.[5] The most noted classicist employed by the BBC was Gilbert Murray, who between 1926 and 1956 made over eighty appearances in front of the microphone. The new medium of television also embraced Classics: in 1936, when the BBC launched the world's first regular high-definition service, those rich enough to afford a television set[6] and who were living within range of the Alexandria Palace station in the north London area could watch the Ginner-Mawer Company performing 'Greek, Egyptian and Neo-Classic Mimetic Dancing'.[7]

This encouragement of classical learning was given added impetus by the creation of the Third Programme on 29 September 1946, a radio station once rather unkindly described as 'dons speaking to dons'.[8] A charge perhaps supported by the broadcast schedule, for on 27 April 1947 when listeners were given the chance to hear extracts from Aristophanes's *The Frogs* broadcast in Greek, 'by members of Cambridge University—introduced by J. T. Sheppard, Provost of

[4] The British Broadcasting Company began broadcasting from London on 18 October 1922, and this company became by Royal Charter on 1 January 1927 the British Broadcasting Corporation.

[5] *Radio Times*, Dec. 1936. The most important record of Graves's broadcasting career with the BBC is the *Radio Times*. This is, however, quite a problematic source to exploit: the annual cumulated volumes of this weekly publication amount to well over 2,000 pages and, unlike *The Listener*, there is no annual index. In addition, by the late 1950s there were seven regional editions of this programme guide. This essay has relied on the Scottish edition of the *Radio Times*. A programme to digitize this important resource began in 2010.

[6] The BBC Television broadcasts were four hours daily: 3 p.m.–4 p.m. and 9 p.m.–10 p.m. In 1936 a Pye television set, with a 5-inch screen, would cost 22 guineas—over £1,000 in today's terms. Such a set would be without sound, which would be supplied by the radio service: information derived from advertisements in the *Radio Times* from 1936 until September 1939, when BBC Television shut down at the outbreak of war.

[7] *Radio Times*, 3 Dec. 1936. Their repertoire included *Spartan War Dance* to music by Schumann, *Bacchic Dancers* (Massenet), and the *Maidens of Athens* (Bauer).

[8] The phrase was coined by P. H. Newby; see Carpenter (1997), 126. One of the proposed titles for this new network was 'the Minerva Programme'.

King's College', with line references provided by the *Radio Times*.[9] In the same year, extracts, in Greek, from Euripides's *The Bacchae* were broadcast, and two years later Phillip Vellacott read extracts, again in the ancient language, from Euripides's *Iphigenia in Tauris*.[10] Latin was not ignored: in 1947 John Sparrow, Warden of All Souls College, Oxford, produced a series of programmes entitled *Latin Poetry* which included contributions from Cyril Connolly (Elegiac), R. C. Trevelyan (Catullus), Rex Warner (Lucretius), and Sparrow himself (Virgil).[11] The Third Programme's *coup de grace* was perhaps the broadcast made by Michael Ventris on 1 July 1952, 'The Cretan Tablets', where he announced to the world the decipherment of Linear B.[12]

Throughout his long creative career of over sixty years, Graves made no secret of the fact that his work as a poet was subsidized by all his other writing activities: 'Though a poet by calling, I make my livelihood by prose-biographies, novels, translations from various languages and so forth.'[13] His output was enormous by any standards: one obituarist calculated that by 1975 he had published 'more than 135 books', and Graves himself claimed that he wrote over 2 million words a year, later edited down to between 150,000 to 200,000 fit enough to be published.[14] His work as a broadcaster provided useful

[9] *Radio Times*, 27 Apr. 1947.This thirty-minute broadcast had followed a transmission of Gilbert Murray's translation of the play in question. That evening's entertainment concluded with a talk by Sir Cyril Burt, 'Is Intelligence Declining With the Decline Of Fertility?'

[10] Val Gielgud, brother of Sir John, Head of Radio Drama and Variety at the BBC from1929 until 1963, recalled in the late 1940s overhearing two actors in the BBC canteen talking about their prospects—the one asked the other if he was 'resting' or working. 'Yes I've got some work on the Third Programme.' To which the other wearily observed, 'Oh then it'll be Troy, Troy, Troy again'. See Gielgud (1957).

[11] It is impossible to be definitive, as neither the *Radio Times* entry nor the files at the BBC Written Archive at Caversham give comprehensive details, but the strong probability is that these programmes gave both the Latin original text and an English translation.

[12] Carpenter (1997), 114.

[13] Graves (1961a), 488.

[14] R. P. Graves (2004), 397. Graves's claim over how many words he produced in a year was heard in the BBC Third Programme *Conversation with Poets*, broadcasted 9 Aug. 1960. In the same programme Graves claimed that he wrote *I, Claudius* because he was 'involved in a land deal and needed to earn £4,000 pretty quick... [the book] made £8,000 in three or four months'. These funds purchased the property at Deyá, Majorca that was to become his permanent home. Permission to quote from Graves's broadcasts has been kindly granted by the BBC and the Robert Graves Estate, who jointly own the copyright.

additional income and a valuable means of promoting works not created under the aegis of the White Goddess. The potential radio audience in Britain in the late 1940s was vast; some 11 million households listened to the BBC.[15] The driving force, as ever in Grub Street, was cash: Graves had a wife and eight children to consider. One of the poet's more endearing traits is his utter frankness, to friends at least, about money: when asked, in 1944, by Alan Hodge what his annual income was, he replied, 'between pals: my income has been £2000 a year since 1927; *Lawrence and the Arabs.* But I don't want it advertised, because what the hell happened to it all?'[16] Graves's joy at the financial pleasures of the American lecture circuit was palpable: 'My God the amount of money in the USA, in a fortnight I cleared $3000. Makes the BBC fees look like canary feed. But canaries must eat.'[17] Again, after a television appearance in 1959 on *Late Night Final* (Independent Television) he exclaimed joyfully, 'they gave me some beautiful clean pounds and I walked off'.[18] Exploiting another new source of income from the United States, in 1960 he sold his manuscripts to the University of Buffalo for $30,000.

The opportunity for gainful employment as a broadcaster was certainly there for someone with Graves's classical education, notoriety, and natural ebullience; but in many ways he seemed, as he himself believed, eminently unqualified. To begin with, there was his voice: 'I don't like my voice . . . aristocratic, Oxford and nasty.'[19] His delivery, even of his own poems, often sounded halting and uncertain. He was described by the radio critic of the *Observer* in 1954 as 'the world's worst broadcaster', a view he enthusiastically

[15] In 1946 the figure for radio licence-holders was 10.7 million, Briggs (1985), appendix C. It was not until 1960 that TV licence-holders exceeded those holding radio licences only.

[16] Undated letter, but written in 1944, O'Prey (1982), 326. Alan Hodge was to collaborate with Graves on two publications, *The Long Weekend: A Social History of Great Britain.1918–1939* (1940) and *The Reader over Your Shoulder* (1943). In the former book the authors describe *Goodbye to All That* as 'neither a war book, nor literary but a reckless autobiography' (p. 216).

[17] BBC Caversham, 19 Feb. 1957, Radio Contributor Files.

[18] 'Calling West Africa: Conversations with Robert Graves', BBC 1960 British Library Sound Archives Catalogue CDA 26462.

[19] 'Calling West Africa'.

shared.[20] Then there were the logistical problems: Graves had since 1929 lived abroad and, save for the war years when he evacuated his family to Galmpton in Devon, he was in Britain, due to tax reasons, for only three or four weeks a year.[21] As to the nation's sole broadcasting agency, he claimed: 'I never listen to the BBC except the News and Tommy Handley.'[22] Graves also believed that all his attempted work for the BBC was cursed; in a letter to Rayner Heppenstall[23] in April 1948 he complained:

> Nothing that I have ever been asked to do for the BBC has ever prospered: there has always been a technical reason for turning it down if it is a script (I have now been paid three times for scripts that were for old work never for one which is new) and when I recorded a broadcast in German they told me it was too slow for use and when I did a Brains Trust[24] I was rude to Joad[25] + never asked again.[26]

Added to this, despite the success of his historical novels like *I, Claudius* (1934) and *Count Belisarius* (1938) and his book on *The Greek Myths* (1955), he did not regard himself as a classicist:

[20] Letter dated January 1954, Radio Contributor Files, BBC Written Archive Centre, Caversham. See essay by Gibson.

[21] The issue of preserving his foreign-domicile status to avoid paying British income tax was to be an issue again in 1961 when he was elected Professor of Poetry at Oxford. The university permitted Graves to give all three obligatory annual lectures in the Michaelmas (autumn) term. It had extended a similar indulgence to his predecessor in the Chair, W. H. Auden. The latter explained to his promoters for the Chair in 1956, 'The winter months are those in which I earn enough dollars to allow me to live here [in Ischia] in the summer and devote myself to the unprofitable occupation of writing poetry': Carpenter (1981), 381. Auden was granted permission to give the three lectures in Hilary (summer) term. Auden's preferred successor in the chair was William Empson, but Empson refused absolutely to stand against Graves: see Empson (2006), 306–7.

[22] Caversham Radio Contributor Files, letter received 29 Apr. 1946.

[23] Features Department, Third Programme.

[24] An immensely popular radio discussion programme (1941–62), which attracted an audience of over 12 million listeners, one in three of the adult population.

[25] C. E. M. Joad, the oleaginous Professor of Philosophy at Birkbeck College, University of London (1930–48), whose public career ended in 1948 when, attempting to travel from London to Exeter without a ticket, he was convicted of defrauding British Railways.

[26] Graves certainly believed in curses: when his manuscript of the *White Goddess* was refused by two different publishers the immediate result was the death of one the editors and the suicide of the other. T. S. Eliot, who accepted the text, for Faber & Faber, was soon awarded the OM—Graves was in no doubt that here was the handiwork of the Goddess. Seymour Smith (1995), 388.

> I am not a Greek scholar, or an archaeologist, or an anthropologist, or a comparative mythologist, but I have a good nose and sense of touch, and think I have securely connected a lot of mythical patterns which were not connected before. Classical faculties will hate me.[27]

Some evidence survives of Graves as a performer on film. There is, of course, the 1965 BBC documentary *The Epic that Never Was*, describing the doomed attempt in 1937 to film *I, Claudius*, directed by Joseph von Sternberg and starring Charles Laughton.[28] In 1967 Graves appeared briefly in a BBC *Omnibus* programme devoted to an analysis Blake's 'Tyger', a poem, of course, Graves later 'revised'.[29]

There is one other performance, and it is rather a sad one: in June 1975 he was interviewed on Thames Television by Llew Gardiner for their London *Today* programme. Graves is clearly very frail and uncertain, and the thirty-minute 'live' interview is therefore sadly halting, rambling, and often simply inconsequential.[30] But the one memory that stayed vivid in the poet's mind even in old age was the conditions that existed on the Western Front in the Great War. It is not the dead and dying men that horrified Graves, but having been an eyewitness to the sixty-odd horses dying in agony in the mud of No Man's Land. He seemed, at this point in the interview, lost in melancholic reverie, saying about that conflict: 'What does it matter? What does it matter?'[31] Later in the interview Graves seems to be being simply mischievous, enjoying his interviewer's obvious discomfort:

GARDINER. Why are there so few poets today?

GRAVES. So few gentlemen . . . A gentleman is defined by his attitude to food and women.

GARDINER. You know you are almost impossible to interview? . . . You should give longer answers

[27] Seymour Smith (1995), 448. But as Seymour-Smith points out, Graves was a good enough Latinist to compose his own Oration when installed as Professor of Poetry at Oxford in 1961, unlike Auden, his predecessor in the chair, who in 1956 employed a 'ghost writer', J. G. Griffith (Jesus College).

[28] Currently (2008) the DVD of *The Epic That Never Was* is usually 'bundled' with the BBC 1976 production of *I, Claudius*; see Gibson's essay, Chapter 14 in this collection.

[29] Graves expanded his views in his essay 'Tyger, Tyger', in Graves (1969), 133–40.

[30] The whole programme can be viewed at the British Film Institute, London.

[31] Could it perhaps be that, in old age, Graves was at this moment recalling his friend Siegfried Sassoon's poem from 1918, 'Does it Matter': 'Does it matter losing your legs, | For people will always be kind . . . '?

GRAVES. I haven't been interviewed that often.
GARDINER. Are you a religious man?
GRAVES. I will be if you like.[32]

There are extant over 400 recordings of Graves's broadcasts at the BBC, in most cases reciting his own poetry.[33] There are, however, a significant number of audio recordings and, in addition, scripts and letters where Graves very directly discusses his attitude to the ancient world. In the post-war years a pattern seems to have emerged in Graves's relationship with the BBC: Graves's loyal agent A. P Watt would offer the latest work, usually in spring, to the Corporation for use on the airwaves and hopefully his client could, when making his annual visit to London, promote the work, either on the airwaves or by stirring some attendant controversy. In the 1940s and 1950s Graves wrote and broadcast on a topic, the life of Jesus, that in a more publicly pious age than today[34] was certain to generate controversy and, possibly, therefore larger sales, both here and more especially in the United States.[35] The two key texts are *King Jesus*,[36] published in 1946, and, seven years later *The Nazarene Gospel Restored*; the former was reasonably successful commercially but the latter not at all so.[37]

[32] In November 1972 Graves accepted an invitation from the Burns Federation to give the 'Immortal Memory' at a Burns Supper to be held in Glasgow and televised by Scottish Television (*TV Times* (Scottish edn.), 25 Jan. 1973). This caused a few eyebrows to be raised in Scotland, given the fact that Graves published opinion that Burns was like John Clare in that both employed a 'charmingly odd . . . dialect': Graves (1959b), 61. No script or recording has survived of the event, but my memory, nearly forty years later, is that Graves began by noting that the ancient Greeks and the Scots employed the same term for a poet (ποιήτης), i.e. maker. He then proceeded to refer to William Dunbar and then to make a series of rather anodyne points about Burns himself.

[33] The audio recordings of Graves's BBC work are to be located at British Library Sound Archive, a department of the British Library in London. This sound archive, with over 1 million recordings is one of the world's most important collections of its kind.

[34] When the British Broadcasting Company started in Britain in 1922 each day began with the Daily Service, and on Sundays broadcasting did not begin until 3.30 p. m. to allow listeners to attend church without the possible distraction of the wireless.

[35] Graves's attitude to some branches of organized religion is made very clear in *Goodbye to All That*: 'It was said that not one soldier in a hundred was inspired by religious feeling of even the crudest kind. It would have been difficult to remain religious in the trenches', Graves (1929), 241. But he made a very sharp distinction between the Catholic chaplains' behaviour at the Front, which he regarded as exemplary, and that of the Anglican padres.

[36] '*King Jesus* sold some 100,000 copies in thirty five years', Seymour-Smith (1995), 384.

[37] But the *Gospel* did win praise from the theologian Reinhold Niebuhr; see Seymour-Smith (1995), 418 and Empson (1988), 519.

In 1949, between the publication of these two revisionist texts, Graves made a broadcast on the Third Programme, 'The Parable of the Talents', that seemed to have caused near-apoplexy to F. H. House the Head of Religious Affairs:

> It is difficult to take this script seriously . . . The opening and closing paragraphs are of course deliberately offensive in that they assert the complete absence of integrity in all Christian New Testament scholars . . . Many listeners would not appreciate the pleasure which Graves takes in trailing his coat.[38]

Despite the title of the talk, Graves in fact dealt with several of the most well-known incidents in the life of Christ; his starting-point was the usual Gravesian premise: the consensus—orthodox, respectable, academic, or devout—was utterly wrong. The revision of the Gospels took place because:

> The Gentile Christians [were forced] during and after the Jewish revolts against Roman rule, to convince the Romans that they themselves were not Jews—especially not militant, nationalistic ones. They were desperately anxious to free their own doctrine as far as possible from the tutelage of the Mosaic law, and therefore went out of their way to libel the Pharisees, who were the official expounders of the law.

This demonization of the Pharisees meant that the sayings and acts of Jesus, who was originally to Graves simply preaching sound Pharisaical doctrine, had to be completely rewritten. The Good Samaritan was not a Samaritan at all but a Pharisee, the victim was from Samaria; and the woman taken in adultery was not in any risk of being stoned to death either before or after Christ's intervention because, 'since the Pharisees had gained control of the Jewish courts . . . no woman had been stoned for adultery either in Judea or Galilee—she was always released on a technicality'.[39] The Parable of the Talents he insisted was a coded reference to the visit of Prince Arcelaus to Rome in 4 BC to seek official endorsement as King of Judaea. In the space of a fifteen-minute talk Graves had, quite deliberately and provocatively, set several hares racing. In 1952 T. S. Gregory (Producer, Talks) wrote to his fellow producer P. H. Newby suggesting that Graves 'be warned off religion . . . [he]

[38] Caversham, Memo 1949 to 'GT' (General Talks?).
[39] Caversham, script Reference SLO 56246; a programme broadcast 9 Sept. 1939.

lacks the diffidence that makes simplicity attractive'.[40] This injunction seems to have been observed.

The problem for the Third Programme concerning Graves was pithily described by John Morris (Controller, Third Programme, 1953–8): 'His [Graves's] previous broadcasts, as you know have not obtained a good AR [Audience Rating] . . . but Graves's [Clarke] lectures are, however, drawing phenomenal audiences in Cambridge.'[41] The Third Programme could never attract a large audience, by the very nature of its programming policy, but it did need to attract an elite, influential, and supportive group of listeners; both the University of Cambridge, and more particularly Oxford, were central to such a listener recruitment plan.[42]

In 1957 Graves was asked to appear on what was then the flagship interview programme, *Frankly Speaking*, on the BBC Home Service.[43] The format was a very simple one: a panel of three interviewers asked a series of unscripted questions over a thirty-minute period; amongst those interviewed on this programme were the conductor Sir Thomas Beecham, filmmaker Walt Disney, and biologist J. B. S. Haldane.[44] The programme had won considerable notoriety at the outset, in November 1953, when the guest was Evelyn Waugh and the questions were nakedly hostile and clearly designed to provoke the novelist:

[40] Caversham, letter, 14 Mar. 1952. Newby a noted novelist, won the first Booker Prize in 1969, and was the producer most responsible for commissioning programmes dealing with contemporary literature themes. He was made Controller of the Third Programme in 1958.

[41] Caversham, letter, 19 Oct. 1954. In 1948 only two people in a thousand listened to the Third Programme, Carpenter (1997), 84.

[42] '[BBC] Traineeships for Graduates began in 1954. Competition for the eight or so places was immense—'800 odd applicants for 1954 when the scheme was open to men and women—and 500 when it was restricted to men', noted the BBC in 1955, giving no reason as to the exclusion of women. 'The first year's recruits [were] all from Oxford.' Carpenter (1997), 129. There were, too, severe reception problems in the early years: the Third Programme only became a genuinely national UK radio channel after 1951, five years after its first broadcast. See Carpenter (1997), 106.

[43] By this time there were three BBC radio channels: the Third Programme; the Home Service, offering a mixture of drama, music, plus what was called in the BBC 'the spoken word'; and the Light Programme, offering 'light entertainment', i.e. popular music and variety acts. It is difficult not to see this arrangement as mirroring the English class system, much in the same way as British Railways, in the same period offered travellers First, Second, and Third Class fares.

[44] Just as today, very little broadcasting—apart from the news, variety, and sport—was 'live'. In the case of this programme, the interview was recorded on 9 May 1957, a verbatim transcription was made, checked, and edited, then finally the transmission was made on 30 May. The final programme was timed at 28 minutes, 10 seconds.

'Are you a facile writer?' 'Have you ever wanted to kill someone?' 'Would you act as a public executioner?' were some of the deliberately provocative questions posed.[45] Waugh being Waugh, he took his revenge in prose: four years later, in his last major work of fiction, *The Ordeal of Gilbert Pinfold*, the eponymous hero is nearly driven insane by a young man from the BBC:

> The commonplace face [of the BBC interviewer] above the beard, became slightly sinister, the accentless but insidiously plebeian voice, menacing. The questions were civil enough in form but Mr Pinfold thought he could detect an underlying malice . . . Anyone sufficiently eminent to be interviewed . . . must have something to hide, must be an impostor . . . There was the hint of the underdog's snarl which Mr Pinfold recognised from his press cuttings.[46]

Graves's ordeal was to be of a far more benign nature, but as usual the poet's first concern was money; on receiving the invitation to appear on the programme he wrote to the BBC: 'Is this only an honour and a free meal (coffee incl.) or is the distinguished guest paid? If it is not too bad and I shall come up anyway and speak even more freely.'[47] The chairman of the panel was the broadcaster and editor of *Punch* magazine, Malcolm Muggeridge,[48] together with the playwright Paul Dehn and the archaeologist and television 'celebrity' Professor Glyn Daniels.[49] At the outset Graves is asked what is his favourite of his own works, and he replies it is *The Real David Copperfield*; it 'got a real slanging everywhere. I am afraid it will never be published again, so it will continue to be my favourite book.'[50] He is then challenged by Muggeridge about his prolixity:

[45] The whole interview can be heard on CD released by the British Library, in 2008, under the title *The Spoken Word: BBC* series [NSACD 34]. Despite the interview being such an ill-tempered affair, Waugh manages to finish on a very touching grace-note: when asked how he wants to be remembered, he says: 'For people of their charity to pray for my soul as a sinner.'

[46] Waugh (1957), 14–15.

[47] He was paid 25 guineas for his appearance.

[48] Graves had published articles in *Punch* during Muggeridge's editorship (1952–7).

[49] This was not the panel that 'interviewed' Waugh.

[50] Caversham, Radio Contributor File. The *David Copperfield* book, published in 1932, is the most notorious example of Graves 'putting it right' with another author's text. Other examples include, as already noted Blake's 'Tyger' and Keats's 'La Belle Dame sans Merci', in Graves and Hodge (1943), 35, which includes a considerable 'howler', unnoticed, it seems, by reviewers. In the first edition of *The Reader over Your Shoulder* the authors provide an analysis of the tenth stanza of Keats's '*La Belle Dame*

> Well writing is my profession; I know no other; I cannot dig; to beg I am ashamed, and I find it comes more—it comes easier to me than it did although I still have to write every page five times over, and living in Majorca, I have no alternative but to write, because the only alternative there to writing is drinking. And I don't really enjoy drinking to get drunk.[51]

Then he is asked about his working day:

> About half-past-eight I am ready to work and I start working and then half-an-hour later I have to give Latin lessons to the children because that's part of the household economy, then a bit later comes their Scripture lesson. And then I am free to go on working and it's very nice and I work till about lunchtime which is about quarter-past-one . . . and then I've got to send off the work I've done in the morning to the bus, because I've got a secretary who lives in another village.[52]

At this Graves is asked, by Muggeridge, about theology. 'Don't let's talk about theology; let's talk about history.' The poet then expresses his enthusiasm for Suetonius, an 'extremely practical and obviously a very good man', but continues by dismissing Rome's most noted historian: 'whereas a person like Tacitus I would never translate because to me he is so unpleasant.'[53] Frustratingly, none of the interviewers pursue Graves on this last point. Then, rather perversely, Graves talks about translating another ancient writer, Lucan, he also disliked:

> I got involved accidentally in translating Lucan and I hated every minute of it—until finally the time came in which I wrote the Introduction, and there I let myself go, and Mr Rieu who was the General

sans Merci' and provide a correct version of the quatrain: 'I saw pale kings and princes too, | Pale warriors, death pale were they all— | They cried 'La Belle Dame Sans Merci | Hath thee in thrall.' However, in the second, abridged edition (1947, p. 35) and in the much more widely read paperback edition (1965, p. 35) the last line appears as 'Thee hath in thrall'. This is not just an error of transposition but completely subverts the meaning of the poem and may have misled readers unfamiliar with it.

[51] Caversham, Radio Contributor File.

[52] Caversham, Radio Contributor File. Graves always created his manuscripts in long hand, apart from *Goodbye to All That* which he dictated, possibly for reasons of speed. 'Can't use a typewriter-trained myself not to use it . . . the pen remains personal . . . I think through my pen, not through my brain.' *Calling West Africa: Conversations with Robert Graves.* 1960 British Library Sound Archive.

[53] 'The greatest of the Roman historians', Syme (1939): the opening sentence of that majestic work.

> Editor said 'if you dislike Lucan so much, why do you translate him?' And so then I had to explain at the end that just because I disliked him, it didn't mean that other people wouldn't be grateful for the translation, he's a very important man because he started I think the Hollywood costume film, the Sunday journalism and all the things that go with the popular modernist movement.[54]

Finally Graves is asked about his library in Majorca, a necessary tool for any translator: 'I've got a small library in which there is nothing but plain texts and reference books . . . oh there's a place where you keep all your Simenons and Agatha Christies and Selwyn Jepsons and Erle Stanley Gardners.'[55] Graves seems very much in control of this interview from start to finish, and it must be regarded as an opportunity lost to challenge some of the poet's more eccentric opinions.[56]

In March 1956 Graves approached the Third Programme with the idea of making three programmes entitled 'Why I Hate the Romans', a proposal that initially P. H. Newby, Assistant Head of Talks, dismissed out of hand as 'quite unsuitable for the Third Programme'.[57] The attraction of giving a talk on the Third Programme was that the material stood a very good chance of appearing in the BBC's own weekly arts magazine, the *Listener*.[58] This proposal was eventually adopted by the station under the general title of 'The

[54] 'Lucan may be called the father of yellow journalism, for his love of sensational detail, his unprincipled reportage, and his disregard of continuity between to-day's and yesterday's rhetoric . . . [he] may also be called the father of the costume-film. If lopped of all the digressive rhodomonade, the *Civil Wars* is a script which could be put almost straight on the floor. It consists of carefully chosen, cunningly varied, brutally sensationalised scenes, linked by a tenuous thread of historical probability, and alternated with soft interludes in which deathless courage, supreme self-sacrifice, memorable piety, Stoic virtue, and wifely devotion are expected to win favour from the great sentimental box-office public.' Graves (1956), 13–14.

[55] Given that Graves was only in Britain for two to three weeks a year, and also given the fact that between 1950 and 1957 he produced three major translations for Penguin (Apuleius, Lucan, and Suetonius) plus *The Greek Myths*, all of which represented a very important source of income, the meagreness of the library described is, to say the least, somewhat puzzling.

[56] The full script is available at Caversham, and the British Library Sound Archive has full recording of the programme, Reference 1CDR 003155.

[57] Memo to Donald Boyd dated 5 Apr. 1956, Scripts B/CTP Caversham.

[58] This magazine was launched in 1929 to capture 'the fugitive word in print' (Lord Reith's phrase). Because of its Charter the BBC was forbidden to take any political stance, so the *Listener* was an apolitical arts journal, publishing reviews and the odd commissioned article; but the bulk of any edition was made up of extracts from, or the complete transcript of, programmes broadcast by the BBC in Britain or on its overseas services. In addition, the *Listener* from the 1930s onwards published new poems by

Cultured Romans', although in private Graves referred to these broadcasts as 'Why I hate the bloody Romans'.[59] The first of the three thirty-minute programmes was broadcast on 20 February 1957 and reprinted in the *Listener*.[60] It dealt with the Etruscans, to whom the later Roman culture, in Graves's view, owed everything, including their military traditions. The Romans were 'all . . . Etruscan . . . their weapons, armour, close-order drill, defensive walls, the layout of their camps, their legionary formation, their discipline, awards for personal valour and triumphs—everything of that sort. Roman law was Etruscanised Latin law.' Added to this, Graves airily insists: 'A sense of national doom plagued the Etruscans, much as it later plagued the Incas of Mexico [*sic*] and gave the savage Spanish conquistadores their chance.' He concludes by dealing with the issue of the Etruscan language: 'Etruscan inscriptions can now be read but, apart from a few words in common sepulchral formulas not yet translated.' The broadcast produced the expected response in the letters page of the *Listener*: R. D. Greenaway of Bristol described it as: 'inaccurate . . . misleading . . . hypotheses probable or improbable are stated as fact and inaccuracy degenerates into such nonsense as the absurd remark about the "Incas of Mexico".'[61] Equally predictably, Graves brushes aside such comments with the air of a medieval pope wearily dismissing a minor schematic: 'If Mr Greenaway thinks that I am going to get into a learned dog-fight . . . he errs . . . Yes: wasn't that curious—my Freudian slip of 'Mexico' for 'Peru'. Nobody else noticed it.'[62]

The second programme in the series, entitled 'The Most Cultured of All the Romans', dealt with Nero, and again Graves adopts his familiar *contra mundum* stance. The Emperor was not a 'psychotic' like Caligula or suffering from 'megalomania' like Lord Byron; he was simply an 'ordinary, unlovable Roman'. Nero demonstrated 'the unrepressed cultural ambitions of a Roman—just as Alexander the

Graves. At its peak, in the mid-1950s, it had a circulation of 150,000 readers, but it ceased publication in 1991. It is worth pointing out, too, that the weekly guide to BBC programmes, the *Radio Times*, fiercely guarded its monopoly on programming details for the week ahead; newspapers were not allowed to print full broadcasting details. The *Radio Times* would contain short 'puffs' for forthcoming programmes and a Graves broadcast would regularly feature in these advance promotions.

[59] Letter dated 30 Mar. 1956, BBC Written Archive Centre, Caversham Radio Contributor Files 41–62.

[60] *Listener*, 28 Feb. 1957, pp. 341–2.

[61] *Listener*, 7 Mar. 1957, pp. 386–7.

[62] *Listener*, 14 Mar. 1957, p. 428.

Great (whom I find an almost equally nasty character) was able to demonstrate those of a Macedonian.'[63]

The final programme, 'An Even More Cultured Roman', dealt with Virgil and Lucan. The charge-sheet against the latter remains the same: he was 'the father of modern journalism [and] his love of sensational details', but Graves's distaste for Virgil is palpable:

> Virgil's shyness, his literary perfectionism, his temperance, his idealism, his valetudinarianism, his avoidance of bawdy society, and his notorious passion for beautiful boys—which in those days could be gratified without loss of reputation—combine to make a recognisable picture. How exquisite the interior decorations of his house on the Esquiline (a gift from Augustus) must have been: especially the gilded bedrooms where sleep kissed the eyelids of Alexander and Cebes, his poetical boy-slaves. This Alexander who appears as Alexis in Virgil's *Bucolics* had been a present from Asinius Pollio, the most enlightened man of his age.[64]

Graves's last major radio broadcast took place in 1960, when he was interviewed for the Third Programme as part of an occasional series entitled *Conversations with Poets*; this was the third in the series; the first had been with Ezra Pound in Rapallo, the second with Hugh MacDiarmid at his home in Langholm on the Scottish borders, and so Graves was interviewed at his home in Majorca. In the second of these two forty-five-minute programmes Graves discusses, amongst other issues, the poets he admires and those he does not:

> 'If a knock came to your door and someone said, "John Milton is here, do you want to see him?"'
> 'Oh I suppose so.'
> 'If a knock came to your door and someone said, "Virgil is here"?
> 'Throw him out!'
> 'If they said , "Homer is here"?'
> 'I would jump up knock everything off the table, rush to greet him, not exactly kneel at his feet but give him a glass of fine wine and roast an ox if I could find one.'[65]

The interviewer, D. G. Bridson, presses Graves on his views on Virgil, and he admits to:

[63] *Listener*, 7 Mar. 1957, p. 379. [64] *Listener*, 31 Mar., p. 472.

[65] British Library National Sound Archive, *Conversations with Robert Graves* [2], Catalogue 1 CDR 0033113.The first programme was broadcast 29 July 1960 and the second part was broadcast 8 August. Both programmes were repeated.

> an extreme dislike . . . Virgil started off with the *Eclogues* . . . drawing room pastorals and managed to secure in 39 BC the patronage of Maecenas who admired the elegance *Eclogues* urged him to write on something less trivial So Virgil who was unwilling to stick his neck out on some political project—the quarrel between Octavian and Mark Antony was ongoing—agreed to compromise and to write in aid of agriculture. 'Very well' said Maecenas 'You have proved yourself the Latin Theocritus now prove yourself the Latin Hesiod . . . ' Nobody ever found the *Georgics* a useful work for farmers. He lacked imagination and knowledge. A more honest poet would have anticipated Goldsmith's *The Deserted Village* to show the impact of Augustus' victories on the Roman countryside . . . Augustus [after Actium] was pondering Maecenas view that Latin literature could challenge at Greek literature in all fields except the Homeric corpus of epic poetry and must conquer this field too . . . Virgil was just the man to write the official Roman epic glorifying the divinely descended Caesars, fated rulers of the world.[66]

It is difficult to know just how in touch Graves was with contemporary Virgilian scholarship, which was enjoying the beginnings of remarkable renaissance as he was making these dismissive remarks.[67] Certainly, one of Graves's circles of British friends, the classicist Hugh Lloyd-Jones, would have been in touch with developments in European and American Virgilian scholarship.[68] Perhaps Graves's attitude to Virgil merely reflects the values of a classical education informed by Victorian values which insisted none could share a pedestal with Homer.[69] The list of writers, both ancient and modern, Graves did not like is a very long one, and one is forced to agree with William Empson: 'I wouldn't bother much about his contempt for Donne, Milton, Dryden, Pope, Wordsworth, Tennyson, Yeats, Eliot and so forth; I only wish he had sounded a bit more as if he liked poetry

[66] The audio recording of this programme is held at the British Library Sound Archives, Reference M7557 W&R-M7558 W & RC 1.

[67] I am grateful to Roger Rees for drawing my attention to this point.

[68] See Graves (1999b), 482–3. Sir Hugh Lloyd-Jones succeeded E. R. Dodds as the Regius Professor of Greek at Oxford, a post he held until retirement in 1989. Friend or no, Jones was in no doubt about the poor quality of Graves' translation of Lucan: 'deplorable', 'Roman Grand Guignol', Lloyd-Jones (1991), 61. Jones also disliked Graves's translation of the *Iliad*: ' Even such a poet as Robert Graves was so much pre-occupied with the anti-heroic reaction that he produced a vey un-poetical translation of the Iliad', Lloyd-Jones (1991), 7.

[69] '[Gladstone] thought much harm had been done through the habit of regarding Homer through Roman spectacles and the severity of these remarks about Virgil might have satisfied even Robert Graves.' Lloyd-Jones (1982), 122.

when it is good.'[70] In this programme Graves makes a very sharp distinction between true poets, who are possessed by shamanistic powers—'a poem is a holy thing produced in a trance'—and those whom he calls, in a derogatory sense, 'classical' poets, whose work is 'musical, carefully designed, architecturally perfect, produced in beautiful editions and taught in innumerable schools, but gives no thrill . . . unlike real poetry'.

This seems to be one of the key objections against Virgil, Milton, Wordsworth, and other canonical poets: they produced work to order and at great length, but without the inspiration of the divine afflatus.

By the 1960s Graves broadcast, if at all, not on the radio but on television, where the audiences and the fees were larger.[71] In 1961, for example, he was invited to appear on a BBC Television arts programme, *Monitor*, to be interviewed by fellow-poet Al Alvarez, but before agreeing the perennial concern is voiced by Graves: 'Can't fifty guineas be an outright fee for my consent to be interviewed and not taxable as a performance?'[72]

Graves certainly perceived his broadcasting career, along with all his other non-poetic activity, as providing a very necessary income, but he was incapable of hack-work in any field; even in the most minor and ill-paid radio programme his scholarship, charm, and huge sense of mischief shined through.[73] His judgement on himself was stoical: 'I don't take myself seriously in public . . . I'm not really interested in other people's poetry . . . the poetry racket.'[74] Graves is perhaps an example of what the noted American film critic Manny Farber called 'termite art . . . ornery, wasteful, stubbornly self-involved, doing go-for-broke art and not caring what comes of it'.[75]

Let us leave the final word with a poet who shares some of Graves's characteristics, C. P. Cavafy:

[70] Empson (1988), 133.

[71] In 1969 he appeared briefly in a documentary about the Queen. He was receiving the Queen's Medal for Poetry, see Seymour-Smith (1995), 535.

[72] Letter dated 1 Apr. 1959.

[73] Not all warmed to Graves's charm: John Cheever confided in his *Journal* that he found Graves to be 'slippery and sinister', Bailey (2009), 427.

[74] 'Calling West Africa: Conversation with Robert Graves', BBC World Service British Library Sound Archive Reference CDA 26462.

[75] 'White Elephant Art versus Termite Art', in Farber (2009), 535. 'Elephant art' aims to 'blow up every situation and character like an affable inner tube with recognisable details and smarmy compassion . . . to reconcile those two supposed long-term enemies—academic and Madison Avenue art' (p. 538).

I sit here, yielding to reverie. I've brought to Art
desires and notions: certain things half-seen—
countenances and figures; certain vague recollections
of love unfinished . . .[76]

[76] 'I've Brought to Art' (1921), in Cavafy (2007), 271. The two writers were concerned with affairs of the heart, but also the byways of antiquity. Cavafy would surely have appreciated Graves's poem 'The Persian Version', and he too was acquainted with the White Goddess: 'How often during my work a fine idea comes to me, a rare image, and sudden-formed lines, and I'm obliged to leave them, because work can't be put off. Then when I go home and recover a bit, I try to remember them but they're gone. And it's quite right. It's as if Art said to me: "I'm not a servant, for you to turn me out when I come, and to come when you want. I'm the greatest lady in the world"'. Liddell (1994), 89.

16

The Anger of Achilles

A Prize-Winning 'Epic for Radio' by Robert Graves

Amanda Wrigley

> Classical scholars do not automatically jump for joy when the name of Robert Graves is mentioned. His excursions into their territory are raids, not pilgrimages—gay assaults, hit-and-run, 'unprofessional', popularizing, irreverent to the point of impudence. Clearly he is not a Classical Scholar: the man can take an ancient text—Apuleius, Suetonius and now Homer—and make it live again in an English as fresh and as pure and as compelling as a morning gale.[1]

In the opening quotation the American teacher, poet, and translator of Greek tragedy Dudley Fitts (1903–68) captures the paradox surrounding Robert Graves's work on classical literature and the ancient world. In this *New York Times* review of Graves's translation of Homer's *Iliad*, Fitts points to both Graves's public popularity and success and also the suspicion with which classical scholars typically viewed his work. This mixed reception of Graves's classical oeuvre forms the backdrop for the present study of the literary and performance life of Graves's version of the *Iliad*, which was first published in 1959 by Doubleday in the United States under the title *The Anger of Achilles* and described as a 'translation' on the title-page. This essay first considers the reception of this version of Homer's epic poem,

[1] Fitts (1959).

before moving on to a consideration of the 1964 radio production of the text which won the coveted Prix Italia the following year. The essay is therefore concerned with focusing attention on the varied scholarly, critical, and public engagements with the various manifestations of *The Anger of Achilles*, emphasizing how Graves's rewritings of antiquity held great popular appeal as both entertainment and (broadly speaking) cultural education, not only for readers and viewers but also for hundreds of thousands of *listeners* who may not, in the main, have been schooled in Classics.

AN *ILIAD* FOR THE 'NON-CLASSICAL PUBLIC'

The brightly coloured cover of the first edition of *The Anger of Achilles*, published by Doubleday in 1959, was illustrated by Ronald Searle (1920–2011), cartoonist for *Punch*, the *New Yorker*, and *Le Monde*.[2] The underlying humour in Searle's lively sketch of Achilles in profile, standing solemnly—and, perhaps, petulantly—in full armour, captures well the flavour of the sentiments expressed on the flyleaf:

> Known the world over as a great epic and a literary classic, the *Iliad* was composed primarily to amuse and is filled with great comedy and biting satire. In *The Anger of Achilles*, Robert Graves has translated the narrative into sharp, clear prose, interpolating the songs into exquisite lyric poetry, and has caught all the rich humor lacking in the usual solemn, pedantic versions of the *Iliad*.[3]

The flyleaf records that Searle's fourteen cartoons within the book are intended to highlight 'the satire accented in this fresh, new rendering of Homer's epic', and it anticipates that the translation 'may shock some scholars'. Indeed, the certainty and confidence with which the first two sentences of the introduction state what are offered as the 'facts' of the *Iliad*'s composition and early performance would have undoubtedly left Homeric scholars and students aggrieved:

> The *Homeridae* ('Sons of Homer'), a family guild of Ionian bards based in Chios, enlarged their ancestor's first short draft of the *Iliad* to twenty-four books, and became comprehensively known as 'Homer'. They earned

[2] McNay (2012). [3] Flyleaf to the first edition: Graves (1959a).

> their livelihood by providing good popular entertainment for such festivals as the All-Ionian at Mount Mycale in Lydia, the All-Athenian at Athens, and the four-yearly homage to their patron Apollo at Delos; also, it seems, by going on circuit to various small royal courts where Greek was spoken, from Asia Minor to Sicily, and perhaps even visiting Spain and Western Morocco.[4]

Graves goes on to set forth some theories on the interpretation of the *Iliad* which were so controversial that one scholar—who is otherwise favourable in his review of the translation itself—suggests 'that the reader ignore completely Graves's introduction'.[5] Where Graves may be more in line with scholarship is in his emphasis on entertainment as a function of Homer's epic poetry. The Homeric epics, he declares, need to be 'rescued from the classroom curse which has lain heavily on them throughout the past twenty-six centuries, and become entertainment once more'.[6] Further along in his introduction, Graves pays homage to the recent translation of the *Iliad* by Richmond Lattimore, published in 1951, but he describes it merely as a 'crib', a literal translation for the use of students. Translations, on the other hand, Graves considers, 'are made for the general, non-Classical public, yet their authors seldom consider what will be immediately intelligible, and therefore readable, and what will not'.[7] It is this perceived failure that Graves seeks to rectify with his own translation of the *Iliad*, which is written in prose with frequent short passages of verse—which he describes as song—'where prose will not suffice' (for example, addresses to gods and Homeric similes).[8] He appoints himself as rescuer of the *Iliad* for readers who wish thoroughly to enjoy it in English translation. Some reviewers considered that this was a much-needed mission in which Graves succeeds. For example, the English literature scholar and literary critic F. W. Bateson (1901–78), writing in the *Observer*, considers that, whereas the fortunes of Homer's *Odyssey* have gone 'up and up', 'The *Iliad* has become more than sophisticated modern flesh can bear . . . the grand style is out to-day . . . A modern translation of the *Iliad* is,

[4] Graves (1959a), 13. For a concise summary of the issues of composition and transmission which continue to be discussed as the 'Homeric question', see Rutherford (1996), 9 ff.

[5] Rexine (1962), 281. [6] Graves (1959a), 13. [7] Graves (1959a), 33.

[8] Graves (1959a), 35. Notably, Steiner (2004) leaves Graves out of his survey of Homeric translation.

therefore, primarily a rescue operation'. He concludes: '*The Anger of Achilles* is a triumphant success.... Here is a Homer who is alive for us... this is a translation to be grateful for. Greekless readers can now see the great Achilles whom *we* knew.'[9]

Bateson's emphasis on the word 'we' makes the interesting assumption that the *Observer* reader has knowledge of Homer in the original ancient Greek. Did other scholars and critics writing with knowledge of the original Greek agree with his estimation? Reviewing the translation in the *Classical World*, Pearl Cleveland Wilson, Professor Emerita of Classics at Hunter College, New York, finds the prose sections more satisfactory than the verse, although 'Graves often fails to represent not only statements made in the original, but also—and an immeasurably greater loss—some feeling expressed by the poet with intensity and power or suggested with poignant subtlety'.[10] The review begins by asserting that 'there is much to disturb those who know and admire and love the original', and concludes with the estimation that Graves's translation is a 'disappointing book'.[11] The poet, writer, and BBC Radio producer Louis MacNeice (1907–63), who had served as a lecturer in Classics early in his career, is very much of the same mind:

> The trouble is that his prose is the wrong sort of prose and his verse the wrong sort of verse.... Prose can be simple and still rhythmical and colourful: Mr Graves on the contrary uses an admass diction and a halting or laboured line. And almost worse is to come when he slips (repeat 'slips') into verse.... The passages he has versified are usually lyrical but he has not kept them lyrical: they jogtrot with John Gilpin or jingle with the verses in Christmas crackers. This is sad and criminal for a poet of Mr Graves's stature.[12]

John E. Rexine, Professor of Classics at Colgate College, offers a review in the *Classical Journal*, the conclusion of which is based less on the book's merits or otherwise as a translation of Homer and more on its wider usefulness. Rexine acknowledges that in the three years since the translation was published it has received 'a good deal of favourable attention'. Although he considers it to be 'not the kind of translation that a Hellenist would write to convey the real essence

[9] Bateson (1960). [10] Cleveland Wilson (1960), 161.

[11] Cleveland Wilson (1960), 157 and 162.

[12] MacNeice (1960). On Graves' 'plain prose style', see Burton, Chapter 7 this volume.

of Homer', he concedes that 'a literary figure such as Graves, through his translations of classical authors, will excite discriminating readers in larger numbers to explore ancient literature than would otherwise be possible'.[13] (Rexine was the reviewer, above, who recommended that the reader ignore the introduction and get on instead with becoming acquainted with this 'entertaining' translation of the *Iliad*.[14])

In the *Hudson Review* a review entitled 'The *Iliad* Rescued: or a Mustache for Mona Lisa' was published by the classical scholar George E. Dimock, who had translated Homer for the prestigious Loeb series of classical texts with facing-page literal translations. Dimock takes Rexine's balanced reasoning further, arguing that 'to take a traditional story and recast it according to the bard's own views of human experience and ideas of literary form' is 'a right and proper thing', noting that 'Homer no doubt did as much'. But his primary criticism of Graves is that he 'is not quite willing to stand independent of the name and fame of his predecessor'.[15] In other words, drawing on the terms commonly applied today to modern-language reworkings of Greek and Roman literature, Graves's *The Anger of Achilles* may more accurately be described as an adaptation or a version rather than a translation, notwithstanding the words 'translated by' on the title-page.[16]

Dimock unpicks the introduction's bold claim that the *Iliad* is a great satire. Graves asserts that it was Homer's intention to portray Agamemnon as 'a weak, truculent, greedy, lying, murderous, boastful, irresolute busybody', with Achilles, Odysseus, and Nestor being no better, in order to satirize the 'semi-barbarous . . . iron-age princes' who ruled in his day.[17] Dimock considers that this 'absolutely incredible' theory gives Graves the freedom to make the *Iliad* ridiculous, and that this ridiculousness is intended to make the poem palatable to what he terms a new, 'anti-intellectual' audience.[18] For some, it must be noted, Graves's discussion of perceived satiric threads in the *Iliad* was welcome. Peter Green, writing in the *Times Literary Supplement*, comments that: 'He emphasizes wherever possible—and for this at least he deserves our gratitude—the too-often neglected

[13] Rexine (1962), 281. [14] Rexine (1962), 282.
[15] Dimock (1960), 293.
[16] On the development of the vocabulary to describe and define such works in relation to ancient texts, see Hardwick (2003), 9–10.
[17] Graves (1959a), 16. [18] Dimock (1960), 294 and 297.

element of satire and ridicule which Homer infuses into his heroes' exchanges.'[19] Green goes on to note that this is particularly noticeable in passages involving the gods. In the first edition of the translation this sensibility is often underscored by Searle's cartoon-like illustrations: for example, the potentially comic undertones of the scene in *Iliad* 1 in which the great hero Achilles is stopped from attacking Agamemnon by the goddess Athene is represented by the goddess holding the surprised hero back by pulling on his long hair (Graves (1959a), facing p. 48). Graves's economical translation of this scene reads as follows:

> As he stood in doubt, slowly drawing the sword out of its scabbard, Hera, who cared for both contestants, hurriedly sent her step-daughter, Owl-Eyed Athene, to step behind Achilles and catch him by his yellow hair. Turning about in surprise, he recognised the goddess' fierce eyes, though she was invisible to everyone else, and addressed her impatiently: 'What are you doing here, Pallas Athene, daughter of Zeus?' . . .
>
> Athene answered: ' . . . Leave that sword-hilt alone! By all means, give him a tongue-lashing and tell him what punishment he must expect; but abstain from violence . . . .' (Graves (1959a), 44)

Graves and Searle worked in close collaboration on the drawings. In a letter asking Searle whether he would be willing to take on the job of illustrating his translation, Graves records that 'Homer has been making me laugh and laugh'; in another, once Searle has agreed to do the work, he remarks that 'I'll have to write a long introduction pointing out some of Homer's deadpan jokes. There's a nice one in Book XI where that old bore Nestor tells a long story of his youthful adventures to Machoen, his guest, who sits with him drinking a delicious beverage . . . with a barbed arrow still sticking in his shoulder. I should like that one illustrated.' In a later letter, still discussing which scenes should be illustrated, he states: 'It is lovely to think you are fighting by my side, with spear & shield and little pencil.'[20]

The Anger of Achilles, with its easy prose and vivid dialogue, was clearly a commercial success: the translation appeared in several editions on both sides of the Atlantic in the 1960s (see Bibliography); and, indeed, as recently as 2001 it was reprinted by Carcanet Press

[19] Green (1960).

[20] Letters from Robert Graves to Ronald Searle sent between 1958 and 1959 (RGC, Gr 16, 1–13). See Murnaghan, Chapter 3 this volume, for humour in Graves's novel *Homer's Daughter* (1955b), which he also envisaged being turned into a film script.

and in 2009 in the popular Penguin Classics series.[21] What is notable is that publishers clearly enjoyed marketing this rollicking and accessible version of the *Iliad* in cinematic terms: the cover of the 1966 Pyramid Books edition, for example, announces the work as: 'The Epic Tale of the Great Assault on Troy. A Superb Rendition of Homer's *Iliad*.' The commercial success of *The Anger of Achilles* in print certainly lends support to Dimock's view that in the 1960s Graves's work held great appeal for the general reader, and, as we shall see, such cinematic language in the marketing blurbs seems to resonate with Graves's hopes to turn *The Anger of Achilles* into a script for performance, ultimately, on film.

PERFORMING *THE ANGER OF ACHILLES*

> It was quite by chance we heard that Robert Graves would be interested in making a broadcasting adaptation of his own racy, vivid translation [of Homer's *Iliad*]—he wanted to do this as a first step to making a dramatisation for the stage, for television, and the films.[22]

In the early 1960s Graves was talking to the film and theatre director Sam Wanamaker (1919–93) about making, first, a stage dramatization and, later, a film version of *The Anger of Achilles*. Wanamaker testified to much interest in America for this idea. A letter to Graves states that he wanted 'to mount your Trojan War using all sorts of film + projection techniques'.[23] He was in conversation with the Lincoln Center in New York about a production which was likely to cost half a million dollars.[24] By 1967 little progress towards these ends had been made, but the idea was still considered to be a live project. The designs which the Czech set designer Josef Svoboda (1920–2002) presented to the Lincoln Center for this production were considered

[21] In its blurb on this reprint the Penguin Classics website states that the translation 'takes a revered classic back to its roots as popular entertainment' <http://www.penguinclassics.co.uk/books/the-anger-of-achilles/9780140455601> (accessed 16 Feb. 2015).

[22] Raikes (1966).

[23] Letter from Beverley Cross to Robert Graves, 7 Jan. 1963 (RGA).

[24] Letter from Sam Wanamaker to Robert Graves, 17 July 1967 (RGA).

by Wanamaker to form 'a staggeringly exciting concept which surpasses every expectation and hope that I have had'.[25] In 1968, however, the Lincoln Center decided not to proceed with the project, largely because of the enormous budget: 'the price tag, as far as we are concerned, is simply too much.'[26] Wanamaker began to write to a variety of other theatres and foundations for support, and was still writing to Graves as late as 1972 about his efforts to launch a big professional theatre production of *The Anger of Achilles*.[27]

In the meantime—whilst this big idea for a theatre and film *Iliad* seemed continually to falter, and whilst other film versions of Homer's epic poem proved themselves to be more successful in making it to the big screen[28]—a performance version of *The Anger of Achilles* reached something in the region of several hundred thousand people via the radio medium. Not only did this radio performance prove to be continually popular with listeners in its revivals, but it was also deemed to have been an artistic success, winning the Prix Italia in 1965.

Graves had in earlier decades often been approached to write for radio. In 1946, for example, the Producer of Features Rayner Heppenstall (1911–81) invited him to contribute a script for the series 'Imaginary Conversations' (drawn from authors such as Plato, Erasmus, and Boswell) to be broadcast on the Third Programme, the new radio network which would be launched later that year.[29] Graves's response to this invitation starkly demonstrates his ambivalent feelings towards the BBC at this time:

> Nothing that I have ever been asked to do for the B.B.C. has prospered: there has always been some technical reason for turning it down if it is a script; and when I recorded a broadcast in German they told me it was too slow for use and when I did a Brains Trust I was rude to Joad

[25] Letter from Sam Wanamaker to Beverley Cross, 21 Nov. 1967 (RGA).

[26] Letter from Schuyler G. Chapin (Vice-President, Programming, Lincoln Center for the Performing Arts) to Sam Wanamaker, 23 Jan. 1968 (RGA).

[27] For example: 'I am pushing the *Iliad* with the Kennedy Centre as hard as I can': letter from Sam Wanamaker to Robert Graves, 28 May 1972 (RGA). The almost decade-long attempt to stage and film Graves's version of the *Iliad*, although ultimately unsuccessful, prefigures the stage and small-screen production of his 1934 novel *I, Claudius*, which was staged in 1972 and achieved major success as BBC serial later in the 1970s.

[28] e.g. *Helen of Troy* (dir. Robert Wise, 1956) and *L'ira di Achille* [*The Fury of Achilles*] (dir. Marino Girolami, 1962). See Paul (2013).

[29] Letter from Rayner Heppenstall to Robert Graves, 25 Apr. 1946 (RG/S1).

> + never asked again. And as I never listen to the B.B.C. except News + Tommy Handley I must conclude that the radio + I are not in sympathy. But thanks very much all the same.[30]

One can easily understand the frustration of the writer who, as he claimed, had 'been paid three times for scripts which were never used, never for one which was used'.[31]

Heppenstall persisted in his wooing of Graves, countering his anxiety about 'not being one of the boys' by saying that 'I am sure cliques do form, but one of the virtues of the BBC is that it's so large that it can never fall into the hands of a single clique. What is certain is that your prose work is particularly up the street of this department [Features], because of its factual and speculative nature.'[32] In 1952 he wrote to him again about a new series of 'Imaginary Conversations', and by now Graves had become more favourable to the idea of writing for radio,[33] offering a thirty-minute talk on 'The Argonauts' for the Third Programme.[34] Some months later, an internal memo written by Douglas Cleverdon (1903–87), Heppenstall's colleague in the Features Department, notes that 'we should like to recommend very strongly that Robert Graves be commissioned to undertake a major work for the Third Programme. . . . it appears that Graves would be very willing to write something within the range of a work of creative imagination like *The Dark Tower* . . . We should prefer to leave the precise form and subject to Graves's choice.'[35] Accordingly, the Third Programme offered Graves a commission for 'a new and major work of some kind—preferably, but not necessarily in verse, and if possible, dramatic or semi-dramatic in form . . . I know this is

[30] Letter from Robert Graves to Rayner Heppenstall, undated, but stamped 29 Apr. 1946 (RG/S1). C. E. M. Joad (1891–1953), a philosopher, presented the popular radio discussion programme *The Brains Trust* from 1940 to 1948.

[31] Letter from Robert Graves to Rayner Heppenstall, undated, but stamped 29 Apr. 1946 (RG/S1).

[32] Letter from Rayner Heppenstall to Robert Graves, 10 Feb. 1948 (RG/S1).

[33] Letter from Rayner Heppenstall to Robert Graves, 12 Feb. 1952 (RG/S1).

[34] Letter from Robert Graves to P. H. Newby, 2 June 1952; and Talks Booking Requisition, 24 June 1952 (RG/T1). Newby accepted the offer, on condition that it be twenty minutes long; it was broadcast as 'The Geography of the Golden Fleece Legend' on 28 November 1952 (letter from Gilbert Phelps to Robert Graves (RG/T1)).

[35] Internal memo from Douglas Cleverdon to the Assistant Controller of the Third Programme, 13 Oct. 1952 (RG/S1). *The Dark Tower* was Louis MacNeice's 1946 radio masterpiece. On the flyleaf of the Faber edition W. H. Auden is quoted as commenting, 'I consider it the finest radio drama written so far'.

all extremely vague; but that vagueness was really part of Third's intention. They are too eager to broadcast a new work of yours to try laying down the law about its nature.'[36]

The BBC was enthusiastic about persuading authors of standing to write original work for radio, but when the resulting material produced was not fit for broadcasting—either in terms of length, style, or content—much internal hand-wringing accompanied the decision as to whether or not to turn the script into a broadcast. In 1956, for example, Graves proposed a series of three talks on 'Why I Hate the Romans', one of which focused on the Etruscans and another on Nero. An independent reader of the scripts offered the following advice to P. H. Newby, the Chief Assistant for Talks:

> Robert Graves as the child at large in the world of scholarship is now such a well known public character that nobody I think would take these pieces seriously if we put them on. The question is, would they entertain? Of the two, the more outrageous from a scholar's or historian's point of view, + so the more frivolously amusing, perhaps, is that on the Etruscans. If we let it go out, we should have to make it clear to the uninitiated, I suppose, that we were not offering it seriously as historical research but possibly Graves's reputation would do that well enough for us.[37]

Newby writes to Graves with his concerns, and a lively correspondence on such matters as the likelihood that the average Third Programme listener had read Suetonius ensued. Graves insists the talks are well researched and must go out pretty much as they are, since he has no time to recast them; Graves wins the battle, but Newby still privately hopes that he can be encouraged to edit the scripts before broadcast.[38] The three talks, which were broadcast on the Third Programme in 1956 under the title 'The Cultured Romans', generated some anger amongst scholars. The Acting Controller of Talks, J. C. Thornton, relates a conversation he had with the furious Otto Skutsch (1906–90), Professor of Latin at University College, London, as follows: 'I told him that we had not imagined that Robert Graves was making a serious contribution to classical scholarship and that we had put on this talk rather as a *jeu d'esprit*. He said he appreciated this

[36] Letter from [illegible name] to Robert Graves, 19 Dec. 1952 (RG/S1).
[37] Letter from [M. C. H.?] to Peter Newby, 5 Apr. 1956 (RG/T1).
[38] See the correspondence in RG/T1.

point but nevertheless he had found some of his students were taking it seriously and he did think it bad to broadcast a talk which contained errors of fact which could have been corrected.'[39] Another outraged listener, R. D. Greenaway, wrote a long and strong letter to the *Listener* to pick up on several points in the talk which he considered 'in many ways inaccurate and misleading', concluding that 'Mr Graves would do better to stick to poetry'.[40]

As it happens, in 1957, the following year, Graves was invited by the BBC to provide a poetic translation of the scene between Thetis and Achilles in *Iliad* 18.1–147 for one of twelve half-hour programmes of readings of key scenes from the epic poem as translated by a variety of modern poets, for broadcast in 1958.[41] In his letter to Graves, D. S. Carne-Ross (1921–2010) of the Talks Department (who has recently been described as 'the finest critic of classical literature in English translation after Arnold'[42]) notes that the variety of styles of translation offered by the series 'is intended to reflect the varieties of approach possible at the present time to a great traditional poem. The translations are, so far as possible, poets' translations rather than dons' translations.'[43] The idea was an appealing one to Graves, but in his response he regretted that the backlog of work he had to tackle before embarking on an American lecture tour prevented him from accepting the commission.[44] In reply Carne-Ross wrote: 'Indeed, what a pity! It would have been immensely interesting to have seen you at grips with Homer.'[45]

In truth, Graves was already very much 'at grips with Homer', writing *The Anger of Achilles* which, as noted above, was to be published by Doubleday in 1959. It can have been no coincidence, then, that soon after this correspondence with Carne-Ross, Graves's literary agent W. P. Watt wrote to the BBC to inform them of Graves's forthcoming translation, suggesting that the Third

[39] Letter from J. C. Thornton to P. H. Newby, 26 Feb. 1957 (RG/T1).

[40] Typescript copy of letter from R. D. Greenaway written for publication in the *Listener*, 7 Mar. 1957 (RG/T1). These negative responses to Graves's somewhat controversial talks did not, it must be noted, prevent the BBC from repeating the talks in June of the same year.

[41] Letter from D. S. Carne-Ross to Robert Graves, 30 Dec. 1957 (RG/S1).

[42] Kenneth Haynes, in Carne-Ross (2010), 13.

[43] D. S. Carne-Ross to Robert Graves, 30 Dec. 1957 (RG/S1).

[44] Letter from Robert Graves to D. S. Carne-Ross, 8 Jan. 1958 (RG/S1).

[45] Letter from D. S. Carne-Ross to Robert Graves, 14 Jan. 1958 (RG/S1).

Programme might be interested in broadcasting readings from it.[46] In the light of the already planned series, however, Carne-Ross's response to this suggestion could perhaps have been anticipated: 'it does not seem likely that we will be able to place readings from it in the Third Programme since we have just finished a series of twelve readings devoted to new translations of the same poem.'[47] It was as a result of his conversations with Wanamaker that Graves had been struck with the idea of trying out the script on radio, as the best approach to lay the ground for his ambitious theatre and film project.[48] The radio idea may not have had legs in 1958, but in 1961 the University of Oxford elected Graves to the prestigious Professorship of Poetry, and in late 1962—the year in which W. H. Auden described him as England's 'greatest living poet'[49]—Graves's idea to put *The Anger of Achilles* on air, made via his agent, was accepted by the BBC.[50]

Raymond Raikes (1910–98) was in charge of producing the première for the Drama Department, for broadcast in three one-hour parts on the Home Service network. Raikes was a producer for whom radio dramatic sense was of the utmost importance: he had learnt his Classics at Uppingham School and Oxford, but he was no academic purist; rather, he liberally cut and rewrote texts to make them as accessible via radio performance as possible.[51] In his first letter to Graves about *The Anger of Achilles*, he accordingly displays his confidence in both adapting scripts for the comprehension of the listener and understanding where musical and radiophonic sounds are required:

> I have timed the scripts and, finding that they were quite a bit short of the hour, I have extended them, working direct from your translation of the ILIAD (you will notice I have even used a phrase at the start of each from page xii of your introduction). Again, learning that the BBC Home Service hopes to broadcast the three parts at weekly intervals, I have

[46] Letter from W. P. Watt to the Director of Talks, Third Programme, 18 May 1958 (RG/S1). W. P. 'Peter' Watt was writing on behalf of Graves's literary agent, A. P. Watt.

[47] Letter from D. S. Carne-Ross to W. P. Watt, 21 May 1958 (RG/S1).

[48] Letter from Peter Watt to Martin Esslin, 11 Dec. 1962 (RG/T1).

[49] Auden (1962). Auden also wrote, 'on the subject of love, no poet in our time has written more or better' (p. 7). This was part of a series of reviews and criticism in a special issue on Robert Graves in *Shenandoah*.

[50] Memo from Martin Esslin to Peggy Wells, 9 Jan. 1963 (RG/S2).

[51] In his obituary of Raikes, John Tydeman (1998) refers to this tendency. Raikes produced at least twenty Greek and Roman plays over his thirty-year radio career (see Wrigley (2009a), appendix 1).

> tried to make each script self-contained so that a listener should he have missed part 1 and/or part 2 can still enjoy part 3. I have also, as you will see, prepared the scripts for my radio production and have inserted cues for music, both orchestral and radiophonic.[52]

Music was an important part of this production: each of the three hour-long parts was to include between twenty-five to thirty minutes of musical accompaniment specially composed by Roberto Gerhard (1896–1970) for a sizeable orchestra. The score was later described an 'orchestral-cum-radiophonic score', owing to the composer's collaboration with the BBC Radiophonic Workshop: the ensuing 'radiophonic music' was used specifically to accompany scenes involving Athene, Thetis, Aphrodite, and Zeus in order to emphasize their divinity.[53]

The Anger of Achilles was first broadcast as 'The Sunday Play' on the Home Service on three Sunday afternoons, 17, 24, and 31 May 1964. It was billed as an 'Epic for Radio by Robert Graves from his translation of the *Iliad*'. The first part covers Agamemnon's seizure of Achilles' war-prize Briseis and Achilles' subsequent withdrawal from battle; parts two and three deal with the Greeks' reversal, the intervention of the gods, the death of Patroclus at the hands of the Trojan Hector, the subsequent death of Hector at the hands of Achilles, and Achilles' reconciliation with Hector's father, Priam.

Following the première, Raikes devised a 'shortened and tautened' script for a single broadcast on the Third Programme on 10 June 1965, from 8.45–10.20 p.m.[54] This was submitted as the BBC's entry for the prestigious Prix Italia. The script for this begins with a 'SHORT, EVOCATIVE, ORCHESTRAL OPENING', after which a narrator briefly sets the scene: 'Two thousand six hundred years ago in a royal courtyard in Greece . . . an audience, relaxing with wine-cups at their elbows, sat waiting for one of Homer's story-telling sons.'[55] An unspecified 'King' welcomes the bard Phemias (played by Denis Quilley, 1927–2003, who chanted and sang his lines)—whose name clearly owes a substantial debt to the Phemios of the *Odyssey*, the bard of Odysseus' household—upon his arrival from

[52] Letter from Raymond Raikes to Robert Graves, 17 June 1963 (RG/T1).

[53] 'Radiophonic Music in *The Anger of Achilles*', typescript notes (RG/T1). An undated programme note written a couple of years after the radio première describes Gerhard as follows: 'as happy scoring music for a full symphony orchestra as he is making a score for Radiophonics' ('For Transcription Service: A Programme Note', typescript notes (RG/T1)).

[54] Raikes (1966). [55] A copy of this script is in the RGA.

Delos. The script begins with Graves's invocation of the Muse (renamed 'Mountain Goddess'), which is spoken by Phemias who goes on to narrate, over music, the background of the Trojan War, bringing the listener to the moment when Chryses, the priest of Apollo whose daughter Chryseis had been taken by Agamemnon, approaches him to request her return. This structuring technique is used throughout the play—short scenes are interspersed with 'narration over music' by Phemias—thus lending a great economy to the radio storytelling. The dialogue, too, is shortened to give the drama of the tale a fast pace and vivid feel. For example, Graves's published translation of the angry confrontation between Agamemnon and Achilles in Book 1 begins with Achilles addressing Agamemnon thus:

> Son of Atreus, you are the greediest man in the Assembly, as well as the noblest-born! Why should these princes give you a prize of honour [as compensation if he were to return Chryseis to her father]? They have no common stock of booty upon which to draw. What we took from captured cities has already been distributed; and it would not be decent were a particular award withdrawn and made over to you. Send back the girl, as Apollo demands, and later, if Zeus lets us sack some other Trojan fortress, we will vote you three or four times her value.

After a further page of increasingly heated discussion between the two heroes, Agamemnon concludes: 'Yet, let me inform you that, since Apollo insists on robbing me of Chryseis, my own ship and crew will carry her back; and that I shall then visit your hut and compensate myself with your prize of honour, the beautiful Briseis.'[56] In the shortened, prize-winning radio script, this dialogue is rendered much more briefly and to the point as:

ACHILLES (In harsh tones) King Agamemnon, you are the greediest man alive!

AGAMEMNON (Stung) What. Achilles!

ACHILLES Send back the girl, as Apollo demands.

AGAMEMNON (More furious still) So I must surrender Chryseis, and expect no compensation—is that it? You, I suppose, are to keep your prize of honour and leave me chafing empty-handed? No, indeed! I shall visit your hut and recoup my loss with your prize of honour, the beautiful Briseis of Lyrnessus.

[56] Graves (1959a), 42 and 43, his translation of lines from *Iliad* 1.

Following this threat, Achilles of course reaches for his sword, but his fury is checked by the goddess Athene (as mentioned above).

It was this abridged radio version of *The Anger of Achilles* which in 1965 won the Radiotelevisione Italiana Prize (commonly known as the Prix Italia) for a literary and dramatic work for radio; furthermore, Raikes's production of *The Foundling* by Peter Gurney, with music by Humphrey Searle, won the prize for stereophonic radio work. This was the first time since the mid-1950s that the BBC had come away with two prizes in one year, and it was the first time ever that any country had won two prizes for works produced by the same man.[57] Graves had not been able to attend the ceremony himself, but he celebrated the news of the win with a bottle of champagne, poignantly remembering that 'This time 50 years ago I was dining at the Montmorency Chateau Béthune watching my fellow officers who were . . . going to be killed at Loos the next day'.[58] On returning from Florence with his record-breaking two prizes, Raikes wrote to the composer Gerhard as follows: 'I shall be going to a Third Programme meeting on Monday and hope to persuade them to give a further "airing" to the 55 minutes version of *The Anger of Achilles* which I devised specifically for the Italia Prize.'[59]

The *Radio Times* listing for this 1966 production is illustrated by an elaborate drawing, headed 'Radio Italiana Prize 1965', and an appealing and informative article by Raikes:

> How did we set about making this 'epic for radio' which won the Radio Italiana Prize in A.D. 1965? It was quite by chance we heard that Robert Graves would be interested in making a broadcasting adaptation of his own racy, vivid translation—he wanted to do this as a first step to making a dramatisation for the stage, for television, and the films. . . . And then another letter arrived from Robert Graves: 'Homer should be grateful for our having let him have his story without any clever embellishments. I feel that this performance is going to bring us good luck!' His words were prophetically true: originally serialised on three hot Sunday afternoons in May 1964, I shortened and tautened it for the revival as one programme in the Third (June 1965), and the version you

[57] 'Italia Prize Double for BBC Producer from Bromley', BBC Press Service, 12 Oct. 1965 (S452/S4/1).

[58] Letter from Robert Graves to Isla Cameron, 24 Sept. 1965 (RGC, Gr 3, 1–49).

[59] Raymond Raikes to Roberto Gerhard, 8 Oct. 1965 (S452/48/1).

> will hear tonight was awarded the prize in the Palazzo Vecchio in Florence last September. (Raikes (1966))

The 1966 broadcast of the abridged version was heard by an estimated 150,000 Home Service listeners.[60] The choice of network here is interesting. The 1964 première had also been broadcast on the Home in one-hour chunks over three Sundays. In 1965, however, the newly abridged version appeared on the Third Programme, a network which, from its foundation in 1946, had sought to appeal to an already educated and cultured listenership and on which what were thought of as 'highbrow' cultural works—a definition which came to include a great deal of the Greek material subsequently broadcast—were naturally at home. Following the award of the Prix Italia, however, it was revived on the Home Service, which served a much broader audience in terms of 'brow', and this no doubt testifies to its perceived, and actual, wide appeal.[61] As Paul Ferris noted in the *Observer* in response to the 1966 broadcast: 'Poetry and poetry-programmes rarely get further than the Third (a notable exception last week was Robert Graves's *The Anger of Achilles* on the Home Service, a radio spectacular from his translation of the *Iliad*, which won the 1965 Radio Italiana Prize).' Ferris concludes that: 'Programmes like . . . *The Anger of Achilles* are still among the best things that radio has to offer.'[62]

CONCLUSION

In August 1964 Richard Imison, the Script Editor for the BBC Drama Department, wrote to Graves's agent to press for a radio adaptation of *I, Claudius* and *Claudius the God*, to be written either by Graves himself or 'another adaptor of high standing':

> If [the film people] really aren't going to do anything with it and are merely jealously guarding their rights, could you possibly put to them the point of view that a radio production would in no way prejudice any

[60] 'BBC Audience Research Barometer of Listening, Thursday, Week 11, 17 March 1966'.

[61] On radio networks, audiences, and perceptions of cultural 'brow', especially with regard to works drawing on Greek antiquity, see Wrigley (2009*a*) and (2015).

[62] Ferris (1966).

> future plans for a film, and could even be very useful publicity in bringing the books back into the public eye?[63]

Following some further communication between the two men, another letter from Imison followed in which he expressed a wish to commission 'an original work from Mr Graves for Third Programme . . . One idea in particular occurred to us and that was that radio might prove an ideal medium for a new work about Nero.' Most importantly for the subject of this essay, Imison continues by saying that: 'We were enormously pleased with *The Anger of Achilles* and it was extremely popular with the audience.'[64] This fascinating private correspondence bring us back to the fact that, whatever Graves's standing amongst scholars (past and present) and however many feathers he ruffled with his ideas about and interpretations of the ancient world, his rewritings of Greek and Roman antiquity held enormous popular appeal. Audiences for these works—and, as this essay seeks to assert, these not only included readers and viewers but also hundreds of thousands of *listeners*—may not in the main have been schooled in Classics, but their experience of Greece and Rome was made vivid by Graves, who had a remarkable ability to make ancient stories come alive. As an unidentified reader for the BBC put it to P. H. Newby, when considering the radio potential of Graves's 'The Cultured Romans' scripts: 'The question is, would they entertain?'[65] Entertain they clearly did, but—as, indeed, cultural works in printed and audiovisual media rarely fail to do—they also made a significant contribution to the life of the ancient Mediterranean world in the public imagination.

[63] Letter from Richard Imison to Peter Watt, 12 Aug. 1964 (RG/S2).
[64] Letter from Richard Imison to Peter Watt, 19 Aug. 1964 (RG/S2).
[65] Letter from [M. C. H.?] to Peter Newby, 5 Apr. 1956 (RG/T1).

Bibliography

Archival File References

BBC Written Archives Centre

RG/S1 RCONT1, Robert Graves, Scriptwriter, File I, 1939–1962

RG/S2 RCONT12, Robert Graves, Scriptwriter, File II, 1963–1967

RG/T1 Talks, Robert Graves, file 1, 1941–1962

S452/48/1 Raymond Raikes: *The Anger of Achilles*, 1964

S452/S4/1 Raymond Raikes, Italia Prize 1965

St John's College, Oxford

RGA Robert Graves Archive

Special Collections, University of Victoria, Canada

Graves (1935) Letter to John Buchan, 27 March 1935

RGC Robert Graves Collection: Diary of Robert Graves 1935–39

Websites

American Speech Language Hearing Association <http://www.asha.org/public/speech/disorders/stuttering.htm> (accessed 16/07/2013)

Deadline Hollywood <http://www.deadline.com/2011/06/hbo-bbc2-new-make-deal-to-turn-robert-graves-novel-i-claudius-into-epic-miniseries/#more-138836> (accessed 28/05/2012)

Variety 05/09/2007 <http://www.variety.com/article/VR1117971367?refCatId=13> (accessed 01/06/2012)

Manuscript Sources

BBC Written Archive Centre, Caversham: scripts, letters, and internal memoranda relating to Graves employment by the BBC: *Radio Contributor Files 39–72*

Audio Recordings

British Library Sound Archives. On-line catalogue: *cadensa*

Film and Video Recordings

British Film Institute, London

Published Sources

Abbott, H. P. (2005), 'The Future of All Narrative Futures', in J. Phelan and P. J. Rabinowitz (eds.), *A Companion to Narrative Theory*. Blackwell: Oxford. 529–41.

Ackerman, R. (2002), *The Myth and Ritual School*. Routledge: New York.

Acocella, J. (2009), 'Tudor Tales: Hilary Mantel Reconsiders the Life of Thomas Cromwell', *New Yorker*, 19 Oct. 2009 <http://www.newyorker.com/arts/critics/books/2009/10/19/091019crbo_books_acocella?currentPage=all> (accessed 01/06/2012).

Adam Smith, J. (1985), *John Buchan: A Biography*. Oxford University Press: Oxford.

Adler, M. (1979), *Drawing Down the Moon*. Beacon Press: Boston.

Aillagon, J. J. (2008), *Barbarians and Romans: The Birth of a New World*. Skira Editore: Milan.

Alberti, L. Battista (1991), *On Painting*, ed. Martin Kemp. Penguin Classics: Harmondsworth.

Anderson, W. (1969), 'Patrocleia of Homer: A New Version by Christopher Logue. Review by: Warren Anderson', *Comparative Literature Studies* (Special Issue on the Art of Narrative), 6/3: 337–42.

Anglesey, Marquess of (1994), *A History of the British Cavalry, 1816–1919*, Vol. 5: *Egypt, Palestine and Syria, 1914–1919*. Pen & Sword: Barnsley.

Anon (n.d.), 'Raymond Raikes' <http://web.ukonline.co.uk/suttonelms/raymond-raikes.html> (accessed 15/05/2009).

Anon (1956), 'Poetry as Read by the Poet', *Mitcham & Tooting Advertiser; Wallington & Carshalton Advertiser* 14/06/56.

Anon (1960a), 'Robert Graves, Poetry Reading, read by Robert Graves' *Gramophone*, March 1960.

Anon (1960b), 'Sore Thumbs and Poetry Prizes: Mr Robert Graves at Foyle's', *Guardian*, 4 Mar. 1960: 3.

Aristotle (1987), *The Poetics of Aristotle*, trans. Stephen Halliwell. University of North Carolina Press: Chapel Hill, NC.

Ashe, G. (1947), 'The Novelist as Historian', *Tribune*, 2 May 1947.

Ashe, G. (1995), *Discovering the Goddess: A Personal Testimony*. Crescent Moon: Maidstone.

Auden, W. H. (1962), 'A Poet of Honor', *Shenandoah*, 13: 5–11.

Bachofen, J. J. (1861), *Das Mutterrecht: Eine Untersuchung über die Gynaikokratie der alten Welt nach ihrer religiösen und rechtlichen Natur*. Krais & Hoffmann: Stuttgart.

Badsey, S. (2009), *The British Army in Battle and Its Image 1914–1918*. Continuum: London.

Badsey, S. (2008), *Doctrine and Reform in the British Cavalry, 1880–1918*. Ashgate: Aldershot.

Bagnall, R. S. (1993), *Egypt in Late Antiquity*. Princeton University Press: Princeton.

Bailey, B. (2009), *Cheever: A Life*. Knopf: New York.

Baker, J. H. (1987), *Mary Todd Lincoln: A Biography*. W. W. Norton: New York.

Barker, J. W. (1966), *Justinian and the Later Roman Empire*. University of Wisconsin Press: Madison, Wisc.

Barr, J. (2006), *Setting the Desert on Fire: T. E. Lawrence and Britain's Secret War in Arabia, 1916–1918*. Bloomsbury: London.

Bateson, F. W. (1960), 'See the Great Achilles!', *Observer*, 13 Mar. 1960: 21.

Beard, M. (2006), 'Who Wrote *I, Claudius*', in 'A Don's Life', *TLS* 15 Aug. 2006 <http://timesonline.typepad.com/dons_life/2006/08/who_wrote_i_cla.html> (accessed 21/02/2011).

Beard, M. (2007), 'Why Homer Was (Not) a Woman: The Reception of *The Authoress of the Odyssey*', in J. G. Paradis (ed.), *Samuel Butler, Victorian Against the Grain: A Critical Overview*. University of Toronto Press: Toronto.

Becatti, G. (1960), *La Colonna Coclide Istoriata. Problemi storici, iconografici, stilistici*. 'L'Erma' di Bretschneider: Rome.

Bennett, J. (1999), 'Revising for Reasonableness: Robert Graves as Critic and Poet', in Patrick J. Quinn (ed.), *New Perspectives on Robert Graves*. Associated University Presses: London. 19–35.

Bernoulli, C. A. (1924), *J. J. Bachofen und das Natursymbol*. Schwabe: Basel.

Billigmeier, J.-C. and Turner, J. A. (1981), 'The Socio-economic Roles of Women in Mycenaean Greece: A Brief Survey from Evidence of the Linear B Tablets', in Helene P. Foley (ed.), *Reflections of Women in Antiquity*. Gordon & Breach: New York. 1–18.

Bishop, M. C. and Coulston, J. C. N. (2006), *Roman Military Equipment from the Punic Wars to the Fall of Rome*. 2nd edn. Oxbow: Oxford.

Bivar, A. D. H. (1972), 'Cavalry Tactics and Equipment on the Euphrates', *Dumbarton Oaks Papers*, 26: 273–91.

Bivar, A. D. H. (2004), 'Hephthalites', *Encyclopaedia Iranica*, 12. Mazda: New York. 198–201.

Blundell, S. (1995), *Women in ancient Greece*. British Museum Press: London.

Blunden, E. (1928), *Undertones of War*. Penguin: London.

Bond, B. (2008), *Survivors of a Kind: Memoirs of the Western Front*. Hambledon Continuum: London.

Book Review: 'Dickens Brushed Up', *Time*, 26 Mar. 1934.

Books: 'The Golden Fleece', *Time*, 15 Oct. 1945; <http://www.time.com/time/magazine/article/0,9171,792476,00.html#ixzz1NCGqdn2> (accessed 01/04/2011).

Bourke, J. (1999), *An Intimate History of Killing: Face-to-Face Killing in Twentieth-Century Warfare.* Basic Books: New York.

Bradley, J. (2000), *Flags of Our Fathers.* Bantam: New York.

Bradshaw, G. (1988), *The Bear-Keeper's Daughter.* Methuen: London.

Brearton, F. (2008), 'Heaney and the Feminine', in Bernard O'Donoghue (ed.), *The Cambridge Companion to Seamus Heaney.* Cambridge University Press: Cambridge. 73–91.

Brett, G., Martiny, G., and Stevenson, R. B. K. (1947), (eds.) *The Great Palace of the Byzantine Emperors, Being the First Report of the Excavations Carried Out on Behalf of the Walker Trust (University of St Andrews), 1935–38.* University of Edinburgh Press: Edinburgh.

Bridge, A. (1978), *Theodora: Portrait of a Byzantine Landscape.* Cassell: London.

Briffault, R. (1959), *The Mothers*, abridged, introduction by Gordon Rattray Taylor. Allen & Unwin: London.

Briggs, A. (1985), *The BBC: The First Fifty Years.* Oxford University Press: Oxford.

Brittan, S. (1999), 'Graves and the Mythology of Desire', in Patrick J. Quinn (ed.), *New Perspectives on Robert Graves.* Associated University Presses: London. 84–93.

Brittan-Ortiz, S. (1999), 'Priests and Prejudice: Graves, Apuleius and Translated Muses', *Gravesiana*, 2/2: 130–43.

Brooke, R. (1968), *The Letters of Rupert Brooke*, ed. Geoffrey Keynes. Faber & Faber: London.

Brown, M. and Osgood, R. (2009), *Digging Up Plugstreet: The Archaeology of a Great War Battlefield.* J. H. Haynes & Co.: Yeovil.

Browning, R. (1987), *Justinian and Theodora.* Thames & Hudson: London.

Broyles Jr., W. (1984), 'Why Men Love War', *Esquire* (Nov. 1984): 55–65.

Brubaker, L. (2005), 'Gender and Society', in ed. M. Maas (ed.), *The Cambridge Companion to the Age of Justinian.* Cambridge University Press: Cambridge. 427–47.

Bruce, A. (2002), *The Last Crusade: The Palestine Campaign in the First World War.* Thistle Publishing: London.

Buchan, J. (1937), *Augustus.* Hodder & Stoughton: London.

Buchan, J. (1940), *Memory Hold-the-Door.* Musson Book Co.: Toronto.

Buckman, P. and Fifield, W. (1969), 'Robert Graves, The Art of Poetry No. 11', *Paris Review*, 47; <http://www.theparisreview.org/interviews/4178/the-art-of-poetry-no-11-robert-graves> (accessed 20/05/2012).

Budapest, Z. (1990), *Holy Book of Women's Mysteries* Robert Hale: Tonbridge.

Budapest, Z. (1998), *Summoning the Fates: A Woman's Guide to Destiny.* Harmony Books: New York.

Budapest, Z. (1999), *Das magische Jahr: Mythen, Mondaspekte, Rituale. Ein immerwährender Frauenkalender*. Heyne: Munich.

Burlinghame, M. (1994), *The Inner World of Abraham Lincoln*. University of Illinois Press: Urbana and Chicago.

Burton, P. (1995), 'The Values of a Classical Education: Satirical Elements in the *Claudius* Novels of Robert Graves', *Review of English* Studies, 46/182: 191–218.

Butler, S. (1898), *The* 'Iliad' *of Homer, rendered into English prose for the use of who cannot read the original*. Longmans, Green & Co.: London, New York, and Bombay.

Butler, S. (1913), *The Humour of Homer and Other Essays*, ed. R. A. Streatfeild. A. C. Fifield: London.

Butler, S. (1967), *The Authoress of the Odyssey*, with a new Introduction by David Grene. University of Chicago Press: Chicago.

Calder, R. L. (1972), *W. Somerset Maugham and the Quest for Freedom*. Heinemann: London.

Callow, S. (1987), *Charles Laughton: a Difficult Actor*. Methuen: London.

Cameron, A. (1973), *Porphyrius the Charioteer*. Oxford University Press: Oxford.

Cameron, A. (1976), *Circus Factions: Blues and Greens at Rome and Byzantium*. Oxford University Press: Oxford.

Cameron, A. (1993), *The Mediterranean World in Late Antiquity, AD 395–600*. Routledge: London.

Cameron, A. (1985), *Procopius and the Sixth Century*. Duckworth: London.

Cameron, A., Ward-Perkins, B., and Whitby M. (eds.) (2000), *The Cambridge Ancient History*, Vol. 14: *Late Antiquity: Empire and Successors, AD 425–600*. Cambridge University Press: Cambridge.

Canary, R. H. (1980), *Robert Graves*. Twayne: Boston.

Canepa, M. P. (2009), *The Two Eyes of the World: Art and Ritual of Kingship Between Rome and Sasanian Persia*. University of California Press: Berkeley.

Carne-Ross, D. S. (1962), 'Structural Translation: Notes on Logue's *Patrocleia*', *Arion*, 1/2: 27–38; repr. in K. Haynes (ed.), *Classics and Translation: Essays by D.S. Carne-Ross*. Bucknell University Press: Harrisburg, Pa. 152–64.

Carne-Ross, D. S. (2010), *Classics in Translation: Essays by D. S. Carne-Ross*, ed. Kenneth Haynes. Bucknell University Press: Harrisburg, Pa.

Carpenter, H. (1997), *The Envy of the World: Fifty Years of the BBC Third Programme and Radio Three*. Phoenix: London.

Carpenter, H. (1981), *W. H. Auden: A Life*. George Allen & Unwin: London.

Carson, A. (1998), *Eros the Bittersweet*. Dalkley Archive Press: Champaign, Ill.

Carter, D. N. G. (1989), *Robert Graves: The Lasting Poetic Achievement*. Macmillan: Houndmills.

Carter, J. (1928), 'Lawrence of Arabia As Yet Is Unexplained', *New York Times Book Review*, 8 Apr. 1928.

Carver, Lord (2003), *The National Army Museum Book of the Turkish Front, 1914–1918*. Pan: London.

Carver, R. H. F. (2007), *The Protean Ass: The Metamorphoses of Apuleius from Antiquity to the Renaissance*. Oxford University Press: Oxford.

Carver, R. H. F. (2001), 'Quis Ille? The Role of the Prologue in Apuleius' Nachleben', in A. Kahane and A. Laird (eds.), *A Companion to the Prologue of Apuleius' Metamorphoses*. Oxford University Press: Oxford. 163–74.

Castro, G. (1990), *American Feminism: A Contemporary History*. New York University Press: New York.

Cavafy, C. P. (2007), *The Canon*, trans. Stratis Haviaras. Center for Hellenic Studies, Harvard University: Cambridge, Mass.

Christ, C. P. (1979), 'Why Women Need the Goddess', in C. P. Christ and J. Plaskow (eds.), *Womanspirit Rising: A Feminist Reader on Religion*. Harper & Row: San Francisico: 273–87.

Christensen, P. G. (2014), '*Count Belisarius* and Procopius's Wars', *Gravesiana*, 4/1; <http://robertgraves.org/gravesiana>.

Christie, N. J. (2006), *From Constantine to Charlemagne: An Archaeology of Italy, AD 300–800*. Ashgate: Aldershot.

Clark, A. (1961), *The Donkeys*. Hutchison: London.

Claus, H. (1997), 'Whose Film Is It? Alexander Korda's Adaptation of Carl Zuckmayer's Film Script Rembrandt', in Jeff Morrison and Florian Krobb (eds.), *Text into Image: Image into Text*. Rodopi: Amsterdam. 267–75.

Cleveland Wilson, P. (1960), 'Immitis Achilles', *Classical World*, 53/5: 157–62.

Cohen, J. M. (1960), *Robert Graves*. Oliver & Boyd: Edinburgh and London.

Collins, D. (2008), *Magic in the Ancient Greek and Roman World*. Blackwell: Oxford.

Cordell, R. A. (1961), *Somerset Maugham, a Biographical and Critical Study*. Heinemann: London.

Cordell, R. A. (1969), *Somerset Maugham, a writer for all seasons: a biographical and critical study*, 2nd edn. Indiana University Press: Bloomington, Ill.

Cormack, R. and Vassilaki, M. (eds.) (2008), *Byzantium 330–1453*. Royal Academy of Arts: London.

Corrigan, G. (2003), *Mud, Blood and Poppycock: Britain and the First World War*. Cassell: London.

Coulston, J. (2006), 'Introduction', in Lord Mahon, *The Life of Belisarius: The Last Great General of Rome*. Westholme: Yardley. pp. vii–xx.

Coulston, J. C. (1985), 'Roman Archery Equipment', in M. C. Bishop (ed.), *The Production and Distribution of Roman Military Equipment*.

Proceedings of the Second Roman Military Equipment Seminar. BAR International Series 275. British Archaeological Reports: Oxford. 220–366.

Coulston, J. C. (1986), 'Roman, Parthian and Sassanid Tactical Developments', in P. Freeman and D. Kennedy (eds.), *The Defence of the Roman and Byzantine East*. BAR International Series 297. British Archaeological Reports: Oxford. 59–75.

Coulston, J. C. N. (1991), 'The '*draco*' Standard', *Journal of Roman Military Equipment Studies*, 2: 101–14.

Cronin, M. (1996), *Translating Ireland: Translation, Languages, Cultures*. Cork University Press: Cork.

Culham, P. (1987), 'Ten Years after Pomeroy: Studies of the Image and Reality of Women in Antiquity', in Marilyn Skinner (ed.), *Rescuing Creusa: New Methodological Approaches to Women in Antiquity*, special issue of *Helios*, NS 13.2. Texas Tech. University Press: Lubbock, Tex. 9–30.

Curtis, A. (1974), *The Pattern of Maugham: A Critical Portrait*. Hamish Hamilton: London.

Daim, F. (2003), 'Avars and Avar Archaeology: An Introduction', in H. W. Goetz, J. Jarnut, and W. Pohl (eds.), *Regna and Gentes: The Relationship Between Late Antique and Early Medieval Peoples and Kingdoms in the Transformation of the Roman World*. Brill: Leiden. 463–570.

David, D. (1959), 'The Toneless Voice of Robert Graves', *Listener*, 62: 11–13.

Davie, D. (1952), *Purity of Diction in English Verse*. Chatto & Windus: London.

Davis, P. G. (1998), *Goddess Unmasked: The Rise of Neopagan Feminist Spirituality*. Spence Pub.: Dallas, Tex.

Davis, R. (1999), 'The Pastoral Vision of Robert Graves', in Patrick J. Quinn (ed.), *New Perspectives on Robert Graves*. Associated University Presses: London. 209–19.

Dawes, J. (2002), *The Language of War: Literature and Culture in the U.S. from the Civil War Through World War II*. Harvard University Press: Cambridge, Mass.

Day, D. (1963), *Swifter than Reason: The Poetry and Criticism of Robert Graves*. University of North Carolina Press: Chapel Hill, NC.

De Groot, J. (2010), *The Historical Novel*. Routledge: Abingdon.

DeFilippo, J. G. (1992), Review of *Apuleius: Metamorphoses*, trans. J. Arthur Hanson, *American Journal of Philology*, 113/2: 300–3.

Denman, M. C. (2003), 'Nostalgia for a Better Germany: Carl Zuckmayer's Des Teufels General', *German Quarterly*, 76/4: 369–80.

Derrida, J. (1995), *On the Name*, ed. Thomas Dutoit, trans. David Wood, John P. Leavey, Jr, and Ian McLeod. Stanford University Press: Stanford.

Desfossés, Y., Jacques, A. and Prilaux, G. (2008), *L'Archéologie de la Grande Guerre*. Ouest-France: Rennes.

Dewing, H. B. (1914), *Procopius, with an English Translation by H.B. Dewing*, 7 vols. Heinemann: London.

Dignas, B. and Winter, E. (2007), *Rome and Persia in Late Antiquity: Neighbours and Rivals*. Cambridge University Press: Cambridge.

Dimock, George E. (1960), 'The *Iliad* Rescued: or a Mustache for Mona Lisa', *Hudson Review*, 13/2: 293–7.

Dodge, H. (2011), *Spectacle in the Roman World*. Bristol Classical Press: Bristol.

Donald, D. H. (1995), *Lincoln*. Pimlico: London.

Duckworth, A. M. (2004), 'Two Borrowings in Pat Barker's "Regeneration"', *Journal of Modern Literature*. Writing Life/Writing Fiction (Winter), 27/3: 63–7.

Duffy, S. (2010), *Theodora: Actress, Empress, Whore*. Virago: London.

Du Pont, O. (2005), 'Robert Graves's Claudian Novels: A Case of Pseudo-translation', *Target*, 17/2: 327–47.

Dylan, B. (2004), *Chronicles: Volume 1*. Simon & Schuster, New York.

Edward VIII (1999), 'God Save the King', in Brian MacArthur (ed.), *The Penguin Book of Twentieth Century Speeches*, 2nd edn. Penguin: London. 158–9.

Edwards, C. (1997), 'Unspeakable Professions: Public Performance and Prostitution in Ancient Rome', in J. P. Hallett and M. B. Skinner (eds.), *Roman Sexualities*. Princeton University Press: Princeton. 66–95.

Ehrhart, W. D. (1994), 'I Could Not Help My Friend', *Virginia Quarterly Review*, 70: 773–84.

Eliot, T. S. (1954), *Selected Poems*. Faber & Faber: London.

Eller, C. (2000), *The Myth of Matriarchal Prehistory: Why an Invented Past Won't Give Women a Future*. Beacon Press: Boston.

Empson, W. (1988), *Argufying: Essays on Literature and Culture*, ed. J. Haffenden. Hogarth Press: London.

Empson, W. (2006), *Selected Letters*, ed. J. Haffenden. Oxford University Press: Oxford.

Evans, J. A. S. (1996), *The Age of Justinian: The Circumstances of Imperial Power*. Routledge: Abingdon.

Evans, J. A. (2002), *The Empress Theodora, Partner of Justinian*. University of Texas Press: Austin, Tex.

Farber, M. (2009), *Farber on Film: The Complete Film Writings of Manny Farber*, ed. R. Polito. Library of America: New York.

Fauber, L. (1990), *Narses: Hammer of the Goths*. Sutton: Gloucester.

Fehrle, E. (1927/1992), 'Johann Jacob Bachofen und das Mutterrecht', *Neue Heidelberger Jahrbücher*, NF 101–18; repr. in Beate Wagner-Hasel (ed.), *Matriarchatstheorien der Altertumswissenschaft*, Wege der Forschung 651. Wissenschaftliche Buchgesellschaft: Darmstadt. 43–62.

Ferguson, N. (1998), *The Pity of War*. Allen Lane: London.

Ferris, P. (1966), 'Prerecording Pitfalls Exposed', *Observer*, 20 Mar. 1966: 24.

Firla, I. (ed.) (2000), *Robert Graves's Historical Novels*. Peter Lang: Frankfurt a.M. and New York.

Firla, I. and Lindop, G. (eds.) (2003), *Graves and the Goddess: Essays on Robert Graves's The White Goddess*. Susquehanna University Press: Selsingrove, Pa.

Fitts, D. (1959), 'Homer's *Iliad*, Retold in English', *New York Times*, 8 Nov. 1959.

Fitzgerald, F. Scott (1920), *This Side of Paradise*; <http://www.gutenberg.org/files/805/805-h/805-h.htm#link2HCH0005> (accessed005/01/2014).

Fleishman, A. (1971), *The English Historical Novel: Walter Scott to Virginia Woolf*. The John Hopkins Press: Baltimore and London.

Folkart, B. (1998), 'Inventing the Past: Remarks on the Re-enactment of Medieval Poetry', *TTR: traduction, terminologie, redaction*, 11/1: 11–32.

Folkart, B. (2007), *Second Finding: A Poetics of Translation*. University of Ottawa Press: Ottawa.

Ford, R. (2009), *Eden to Armageddon: World War I in the Middle East*. Weidenfeld & Nicolson: London.

Fornara, C. (1983), *The Nature of History in Ancient Greece and Rome*. University of California Press: Berkeley.

Foster, W. (1972), 'Robert Graves Talks to William Foster', *Scotsman*, 12 Aug. 1972.

Frayling, C. (1992), *The Face of Tutankhamun*. Faber & Faber: London.

Frazer, G. (1890), *The Golden Bough*. Macmillan: London.

Frazer, G. (1910), *Totemism and Exogamy: A Treatise on Certain Early Forms of Superstition and Society*, Vol. 3. Macmillan: London.

Frazer, G. (1927), *Man, God and Immortality*, rev. edn. Macmillan: London.

Frazer, G. (1994), *The Collected Works of J. G. Frazer*, 28 vols. Curzon Press: London.

Freud, S. (1915), 'Thoughts for the Times on War and Death: I. The Disillusionment of the War', in E. Jones (ed.), *Sigmund Freud. Collected Papers*. Basic Books: New York. 4. 288–304.

Fukai, S. and Horiuchi, K. (1972), *Taq-i-Bustan*, II. The Tokyo University Iraq–Iran Archaeological Expedition, Report: Tokyo.

Furbank, P. N. (2004), 'On the Historical Novel', *Raritan: A Quarterly Review*, 23/3 94–114.

Fussell, P. (1975), *The Great War and Modern Memory*. Oxford University Press: New York.

Fussell, P. (1989), *Wartime: Understanding and Behavior in the Second World War*. Oxford University Press: New York.

Fussell, P. (2000), *The Great War and Modern Memory*, 2nd edn. Oxford University Press: Oxford.

Fussell, P. (2003), *The Boys' Crusade*. Modern Library: New York.

Gager, J. G. (1999), *Curse Tablets and Binding Spells from the Ancient World.* Oxford University Press: Oxford.

Gaisser, J. H. (2008), *The Fortunes of Apuleius and The Golden Ass: A Study in Transmission and Reception.* Princeton University Press: Princeton.

Garnett, D. (ed.) (1939), *The Letters of T. E. Lawrence.* Doubleday, Doran, & Co.: New York.

Genette, G. (1997), *Paratexts: Thresholds of Interpretation*, trans. J. E. Lewin. Cambridge University Press: Cambridge.

Gibbon, E. (1987), *The History of the Decline and Fall of the Roman Empire*, Vol. 5: *Justinian and the Roman Law.* Folio Society: London.

Gielgud, V. (1957), *British Radio Drama 1922–1956.* Harrap: London.

Goldman, S. (2003), 'White Goddess, Hebrew Goddess: The Bible, the Jews, and Poetic Myth in the Work of Robert Graves', *Modern Judaism*, 23: 32–50.

Göttner-Abendroth, H. (1980), *Die Göttin und ihr Heros—A Study in Matriarchal Religion.* Verlag Frauenoffensive: Munich.

Göttner-Abendroth, H. (1988), *Das Matriarchat* (vol. I), *History of Research on Matriarchy.* Verlag Kohlhammer: Stuttgart.

Göttner-Abendroth, H. (1991a), *The Dancing Goddess: Principles of a Matriarchal Aesthetic.* Beacon Press, Boston.

Göttner-Abendroth, H. (1991b), *Das Matriarchat* (vol. II.1), *Contemporary Matriarchal Societies in East Asia, Indonesia, Pacific Region.* Verlag Kohlhammer: Stuttgart.

Göttner-Abendroth, H. (1995), *The Goddess and her Heros: Matriarchal Religion in Mythology, Fairy-Tales and Poetry.* Anthony Publishing Company: Stow, Mass.

Göttner-Abendroth, H. (2000), *Das Matriarchat* (vol. II.2), *Contemporary Matriarchal Societies in America, India, Africa.* Verlag Kohlhammer: Stuttgart.

Göttner-Abendroth, H. (2001), *Die tanzende Göttin.* Verlag Frauenoffensive: Munich.

Gould Davis, E. (1971), *The First Sex.* G. P. Putnam's Sons: New York.

Grafton, A. (1997), *The Footnote: A Curious History.* Faber & Faber: London.

Grainger, J. D. (2006), *The Battle for Palestine, 1917.* Boydell Press: Woodbridge.

Grant, M. (1987), 'Translating Latin Prose', in W. Radice and B. Reynolds (eds.), *The Translator's Art: Essays in Honour of Betty Radice.* Penguin: Harmondsworth. 81–91.

Grant, M. (1990), 'Introduction', in Robert Graves, *The Transformations of Lucius, Otherwise Known as The Golden Ass*, rev. edn. Penguin: London.

Graves, R. (1925), *The Meaning of Dreams.* Greenberg: New York.

Graves, R. (1927), *Lawrence and the Arabs.* Jonathan Cape: London.

Graves, R. (1929), *Goodbye to All That: An Autobiography.* Cape: London.

Graves, R. (1930), *But it Still Goes On: An Accumulation*. Jonathan Cape: London.

Graves, R. (1934a), *I, Claudius*. Arthur Barker: London/Modern Library: New York.

Graves, R. (1934b), *Claudius the God*. Arthur Barker: London.

Graves, R. (1936a), *Io, Claudio*. Valentino Bompiani: Milan.

Graves, R. (1936b), *Il divo Claudio*. Valentino Bompiani: Milan.

Graves, R. (1938), *Count Belisarius*. Cassell: London.

Graves, R. (1940), *Sergeant Lamb of the Ninth*. Methuen: London.

Graves, R. (1946), *Collected Poems 1938–1945*. American Book—Stratford Press, Inc.: New York.

Graves, R. (1948), *The White Goddess: A Historical Grammar of Poetic Myth*. Creative Age Press: New York.

Graves, R. (1949), *The Common Asphodel: Collected Essays on Poetry, 1922–1949*. Hamish Hamilton: London.

Graves, R. (1950a), *Apuleius. The Golden Ass*. Penguin: Harmondsworth.

Graves, R. (1950b), 'Letter to the Editor', *TLS* 30 June 1950: 405.

Graves, R. (1951a), *The Transformations of Lucius, Otherwise Known as The Golden Ass*. Farrar, Straus & Young: New York.

Graves, R. (1951b), *Occupation: Writer*. Cassell: London.

Graves, R. (1955a), *The Greek Myths*. Penguin: Baltimore.

Graves, R. (1955b), *Homer's Daughter*. Cassell: London/Pyramid Books: New York.; repr. ed. N. Powell (1995), Carcanet: Manchester.

Graves, R. (1955c), 'A Poet and his Public. A Home Service Broadcast', in *The Crowning Privilege*. Cassell: London.

Graves, R. (1956), *Lucan. Pharsalia*. Penguin: Harmondsworth.

Graves, R. (1957a), *Good-bye to All That*. 2nd edn. Doubleday: New York.

Graves, R. (1957b), *Suetonius. The Twelve Caesars*. Penguin: Harmondsworth.

Graves, R. (1959a), *The Anger of Achilles: Homer's Iliad, Translated by Robert Graves, Illustrations by Ronald Searle*. 1st edn. Doubleday: New York.

Graves, R. (1959b), *The Crowning Privilege: Collected Essays on Poetry*. Penguin: Harmondsworth.

Graves, R. (1960a), *The Anger of Achilles*. Cassell: London (reprint ed. N. Powell (1995). Manchester: Carcanet).

Graves, R. (1960b), *Goodbye to All That*, rev. edn. Penguin: Harmondsworth.

Graves, R. (1960c), *The Greek Myths* (Pelican, rev. edn.). Penguin: Harmondsworth.

Graves, R. (1960d), 'The Case for Xanthippe', *Kenyon Review*, 22/4: 597–605.

Graves, R. (1961a), *The White Goddess: A Historical Grammar of Poetical Myth*. Faber & Faber: London.

Graves, R. (1961b), *The Anger of Achilles: Homer's Iliad*. Readers Union: London.

Graves, R. (1962), *The Anger of Achilles: Homer's Iliad.* New English Library: London.

Graves, R. (1963), 'T. E. Lawrence and the Riddle of "S.A."', *Saturday Review*, 15 June 1963.

Graves, R. (1965), 'Moral Principles in Translation', in *Mammon and the Black Goddess* (1st edn. 1962). Cassell: London. 115–39.

Graves, R. (1966), *The Anger of Achilles (Homer's Iliad), Translated by Robert Graves.* Pyramid Books: New York.

Graves, R. (1968), *Antigua, Penny, Puce.* Penguin: Harmondsworth.

Graves, R. (1969), *The Crane Bag and Other Disputed Subjects.* Cassell: London.

Graves, R. (1972), *Difficult Questions, Easy Answers.* Cassell: London.

Graves, R. (1975), *Collected Poems 1975.* Cassell: London.

Graves, R. (1983), *Count Belisarius.* Penguin: Harmondsworth.

Graves, R. (1988), *Collected War Poems.* Cassell: London.

Graves, R. (1991), *Lawrence and the Arabs.* Paragon House: New York.

Graves, R. (1995), *Collected Writings on Poetry*, ed. Paul O'Prey. Carcanet: Manchester.

Graves, R. (1998), *I, Claudius* and *Claudius the God*, ed. Richard Francis. Carcanet: Manchester.

Graves, R. (1999a), *Collected Poems*, 3 vols., ed. B. Graves and D. Ward (vol. 1); ed. Patrick Quinn (vols. 2 and 3). Carcanet: Manchester.

Graves, R. (1999b), *The White Goddess: A Historical Grammar of Poetic Myth*, ed. Grevel Lindop. Faber & Faber: London.

Graves, R. (2000a), *Complete Poems in One Volume*, ed. Patrick Quinn. Carcanet: Manchester.

Graves, R. (2000b), *Goodbye to All That*, rev. edn. Penguin: London.

Graves, R. (2000c), 'Introduction to the *Lives of the Roman Emperors*', in P. Quinn (ed.), *Robert Graves: Some Speculations on Literature, History and Religion.* Carcanet: Manchester. 135–41.

Graves, R. (2000d), *Some Speculations on Literature, History and Religion*, ed. P. Quinn. Carcanet: Manchester.

Graves, R. (2001), *Homer's Daughter; and The Anger of Achilles*, ed. Neil Powell. Carcanet: Manchester.

Graves, R. (2003), *The Complete Poems.* Penguin: London.

Graves, R. (2006a), *Count Belisarius.* Penguin: London.

Graves, R. (2006b), *I, Claudius.* Penguin: London.

Graves, R. (2006c), *Claudius the God.* Penguin: London.

Graves, R. (2007), *Good-bye to All That and Other Great War Writings*, ed. S. Trout. Carcanet: Manchester.

Graves, R. (2009), *The Anger of Achilles.* Penguin: London.

Graves, R. (2011a), *The Greek Myths: The Complete and Definitive Edition*. Penguin: London.

Graves, R. (2011b), *The Golden Fleece*. Penguin: London.

Graves, R. and Riding, L. (1927), *A Survey of Modernist Poetry*. Heinemann: London.

Graves, R. and Riding, L. (eds.) (1937), *Epilogue: A Critical Summary*, Vol III. The Seizin Press: Deyá.

Graves, R. and Hodge, A. (1940), *The Long Weekend: A Social History of Britain 1918–1939*. Faber & Faber: London.

Graves, R. and Hodge, A. (1943), *The Reader Over Your Shoulder: A Handbook for Writers of English Prose*. Jonathan Cape: London.

Graves, R. and Liddell Hart, B. H. (1963), *T.E. Lawrence to His Biographers*. Doubleday: Garden City, NY.

Graves, R. P. (1986), *Robert Graves: The Assault Heroic, 1895–1926*. Weidenfeld & Nicolson: London.

Graves, R. P. (1990), *Robert Graves: The Years with Laura, 1926–40*. Weidenfeld & Nicolson: London/Viking Penguin: New York.

Graves, R. P. (1995), *Robert Graves and the White Goddess, 1940–85*. Weidenfeld & Nicolson: London.

Graves, R. P. (2003), 'Robert Graves and the White Goddess: An Introduction', in Ian Firla and Grevel Lindop (eds.), *Graves and the Goddess: Essays on Robert Graves's 'The White Goddess'*. Associated University Presses: London. 13–24.

Graves, R. P. (2004), 'Robert Graves', in H. C. G. Matthew and B. Harrison (eds.), *The Oxford Dictionary of National Biography*, Vol. 23. Oxford University Press: Oxford.

Graves, W. (2001), *Wild Olives: Life in Majorca with Robert Graves*. Pimlico: London.

Greatrex, G. and Lieu, S. N. C. (2002), *The Roman Eastern Frontier and the Persian Wars*, Vol. 2: *AD 363–630, A Narrative Sourcebook*. Routledge: London.

Green, P. (1960), 'The Face of Agamemnon', *TLS* 17 June 1960: 384.

Green, P. (1961/2), 'Robert Graves as Historical Novelist', *Critic*, 20: 46–50.

Green, P. (1983), 'All That Again (Robert Graves)', *Grand Street*, 2/2: 89–119.

Green, P. (1999), 'War and Morality in Fifth-Century Athens: The Case of Euripides' *Trojan Women*', *Ancient History Bulletin*, 13/3: 97–110.

Greenspun, R. (1965), 'The Epic That Never Was: "I, Claudius" Recalled', *New York Times* <http://movies.nytimes.com/movie/review?res=9A03E5DB1F3AEE34BC4851DFBF668382679EDE> (accessed 29/05/2012).

Greenwood, E. (2009), 'Sounding Out Homer: Christopher Logue's Acoustic Homer', *Oral Tradition*, 24/2: 503–18.

Greenwood, E. (2006), *Thucydides and the Shaping of History*. Duckworth: London.

Gregory, H. (1961), 'Faithful to a Goddess and a Queen', *New York Times Book Review*, 16 July 1961.

Griffin, J. (1992), 'Virgil', in Richard Jenkyns (ed.), *The Legacy of Rome: A New Appraisal*. Oxford University Press: Oxford. 125–50.

Gross, A. (ed.) (1938), *A to Z Atlas and Guide to London and Suburbs*. Geographers Map Co.: London; reprint edn. 2008.

Haldon, J. (2000), *The Byzantine Wars: Battles and Campaigns of the Byzantine Era*. History Press: Stroud.

Halsall, G. (2003), *Warfare and Society in the Barbarian West, 450–900*. Routledge: London.

Handford, S. A. (1951), *Caesar: The Conquest of Gaul*. Penguin: Harmondsworth.

H[arding], D. W. (1935), Review of Robert Graves, *Claudius the God*, *Scrutiny*, 3/4: 421–2.

Harding, E. (1972), 'Lonely Hero Treads Uncertain Road to Power', *Yorkshire Evening Post*, 15 July 1972.

Hardwick, L. (2003), *Reception Studies*, no. 33, *Greece & Rome New Surveys in the Classics* series. Oxford University Press: Oxford.

Hare, S. (1995), *Penguin Portrait: Allen Lane and the Penguin Editors, 1935–1970*. Penguin: Harmondsworth.

Harrison, J. E. (1907), *Prolegomena to the Study of Greek Religion*. Cambridge University Press: Cambridge.

Harrison, S. J. (1990), 'The Speaking Book: The Prologue to Apuleius' *Metamorphoses*', *Classical Quarterly*, NS 40: 507–13.

Hart, P. (2008), *1918: A Very British Victory*. Weidenfeld & Nicolson: London.

Hartnoll, P. and Found, P. (eds.) (1996), *The Concise Oxford Companion to Theatre*, 2nd edn. Oxford University Press: Oxford.

Haslett, M. and Haslett, I. (2009), 'Buchan and the Classics', in K. Macdonald (ed.), *Reassessing John Buchan: Beyond The Thirty-Nine Steps*. Pickering & Chatto: London. 17–27.

Hastings, S. (2009), *The Secret Lives of Somerset Maugham*. John Murray: London.

Heintz, F. (1998), 'Circus Curses and their Archaeological Contexts', *Journal of Roman Arachaeology*, 11: 337–42.

Henderson, J. (1998), *Fighting for Rome: Poets and Caesars, History and Civil War*. Cambridge University Press: Cambridge.

Hendrickson, G. L. (1915), 'A Witticism of Asinius Pollio', *American Journal of Philology*, 36/1: 70–5.

Herbert, K. (1956), Review of Graves, *The Greek Myths*, *Classical Journal*, 51/4: 191–2.

Herr, M. (1977), *Dispatches*. Knopf: New York.

Hesling, W. (2007), 'Artist Legends and the Historical Film: Alexander Korda's *Rembrandt* (1936)', in Leen Engelen and Roel Vande Winkel (eds.), *Perspectives on European Film and History*. Academia Press: Gent. 76–109.

Hirvonen, K. (1968/1992), 'Matriarchal Survivals in Homer', Suomaleinen Tiedeakatemia, *Annales Academiae Scientiarum Fennicae* Se. B tom 151. Helsinki, 8–19, 34–6, 44–6, 50–4; repr. in Beate Wagner-Hasel(ed.), *Matriarchatstheorien der Altertumswissenschaft*, Wege der Forschung 651. Wissenschaftliche Buchgesellschaft: Darmstadt. 149–67.

Hobson, H. (1965), 'The Epic That Never Was', *Christian Science Monitor*, 27 Dec. 1965.

Hobson, H. (1972), 'Great Romantic', *Sunday Times*, 16 July 1972.

Hoffman, D. (1967), *Barbarous Knowledge: Myth in the Poetry of Yeats, Graves and Muir*. Oxford University Press: New York.

Hölkeskamp, K.-J. (2001), 'Marathon. Vom Monument zum Mythos', in D. Papenfuß and V. M. Strocka (eds.), *Gab es das griechische Wunder? Griechenland zwischen dem Ende des 6. und der Mitte des 5. Jahrhunderts v. Chr.* Von Zabern: Mainz. 329–53.

Hopkins, C. (1999), 'Robert Graves and the Historical Novel in the 1930s', in P. J. Quinn (ed.), *New Perspectives on Robert Graves*. Susquehanna University Press: Selingsgrove, Pa. 128–35.

Howald, E. (1926), *Der Kampfum Creuzers Symbolik: Eine Auswahl von Dokumenten*. Mohr: Tübingen.

Hoyland, J. O. (2011), 'Contesting Marathon: Billows, Krentz, and the Persian Problem', *Classical Philology*, 106/3: 265–77.

Hughes, I. (2009), *Belisarius: The Last Roman General*. Pen & Sword: Barnsley.

Hynes, S. (1997), *The Soldiers' Tale: Bearing Witness to a Modern War*. Penguin: New York.

Jacobsen, T. C. (2009), *The Gothic War: Rome's Final Conflict in the West*. Westholme: Yardley.

James, L. (1995), *The Golden Warrior: The Life and Legend of Lawrence of Arabia*. Abacus: London.

Janowitz, N. (2001), *Magic in the Roman World: Pagans, Jews and Christians*. Routledge: London.

Jarrell, R. (1969), *Third Book of Criticism*. Farrar, Straus & Giroux: New York.

Jennings, E. (1960), 'Poetry on Record', *Guardian*, 9 June 1960.

Johns, C. (1982), *Sex or Symbol? Erotic Images of Greece and Rome*. BCA c/o British Museum Press: London.

Johnson, S. (2000), *Samuel Johnson: The Major Works*, ed. D. J. Greene. Oxford University Press: Oxford.

Jones, A. H. M. (1964), *The Later Roman Empire, 284–602: A Social, Economic and Administrative Survey*. Blackwell: Oxford.

Joshel, S. R. (2001), '*I, Claudius*: Projection and Imperial Soap Opera', in S. Joshel, M. Malamud, and D. T. Maguire, (eds.), *Imperial Projections: Ancient Rome in Modern Popular Culture*. The Johns Hopkins University Press: Baltimore. 119–61.

Joshua, E. (2001), *Pygmalion and Galatea: The History of a Narrative in English Literature*. Ashgate: Aldershot.

Kahane, A. and Laird, A. (2001), *A Companion to the Prologue of Apuleius' Metamorphoses*. Oxford University Press: Oxford.

Kaldellis, A. (2004), *Procopius of Caesarea: Tyranny, History and Philosophy at the End of Antiquity*. University of Pennsylvania Press: Philadelphia.

Kaplan, C. M. (1995), 'Conquest as Literature, Literature as Conquest: T. E. Lawrence's Artistic Campaign in *Seven Pillars of Wisdom*', *Texas Studies in Literature and Language*, 37/1: 72–97.

Katovsky, B. and Carlson, T. (2004), *Embedded*. Lyons Press: Guilford, Conn.

Kawin, B. F. (1977), *Faulkner and Film*. Fredric Ungar: New York.

Kenner, H. (1956), 'Homer's Sticks and Stones', *James Joyce Quarterly*, 6: 285–98.

Kenyon, D. (2011), *Horsemen in No Man's Land. British Cavalry and Trench Warfare, 1914–1918*. Pen & Sword: Barnsley.

Kerényi, K. (1956), '*The Greek myths 2bde*. by Robert Graves. Review by: Karl Kerényi', *Gnomon*, 28/7: 553–5.

Kersnowski, F. L. (1989), *Conversations with Robert Graves*. University Press of Mississippi: Jackson, Miss.

Kersnowski, F. L. (2002), *The Early Poetry of Robert Graves: The Goddess Beckons*. University of Texas Press: Austin, Tex.

King, B. (2009), *Robert Graves: A Biography*. Haus Publishing: London.

Knox, B. (1990), Introduction to Robert Fagles (trans.), *Homer. The Iliad*. Penguin: New York. 3–67.

Koelb, C. (2000), 'The Medium of History: Robert Graves and the Ancient Past', in J. L. Halio and B. Siegel (eds.), *Comparative Literary Dimensions: Essays in Honor of Melvin J. Friedman*. University of Delaware Press: Newark, Del. 31–47.

Korda, M. (2010), *Hero: The Life and Legend of Lawrence of Arabia*. Harper: New York.

Korda, M. (2011), *Hero: The Life and Legend of Lawrence of Arabia*. Aurum: London.

Kossman, N. (2001), *Gods and Mortals: Modern Poems on Classical Myths*. Oxford University Press: Oxford.

Kovic, R. (1976), *Born on the Fourth of July*. McGraw Hill: New York.

Krabbe, J. K. (1989), *The Metamorphoses of Apuleius*. P. Lang: New York.

Kronick, J. G. (1999), *Derrida and the Future of Literature*. State University of New York Press: Albany, NY.

Lanchester, E. (1938), *Charles Laughton & I*. Faber & Faber: London.

Lanwerd, S. (1992), *Mythos, Mutterrecht und Magie*. Dissertation, Berlin.

Latte, Kurt (1940), 'Livy's *Patavinitas*', *Classical Philology*, 35/1: 56–60.

Laubscher, H. P. (1975), *Die Reliefschmuck des Galeriusbogens in Thessaloniki*. Mann: Berlin.

Lawrence, A. W. (ed.) (1937), *T.E. Lawrence, by His Friends*. Doubleday, Doran & Co.: Garden City, NY.

Lawrence, T. E. (1926), *The Seven Pillars of Wisdom. A Triumph*. Doubleday, Doran & Co.: London.

Lawrence, T. E. (1935), *The Seven Pillars of Wisdom*. Doubleday, Doran & Co.: Garden City, NY.

Lee, A. D. (2005), 'The Empire at War', in M. Maas (ed.), *The Cambridge Companion to the Age of Justinian*. Cambridge University Press: Cambridge. 113–33.

Lendvai, P. (2002), *The Hungarians*, trans. Ann Major. Hurst & Co.: London.

Leonard, J. (2001), 'The Construction of Authenticity in the Claudius Novels', *Gravesiana*, 2/3–4: 259–72.

Liddell, R. (1994), *Cavafy: A Critical Biography*. Duckworth: London.

Liddell Hart, B. H. (1934), *'T. E. Lawrence' in Arabia and After*. Jonathan Cape: London.

Lincoln, B. (1999), *Theorizing Myth: Narrative, Ideology and Scholarship*. University of Chicago Press: Chicago.

Lindop, G. (2003), 'The White Goddess: Sources, Contexts, Meanings', in Ian Firla and Grevel Lindop (eds.), *Graves and the Goddess*. Associated University Presses: London. 25–39.

Ling, R. (2011), 'Faber and Irish Literature', in C. Hutton and P. Walsh (eds.), *The Oxford History of the Irish Book*, Vol. 5: *The Irish Book in English 1891–2000*. Oxford University Press: Oxford. 562–75.

Liveley, G. (2005), *Ovid: Love Songs*. Duckworth: London.

Lloyd-Jones, H. (1982), *Blood for the Ghosts: Classical Influences in the Classics in the Nineteenth and Twentieth Centuries*. Duckworth: London.

Lloyd-Jones, H. (1991), *Greek in a Cold Climate*. Duckworth: London.

Logue, C. (1962), *Patrocleia*: Book 16 of Homer's *Iliad* freely adapted into English by Christopher Logue. Scorpion Press: Lowestoft.

Louis, M. K. (2009), *Persephone Rises, 1860–1927*. Ashgate: Farnham.

Lowe, N. (2005), 'Killing the Graves Myth: A Creative Retelling of the Greek Myth Cycle', *TLS* 23 Dec. 2005.

Lowell, R. (2005), *Letters*, ed. S. Hamilton. Faber & Faber: London.

Lownie, A. (1995), *John Buchan: The Presbyterian Cavalier*. McArthur & Co.: Toronto.

Lucas, F. L. (1950), 'The Golden Ass', *Times Literary Supplement*, 2 June 1950: 336.

Maas, M. (ed.) (2005), *The Cambridge Companion to the Age of Justinian*. Cambridge University Press: Cambridge.

MacCormack, S. G. (1981), *Art and Ceremony in Late Antiquity*. University of California Press: Berkeley.

MacDonald, D. B. (1928), 'The Legendary Lawrence', *Yale Review*, NS 18 (Sept. 1928): 176–7.

MacNeice, L. (1946), *The Dark Tower*. Faber & Faber: London.

MacNeice, L. (1960), 'On First Looking into Graves's Homer', *Guardian*, 11 Mar. 1960: 7.

Madigan, E. (2011), *Faith Under Fire: Anglican Army Chaplains and the Great War*. Palgrave Macmillan: Basingstoke.

Mahon, Lord (1829), *The Life of Belisarius*, 1st edn. John Murray: London.

Mahon, Lord (1848), *The Life of Belisarius*, 2nd edn. John Murray: London.

Mahon, Lord (2006), *The Life of Belisarius: The Last Great General of Rome*, Introduction by Jon Coulston. Westholme: Yardley, Pa.

Malamud, M. (2009), 'Tacitus and the Twentieth-century Novel', in A. J. Woodman (ed.), *The Cambridge Companion to Tacitus*. Cambridge University Press: Cambridge.

Mango, C. (1981), 'Daily Life in Byzantium', *Jahrbuch der Österreichischen Byzantinistik*, 31/1: 337–53.

Marincola, J. (1997), *Authority and Tradition in Ancient Historiography*. Cambridge University Press: Cambridge.

Marler, J. (2006), 'The Myth of Universal Patriarchy: A Critical Response to Cynthia Eller's Myth of Matriarchal Prehistory', *Feminist Theology*, 14/2: 163–87.

Marmontel, J. F. (1767), *Bélisaire*. Merlin: Paris.

McCarthy, C. (1985), *Blood Meridian, or, The Evening Redness in the West*. Random House: New York.

McFee, W. (1928), 'A Poor Second: Lawrence and the Arabian Adventure', *New York Herald Tribune*, 24 June 1928: 7.

McGuinness, P. (1999), 'Robert Graves, Modernism, and the "Poetic Body"', in P. J. Quinn (ed.), *New Perspectives on Robert Graves*. Associated University Presses: London. 46–61.

McNamara, M. (2012), 'Critic's Notebook: "I, Claudius" left its bloody, sinister mark on TV drama', *LA Times*, 6 May 2012 <http://articles.latimes.com/2012/may/06/entertainment/la-ca-critics-notebook-claudius-20120506> (accessed 20/05/2012).

McNay, M. (2012), 'Ronald Searle Obituary', *Guardian*, 3 Jan. 2012; online at <www.guardian.co.uk/books/2012/jan/03/ronald-searle> (accessed 18 June 2012).

McPherson, J. M. (1990), *Abraham Lincoln and the Second American Revolution*. Oxford University Press: New York and Oxford.

Mehoke, J. S. (1975), *Robert Graves: Peace-Weaver*. Mouton: The Hague.

Meredeen, S. (2008), *The Man who Made Penguins: The Life of Sir William Emry Williams*. Darien-Jones: Stroud.

Milton, G. F. (1928), 'Colonel Lawrence Again', *The Nation*, 126 (16 May 1928): 567–8.

Mitchell, S. (2007), *A History of the Later Roman Empire, AD 284–641*. Blackwell: Oxford.

Mode, M. and Tubach, J. (eds.) (2006), *Arms and Armour as Indicators of Cultural Transfer: The Steppes and the Ancient World from Hellenistic Times to the Early Middle Ages*. Dr Ludwig Reichert: Wiesbaden.

Moorhead, J. (2001), *The Roman Empire Divided, 400–700*. Longman: Harlow.

Morgan, Ll. (2000), 'The Autopsy of C. Asinius Pollio', *Journal of Roman Studies*, 90: 51–69.

Morgan, T. (1980), *Somerset Maugham*. Jonathan Cape: London.

Morrison, B. (1980), *The Movement: English Poetry and Fiction of the 1950s*. Oxford University Press: Oxford.

Müller, T. (2009), 'Gerty McDowell, Poetess: Butler's *The Authoress of the Odyssey* and the Nausicaa Episode of *Ulysses*', *Twentieth-Century Literature*, 58/3: 378–92.

Müller-Wiener, W. (1977), *Bildlexikon zur Topographie Istanbuls. Byzantion-Konstantinupolis-Istanbul bis zum Beginn des 17. Jahrhunderts*. Wasmuth: Tübingen.

Muggeridge, M. (1965), 'Robert Graves', *Radio Times*, 11 Nov. 1965.

Murnaghan, S. (2009), 'Myths of the Greeks: The Origins of Mythology in the Works of Edith Hamilton and Robert Graves', *Classical Bulletin*, 84/1: 81–9.

Murnaghan, S. and Roberts, D. H. (n.d.), 'Antiquity for Girls', unpublished paper.

Murray, M. (1921), *The Witch Cult in Western Europe*. Clarendon Press: Oxford.

Murray, M. (1933), *The God of the Witches*. Sampson Low, Marston & Co.: London.

Murray, O. (1993), *Early Greece*, 2nd edn. Harvard University Press: Cambridge, Mass.

Nicholson, J. (1942), 'My Father—Robert Graves', *Lilliput*, 10/4 (58): 283–6.

Novokhatko, A. A. (2009), *The Invectives of Sallust and Cicero: Critical Edition with Introduction, Translation and Commentary*. Walter de Gruyter: Berlin and New York.

O'Brien, T. (1973), *If I Die In a Combat Zone Box Me Up and Ship Me Home*. Delacorte: New York.

O'Brien, S. (2001), 'A Muse of Fire: Sean O'Brien Salutes the Poetry of Robert Graves, Collected in *The Complete Poems in One Volume*', *Guardian*, 13 Jan. 2001; <http://www.guardian.co.uk/books/2001/jan/13/poetry> (accessed 01/06/2012).

O'Brien, T. (1990), *The Things They Carried*. Houghton Mifflin: Boston.

O'Prey, P. (ed.) (1982), *In Broken Images: Selected Letters of Robert Graves 1914–1946*. Hutchinson: London.

O'Prey, P. (ed.) (1984), *Between Moon and Moon: Selected Letters of Robert Graves 1946–1972*. Hutchinson: London.

O'Rourke, M. (2004), 'Hermetic Hotties. What is Anne Carson Doing on the L Word', *Slate*, 11 Feb. 2004 <http://www.slate.com/articles/news_and_politics/assessment/2004/02/hermetic_hotties.html> (accessed 04/12/2014).

Olovsdotter, C. (2005), *The Consular Image: An Iconological Study of the Consular Diptychs*. BAR International Series 1376. British Archaeological Reports: Oxford.

Orlans, H. (1993), *Lawrence of Arabia, Strange Man of Letters: The Literary Criticism and Correspondence of T. E. Lawrence*. Fairleigh Dickinson University Press: Rutherford, NJ.

Osgood, J. (2011), *Claudius Caesar: Image and Power in the Early Roman Empire*. Cambridge University Press: Cambridge.

Owen, W. (1967), *Collected Letters*, ed. H. Owen and J. Bell. Oxford University Press: London.

Palaima, T. (2000), 'Courage and Prowess Afoot in Homer and the Vietnam of Tim O'Brien', *Classical and Modern Literature*, 20/3: 1–22.

Palaima, T. (2001), Review of Tritle (2000), *Times Higher Education Supplement*, 16 Feb. 2001: 30.

Palaima, T. (2002), Review of Dawes (2002), *Times Higher Education Supplement*, 12 Apr. 2002: 24.

Palaima, T. (2003), Review of Tatum (2003), *Times Higher Education Supplement*, 13 June 2003: 28.

Palaima, T. (2005), 'Why Do Wars Begin?', in H. Swain (ed.), *Big Questions in History*. Jonathan Cape: London. 129–34.

Palaima, T. (2007), 'Civilian Knowledge of War and Violence in Ancient Athens and Modern America', in M. Cosmopoulos (ed.), *Experiencing War: Trauma and Society from Ancient Greece to the Iraq War*. Ares Press: Chicago. 9–34.

Palaima, T. and Tritle, L. (2013), 'Epilogue: The Legacy of War in the Classical World', in B. Campbell and L. Tritle (eds.), *The Oxford Handbook of Warfare in the Classical World*. Oxford University Press: Oxford. 726–42.

Pallottino, M. (1937), Untitled note, *Roma*, vol. XV: 179–80.

Pallottino, M. (1940), 'Profili d'Augusto', *Roma*, vol. XVIII: 168–78.

Paolucci, A. (1971), *Ravenna. Una guida d'arte*. Edizioni Salera: Ravenna.

Paribeni, R. (1937), 'Review of Robert Graves's *Io Claudio* and *Il divo Claudio*', *Roma*, vol. XV: 148.

Paribeni, R. (1938), *Augusto*. Reale Accademia d'Italia: Rome.

Parker, D. (1960), 'Poets on Record', *Weekly Post*, 3 Dec. 1960.

Paul, J. (2013), *Film and the Classical Epic Tradition*. Oxford University Press: Oxford.

Pavlovskis-Petit, Z. (2000), 'Apuleius', in O. Classe (ed.), *Encyclopedia of Literary Translation into English*, vol. 2. Fitzroy Dearborn: London. 60–2.

Peucker, B. (2004), 'The Fascist Choreography: Riefenstahl's Tableaux', *Modernism/Modernity*, 11/2: 279–97.

Pharand, M. W. (2003), 'Greek Myths, White Goddess: Robert Graves Cleans Up a "Dreadful Mess"', in Ian Firla and Grevel Lindop (eds.), *Graves and the Goddess: Essays on Robert Graves's The White Goddess*. Susquehanna University Press: Selsingrove, Pa.

Pharand, M. W. (2007), Poetic Mythography: The Genesis, Rationale and Reception of *The Greek Myths*. *Gravesiana*, 3/1: 56–73.

Piccirillo, M. (1992), *The Mosaics of Jordan*. American Center of Oriental Research: Amman.

Polascheck, E. (1932), 'Wiener Grabfunde aus der Zeit des untergehenden römischen Limes', *Wiener Prähistorische Zeitschrift*, 19: 239–66.

Postlethwaite, N. (1995), 'Homer's *Odyssey* and Lawrence's', *Journal of the T. E. Lawrence Society*, 5/1: 45–55.

Potter, D. S. (1999), 'Entertainers in the Roman Empire', in D. S. Potter and D. J. Mattingly (eds.), *Death and Entertainment in the Roman Empire*. University of Michigan Press: Ann Arbor, Mich. 256–325.

Prescott, O. (1959), 'Books of the Times', *New York Times*, 16 Nov. 1959: 29.

Presley, J. W. (1976), *The Robert Graves Manuscripts and Letters at Southern Illinois University: An Inventory*. Whitston Publishing Co.: Troy, NY.

Presley, J. W. (1997), 'Narrative Structure in Graves' Historical Fiction', *Gravesiana*, 1/3: 292–304.

Presley, J. W. (1999), 'Claudius: The Scripts', *Literature/Film Quarterly* (Salisbury State University, Md.) 27/3: 167–72.

Prokopios (2010), *The Secret History, with Related Texts*, ed. and trans. with an introduction by A. Kaldellis. Hackett: Indianapolis.

Psilopoulos, D. (1999), 'Robert Graves, the Esoteric Tradition, and the New Religion', in P. J. Quinn (ed.), *New Perspectives on Robert Graves*. Susquehanna University Press: Selinsgrove, Pa. 159–71.

Quigly, I. (1965), 'Bloody Epics', *Spectator*, 24 Dec. 1965.

Quinn, P. J. (1999), 'The Breaking of the Spell: Graves's Dissatisfaction Poetry of 1937', in P. J. Quinn (ed.), *Perspectives on Robert Graves*. Associated University Presses: London. 94–103.

Quinn, P. J. (ed.) (1999a), *New Perspectives on Robert Graves*. Susquehanna University Press: Selinsgrove, Pa.

Radio Times, 1923–85.

Raby, J. (1987), 'Mehmed the Conqueror and the Equestrian Statue of the Augusteion', *Illinois Classical Studies*, 12/2: 305–13.

Raikes, R. (1966), '*The Anger of Achilles*', *Radio Times*, 10 Mar. 1966: 49.

Rance, P. (2005), 'Narses and the Battle of Taginae (Busta Gallorum) 552: Procopius and sixth-century warfare', *Historia*, 54: 424–72.

Ranke-Graves, R. von. (1987), *Griechische Mythologie: Quellen und Deutung*, trans. Hugo Steinfeld. Rowohlt Taschenbuch Verlag GmbH: Reinbek.

Ravegnani, G. (1988), *Soldati di Bisanzio in età Giustinianea*. Jouvence: Rome.

Reid, W. (2006), *Architect of Victory: Douglas Haig*. Birlinn: Edinburgh.

Reilly, C. (1998), 'An Interview with Joseph Heller', *Contemporary Literature*, 39/4: 507–22.

Remarque, E. M. (1929), *All Quiet on the Western Front*. Little, Brown & Co.: Boston.

Renault, M. (1972), *The Persian Boy*. Longman: London.

Renfrew, C. and Wagstaff, J. M. (1982), *An Island Polity: The Archaeology of Exploitation in Melos*. Cambridge University Press: Cambridge.

Rexine, J. E. (1962), '*The Anger of Achilles: Homer's Iliad*, translated by Robert Graves', *Classical Journal*, 57/6: 281–2.

Richards, V. (1936), *Portrait of T. E. Lawrence: The Lawrence of the Seven Pillars of Wisdom*. Jonathan Cape: London.

Riding, L. (1937), *A Trojan Ending*. Constable: London.

Riding, L. (1939), *Lives of Wives*. Cassell: London.

Roberts, D. (1996), *Minds at War: The Poetry and Experience of the First World War*. Saxon Books: Burgess Hill, West Sussex.

Robertson, D. S. (1951), Review of *The Transformations of Lucius, otherwise known as The Golden Ass* by Lucius Apuleius, translated by Robert Graves. *Classical Review*, 1/3–4: 241–2.

Robinson, A. (2002), *The Life and Work of Jane Ellen Harrison*. Oxford University Press: Oxford.

Rose, H. J. (1911/1992), 'On the Alleged Evidence for Mother-Right in Early Greece', *Folklore*, 22/3: 277–91; repr. in Beate Wagner-Hasel (ed.), *Matriarchatstheorien der Altertumswissenschaft*, Wege der Forschung 651. Wissenschaftliche Buchgesellschaft: Darmstadt. 30–42.

Rose, H. J. (1928), *A Handbook of Greek Mythology*. Methuen: London.

Rose, H. J. (1955), Review of *The Greek Myths*, *Classical Review*, NS 5/2: 208–9.

Rouse, W. H. D. (1937), *The Story of Odysseus: A Translation of Homer's 'Odyssey' into Plain English*. Thomas Nelson & Sons: London.

Rovere, R. H. (1951), 'Review of *The Golden Ass* by Robert Graves', *New Yorker*, 29 Sept. 1951: 122.

Rushdie, S. (1991), *Imaginary Homelands: Essays and Criticism, 1981–1991*. Granta: London.

Rutherford, R. (1996), *Homer*, no. 26 in *Greece & Rome: New Surveys in the Classics* series. Oxford University Press: Oxford.

Safran, L. (1993), 'Points of View: The Theodosian Obelisk Base in Context', *Greek, Roman and Byzantine Studies*, 34: 409–35.

Sagar, K. (2009), 'Ted Hughes and the Classics', in Roger Rees (ed.), *Ted Hughes and the Classics*. Oxford University Press: Oxford. 1–24.

Sanders, A. (1978), *The Victorian Historical Novel 1840–1880*. Macmillan: Basingstoke.

Sassoon, S. (1918), *Memoirs of a Fox-Hunting Man*. Faber & Faber: London.

Sassoon, S. (1937), *The Complete Memoirs of George Sherston*. Faber & Faber: London.

Scott, R. (2006), 'Narrating Justinian: From Malalas to Manasses', in John Burke, Ursula Betka, and Roger Scott (eds.), *Byzantine Narrative: Papers in Honour of Roger Scott*. Australian Association for Byzantine Studies: Melbourne. 29–46.

Scott, W. (2006), *Count Robert of Paris*. Edinburgh University Press: Edinburgh.

Scott Smith, R. and Trzaskoma, S. M. (eds.) (2007), *Apollodorus' Library and Hyginus' Fabulae*. Hackett: Indianapolis.

Seymour, M. (1995), *Robert Graves: Life on the Edge*. Doubleday: London.

Seymour, M. (2003), *Robert Graves: Life on the Edge*. Scribner: London.

Seymour-Smith, M. (1982), *Robert Graves: His Life and Work*. Hutchinson London/Holt, Rinehart & Winston: New York.

Seymour-Smith, M. (1995), *Robert Graves: His Life and Work*, 2nd edn. Bloomsbury: London.

Shay, J. (1994), *Achilles in Vietnam: Combat Trauma and the Undoing of Character* Athenaeum: New York.

Sheffield, G. (2001), *Forgotten Victory: The First World War. Myths and Realities*. Headline: London.

Silverberg, R. (1975), *Up the Line*. Sphere: London.

Sjöö, M. and Mor, B. (1987), *The Great Cosmic Mother: Rediscovering the Religion of the Earth*. Harper & Row: San Francisico.

Smeds, J. (1990), 'Graves, Bachofen and the Matriarchy Debate', *Focus on Robert Graves and His Contemporaries*, 1/10: 1–17.

Smith, W. S. (2001), 'Review of E. J. Kenney, *Apuleius, The Golden Ass or Metamorphoses, International Journal of Classical Tradition*', 7/3: 435–8.

Snipes, K. (1979), *Robert Graves*. Frederick Ungar Publishing Co.: New York.

Sorley, C. H. (1916), *Marlborough and Other Poems*. Cambridge University Press: Cambridge.

Spender, S. (1973), 'Poems 1970–72; Like Prospero, sure of his wand, his kingship and his splendor By Robert Graves', *New York Times Book Review*, 11 Mar. 1973 <http://select.nytimes.com/gst/abstract.html?res=FA0612FB3F54137A93C3A81788D85F478785F9> (accessed 01/06/2012).

Stanton, F. (1978), 'Television and the Book', in John Y. Cole (ed.), *Television, the Book, and the Classroom*. Library of Congress: Washington, DC.

Starhawk (1979), *The Spiral Dance: A Rebirth of the Ancient Religion of the Great Goddess*. Harper & Row: San Francisco.

Steiner, G. (2004), 'Homer in English Translation', in Robert Fowler (ed.), *The Cambridge Companion to Homer*. Cambridge University Press: Cambridge. 363–75.

Stone, M. (1976), *When God Was a Woman*. Dial Press: New York.

Suttie, I. D. (1935), *Origins of Love and Hate*. Kegan Paul, Trench, Trubner & Co.: London.

Swan, G. S. (1994), 'Who was Homer's Daughter? Robert Graves and T. E. Lawrence', *Focus on Robert Graves and his Contemporaries*, 2/2: 17–21.

Swanson, R. A. (1957), 'Graves's "Hercules at Nemea"', *Explicator*, 15/9: 56.

Syme, R. (1939), *The Roman Revolution*. Clarendon Press: Oxford.

Syme, R. (1956), *Tacitus*, 2 vols. Clarendon Press: Oxford.

Syvänne, I. (2004), *The Age of the Hippotoxotai: Art of War in Roman Military Revival and Disaster (491–636)*. Acta Universitatis Tamperensis 994. Tampere University Press: Tampere.

The Listener, 1929–85.

Talbot Rice, D. (ed.) (1958), *The Great Palace of the Byzantine Emperors: Second Report*. Edinburgh University Press: Edinburgh.

Tatum, J. (2003), *The Mourner's Song: War and Remembrance from the Iliad to Vietnam*. University of Chicago Press: Chicago.

Terkel, S. (1997), *The Good War: Oral History of World War Two*. New edn. New Press: New York.

Terry, W. (1984), *Bloods*. Ballantine Books: New York.

Thomas, C. G. (1973/1992), 'Matriarchy in Early Greek', *Arethusa*, 6:173–95; repr. in Beate Wagner-Hasel (ed.), *Matriarchatstheorien der Altertumswissenschaft*, Wege der Forschung 651. Wissenschaftliche Buchgesellschaft: Darmstadt. 195–219.

Thomas, L. (1927), 'Lawrence of Arabia: Who He Was and What He Did', *The World's Work*, 54/4: 362–8.

Todman, D. (2005), *The Great War: Myth and Memory*. Hambledon Continuum: London.

Toepffer, J. A. F. (1889), *Attische Genealogien*. Weidmann: Berlin.

Tokes, Rudolf L. (1970), Reviewed work(s): *Az 1918-as Magyarorszagi Polgari Demokratikus Forradalom*, by Tibor Hajdu; *A Magyarorszagi*

Tanacskoztarsasag, by Tibor Hajdu; *Ausztria es a Magyarorszagi Tanacskoztarsasag*, by Sandor Gabor, *Slavic Review*, 29/4: 732–4.
Töpfer K. M. (2011), *Signa Militaria. Die römischen Feldzeichen in der Republik und im Prinzipat*. Schnell & Steiner: Mainz.
Tougher, S. (2008a), *The Eunuch in Byzantine History and Society*. Routledge: London and New York.
Tougher, S. (2008b), 'The Renault Bagoas: The Treatment of Alexander the Great's Eunuch in Mary Renault's *The Persian Boy*', *New Voices in Classical Reception Studies*, 3: 77–89.
Trengrove, G. (1986), 'What is Robert Graves Playing At?', in C. J. Brumfit and R. A. Carter (eds.), *Literature and Language Teaching (Oxford Applied Linguistics)*. Oxford University Press: Oxford. 60–9.
Tritle, L. (2000), *From Melos to My Lai: War and Survival*. Routledge: London and New York.
Tuplin, C. (2010), 'Marathon: In Search of a Persian Dimension', in K. Buraselis and K. Meidani, *Μαραθών: η μάχη και ο αρχαίος Δήμος/ Marathon: the Battle and the Ancient Deme*. Kardamitsa: Athens. 251–74.
Tydeman, J. (1998), 'Obituary: Raymond Raikes', *Independent*, 8 Oct. 1998: 6.
Unsworth, B. (2006), 'Introduction', to Robert Graves, *I Claudius*. Penguin: London.
Valiente, D. (2000), *Charge of the Goddess*. Hexagon: Berkeley.
Vandiver, E. (1999), '"Millions of the Mouthless Dead": Charles Hamilton Sorley and Wilfred Owen in Homer's Hades', *International Journal of the Classical Tradition*, 5: 432–55.
Vandiver, E. (2010), *Stand in the Trench, Achilles: Classical Receptions in British Poetry of the Great War*. Oxford University Press: Oxford.
Vanezis, P. (2002), *I, Claudius: A Television Epic*. BBC Worldwide: London.
Venuti, L. (1995), *The Translator's Invisibility: A History of Translation*. Routledge: London.
Vidal, G. (1963), *Rocking the Boat*. Heinemann: London.
Vidal, G. (1964), *Julian*. Heinemann: London.
Vidal, G. (1999), 'Introduction' to *Of Human Bondage* by Somerset Maugham. Modern Library: New York. ii–xxiv.
Virgil (1953), *The Aeneid of Virgil: A New Verse Translation By C. Day Lewis*. Doubleday Anchor Books: New York.
Virgil (1997), *Virgil's Aeneid*, trans. John Dryden, ed. Frederick M. Keener. Penguin: Harmondsworth.
Virgil (2005), *Aeneid*, trans. Stanley Lombardo, intro. W. R. Johnson. Hackett: Indianapolis.
Von Sternberg, J. (1965), *Fun in a Chinese Laundry*. Colliers Books: New York.
Vonnegut, K. (1969), *Slaughterhouse-Five Or the Children's Crusade: A Duty-Dance With Death*. Delacorte: New York.

Wallace, D. (2005), *The Woman's Historical Novel: British Women Writers, 1900–2000*. Palgrave Macmillan: Basingstoke.

Walsh, P. G. (1961), *Livy: His Historical Aims and Methods*. Cambridge University Press: Cambridge.

Walsh, P. G. (trans.) (1994), *Apuleius: The Golden Ass*. Oxford University Press: Oxford.

Wain, J. (1960), 'Speech on Record', *Observer*, 11 Sept. 1960.

Ward, D. (2003), 'God and the Goddess: The Muse and the "Muses"', in Ian Firla and Grevel Lindop (eds.), *Graves and the Goddess: Essays on Robert Graves's The White Goddess*. Susquehanna University Press: Selsingrove, Pa. 88–98.

Wardle, I. (1972), 'I, Claudius; Queen's', *The Times*, 12 July 1972.

Waugh, E. (1957), *The Ordeal of Gilbert Pinfold: A Conversation Piece*. Chapman & Hall: London.

Weil S. (1939), *L'Iliade ou le Poème de la Force*, trans. M. McCarthy. Politics Pamphlet No. 1: New York.

Wells, H. G. (1928), 'Changes in the Arts of War. Are Armies Needed Any Longer? The Twilight of the Guards', in H. G. Wells, *The Way the World Is Going. 26 Articles and a Lecture by H.G. Wells*. Ernst Benn: London. 134–46.

Whitmarsh, T. (2002), 'What Samuel Butler Saw: Classics, Authorship and Cultural Authority in Late Victorian England', *Proceedings of the Cambridge Philological Society*, 48: 66–86.

Wilson, J. (1990), *Lawrence of Arabia: The Authorised Biography of T. E. Lawrence*. Minerva: London.

Winkler, J. J. (1985), *Auctor & Actor: A Narratological Reading of Apuleius'* Golden Ass; University of California Press: Berkeley.

Winkler, J. J. (1990), 'Penelope's Cunning and Homer's', in *The Constraints of Desire: The Anthropology of Sex and Gender in Ancient Greece*. Routledge: London. 129–61.

Wiseman, Peter (1979), *Clio's Cosmetics: Three Studies in Greco-Roman Literature*. Leicester University Press: Leicester.

Wood, J. (2012), 'Invitation to a Beheading: The Thomas Cromwell Novels of Hilary Mantel', *New Yorker*, 7 May 2012 <http://www.newyorker.com/arts/critics/books/2012/05/07/120507crbo_books_wood?currentPage=all> (accessed 01/06/2012).

Woodhead, A. G. (1990), 'Conflict and Ancient Society', in J. W. Allison (ed.), *Conflict, Antithesis, and the Ancient Historian*. Ohio State University Press: Columbus. 1–24.

Woodman, A. J. (1988), *Rhetoric in Classical Historiography: Four Studies*. Croom Helm: London and Sydney.

Woodward, D. R. (2006), *Hell in the Holy Land: World War I in the Middle East*. University of Kentucky Press: Lexington, Ky.

Woodworth, D. C. (1935), 'Review of *I Claudius*', *Classical Journal*, 30/6: 366–9.

Woolger. J. B. and Woolger, R. J. (1990), *The Goddess Within: A Guide to the Eternal Myths that Shape Women's Lives*. Rider: London.

Wrigley, A. (2005), 'Aeschylus' *Agamemnon* on BBC Radio, 1946–1976', *International Journal of the Classical Tradition*, 12/2: 216–44.

Wrigley, A. (2007), 'Stages of Imagination: Greek Plays on BBC Radio', in Christopher Stray (ed.), *Remaking the Classics: Literature, Genre and Media in Britain, 1800–2000*. London: Duckworth. 57–73.

Wrigley, A. (2009a), 'Engagements with Greek Drama and Homeric Epic on BBC Radio in the 1940s and 1950s', doctoral thesis submitted to the Department of Classical Studies, The Open University.

Wrigley, A. (2009b), 'Louis MacNeice's Radio Classics: 'all so unimaginably different'?', in Dunstan Lowe and Kim Shahabudin (eds.), *Classics For All: Reworking Antiquity in Mass Culture*. Cambridge Scholars Publishing: Cambridge. 39–61.

Wrigley, A. (2010), 'A Wartime Radio *Odyssey*: Edward Sackville-West and Benjamin Britten's *The Rescue* (1943)', *The Radio Journal: International Studies in Broadcast and Audio Media*, 8/2: 81–103.

Wrigley, A. (2014), 'Aristophanes at the BBC, 1940s–1960s', in S. Douglas Olson (ed.), *Ancient Comedy and Reception: Essays in Honor of Jeffrey Henderson*. Walter de Gruyter: Berlin and Boston. 849–70.

Wrigley, A. (2015), *Greece on Air: Engagements with Ancient Greece on BBC Radio, 1920s–1960s*. Oxford: Oxford University Press.

Wrigley, A. and Harrison, S. (eds.) (2013), *Louis MacNeice: The Classical Radio Plays*. Oxford University Press: Oxford.

Yourcenar, M. (1990), *Memoirs of Hadrian*, trans. G. Frick. Noonday Press: New York.

Ziolkowski, T. (2005), *Ovid and the Moderns*. Cornell University Press: Ithaca, NY.

Zuckmayer, C. (1970), *A Part of Myself*, trans. Richard and Clara Winston. Harcourt Brace: New York.

Index

Abderos 167
Achilles 17–18, 150, 167, 192–3, 199–200, 208, 251, 316, 318–20, 325, 327–9
Ackerman, Robert 185
Adlington, William 127–8, 138, 141, 146, 157
Aeneas 107, 208
Aeneas of Lydda 107
Aeneid 13, 205, 209
Aeschylus 251, 254
Aethon 64, 70, 73
Agamemnon 17–18, 36, 148, 150, 191–3, 207, 244–5, 253, 319, 327–8
Agamemnon 254
Agathias 92
Agrippina the Elder 106
Agrippina the Younger 28, 286
Agrius 199
Ainslie, Ricardo 237
Ajax 208
Akan 169
Alberti, Leon Battista 227
Alexander the Great 9, 309–10
Allenby, Edmund, General 116, 124, 132, 159
Alpheius 226
Alvarez, Al 312
Ameinius 226
Amis, Kingsley 162
Ammianus Marcellinus 93
anachronism (translation) 16, 32–4, 37, 155, *see also* historical novel
analeptic writing technique 19, 276–7
Ancaeus 212–13
Anchises 215
Andromache 215
Andromeda 190
Anouilh, Jean 294
Antiope 166
Antonina 79, 89–91, 95, 99–102, 104–6, 108, *see also* Belisarius
Antony, Mark 260
Aphrodite 69–70, 73–4, 166, 213, 215, 238, 327
Apollinaris 83
Apollo 17, 187, 192–4, 206, 209–10, 317, 328
Apollo, Library of 51–3
Apollodorus 198–9, 213
Apollonian 170, 204, 209–10
Appius Claudius 148–9
Apuleius, Lucius 123–32, 134–50, 157, 163, 202, 208, 308, 315
archaeology 60, 120, 198
Archilocus 234
Ares 199
Ariadne 218
Aristophanes 126, 130–1, 209, 242, 251, 254, 298
Aristotle 37–41
Artemis 6, 191–3, 226
Ashe, Geoffrey 276–7
Atalanta 202, 215
Athene/Athena 70, 178, 187, 208, 320, 327, 329
Athens 135, 218, 251, 253, 317
Auden, W. H. 4, 11, 202, 204, 301–2, 323, 326
Augustus 35, 48, 54, 82, 258–72, 283, 289, 311
Austen, Jane 22
autobiography 3, 10, 24, 28, 54, 59, 61–3, 65, 67, 86, 116, 237, 285, 300, *see also* biography
Authoress of the Odyssey, The 60–3, 68–9

Bachofen, Johan Jakob 168, 170–2, 174–6
Bagoas 78
Baldwin, Stanley 262, 272
Baucis 217–18
Beecham, Sir Thomas 305
Bel 190
Belisarius 77–122, 130
Bellerophon 218–19

Belloc, Hilaire 147
Bergman, Ingrid 57–8, 287, 289
Bernoulli, Carl Albrecht 171
Bessas 109–10
Bildungsroman 285, 292
biography 37, 141, 237, *see also* autobiography
of Augustus (by John Buchan) 260, 265–6, 270, 272, 275
of Belisarius 80, 82, 84, 94
of Lawrence, T. E. 126, 132–7, 140, 159
Biró, Lajos 278–9, 284
Blake, William 202, 302, 306
Blunden, Edmund 6, 10, 118, 204, 211
Boccaccio, Giovanni 124, 129
Bogart, Humphrey 252
Boland, Bridget 280, 288–9
Bolt, Robert 10, 294
Bond, Edward 290
Boswell, James 322
Bracciolini, Poggio 152–3
Bramble, John 153
Bridges, Robert 202, 211
Briffault, Robert 171
Briseis 327–8
British Broadcasting Corporation (BBC) 2, 77, 118, 265, 267, 291–2, 297–303, 305–6, 308–9, 312, 318, 322–31
Home Service 297, 305, 326–7, 330
Light Programme 305
Third Programme 298–9, 304–5, 308, 310, 322–4, 326–7, 329–31
Brooke, Rupert 205–6
Brown, Christy 291
Broyles, Bill 237
Brutus 48
Buchan, John 255–6, 260, 265–72
Bunyan, John 154
Burkert, Walter 174
Burnett, John 237
Butler, Samuel 57–63, 68–9
Byron, Lord 216 309

Caesar, Julius 43, 66–7, 81, 108, 151, 157, 204, 251, 259, 261, 264–5, 271
Calchas 192
Caligula 279, 289, 293–4, 309
Callimachus 186
Callinus 234
Calypso 73, 75
Cambridge Ritualists 181
Carlyle, Thomas 49
Carne-Ross, D. S. 15, 17, 325–6, *see also* BBC
Cartledge, Paul 237
Cassiodorus 83, 92
Cassius, Dio 43, 276, 286, 292
Cato the Younger 272
Catullus 54, 75–6, 127, 205, 299
Cavafy, C. P. 312–13
Cephisus 225
Cerberus 209, 236
Cerdo 72, 160
Cervantes, Miguel de 124, 129
Chesterton, G. K. 147
Chapman, George 157
Charybdis 74, 155
Chimaera 219
Chosroes II 112
Christianity 79, 82–3, 86–9, 95–6, 101, 106–8, 114, 124, 128, 145, 179, 189, 254, 304
Christie, Agatha 308
Chryseis 150, 328
Chryses 328
chthonian mythography 173
Churchill, Winston 81–2
Circe 6, 73–5, 214
civil war 3, 13, 78, 100, 148, 268, 280, 292, 294, 308
Claudian 83
Claudius Caesar 2–3, 8–9, 22–3, 26, 28–37, 40, 43–54, 62, 66–7, 71, 77, 255, 260–2, 275–7, 280–3, 285–8, 290, 292–5
Claudius (novels) 8–9, 12, 24–5, 37, 39–40, 46, 57, 77–8, 80, 84, 86–7, 91, 118, 121, 143, 255–7, 260, 275, 277, 282, 288, 292, 330
Cleverdon, Douglas 323, *see also* BBC
Clymene 165
Clytaemnestra 192–3
Clytoneus 64, 70, 154
Coardi, Carlo 257
Cohen, Lester 278, 284, 293
Coleridge, Samuel Taylor 41, 127, 131–2, 202
colloquialism 150, 154–6
communism 263
Connolly, Cyril 299

Constantinople 78, 80–2, 89, 93–5, 102, 104–5, 108, 117
Cooper, Gary 282
Craiglockhart War Hospital 235
Cranmer, Thomas 10
creation myth 178
Cromwell, Oliver 265
Cromwell, Thomas 9–10
Ctimene 63–4
Cupid 131, 139
Cyclops 71
Cymbeline 264
Cyrus the Great 87

Daniels, Glyn 306, *see also* BBC
Dante Alighieri 208–9, 231–2
Daphne 193–4
Daphoene 194
Darius I 246–7
Davis, Elizabeth Gould 176, 178
Davy, Nelle 294
Day Lewis, Cecil 4, 13, 127, 144, 202, 204
Defoe, Daniel 32
Dehn, Paul 306
Deidameia 193
Derrida, Jacques 38
Dickens, Charles 32
Dietrich, Marlene 278, 284
Dillow, Gordon 237
Dimock, George E. 319, 321, *see also* BBC
Diodorus Siculus 152–3
Diomedes 167
Dionysian 170, 209–10
Dionysus 166, 209, 218, 236
Disney, Walt 305
divination 105
Dodds, E. R. 311
Donne, John 311
Drusus the Elder 261–2
Dryden, John 13, 143, 202
Duncalf, Bill 275, 292
Dylan, Bob 19

Echo 226, 228
Edelman, Bernard 237
Edward VIII (abdication) 281
cummings, e. e. 202
Ehrhart, Bill 237
Eliot, George 32
Eliot, T. S. 202, 208, 211, 221, 301, 311
Empson, William 301
Epic that Never Was, The 275, 292, 302
Erasmus, Desiderius 322
Eros 73, 226–7
Etruscans 309, 324
Eugenius 79, 86, 88–92, 95–6, 100, 117
Eumaeus 64, 69, 71–2, 160
eunuch, eunuchood 78–9, 87–92
Euripides 236, 254, 299
Eurymachus 64
Eurymedusa 71
Eurypylus 199
Eusebius 83

Farber, Manny 312
fascism 256–7, 259–60, 263–5, 270–3, 292–3
Fellini, Federico 289
female authorship 58, 60–1
Fielding, Henry 32, 124, 129
film
  The Anger of Achilles 321–2, 326, 329
  cinema 18, 24, 267, 305, 308
  Homer's Daughter 57–8, 320
  I, Claudius/ Claudius the God 9, 27, 57, 264, 268, 275–95, 302, 330–1, *see also* Alexander Korda
  Lawrence, T. E. 133
  war 120–1, 133, 237–8, 252
First World War 3, 6, 13, 67, 114, 119–20, 233–5, 238–40, 242, 252, *see also* Western Front
Fitts, Dudley 315
Fitzgerald, F. Scott 224
Ford, Ford Madox 10
Frazer, J. G. 170, 172–7, 181, 184, 188, 211–12
Freud, Sigmund 179, 189, 225, 227, 230, 238
  Freudian narcissist 228, 230
  Freudian theory and analysis 211, 224–30, 232, 235
Fronto 83
Frost, Robert 202
Fussell, Paul 235, 239, 245–6, 250

Galatea 213–14, 216
Galerius 103
Gardiner, Llew 302–3
Gardner, Ava 196, 297
Gardner, Eric Stanley 308
gender 58, 70–3, 78, 87–92, 96

Gerhard, Roberto 327, 329, *see also* music
Germanicus 29, 36, 106
George V 266
George VI 266
Gibbon, Edward 83, 93–5
Gill, Eve 68
Gilpin, John 318
Glauce 199
Glaucus 49, 166
Glenville, Peter 288–9
Glover, A. S. B. 152, 183, 195–6
Godwin, William 41
Golden Bough, The 172, 184, 188, 211
Goldman, James 294
Golzius, Hendrick 1
Gorgo 71
Göttner-Abendroth, Heide 177
Gowers, Ernest 161
Goya, Francisco 1
Graves, Alfred Perceval 2, 156, 201
Graves, Beryl 5, 128, 288, *see also* Beryl Pritchard
Graves, Robert von Ranke
  Anger of Achilles, The 15, 17, 144, 149–54, 158, 237, 245, 250, 315–31
  Antigua, Penny, Puce 155
  Count Belisarius 3, 77–97, 99–101, 106, 108, 112–14, 117–19, 121, 130, 152, 155, 301, *see also* historical novel
  Good-bye to All That 3, 6, 10, 46, 72, 75, 86, 91, 105, 109, 116–21, 128, 285, 293, 300, 303, 307
  Golden Ass, The 144
  Golden Fleece, The 3–4, 59, 155, 169, 183, 212, 219
  Greek Myths, The 12, 61, 165, 168, 171, 175–7, 180–6, 189, 191, 193–8, 213, 225, 227, 308, *see also* myth, Greek.
  Homer's Daughter 57–76, 144, 154, 158, 160, 287, 320
  I,Claudius & *Claudius the God* 3, 5, 8–10, 21–41, 43–55, 57, 62–3, 66–7, 77–8, 93, 100, 106, 119, 125, 129, 155, 212, 255–6, 260–1, 268, 275–95, 299, 302, 322, 330, *see also* historical novel
  King Jesus 19, 86, 155, 169, 303
  Lawrence and the Arabs 3, 117, 126, 131–2, 134–6, 139, 159–60, 267, 300
  Nazarene Gospel Restored, The 303
  Pharsalia 144, 148, 151, 157–8, 234, 307, 310
  Proceed Sergeant Lamb 81
  Real David Copperfield, The 12, 45, 306
  Sergeant Lamb of the Ninth 81, 88, 155
  Seven Days in New Crete 25, 155
  Twelve Caesars, The 43, 144, 149, 151, 153, 158, 161, *see also* Suetonius
  White Goddess, The 1, 19, 31, 59, 71–2, 75, 87, 138, 143, 145–6, 158, 163, 168–9, 179, 183, 186–91, 193, 195, 201, 203–4, 211, 301, *see also* Akan; iconotropy; matriarchy
  Wife to Mr Milton 155
  Poetry:
    'A Dead Boche' 248–50
    'A Dedication of Three Hats' 6–7
    'Adventure, The' 247
    'A Former Attachment' 223
    'Anchises to Aphrodite' 215–16
    'An Idyll of Old Age' 217–18
    'As It Were Poems' 208
    'At First Sight' 231–2
    'Beatrice and Dante' 231–2
    'Cuirassiers of the Frontier, The' 208
    'Down, Wanton, Down!' 223
    'Ecstasy of Chaos' 232
    'Escape' 208, 234
    'First Funeral, The' 247–8, 250
    'Galatea and Pygmalion' 213–14
    'Heroes in their Prime' 218–19
    'Hippopotamus's Address to the Freudians' 211
    'I'd Die For You' 222
    'Judgment of Paris' 215
    'Leda' 6
    'Legion, The' 207–8
    'Lyceia' 6
    'Man Does, Woman Is' 231
    'My Name and I' 221
    'Next War, The' 240
    'Ovid in Defeat' 216–17
    'Persian Version, The' 7–8, 243–4, 246, 313

'Prison Walls' 223
'Prometheus' 6
'Pygmalion to Galatea' 213–14
'Second-Fated, The' 31
'Singleness in Love' 224
'Theseus and Ariadne' 218
'To Put It Simply' 231
'Ulysses' 6, 74–5
Interactions and themes:
Charterhouse 3, 59, 203, 205, 243
Christianity and Graves 86, 95, 107, 145, 179
footnotes 30, 136, 150–1, 157, 198
Latin poetry 203–4. 242
love 6–7, 16, 50, 64, 69–70, 73–5, 90, 92, 105, 168, 176, 193, 205, 210, 213–19, 222–32, 243, 254, 281, 284, 286, 326
love poetry 5, 7, 76, 222, 225, 231
muse 4, 6, 19, 144, 212–14, 297
mythography (Robert Graves) 191–5
poetic myth 187–8, *see also The White Goddess*
'potboilers' 3, 39–40, 57, 84–5, 97, 143, 255, 283
reading voice 11
relationships: *see* relationships; Nancy Nicholson; Beryl Pritchard; Laura Riding; male-female domination; eunuchs; sadomasochism
religion 61, 73, 86–7, 95–6, 145, 160, 170–9, 182–4, 188–9, 211–12, 303–4
sadomasochism 91, 100, 286, *see also* Sacher-Masoch
self-presentation 59
sources 22, 29–30, 43–4, 83, 92–6, 101–4
stutter 31
translations 13–18, 143–63, *see also* plain prose; colloquialism
Virgil 50, 152, 202–5, 208, 219, 234, 310–12
war, war experiences 13, 108, 116–19, 235–54, *see also* First World War; Western Front
Graves, Sally 83
Greeks 4, 7, 17–18, 44–5, 47, 150, 173, 184, 189, 192–3, 199, 212, 234, 236, 245, 251, 253, 303, 327
Green, Peter 20, 148, 319–20
Grégoire, Henri 81
Gregory, T. S. 304
Grimal, Pierre 170
Groddeck, Georg 179
Guinness, Alec 287–90
gynaecocracy 173, *see also* matriarchy, White Goddess

Hades 18, 236
Hadrian 69, 258
Haig, Field Marshal Douglas 116, 120
Haldane, J. B. S. 305
Handford, S. A. 151
Handley, Tommy 301, 323
Hannay, Richard 265
Harding, D.W. 21–5, 41
Hardy, Thomas 202, 210
Harith, King 107
Harrison, Jane Ellen 174–6, 184, 205, 212
Harrower, John 298
Head, June 278
Heaney, Seamus 203
Hebrew (religion) 188–9
Hector 167, 215, 254, 327
Hedges, Chris 237
Hegel, G. W. F. 41
Helen of Troy 44, 207, 215
Heller, Joseph 251
Hemingway, Ernest 236
Heppenstall, Rayner 301, 322–3, *see also* BBC
Hera 190, 215, 226, 320
Heracles/Hercules 4, 152–3, 167, 190
Herbert, Kevin 197–8, 237
Hermes 217–18
Herod Agrippa 36, 86
Herod the Great 87
Herodotus 7, 35, 47, 113, 167, 246
Hersh, Seymour 237
Herzog, Werner 237
Hesiod, 174, 186, 253, 311
Hesionë 190
Hodge, Alan 83, 154, 295, 300
Holland, Philomen 157
Homer 6, 14, 16, 17–18, 22, 44–5, 58–60, 64, 71, 73, 75, 149–50, 152, 158, 162, 174, 202, 204–7, 209, 215, 219, 234, 237, 245, 249, 250, 251–2, 287, 310–11, 315–22, 325, 327, 329
Homer *Iliad* 17, 234, 237, 250, 315, 321, *see also* Troy; Trojan War
Homer *Odyssey* 75–6, 317

Homeric 18, 45, 60–1, 64–5, 68, 70, 73, 109–10, 152, 160, 206–7, 245, 253, 311, 316–17
Horace 205
House, F. H. 304
Housman, A. E. 157–8, 211
Hippolyte 166, 199
Hippolytus 166–7
historical novel 8–10, 21–41, 48–54, 62–3, 65–76, 85, 92–6, *see also* poetry and history
 historiographical veracity 30–2, 35, 45
Hitchcock, Alfred 267
Hitler, Adolf 119, 259, 293
Hughes, Ted 203
Hussey, John 81
Hydra 190

iconotropy 168–9, 185, 191
Idas 193
Iliad 14–18, 143–4, 157–9, 162, 186, 205, 234, 237, 244, 250–4, 311, 315–30, *see also* Homer
Imison, Richard 330, *see also* BBC
Incitatus 280
Iphigeneia 190–3
Isherwood, Christopher 290

James Tait Black prize 256
Jannings, Emil 278
Jason 219
Jephthah 190, 193
Jepson, Selwyn 58, 68, 196, 308
Jerome 83, 89, 95
Joad, C. E. M. 301, 322–3
John the Epicure 107
Johnson, Samuel 23, 157, 202
Josephus 43, 144, 294
Joyce, James 32, 61, 205, 286
Julian 93, 107
Julio-Claudian 46, 262, 280
Jung, C. G. 179, 189
Juno 13–14, 205
Jupiter the Deliverer 147
Justinian I 79–83, 87, 89–93, 99–107

Kagan, Donald 237
Kant, Immanuel 41
Keats, John 128, 202, 209–10, 306
Kemp, Harry 264
Kerényi, Karl 165, 170, 174, 178
King, Mackenzie 266, 268
Klages, Ludwig 171
Købke, Christen 1
Korda, Alexander 9, 27, 85, 267, 275–89, 293
Korda, Vincent 283, 287, 293

Landor, Walter Savage 202
Lane, Allen 123, 162, 196
Lang, Andrew 6
Laodamas 63–4
Last Days of Pompeii 49
Last, Hugh 269
Lattimore, R. A. 14, 17, 158, 317
Laughton, Charles 275, 278, 280–3, 293–4, 302
Lauis 167
Lawrence, D. H. 286
Lawrence, T. E. 3–4, 26–7, 31, 40, 44, 50, 80–3, 95, 101, 117, 121, 123–42, 144, 158–61, 202, 236–7, 267, 282, *see also Seven Pillars of Wisdom*
Leavis, F. R. 23, 162
Leda 6, 214–15
Leiriope 225
Lethe 209
Leto 17
Leucippus 194
Lewis, Alun 202
Liddell Hart, Basil 3, 81–2, 96, 121
Lincoln, Abraham 294
Linear B 174, 299
Livia 31, 36, 44, 46, 54, 77, 87, 91, 261–2, 283, 289
 and Laura Riding 261–2
Livy 32–5, 43–54, 66–7
Lloyd-Jones, Hugh 311
Logue, Christopher 14, 16–17
Lombardo, Stanley 13–14, 17–18
Loren, Sophia 297
Lowe, Nick 197
Lowell, Robert 297
Lucan 144, 148, 151, 157–8, 234, 307–8, 310–11
Lucas, F. L. 147
Lucian 65
Lycurgus 167
Lyly, John 154
Lytton, Bulwer 49

Macaulay, Thomas 49
McCarthy, Cormac 245–6, 249
MacDiarmid, Hugh 310
Macdonald, George 298

Mackenzie, Compton 286
MacNeice, Louis 144, 318, 323, *see also* BBC
Machaon 199
Maecenas 311
Maenads 194, 212
magic 59, 104–6, 119, 140, 145, 172, 187, 212, 224
Magnani, Anna 287–9
Mahon, Lord 81–2, 84–5, 94–6, 99, 106, *see also* Viscount Stanhope
Malalas 83
male-female domination 101, *see also* relationships; Sader-Masoch; Graves, Robert: sadomasochism
Mallory, George 205
Manfredi, Valerio Massimo 9
Mantel, Hilary 9–10
Mapplethorpe, Robert 1
Marathon, Battle of 7–8, 244, 247, 251
Marduk 190
Marlowe, Christopher 143, 157
Marpessa 193
Marsh, Edward 205–6, 255–6
Masefield, John 3, 205, 211
matriarchy 12, 170–8, 187, 212–13, *see also* gynaecocracy
Matthews, Julie 27, 279
Matthews, Tom 27, 212, 255
Maugham, Somerset 275, 283–7, 292–3
Maximianus 102
Melanippe 199
Memoirs of Hadrian 69
Menelaus 192, 215
Mentor 63–5, 69
Messalina 28, 31, 36, 78, 87, 91, 275, 282–4, 286, 288–9, 292
Meyrowitz, E. 169
military equipment 109–17, *see also Count Belisarius*
Milligan, Spike 161
Milton, John 202, 207, 297, 310–12
Minoan culture 174, 187, 190, 194
Minotaur 218
Modestus 79, 92, 108–9
Momigliano, Arnaldo 44
Mommsen, Theodor 269
Monahan, William 292
Montrose, Marquess of 265
Moon-Goddess 168, 187, 194
Mor, Barbara 178
Morris, John 305
Morris, William 201
Morrison, Joan 237
Morte D'Arthur 126, 131
Mortimer, John 289–91
Mother Earth 193–4
mother goddess 87, 169–70, 172–5, 178, *see also* matriarchy; White Goddess; gynaecocracy
Muggeridge, Malcolm 1, 306–7
Murray, Gilbert 211, 266, 298–9
Murray, Margaret 177
Murray, Oswyn 8
Muse 20, 71–2, 187, 163, 204, 210, 267, 328, *see also* Graves, Robert: muse
music, musicians 11, 18–20, 105, 151, 187, 204–5, 210, 238, 298, 305, 327–9
Mussolini, Benito 257, 259, 264–5, 272
Mycenae 70, 174, 176
myth:
  Celtic 146, 150, 161, 184, 187, 189
  Greek 165, 180, 181–200, 212, 219, *see also The Greek Myths*
mythology 24, 61, 137, 150, 167–8, 174, 177, 182–3, 189, 195, 198–9, 211, 234

Narcissus 225–9, 232, 280
Narses 79, 89–91, 85, 108
Nausicaa 57–76, 160, 205, 287
Neoptolemus 193
Nero 28, 151, 157, 309, 324, 331
Nestor 219, 319–20
neurasthenia 239
Newby P. H. 298, 304–5, 308, 323–4, 331, *see also* BBC
Nicholson, Ben 3
Nicholson, Jenny 287–9
Nicholson Nancy 3, 87, 101, 286–7
Niebuhr, Reinhold 303
Nietzsche, Friedrich 187, 209–10
Nilsson, Martin 165
Niobe 215
nymph 168, 176, 188, 193–4, 213, 225–6
numismatics 102–3

Oberon, Merle 284
O'Brien, Tim 236–7, 243, 245–6, 248–50, 252–4
Octavius, Caius (Octavian) 259, 269, 311, *see also* Augustus
Odom, Jesse 237

Odysseus 64, 68–9, 73–5, 162, 181, 192, 207–8, 319, 327
Odyssey 6, 16, 57–76, 127, 140, 144, 154, 158–62, 205, 207, 253, 317, 327, *see also* Homer
Oeax 191
Oenomaus 167
oracle 148, 167, 210
Orbison, Roy 19
Orestes 191–3
Orwell, George 161–2, 236
Otrere 199
Ovid 50, 186, 194, 203, 213, 216–19, 228
Owen, Wilfrid 6, 118, 211, 235, 237, 239–40, 242, 245–6

Palamedes 191–2
Pallas Athene, *see* Athene
Pallottino, Massimo 270–3
Paribeni, Roberto 257–60, 263, 265
Paris 207, 215,
Pasiphaë 193–4
Patroclus 14, 327
Patterson, Charles 237
Paul (apostle) 61, 89, 107, 163
Pegasus 218
Pelasgians 168–9, 178, 189
Peleus 17
Pelops 166, 191
Penelope 6, 64, 69, 73–5, 160, 205
Penguin 26, 28, 123, 128, 137, 141, 144, 149, 151–3, 162, 181–3, 195–6, 284, 308, 321
Penthesileia 199–200
Pericles 252
peritexts 27–30, *see also* historical novel
Perseus 190
Peter (disciple) 107, 115
Petronius 43, 124
Phaedra 166, 199
Phaethon 165, 167
Phemias 327–8
Phemios/Phemius 69, 73, 327
Philemon 217–18
Photius 43, 192
plain prose style (translation) 144–9, 153–4, 156, 158–62, 318
Plato 227, 252, 322
Plotina 69
Plutarch 43, 194, 211
poetry 2–7, 11, 15–16, 19–20, 23–4, 50, 84, 85, 96, 125, 144, 156–7, 160, 187, 201–32, 242, 253–4, 267, 301–3, 311–12, 317, 326, 330
  and history 38–9, 45, 66
  and politics 263–4
  and prose 39–41, 158, 163, 204
  and women 60–1, 71–2, 160
  war poetry 6, 13, 120, 233–4, 238
Pollio, Asinius 33–5, 45–50, 53–4, 66–7
Polybius 35, 51, 53, 62
Polyphemus 162
Pontius Pilate 86
Pope, Alexander 143, 202, 311
Porphyrion 96
Poseidon 69, 73–4, 154
Post-traumatic stress (PTS) 235, 239, 245
Pound, Ezra 16, 144, 157, 202, 221, 267, 310
Priam 199, 327
Price, Will 287–9
priestess 124, 129, 168, 174–5, 190–4, 210, 212
Pritchard, Beryl 4–5, 288
Procne 64
Procopius 79, 83–4, 87, 92, 96, 99, 101–3, 106, 108, 110–13
Procrustes 218
prophecy 22
Proserpine 209–10
Prote 165
Psyche 131, 139
Pulman, Jack 5, 291
Pygmalion 213–14, 216

Quilley, Dennis 327

Radice, Betty 128, 152
radio broadcasts 10, 15, 150, 265, 295, 298–301, 305–7, 309–10, 312, 316, 318, 322–31, *see also* BBC
Raikes, Raymond 326–7, 329–30, *see also* BBC
Raleigh, Sir Walter 265
Ranke, Amelia von 2–3
Ranke, Leopold von 3, 27, 46
Rawlings, Marjorie Kinnan 257
relationships:
  authorial presence/absence 31
  Belisarius and Justinian 79
  Graves and Apuleius 128
  Graves and BBC 303
  Graves and Buchan 267
  Graves and Butler 61

Graves and Claudius 289, *see also I, Claudius*, Claudius Caesar
Graves's domestic 3–4, 13, 31, 87, 100, 125, 214–15, 275, 283–4, 286, 292
Intellectual, W. H. R. Rivers 235
Intertextual 191
novel and epic 68
novel and history 25–6, 92
poetry 38
poet and muse 213
religion:
practice 59, 61, 95, 167–9, 172–5, 187–190, 210, 212, 214–15, 262, 303, *see also* magic
thought & knowledge 40, 79, 86, 104, 125, 137, 140, 142, 145, 168, 174, 182, 215, 303
Remarque, Erich 249, 253–4
Renault, Mary 9, 78, 93, 97
Rexine, John E. 318–19
Rhode 165
Richardson, J. S. 277, 288
Richardson, Tony 289–90
Richmond, Ian A. 280
Riding, Laura 3, 5, 31, 62, 78, 80, 84–8, 91–2, 97, 100–5, 118, 125, 202, 214–15, 255–7, 261–4, 275, 283–6, 292
Riefenstahl, Leni 279, 293
Rieu, E. V. 145, 151–2, 154, 158, 160, 162, 181–2, 195, 307
Rivers, W. H. R. 4, 87, 211, 235
Romanticism 39
romanticism 131, 224
Rome
ancient 9, 13–14, 23, 34, 44, 46, 48, 50, 66–7, 77, 79, 103, 109, 151, 153, 208, 257–8, 276–7, 280, 286, 304, 307, 331
empire 54, 78–9, 82–3, 85–7, 108–9, 112, 115, 258–9, 261, 264–5, 269, 271, 281
modern 259, 265, 270, 283, 286–8, 292–3
Romans 109, 251, 271, 298, 304, 308–9, 324, 331
Roosevelt, F. D. 257, 266
Rose, H. J. 194, 196, 198
Rossellini, Roberto 58, 288–9
Rossetti, Dante Gabriel 201
Rouse, W. H. D. 162
Rowe, Nicholas 157
Rushdie, Salman 141
Ruskin, John 201

Sacher-Masoch, Leopold von 286, *see also* male-female domination; relationships; Laura Riding; Graves, Robert: sadomasochism
sacrifice, women 190–3
Santayana, George 257
Sappho 210, 227
Sassoon, Siegfried 3, 6, 8, 10, 45, 59–60, 118, 121, 159, 203, 206–7, 211, 235, 237, 239, 241, 245, 249, 282, 302
Schiesari, Nancy 237
Scipio Africanus 81–2
Scott, Sir Walter 8–9, 48–9, 84, 97, 202
Scylla 74, 155
Searle, Humphrey 329
Searle, Ronald 316, 320
Seneca the Elder 47
Seneca the Younger 31, 43, 47
Seven Pillars of Wisdom 117, 125–6, 132–3, 137, 159–60, *see also* Lawrence, T. E.
Shane (film character) 252
Shaw, George Bernard 147, 205
Shepherd, J. T. 298
Sheridan, Jim 291–2
Sibyl 209
Sidney, Sir Philip 41, 154
Sillitoe, Alan 161
Simenon, Georges 308
Silverius 92
Sirens 74
Sjöö, Monica 178
Skelton, John 128, 152–3, 202
Skutsch, Otto 324
Sledge, E. B. 237
Smith, Rolando Hinojosa 237
Smith, William 82, 170, 183, 186
Smollett, Tobias 124, 129
Somme, Battle of the 3, 15, 208,
Sophocles 208, 254
Sorley, Charles Hamilton 128, 206–7
Spanish Civil War 3, 78, 100, 268, 292
Sparrow, John 299
Spinoza, Baruch 286
Stanhope, Viscount *see* Lord Mahon
Steinbeck, John 257
Steiner, Rudolf 179
Sternberg, Josef von 278–82, 284, 286, 293
Sterne, Laurence 32

Stone, Merlin 177
Suetonius 30, 37, 43, 54, 93, 144, 149, 151, 153, 157–8, 161, 276, 283, 286, 292, 307–8, 315, 324
Suttie, Ian D. 225, 229–31
Svoboda, Josef 321
Swinburne, A. S. 202, 210
Syme, Ronald 48, 53–4, 260, 269–70, 307

Tacitus 29–30, 43, 83, 286, 292, 307
Talthybius 192
T'ang Tai-tsung 114
Tatum, James 237
Taylor, Geoffrey 101
Teiresias 225
Telamon 208
Telemachus 63, 154, 160
Telephus 199
Tempe 194
Tennyson, Alfred 201, 311
Terkel, Studs 254
Terry, Wallace 237
theatre 106, 236, 289–91, 321–2, 326
Theocritus 311
Theodora 79, 87, 89, 95–6, 99–100, 102–6, *see also* Justinian
Theodosius I. 92, 103, 105
Theophanes 83
Thermopylae, Battle of 246
Thersites 199–200, 251, 253
Theseus 166, 199, 218–19
Thetis 199, 325, 327
Thomas, Dylan 202
Thomas, Lowell 124, 126, 129, 134–5
Thornton, J. C. 324, *see also* BBC
Thucydides 35, 47, 83, 252, 19,
Tiberius 35, 290
Trajan 103, 258
Trevelyan, R. C. 299
Tritle, Larry 237
Troy 13–14, 44, 68, 74, 148, 167, 191, 199, 206, 215, 219, 236, 299, 321, *see also* Homer; Trojan War; *Iliad*
Trojan War 97, 167, 208, 321, 328
truth (historical) 92–6
Twain, Mark 278, 280
Tyrtaeus 234

Universum Film (UFA) 278

Vanezis, Paul 292
Vegetius 83
Vellacott, Phillip 299
Velvet Underground, The 18
Ventris, Michael 299
Vera Historia 65
Vermeer, Johannes 1
Vidal, Gore 92–3, 97, 284
Vidor, King 288
Virgil 50, 152, 202–5, 208, 219, 234, 310–12
Vonnegut, Kurt 243, 248

Wales 75, 184
Wallace, Lew 8
Walpole, Horace 269
Walsh, P. G. 140–1
Wanamaker, Sam 321–2, 326
Warner, David 289–91
Warner, Rex 299
war poets, Greek 234
Wassermann, Jakob 8
Watt, A. P. 303, 325
Waugh, Evelyn 305–6
Way of All Flesh, The 60–1
Wayne, John 252, 254
Wells, H. G. 205
Western Front 109, 112, 114, 116, 118–21, 302, *see also* First World War
White Goddess (deity) 124, 129–30, 160, 195, 210, 212–13, 219, 300, 313, *see also* Graves, Robert; *The White Goddess*
Wiccan 179
Williams, W. E. 162
Wilson, Pearl Cleveland 318
Wimsatt, W. K. 41
Wolff, Tobias 237
Woodhead, A. G. 251
Woodworth, Dorothea Clinton 21–2, 41
Woolf, Virginia 32
Woolger, Jennifer 178
Woolger, Roger 178
Wordsworth, William 207, 311–12
World War 1 *see* First World War, Western Front

Xerxes 246

Yeats, W. B. 6, 11, 202, 215, 311
Yourcenar, Marguerite 69

Zeus 6, 17–18, 166, 192, 199, 212, 214–15, 217–18, 226, 320, 327–8
Zuckmayer, Carl 278–9, 284, 293